STOP!

This is the back of the book!
You wouldn't want to spoil a great ending!

This book is printed "manga-style," in the authentic Japanese right-to-left format. Since none of the artwork has been flipped or altered, readers get to experience the story just as the creator intended. You've been asking for it, so TOKYOPOP® delivered: authentic, hot-off-the-press, and far more fun!

DIRECTIONS

If this is your first time reading manga-style, here's a quick guide to help you understand how it works.

It's easy... just start in the top right panel and follow the numbers. Have fun, and look for more 100% authentic manga from TOKYOPOP®!

ALSO AVAILABLE FROM ☺TOKYOPOP®

MANGA

.HACK//LEGEND OF THE TWILIGHT
@LARGE
ABENOBASHI: MAGICAL SHOPPING ARCADE
A.I. LOVE YOU
AI YORI AOSHI
ALICHINO
ANGELIC LAYER
ARM OF KANNON
BABY BIRTH
BATTLE ROYALE
BATTLE VIXENS
BOYS BE...
BRAIN POWERED
BRIGADOON
B'TX
CANDIDATE FOR GODDESS, THE
CARDCAPTOR SAKURA
CARDCAPTOR SAKURA - MASTER OF THE CLOW
CHOBITS
CHRONICLES OF THE CURSED SWORD
CLAMP SCHOOL DETECTIVES
CLOVER
COMIC PARTY
CONFIDENTIAL CONFESSIONS
CORRECTOR YUI
COWBOY BEBOP
COWBOY BEBOP: SHOOTING STAR
CRAZY LOVE STORY
CRESCENT MOON
CROSS
CULDCEPT
CYBORG 009
D•N•ANGEL
DEARS
DEMON DIARY
DEMON ORORON, THE
DEUS VITAE
DIABOLO
DIGIMON
DIGIMON TAMERS
DIGIMON ZERO TWO
DOLL
DRAGON HUNTER
DRAGON KNIGHTS
DRAGON VOICE
DREAM SAGA
DUKLYON: CLAMP SCHOOL DEFENDERS
EERIE QUEERIE!
ERICA SAKURAZAWA: COLLECTED WORKS
ET CETERA
ETERNITY
EVIL'S RETURN
FAERIES' LANDING
FAKE
FLCL
FLOWER OF THE DEEP SLEEP
FORBIDDEN DANCE
FRUITS BASKET
G GUNDAM
GATEKEEPERS
GETBACKERS

GIRL GOT GAME
GRAVITATION
GTO
GUNDAM SEED ASTRAY
GUNDAM SEED ASTRAY R
GUNDAM WING
GUNDAM WING: BATTLEFIELD OF PACIFISTS
GUNDAM WING: ENDLESS WALTZ
GUNDAM WING: THE LAST OUTPOST (G-UNIT)
HANDS OFF!
HAPPY MANIA
HARLEM BEAT
HYPER POLICE
HYPER RUNE
I.N.V.U.
IMMORTAL RAIN
INITIAL D
INSTANT TEEN: JUST ADD NUTS
ISLAND
JING: KING OF BANDITS
JING: KING OF BANDITS - TWILIGHT TALES
JULINE
KARE KANO
KILL ME, KISS ME
KINDAICHI CASE FILES, THE
KING OF HELL
KODOCHA: SANA'S STAGE
LAGOON ENGINE
LAMENT OF THE LAMB
LEGAL DRUG
LEGEND OF CHUN HYANG, THE
LES BIJOUX
LILING-PO
LOVE HINA
LOVE OR MONEY
LUPIN III
LUPIN III: WORLD'S MOST WANTED
MAGIC KNIGHT RAYEARTH I
MAGIC KNIGHT RAYEARTH II
MAHOROMATIC: AUTOMATIC MAIDEN
MAN OF MANY FACES
MARMALADE BOY
MARS
MARS: HORSE WITH NO NAME
MINK
MIRACLE GIRLS
MIYUKI-CHAN IN WONDERLAND
MODEL
MOURYOU KIDEN: LEGEND OF THE NYMPH
NECK AND NECK
ONE
ONE I LOVE, THE
PARADISE KISS
PARASYTE
PASSION FRUIT
PEACH FUZZ
PEACH GIRL
PEACH GIRL: CHANGE OF HEART
PET SHOP OF HORRORS
PHD: PHANTASY DEGREE
PITA-TEN
PLANET BLOOD
PLANET LADDER

10.19.04

ALSO AVAILABLE FROM TOKYOPOP

PLANETES
PRESIDENT DAD
PRIEST
PRINCESS AI
PSYCHIC ACADEMY
QUEEN'S KNIGHT, THE
RAGNAROK
RAVE MASTER
REALITY CHECK
REBIRTH
REBOUND
REMOTE
RISING STARS OF MANGA™, THE
SABER MARIONETTE J
SAILOR MOON
SAINT TAIL
SAIYUKI
SAMURAI DEEPER KYO
SAMURAI GIRL™ REAL BOUT HIGH SCHOOL
SCRYED
SEIKAI TRILOGY, THE
SGT. FROG
SHAOLIN SISTERS
SHIRAHIME-SYO: SNOW GODDESS TALES
SHUTTERBOX
SKULL MAN, THE
SNOW DROP
SORCERER HUNTERS
SOUL TO SEOUL
STONE
SUIKODEN III
SUKI
TAROT CAFÉ, THE
THREADS OF TIME
TOKYO BABYLON
TOKYO MEW MEW
TOKYO TRIBES
TRAMPS LIKE US
UNDER THE GLASS MOON
VAMPIRE GAME
VISION OF ESCAFLOWNE, THE
WARCRAFT
WARRIORS OF TAO
WILD ACT
WISH
WORLD OF HARTZ
X-DAY
ZODIAC P.I.

NOVELS

CLAMP SCHOOL PARANORMAL INVESTIGATORS
SAILOR MOON
SLAYERS

ART BOOKS

ART OF CARDCAPTOR SAKURA
ART OF MAGIC KNIGHT RAYEARTH, THE
PEACH: MIWA UEDA ILLUSTRATIONS
CLAMP NORTH SIDE
CLAMP SOUTH SIDE

ANIME GUIDES

COWBOY BEBOP
GUNDAM TECHNICAL MANUALS
SAILOR MOON SCOUT GUIDES

TOKYOPOP KIDS

STRAY SHEEP

CINE-MANGA®

ALADDIN
CARDCAPTORS
DUEL MASTERS
FAIRLY ODDPARENTS, THE
FAMILY GUY
FINDING NEMO
G.I. JOE SPY TROOPS
GREATEST STARS OF THE NBA
JACKIE CHAN ADVENTURES
JIMMY NEUTRON: BOY GENIUS, THE ADVENTURES OF
KIM POSSIBLE
LILO & STITCH: THE SERIES
LIZZIE MCGUIRE
LIZZIE MCGUIRE MOVIE, THE
MALCOLM IN THE MIDDLE
POWER RANGERS: DINO THUNDER
POWER RANGERS: NINJA STORM
PRINCESS DIARIES 2, THE
RAVE MASTER
SHREK 2
SIMPLE LIFE, THE
SPONGEBOB SQUAREPANTS
SPY KIDS 2
SPY KIDS 3-D: GAME OVER
TEENAGE MUTANT NINJA TURTLES
THAT'S SO RAVEN
TOTALLY SPIES
TRANSFORMERS: ARMADA
TRANSFORMERS: ENERGON

10.19.04T

When love is war,
she takes no prisoners.

Neck and Neck™

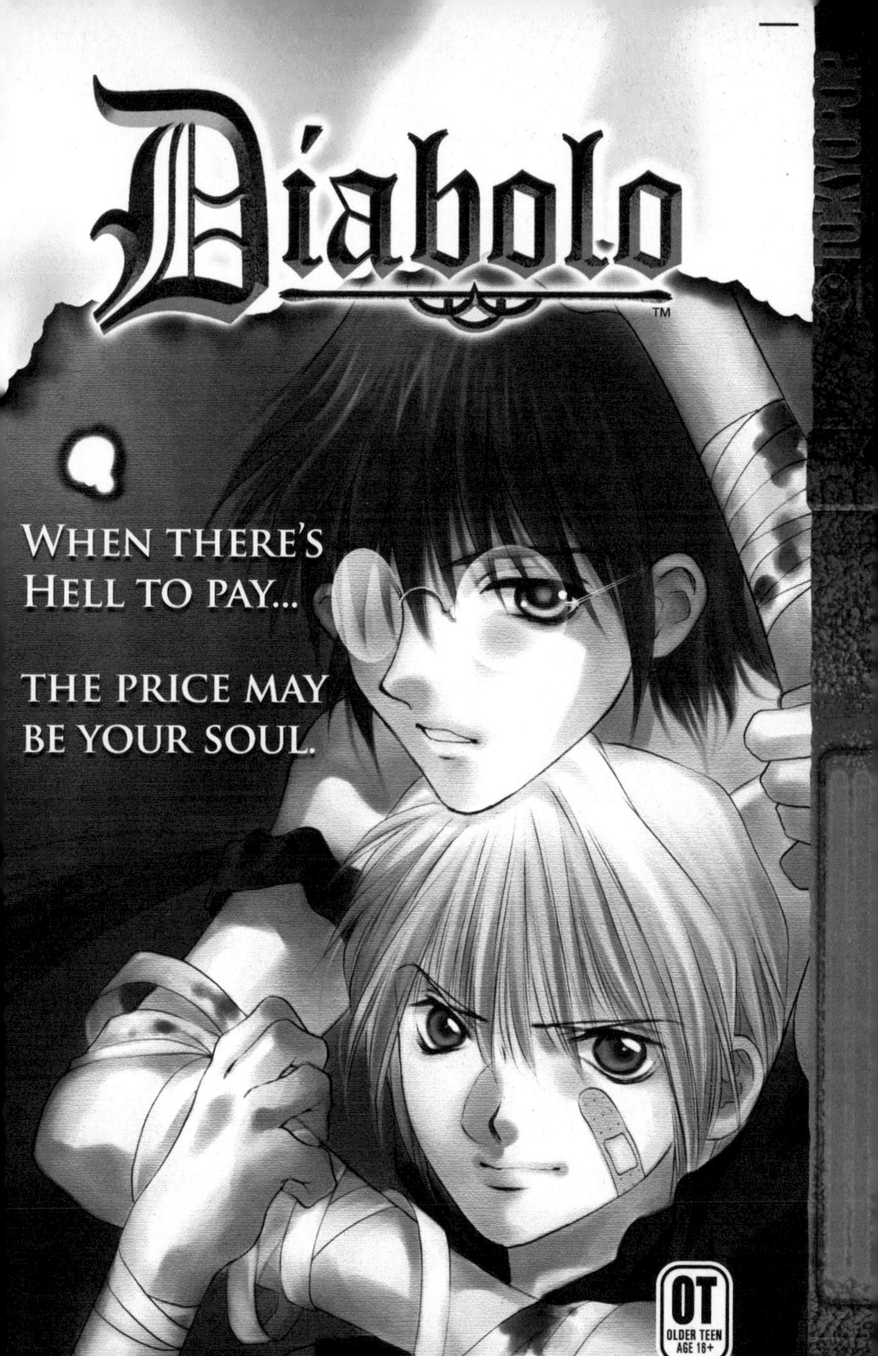
Diabolo
TM
WHEN THERE'S HELL TO PAY...
THE PRICE MAY BE YOUR SOUL.
OT
OLDER TEEN AGE 16+
TOKYOPOP

Dear Diary,
I'm starting to feel

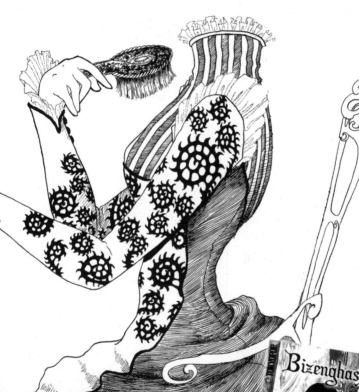

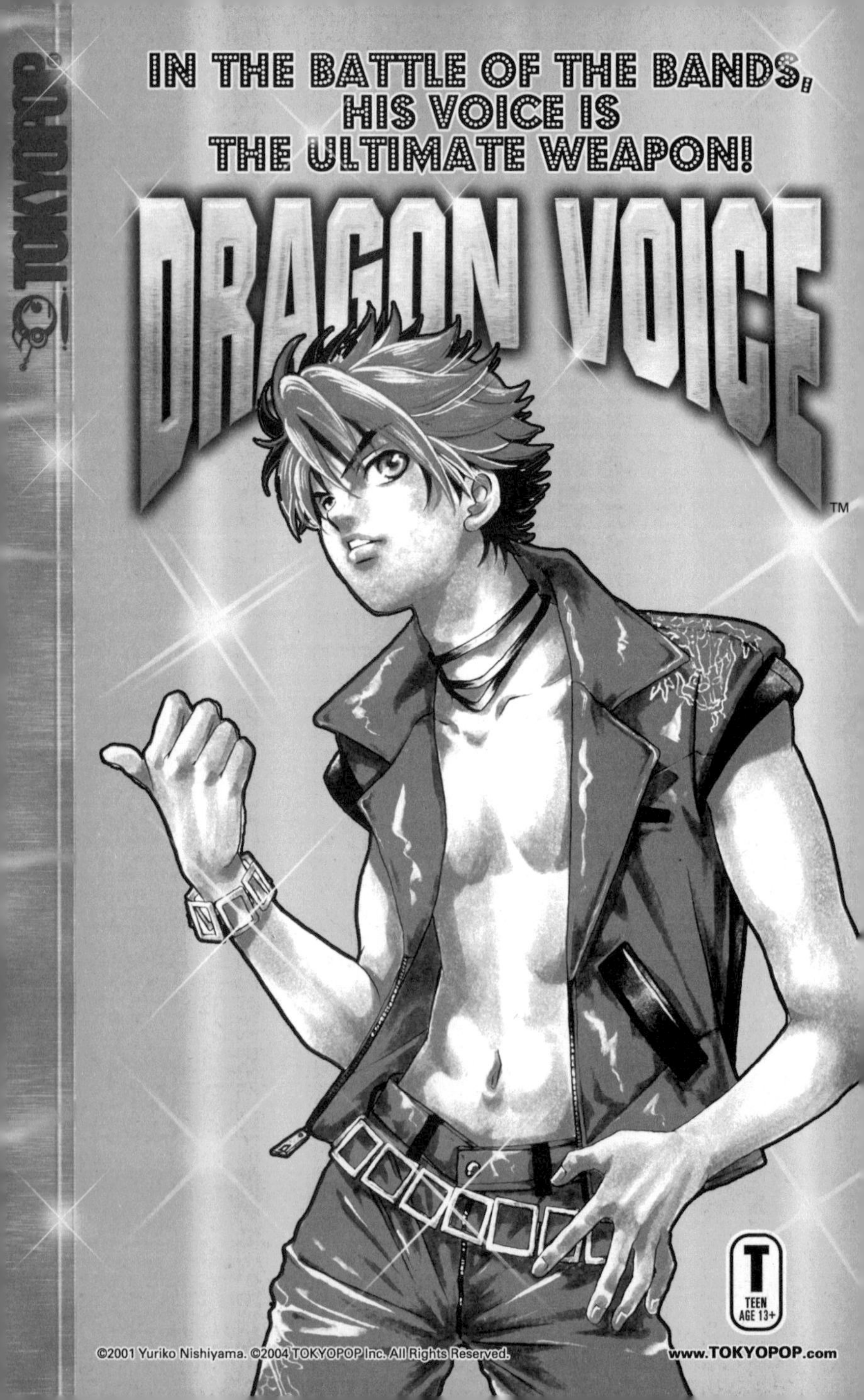
TOKYOPOP
IN THE BATTLE OF THE BANDS, HIS VOICE IS THE ULTIMATE WEAPON!
DRAGON VOICE™
T TEEN AGE 13+
©2001 Yuriko Nishiyama. ©2004 TOKYOPOP Inc. All Rights Reserved.
www.TOKYOPOP.com

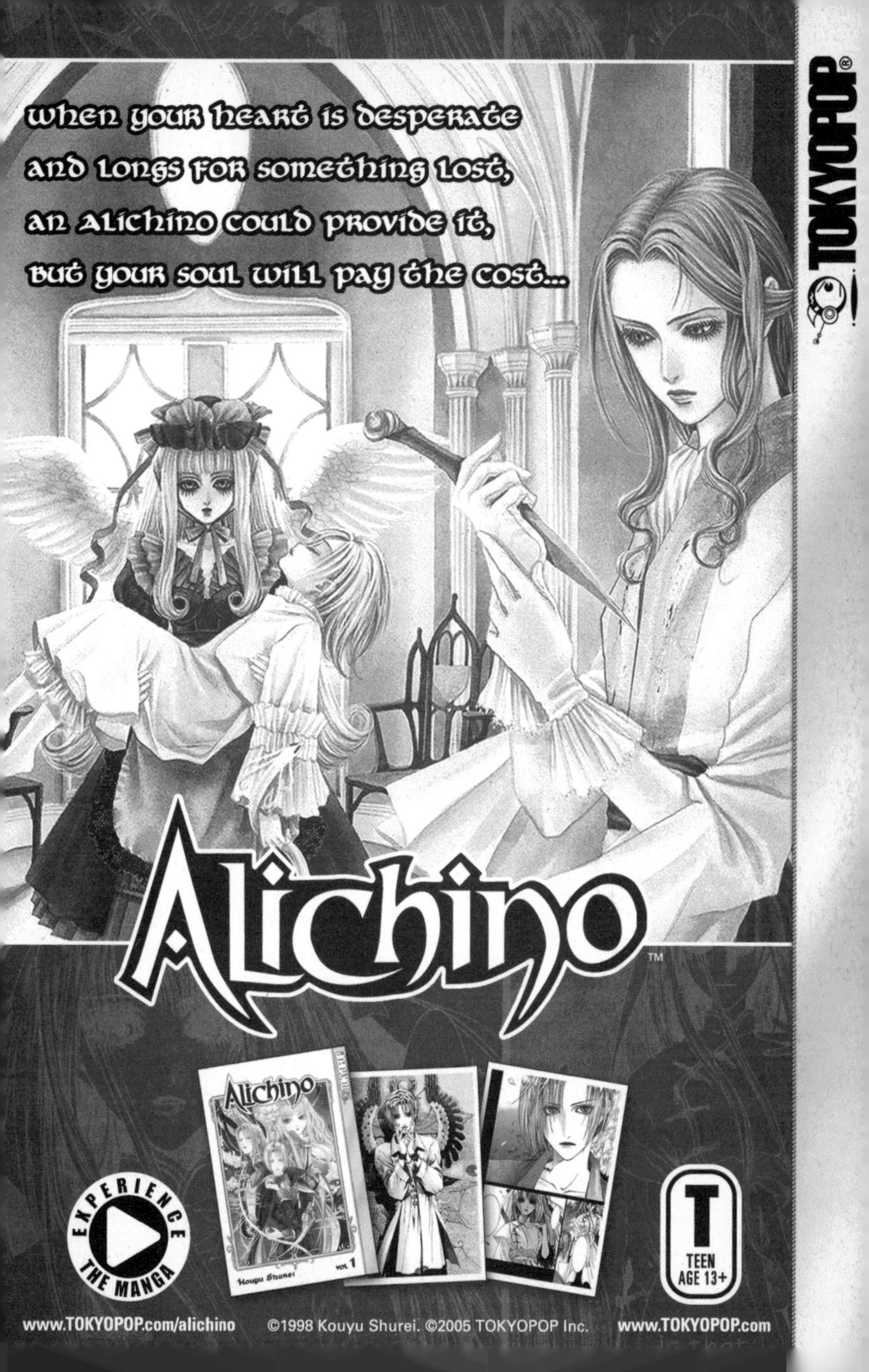

WHEN YOUR HEART IS DESPERATE
AND LONGS FOR SOMETHING LOST,
AN ALICHINO COULD PROVIDE IT,
BUT YOUR SOUL WILL PAY THE COST...
Alichino™
Alichino
Kouyu Shurei
VOL 1
EXPERIENCE THE MANGA
T
TEEN AGE 13+
TOKYOPOP®
www.TOKYOPOP.com/alichino
©1998 Kouyu Shurei. ©2005 TOKYOPOP Inc.
www.TOKYOPOP.com

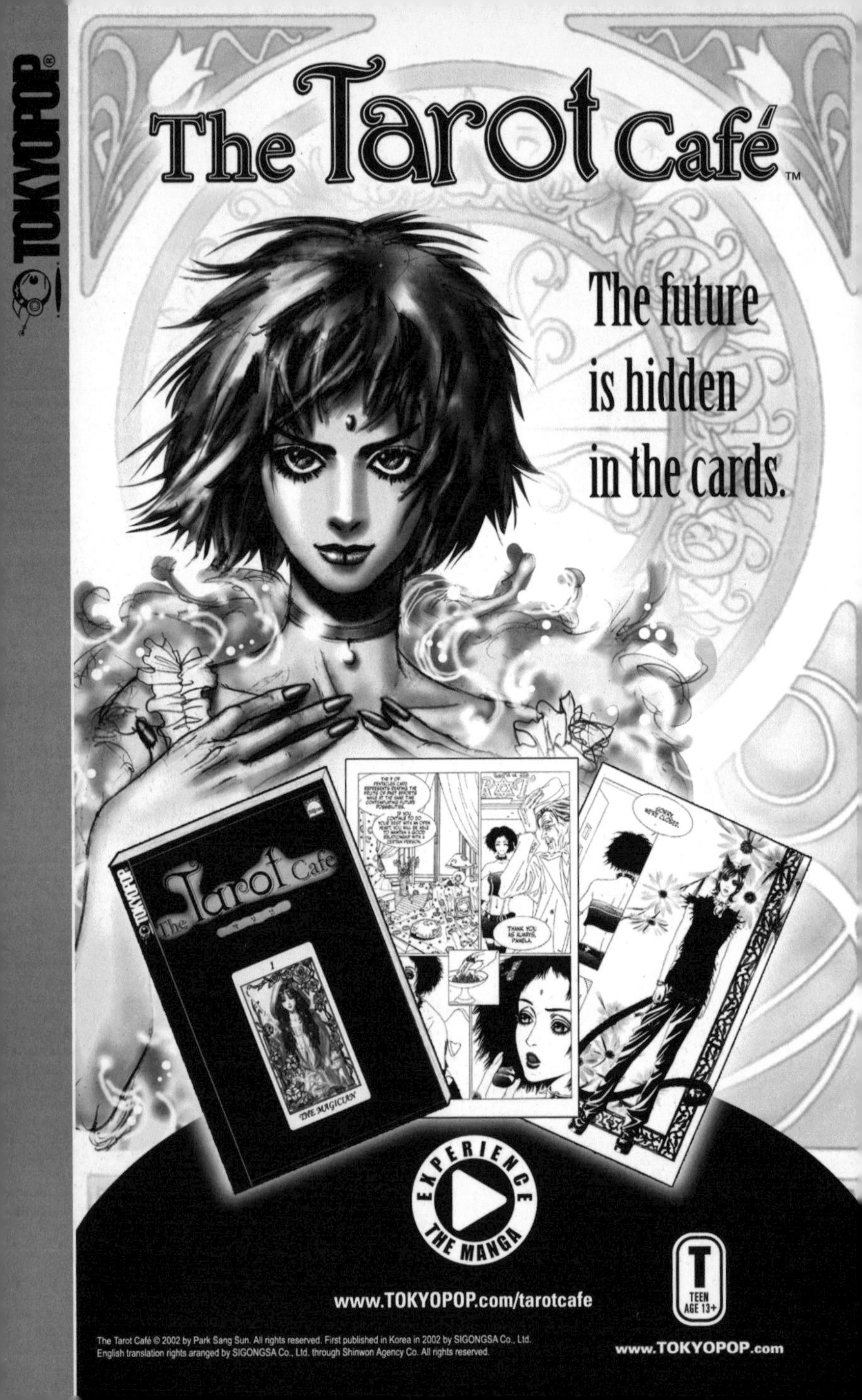
TOKYOPOP®
The Tarot Café™
The future is hidden in the cards.
TOKYOPOP
The Tarot Cafe
THE MAGICIAN
EXPERIENCE THE MANGA
T
TEEN AGE 13+
www.TOKYOPOP.com/tarotcafe
The Tarot Café © 2002 by Park Sang Sun. All rights reserved. First published in Korea in 2002 by SIGONGSA Co., Ltd.
English translation rights aranged by SIGONGSA Co., Ltd. through Shinwon Agency Co. All rights reserved.
www.TOKYOPOP.com

Volume 10

By
Maki Murakami

HAMBURG // LONDON // LOS ANGELES // TOKYO

Gravitation Vol. 10
Created by Maki Murakami

Translation - Ray Yoshimoto
English Adaptation - Jamie S. Rich
Copy Editors - Aaron Sparrow and Troy Lewter
Retouch and Lettering - Eric Pineda
Production Artist - James Dashiell
Cover Design - Raymond Makowski

Editor - Paul Morrissey
Digital Imaging Manager - Chris Buford
Pre-Press Manager - Antonio DePietro
Production Managers - Jennifer Miller and Mutsumi Miyazaki
Art Director - Matt Alford
Managing Editor - Jill Freshney
VP of Production - Ron Klamert
President and C.O.O. - John Parker
Publisher and C.E.O. - Stuart Levy

A  Manga

TOKYOPOP Inc.
5900 Wilshire Blvd. Suite 2000
Los Angeles, CA 90036

E-mail: info@TOKYOPOP.com
Come visit us online at www.TOKYOPOP.com

ISBN: 1-59182-342-0

First TOKYOPOP printing: February 2005
10 9 8 7 6 5 4
Printed in the USA

THE MEMBERS OF THE GRAVITATION BAND

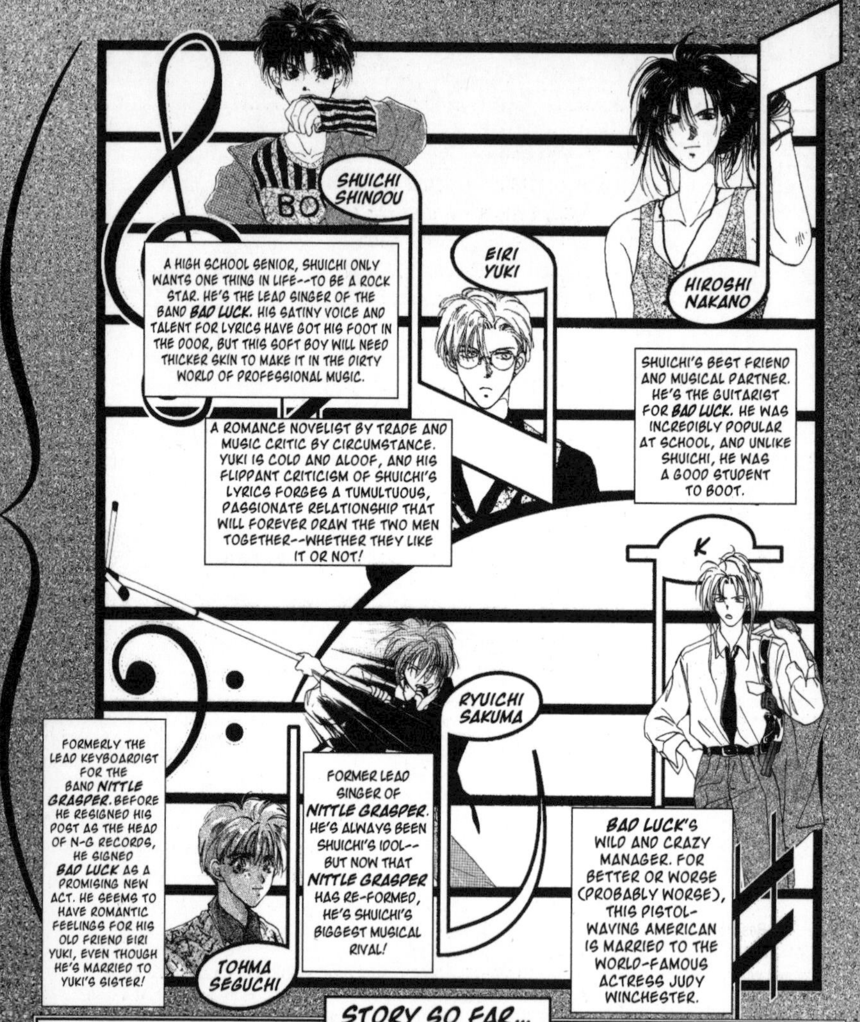
SHUICHI SHINDOU
A HIGH SCHOOL SENIOR, SHUICHI ONLY WANTS ONE THING IN LIFE--TO BE A ROCK STAR. HE'S THE LEAD SINGER OF THE BAND ***BAD LUCK***. HIS SATINY VOICE AND TALENT FOR LYRICS HAVE GOT HIS FOOT IN THE DOOR, BUT THIS SOFT BOY WILL NEED THICKER SKIN TO MAKE IT IN THE DIRTY WORLD OF PROFESSIONAL MUSIC.
HIROSHI NAKANO
SHUICHI'S BEST FRIEND AND MUSICAL PARTNER. HE'S THE GUITARIST FOR ***BAD LUCK***. HE WAS INCREDIBLY POPULAR AT SCHOOL, AND UNLIKE SHUICHI, HE WAS A GOOD STUDENT TO BOOT.
EIRI YUKI
A ROMANCE NOVELIST BY TRADE AND MUSIC CRITIC BY CIRCUMSTANCE. YUKI IS COLD AND ALOOF, AND HIS FLIPPANT CRITICISM OF SHUICHI'S LYRICS FORGES A TUMULTUOUS, PASSIONATE RELATIONSHIP THAT WILL FOREVER DRAW THE TWO MEN TOGETHER--WHETHER THEY LIKE IT OR NOT!
K
BAD LUCK'S WILD AND CRAZY MANAGER. FOR BETTER OR WORSE (PROBABLY WORSE), THIS PISTOL-WAVING AMERICAN IS MARRIED TO THE WORLD-FAMOUS ACTRESS JUDY WINCHESTER.
RYUICHI SAKUMA
FORMER LEAD SINGER OF ***NITTLE GRASPER***. HE'S ALWAYS BEEN SHUICHI'S IDOL--BUT NOW THAT ***NITTLE GRASPER*** HAS RE-FORMED, HE'S SHUICHI'S BIGGEST MUSICAL RIVAL!
TOHMA SEGUCHI
FORMERLY THE LEAD KEYBOARDIST FOR THE BAND ***NITTLE GRASPER***. BEFORE HE RESIGNED HIS POST AS THE HEAD OF N-G RECORDS, HE SIGNED ***BAD LUCK*** AS A PROMISING NEW ACT. HE SEEMS TO HAVE ROMANTIC FEELINGS FOR HIS OLD FRIEND EIRI YUKI, EVEN THOUGH HE'S MARRIED TO YUKI'S SISTER!

STORY SO FAR...

SHUICHI SHINDOU IS DETERMINED TO BE A ROCK STAR...AND HE'S OFF TO A BLAZING START! HIS BAND, ***BAD LUCK***, IS SIGNED TO THE N-G RECORD LABEL, AND THEIR ALBUM HAS JUST GONE PLATINUM! WITH THE ADDITION OF HIS NEW MANAGER--THE GUN-TOTING AMERICAN MANIAC NAMED "K"--SHUICHI IS POISED TO TAKE THE WORLD HOSTAGE! ALL THE WHILE, SHUICHI COPES WITH HIS ROLLER-COASTER RELATIONSHIP WITH THE MYSTERIOUS WRITER EIRI YUKI. THEIR SECRET ROMANCE HAS HIT A FEW JARRING NOTES, PROVING THAT LOVE ISN'T ALWAYS HARMONIOUS. HOW LONG CAN THEY REMAIN INEXORABLY INTERTWINED, HELD TOGETHER BY A FORCE AS STRONG AS GRAVITY? CONFRONTED BY A VORACIOUS PACK OF REPORTERS, YUKI SURPRISINGLY ADMITS TO A SHOCKED WORLD THAT HE AND SHUICHI ARE INDEED LOVERS! FUELED BY JEALOUSLY, SEGUCHI ORDERS SHUICHI TO BREAK UP WITH EIRI. SHUICHI CONTEMPLATES LEAVING N-G IN ORDER TO SALVAGE HIS ROMANCE, BUT ALL IS FOR NAUGHT--IN A SHOCKING MOVE, EIRI DUMPS ***HIM***! K TRIES IN VAIN TO HELP A DEVASTATED SHUICHI RECOVER, BUT THE SURPRISES JUST KEEP COMING: SHUICHI IS KIDNAPPED...AND PUT ON A PLANE TO R-O-C-K IN THE U.S.A.! SHUICHI'S NEW MANAGER AT XMR RECORDS--THE VOLATILE REIJI (A.K.A. RAGE)--IS DETERMINED TO MAKE HIM AN AMERICAN SUPERSTAR. ALTHOUGH SHUICHI CONTEMPLATES NORTH AMERICAN FAME, HIS UNDYING LOVE FOR YUKI ULTIMATELY LEADS HIM BACK TO JAPAN. THERE'S JUST ONE PROBLEM: THE INSANELY JEALOUS RAGE HAS DECIDED TO FOLLOW HIM BACK HOME--IN HER GIANT, ROBOTIC FLYING PANDA!

CONTENTS

track 42 —————————————— 7
track 43 —————————————— 47
track 44 —————————————— 89
track 45 —————————————— 133
bonus track ————————————— 183

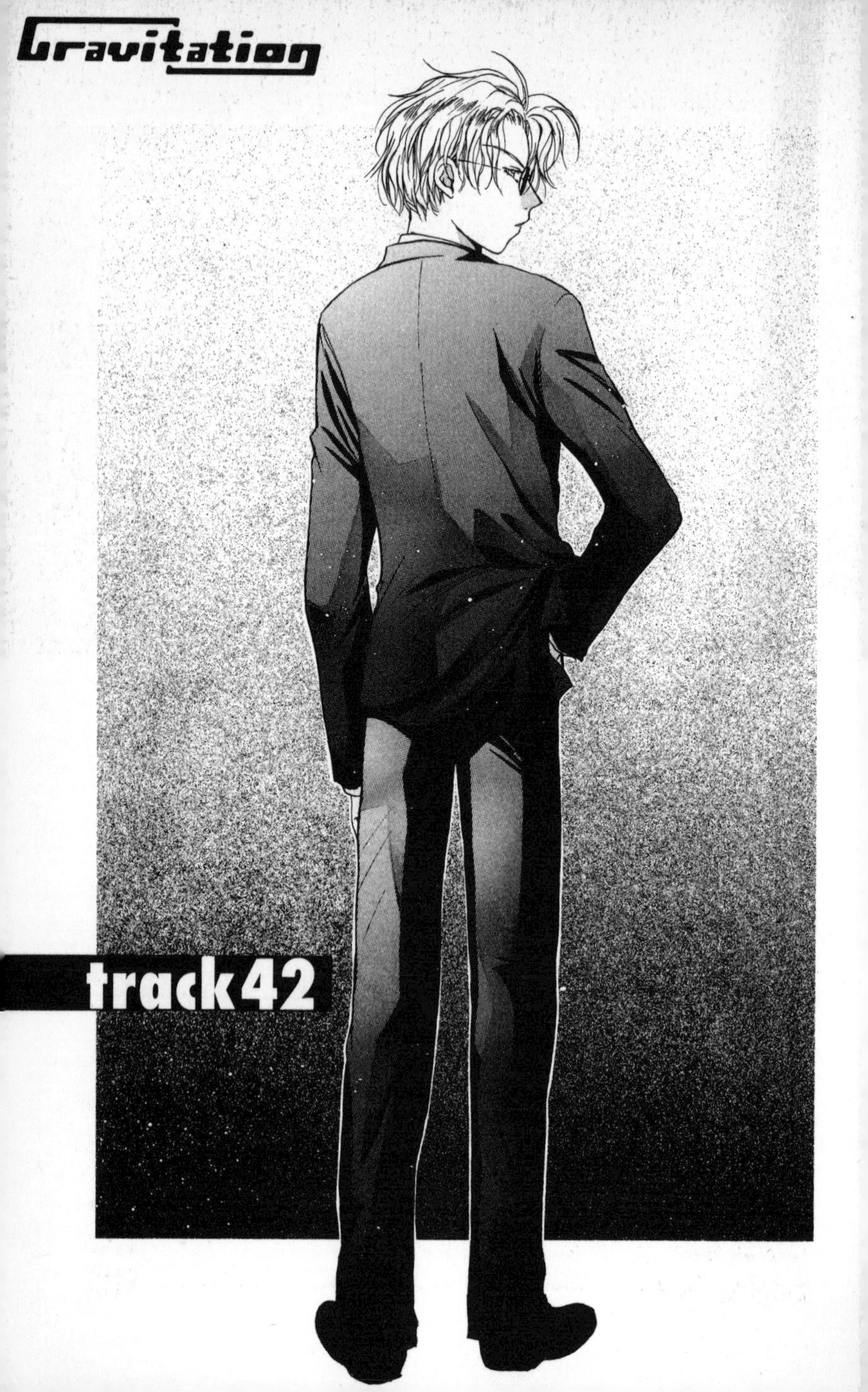
Gravitation
track 42

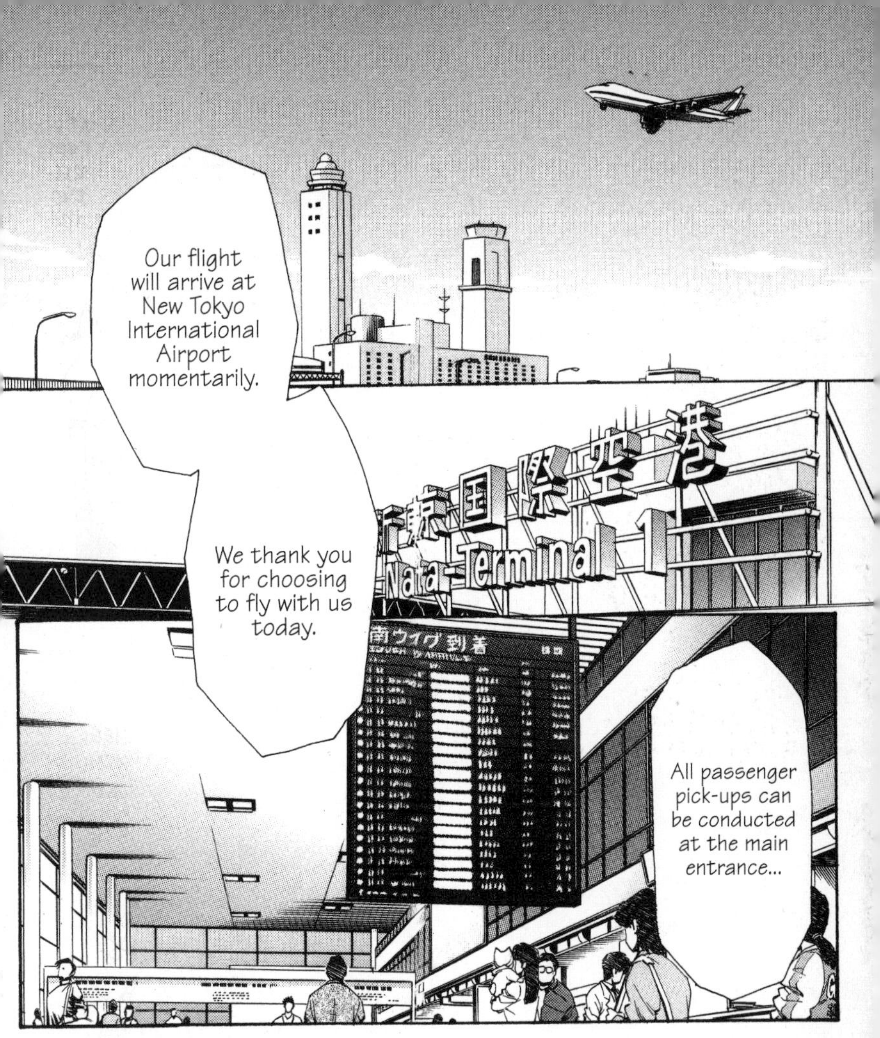
Our flight will arrive at New Tokyo International Airport momentarily.
We thank you for choosing to fly with us today.
All passenger pick-ups can be conducted at the main entrance...

ABOUT GRAVITATION TRACK 42

Hello, everyone--Maki Murakami, here. Long time no see. We're in double digits now, all the way to book 10. Thank you for all your support. (Personally, I think this book is the most uninteresting volume so far, but hopefully you readers were fooled into buying it.) So, how long is this manga going to continue? (You must be happy...?) I can't even think of interesting ideas to fill this dead space here, anymore. So...about the best I can manage is a flower garden... Well, see you soon!! Don't forget to buy book 11!

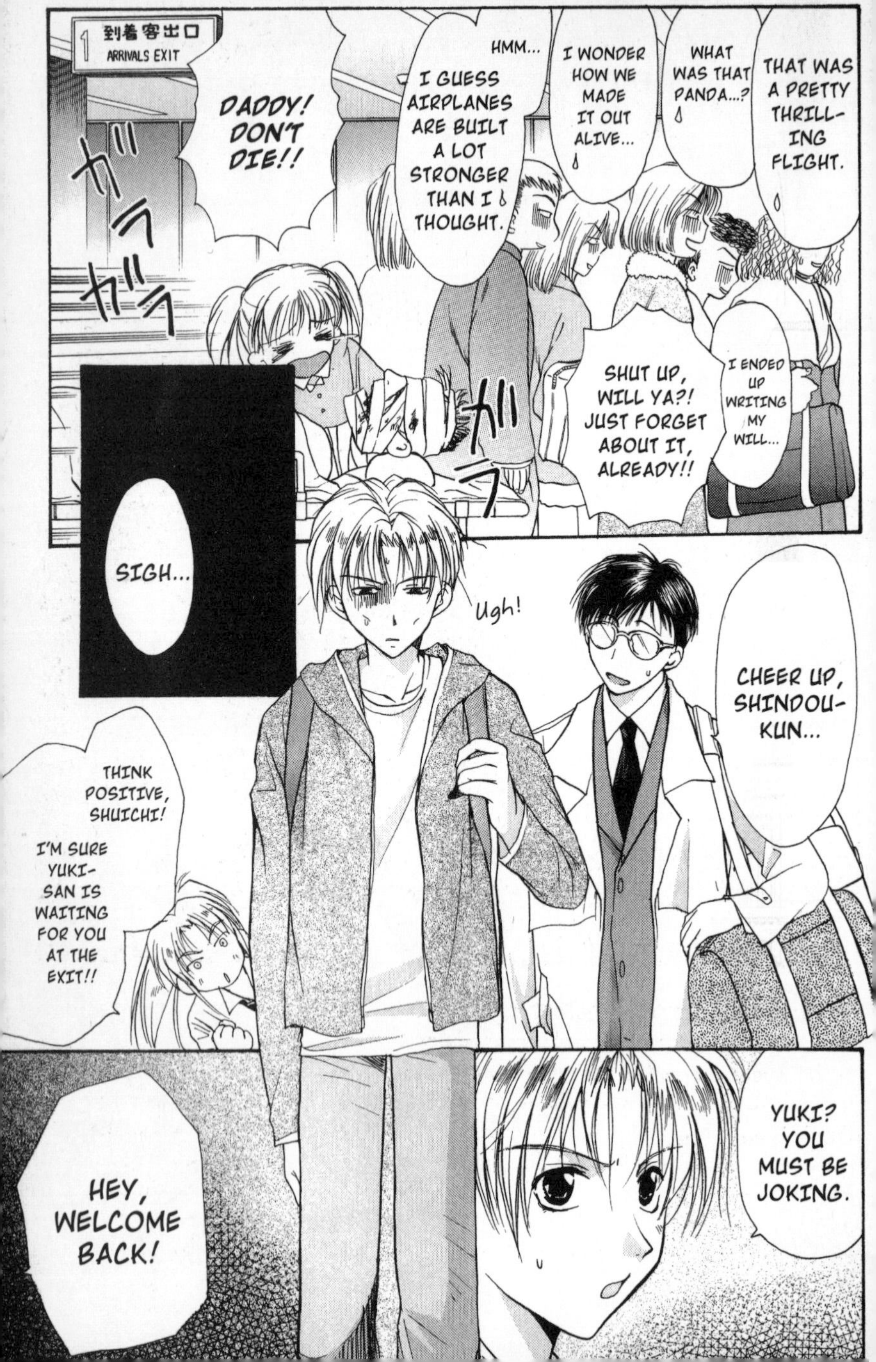
THAT WAS A PRETTY THRILLING FLIGHT.
WHAT WAS THAT PANDA...?
I WONDER HOW WE MADE IT OUT ALIVE...
HMM... I GUESS AIRPLANES ARE BUILT A LOT STRONGER THAN I THOUGHT.
DADDY! DON'T DIE!!
1 到着客出口 ARRIVALS EXIT
ガラ
ガラ
I ENDED UP WRITING MY WILL...
SHUT UP, WILL YA?! JUST FORGET ABOUT IT, ALREADY!!
ガラ
CHEER UP, SHINDOU-KUN...
Ugh!
SIGH...
THINK POSITIVE, SHUICHI!
I'M SURE YUKI-SAN IS WAITING FOR YOU AT THE EXIT!!
YUKI? YOU MUST BE JOKING.
HEY, WELCOME BACK!

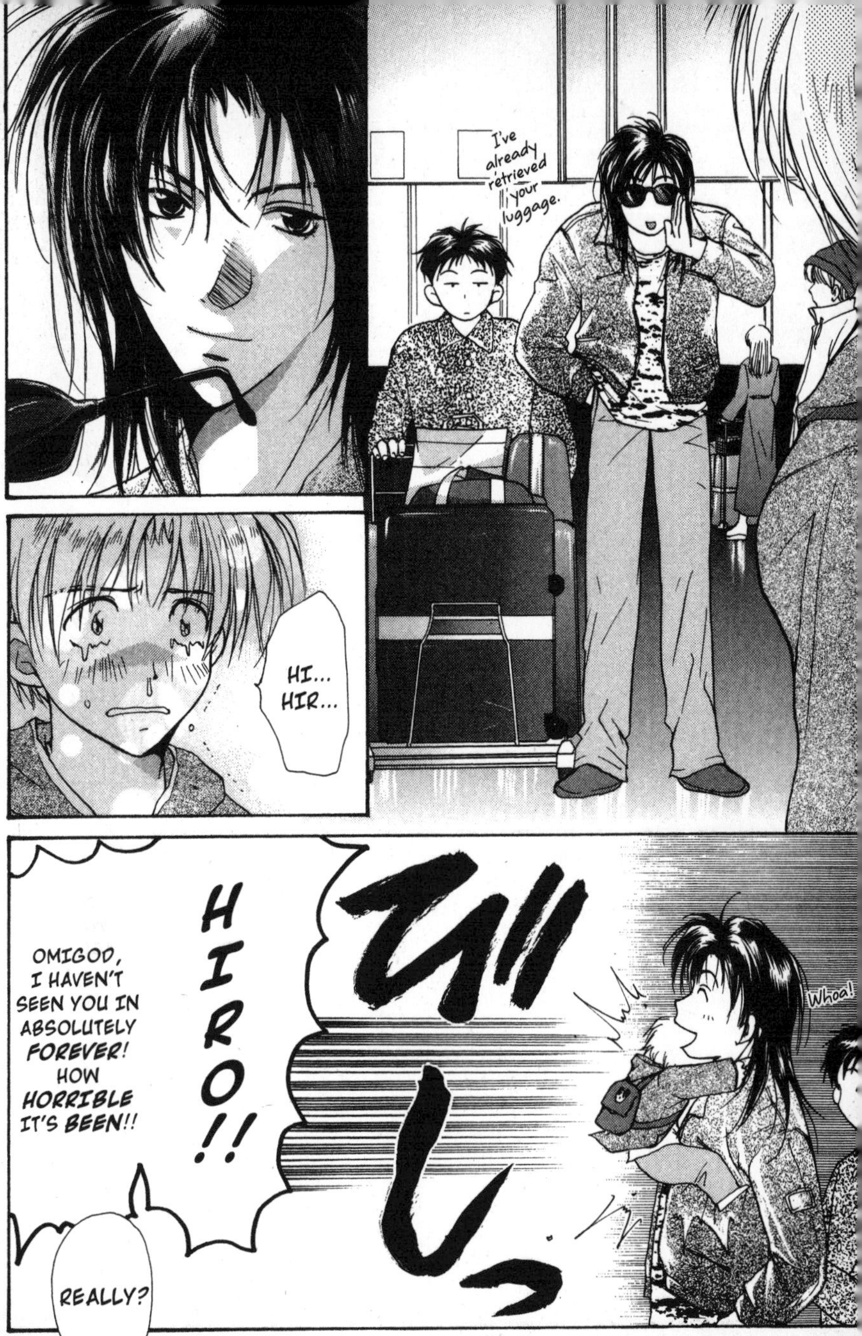
I've already retrieved your luggage.
HI... HIR...
Whoa!
びしっ
HIRO!!
OMIGOD, I HAVEN'T SEEN YOU IN ABSOLUTELY *FOREVER*! HOW *HORRIBLE* IT'S *BEEN*!!
REALLY?

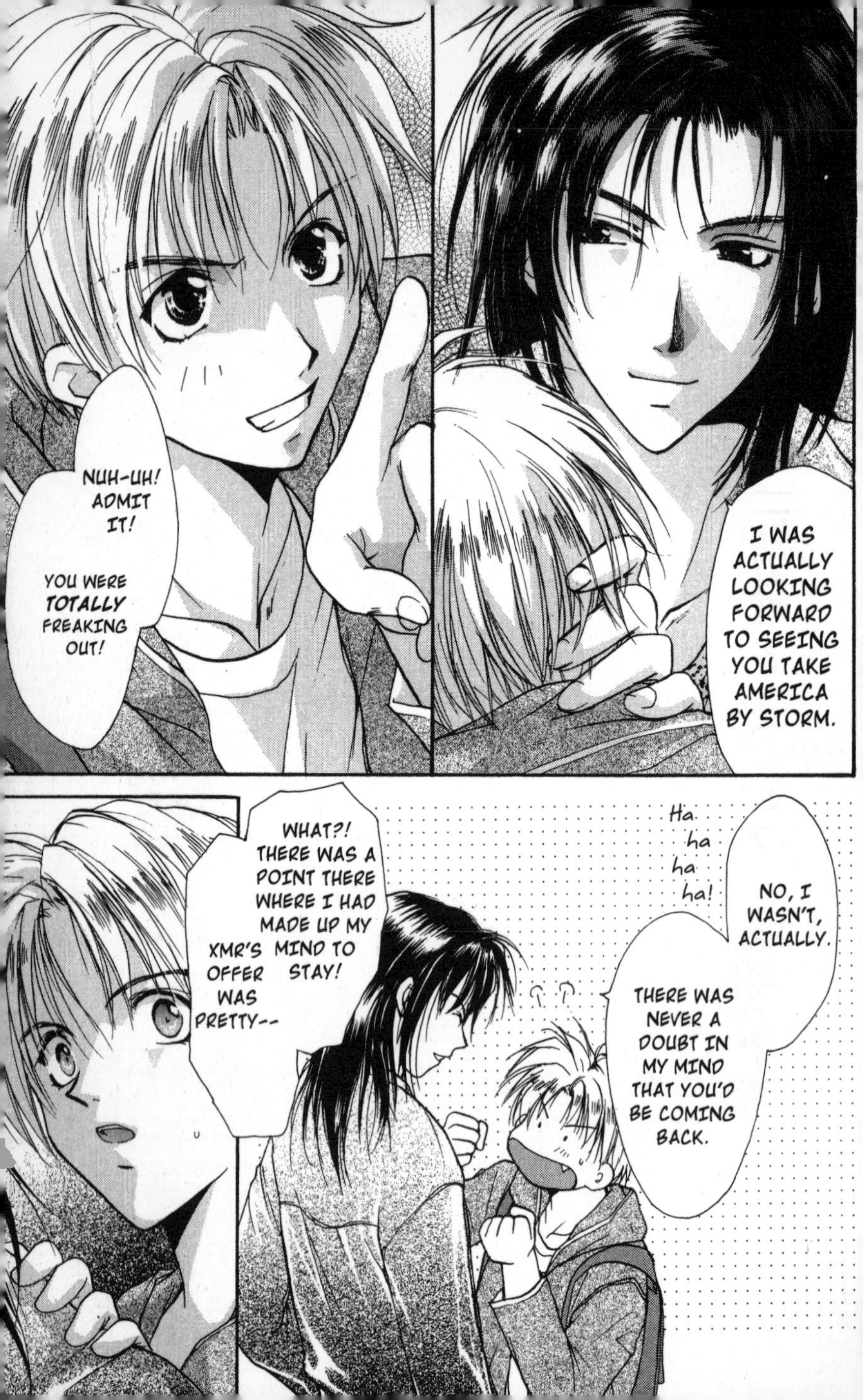
I WAS ACTUALLY LOOKING FORWARD TO SEEING YOU TAKE AMERICA BY STORM.
NUH-UH! ADMIT IT!
YOU WERE *TOTALLY* FREAKING OUT!
Ha ha ha ha!
NO, I WASN'T, ACTUALLY.
THERE WAS NEVER A DOUBT IN MY MIND THAT YOU'D BE COMING BACK.
WHAT?! THERE WAS A POINT THERE WHERE I HAD MADE UP MY MIND TO STAY!
XMR'S OFFER WAS PRETTY--

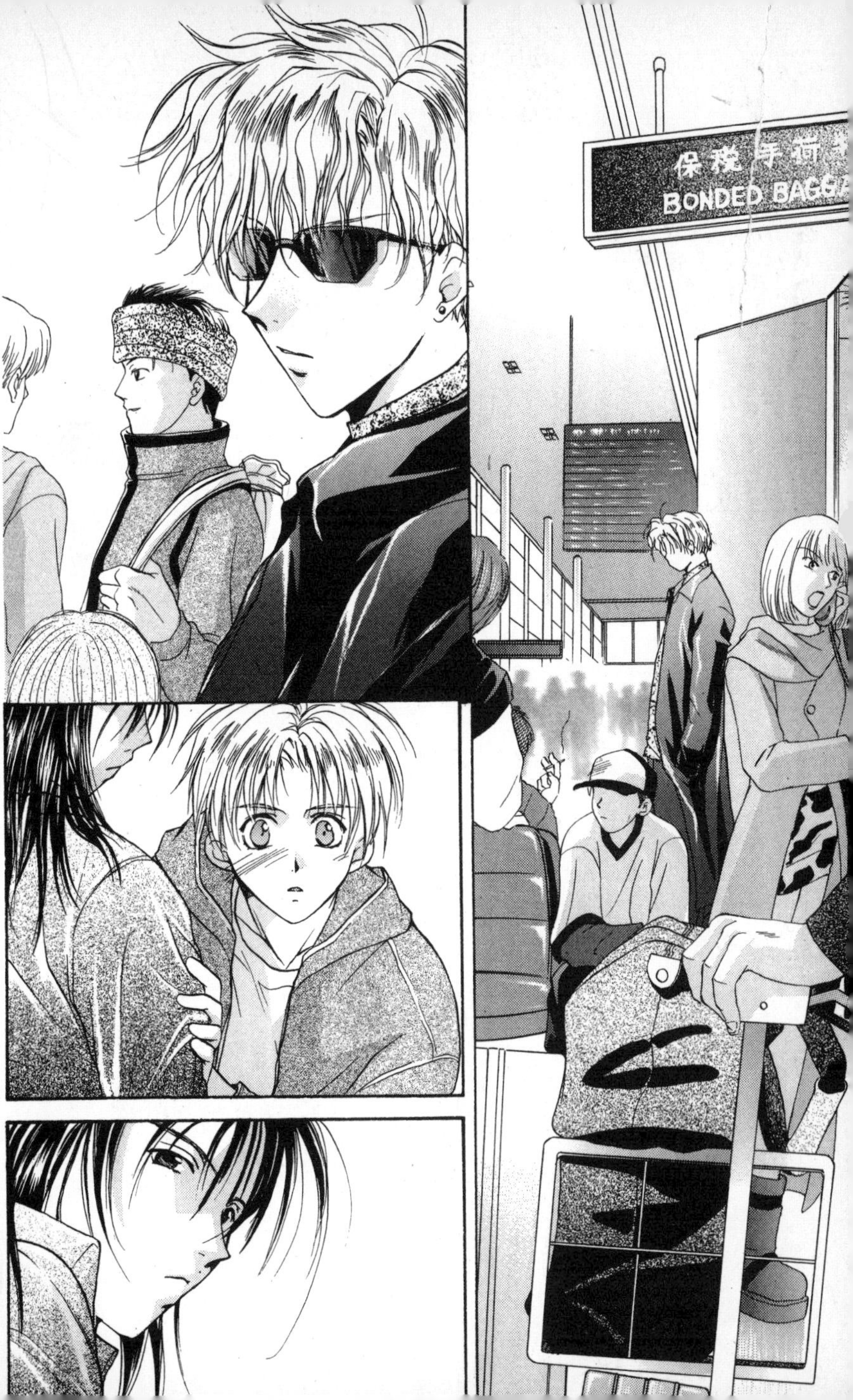

BONDED BAGGA

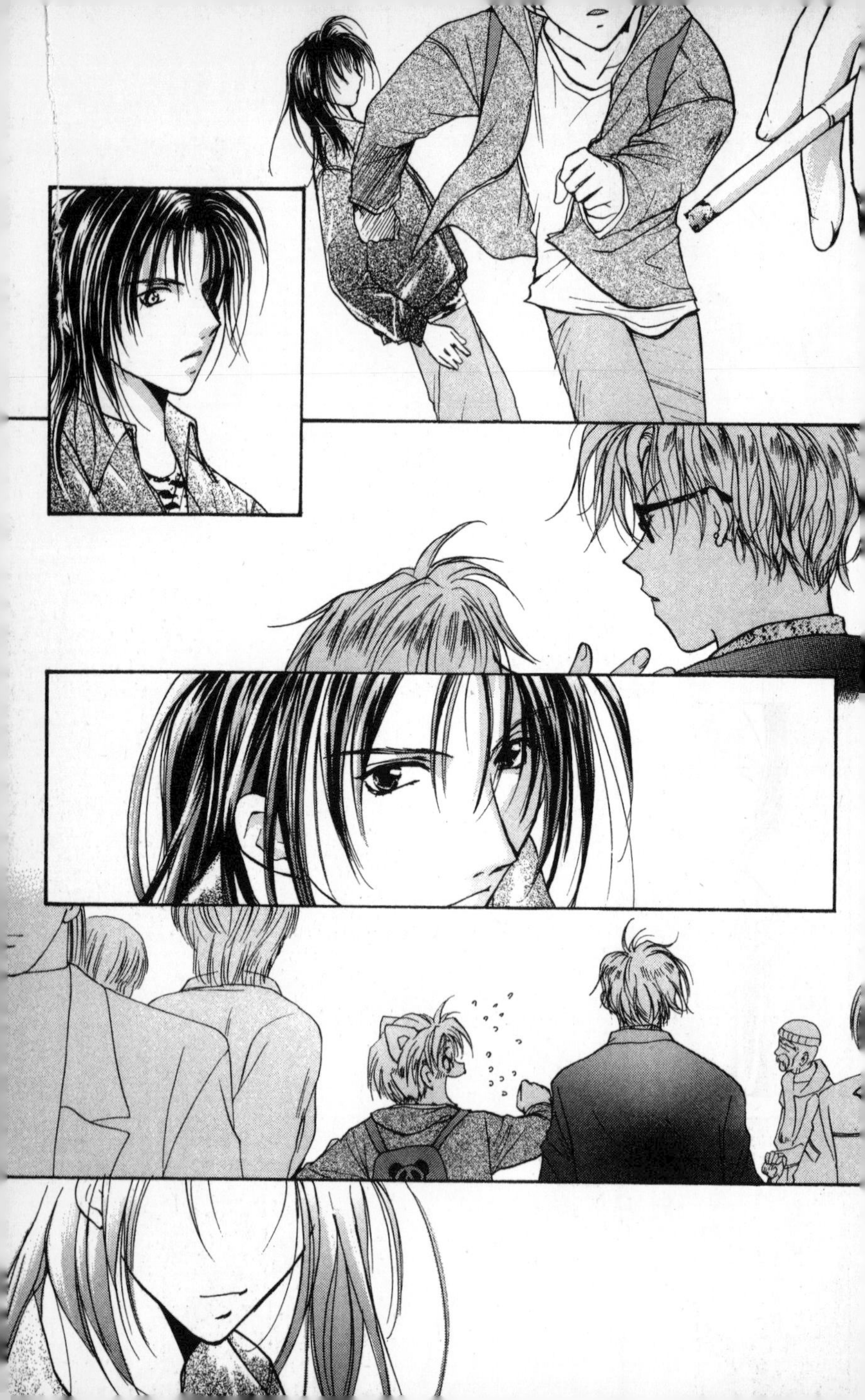

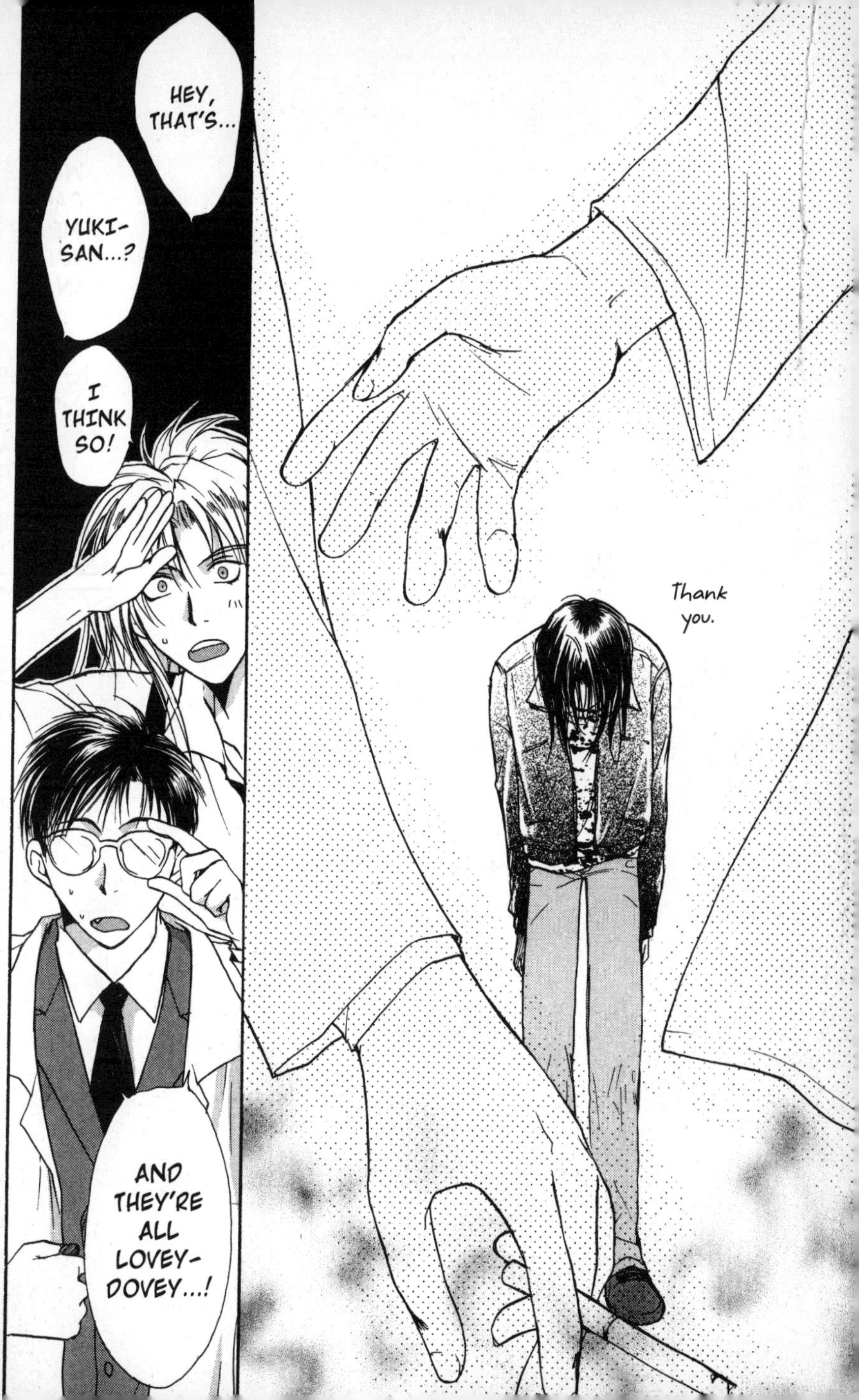
Thank you.
HEY, THAT'S...
YUKI-SAN...?
I THINK SO!
AND THEY'RE ALL LOVEY-DOVEY...!

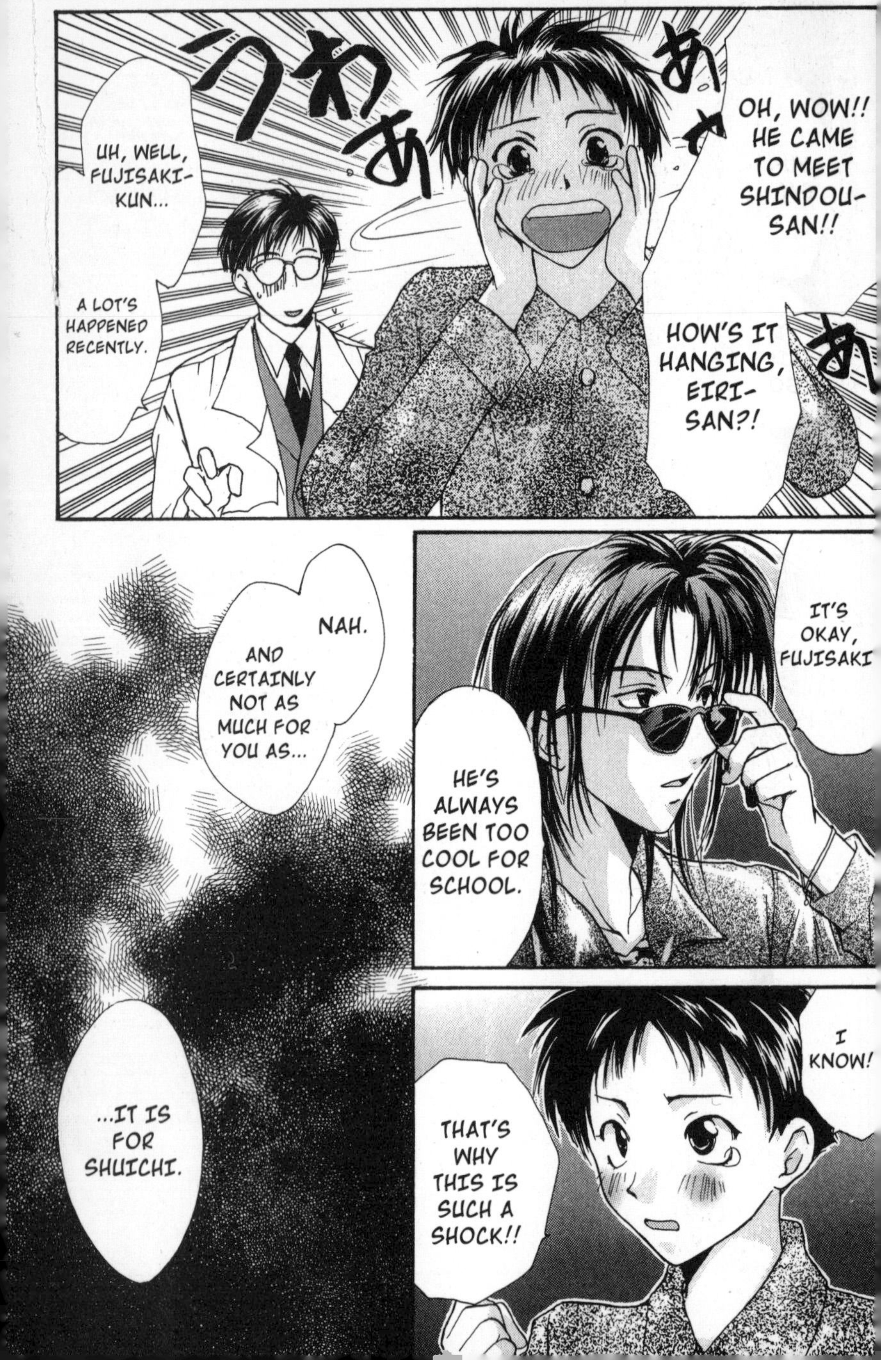
OH, WOW!! HE CAME TO MEET SHINDOU-SAN!!
HOW'S IT HANGING, EIRI-SAN?!
あああ
うわあ
UH, WELL, FUJISAKI-KUN...
A LOT'S HAPPENED RECENTLY.
IT'S OKAY, FUJISAKI
HE'S ALWAYS BEEN TOO COOL FOR SCHOOL.
I KNOW!
THAT'S WHY THIS IS SUCH A SHOCK!!
NAH.
AND CERTAINLY NOT AS MUCH FOR YOU AS...
...IT IS FOR SHUICHI.

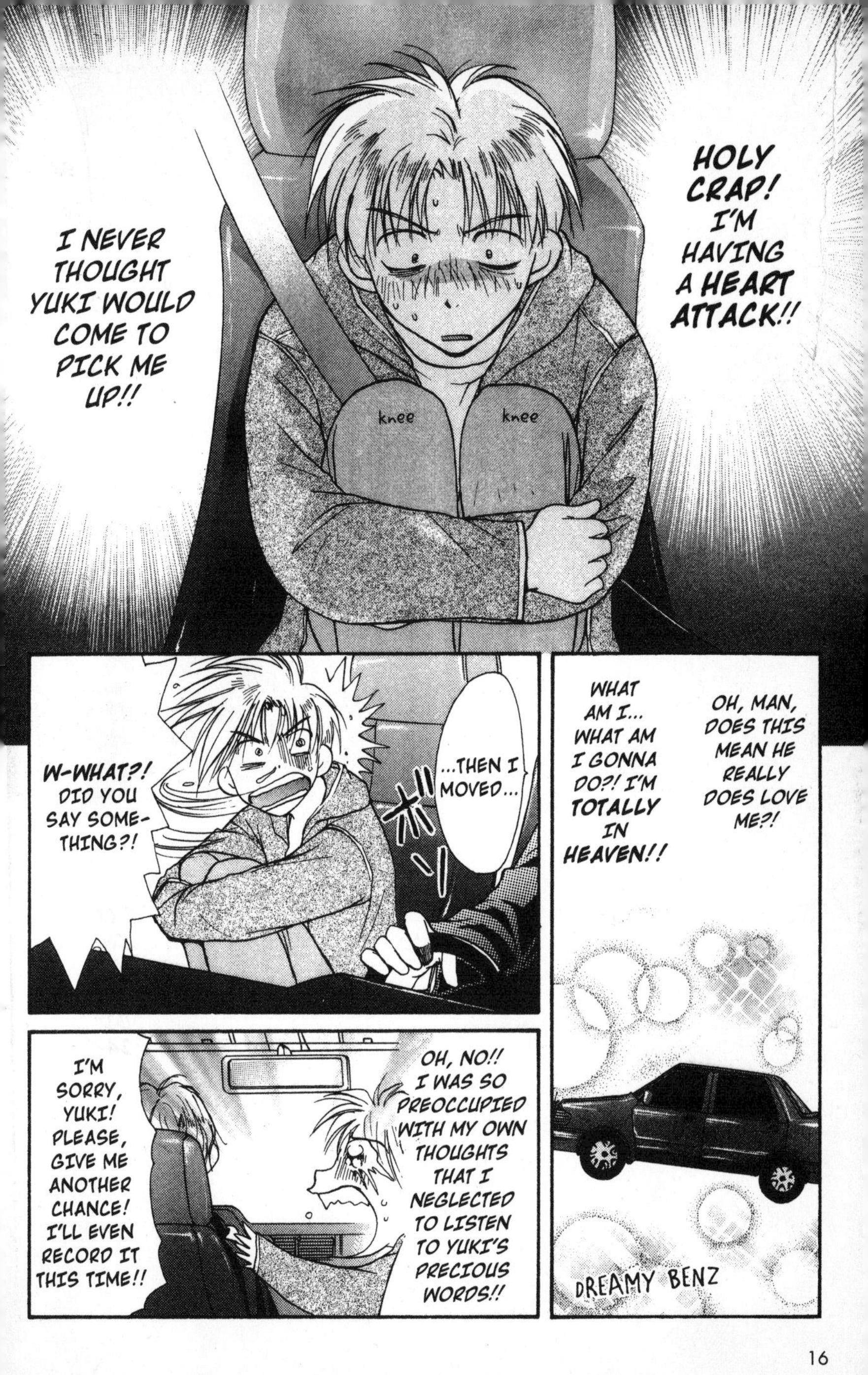
HOLY CRAP! I'M HAVING A HEART ATTACK!!
I NEVER THOUGHT YUKI WOULD COME TO PICK ME UP!!
knee
knee
OH, MAN, DOES THIS MEAN HE REALLY DOES LOVE ME?!
WHAT AM I... WHAT AM I GONNA DO?! I'M TOTALLY IN HEAVEN!!
DREAMY BENZ
...THEN I MOVED...
W-WHAT?! DID YOU SAY SOME-THING?!
OH, NO!! I WAS SO PREOCCUPIED WITH MY OWN THOUGHTS THAT I NEGLECTED TO LISTEN TO YUKI'S PRECIOUS WORDS!!
I'M SORRY, YUKI! PLEASE, GIVE ME ANOTHER CHANCE! I'LL EVEN RECORD IT THIS TIME!!

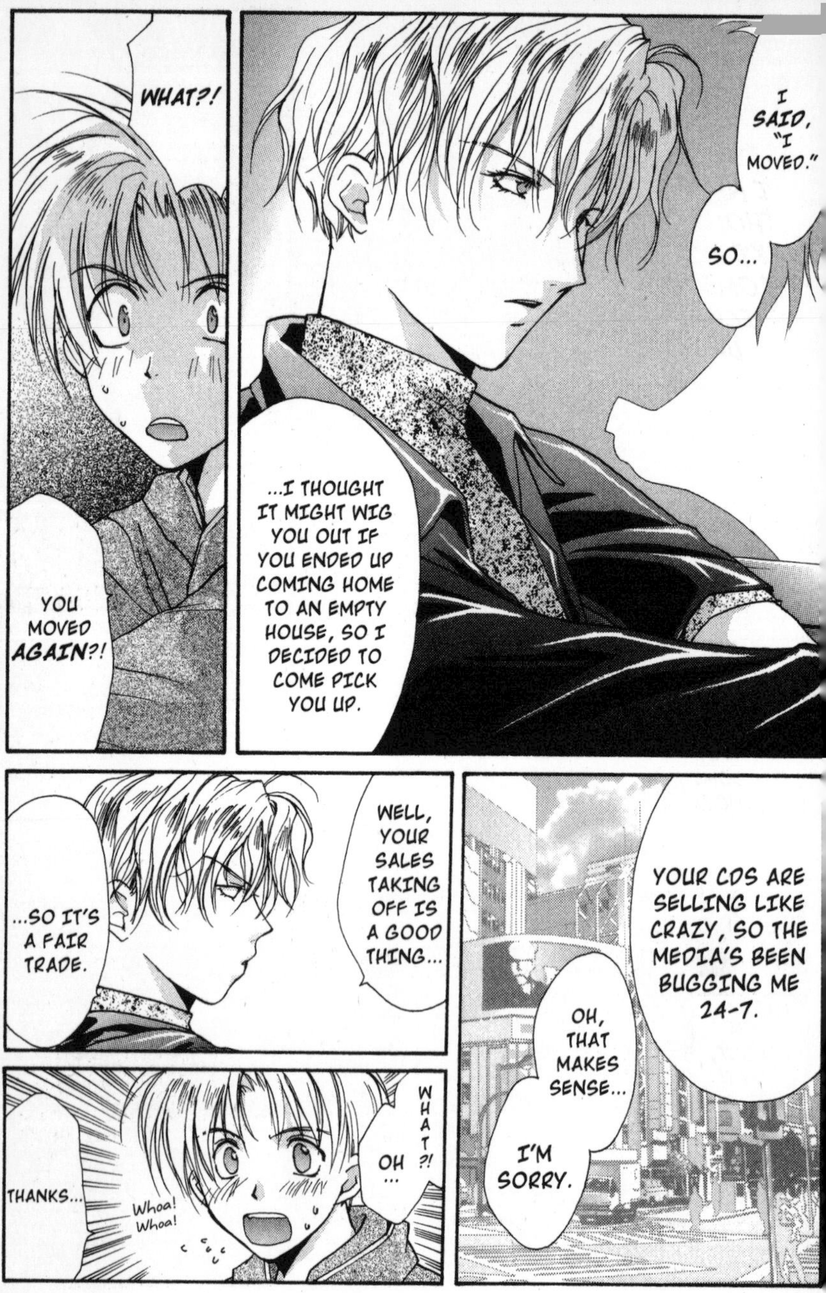
I SAID, "I MOVED."
SO...
...I THOUGHT IT MIGHT WIG YOU OUT IF YOU ENDED UP COMING HOME TO AN EMPTY HOUSE, SO I DECIDED TO COME PICK YOU UP.
WHAT?!
YOU MOVED **AGAIN**?!
YOUR CDS ARE SELLING LIKE CRAZY, SO THE MEDIA'S BEEN BUGGING ME 24-7.
OH, THAT MAKES SENSE...
I'M SORRY.
WELL, YOUR SALES TAKING OFF IS A GOOD THING...
...SO IT'S A FAIR TRADE.
WHAT?!
OH...
Whoa! Whoa!
THANKS...

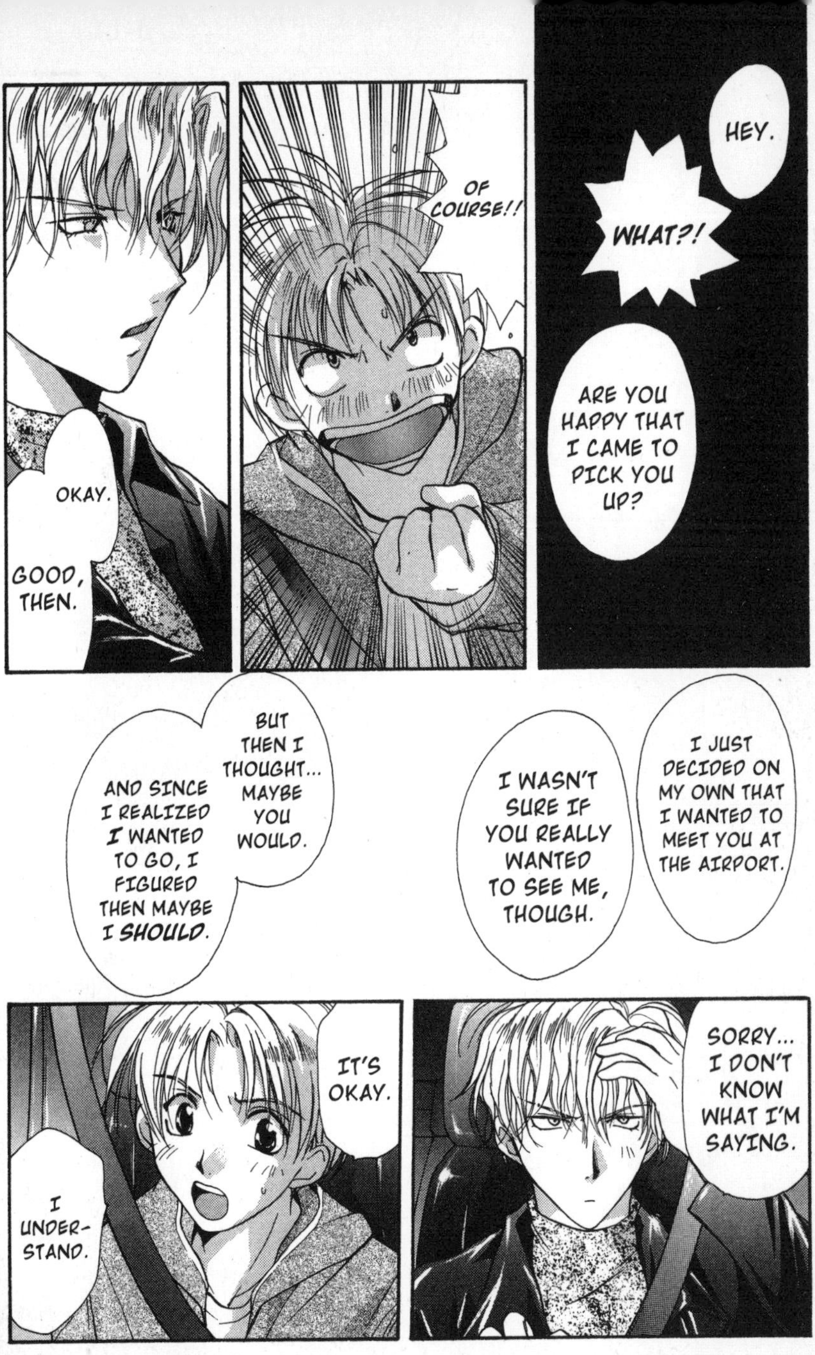
HEY.
WHAT?!
ARE YOU HAPPY THAT I CAME TO PICK YOU UP?
OF COURSE!!
OKAY.
GOOD, THEN.
I JUST DECIDED ON MY OWN THAT I WANTED TO MEET YOU AT THE AIRPORT.
I WASN'T SURE IF YOU REALLY WANTED TO SEE ME, THOUGH.
BUT THEN I THOUGHT... MAYBE YOU WOULD.
AND SINCE I REALIZED *I* WANTED TO GO, I FIGURED THEN MAYBE I **SHOULD**.
SORRY... I DON'T KNOW WHAT I'M SAYING.
IT'S OKAY.
I UNDER-STAND.

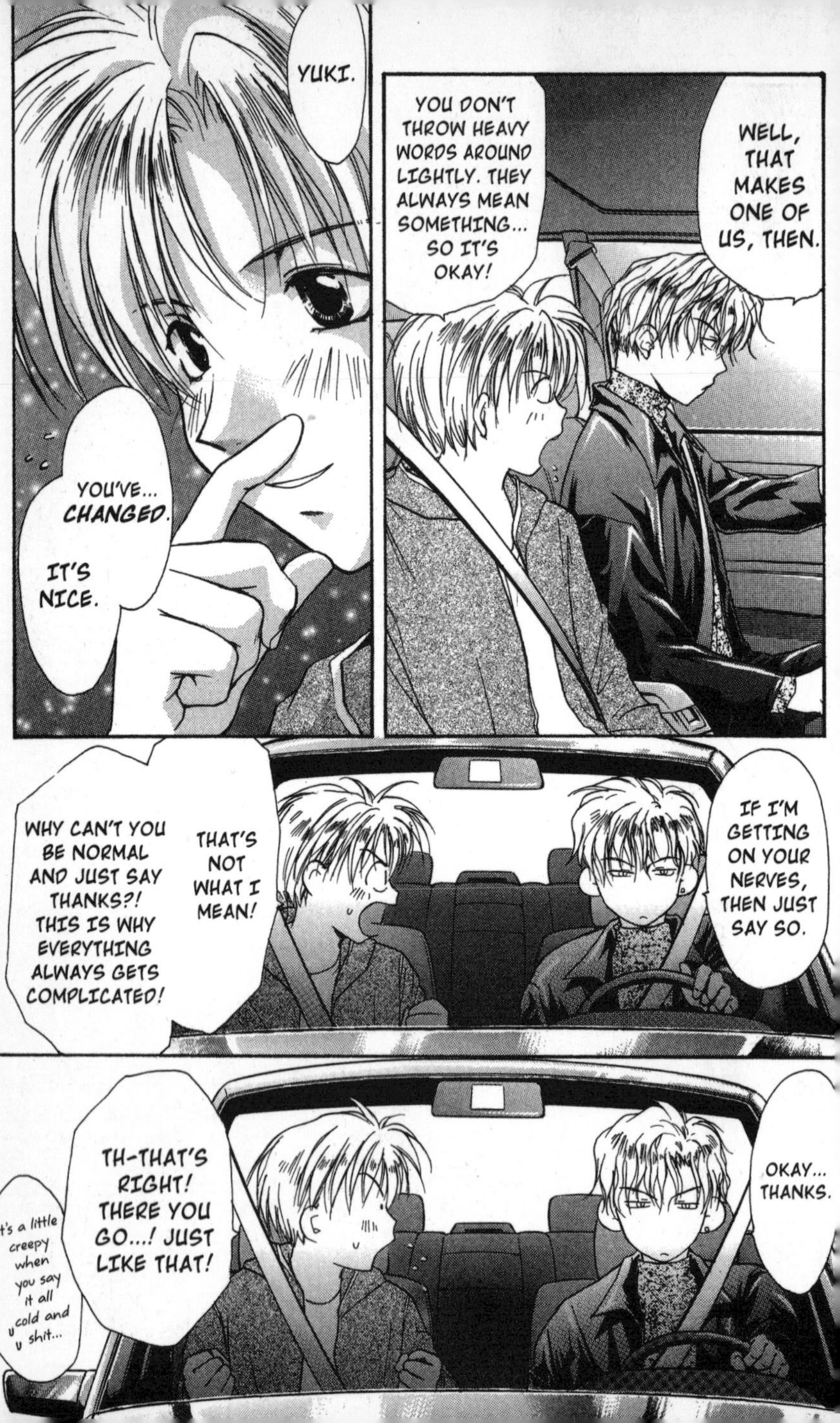
WELL, THAT MAKES ONE OF US, THEN.
YOU DON'T THROW HEAVY WORDS AROUND LIGHTLY. THEY ALWAYS MEAN SOMETHING... SO IT'S OKAY!
YUKI.
YOU'VE... CHANGED.
IT'S NICE.
IF I'M GETTING ON YOUR NERVES, THEN JUST SAY SO.
THAT'S NOT WHAT I MEAN!
WHY CAN'T YOU BE NORMAL AND JUST SAY THANKS?! THIS IS WHY EVERYTHING ALWAYS GETS COMPLICATED!
OKAY... THANKS.
TH-THAT'S RIGHT! THERE YOU GO...! JUST LIKE THAT!
It's a little creepy when you say it all cold and shit...

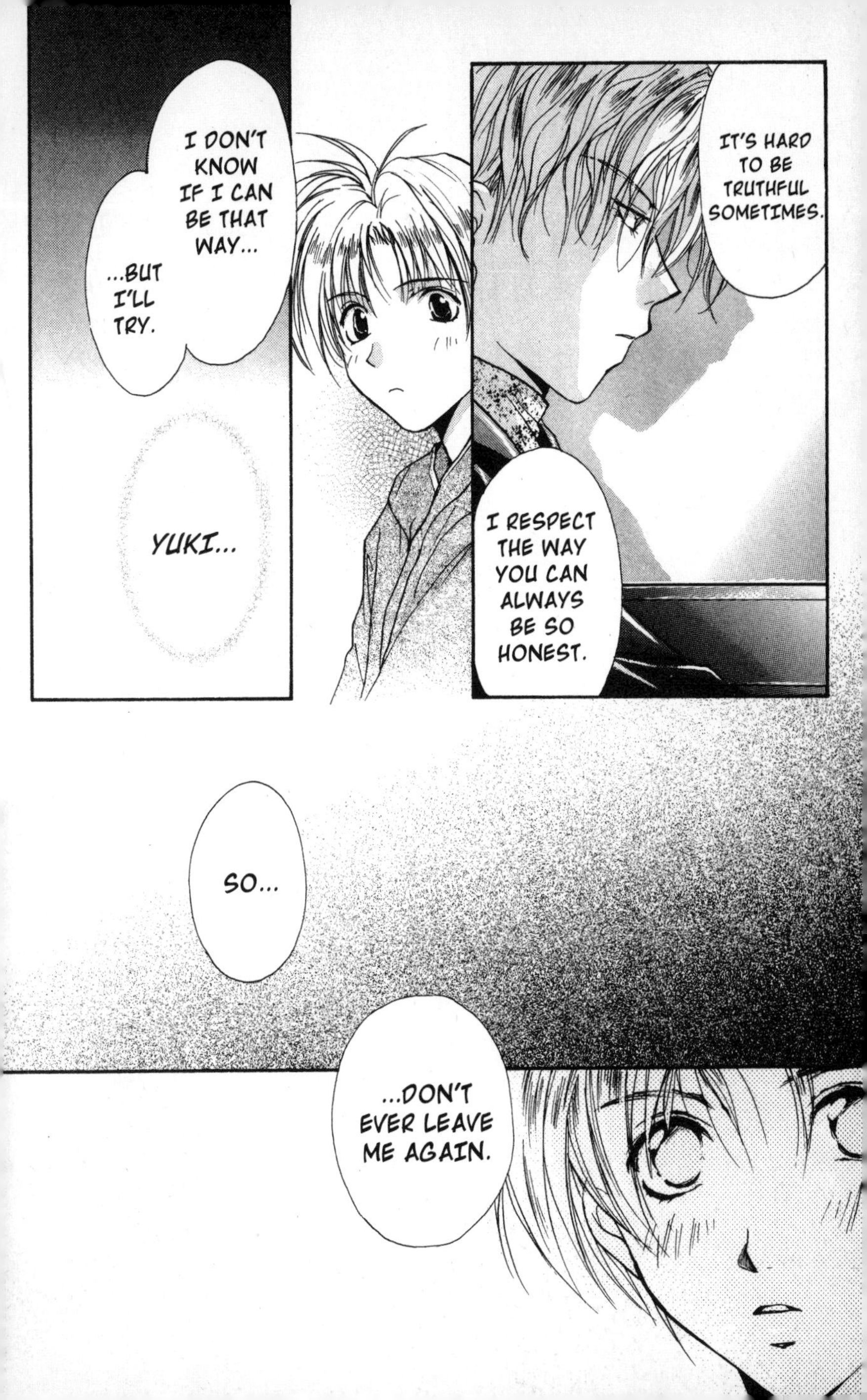
IT'S HARD TO BE TRUTHFUL SOMETIMES.
I RESPECT THE WAY YOU CAN ALWAYS BE SO HONEST.
I DON'T KNOW IF I CAN BE THAT WAY...
...BUT I'LL TRY.
YUKI...
SO...
...DON'T EVER LEAVE ME AGAIN.

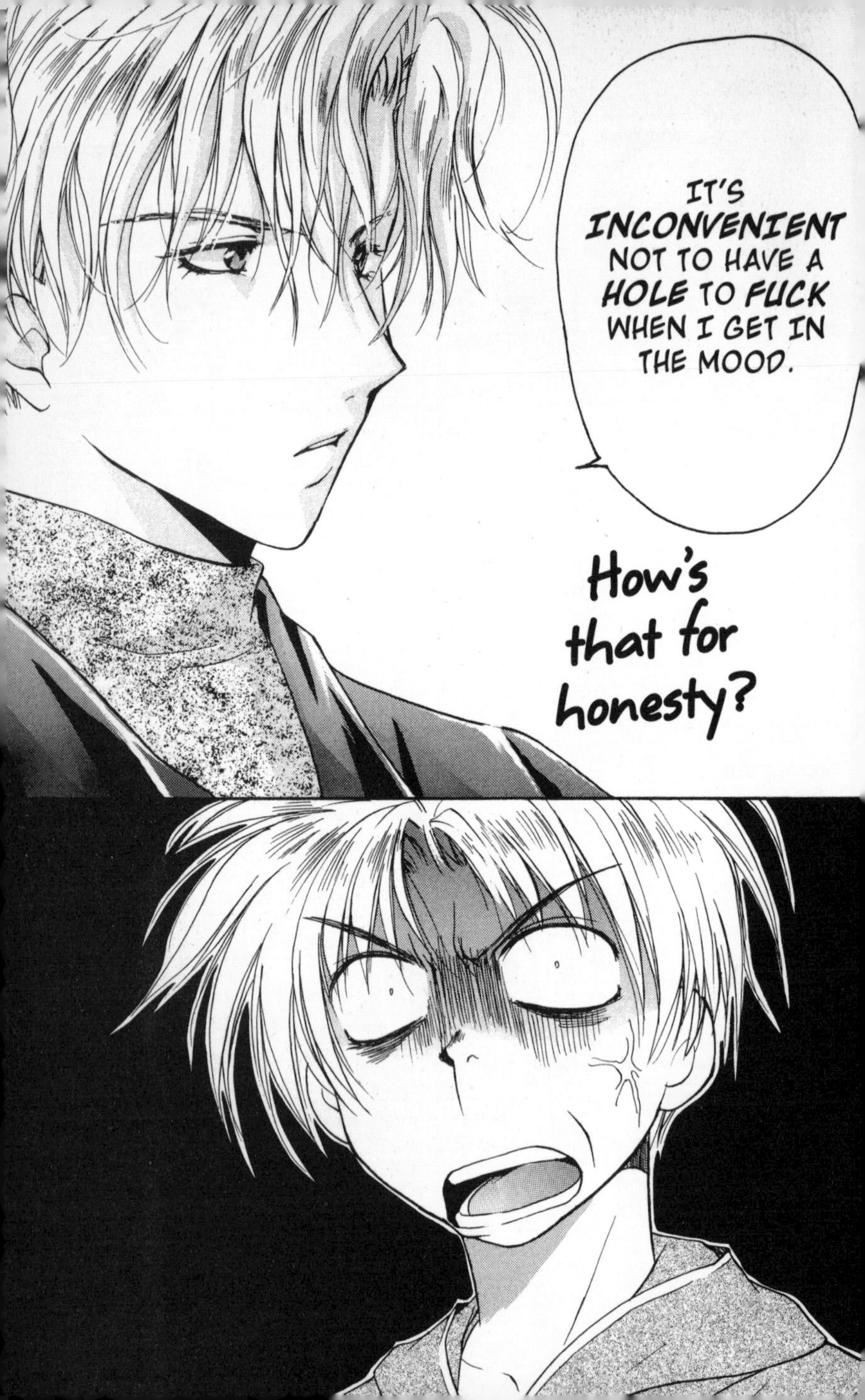
IT'S **INCONVENIENT** NOT TO HAVE A **HOLE** TO **FUCK** WHEN I GET IN THE MOOD.
How's that for honesty?

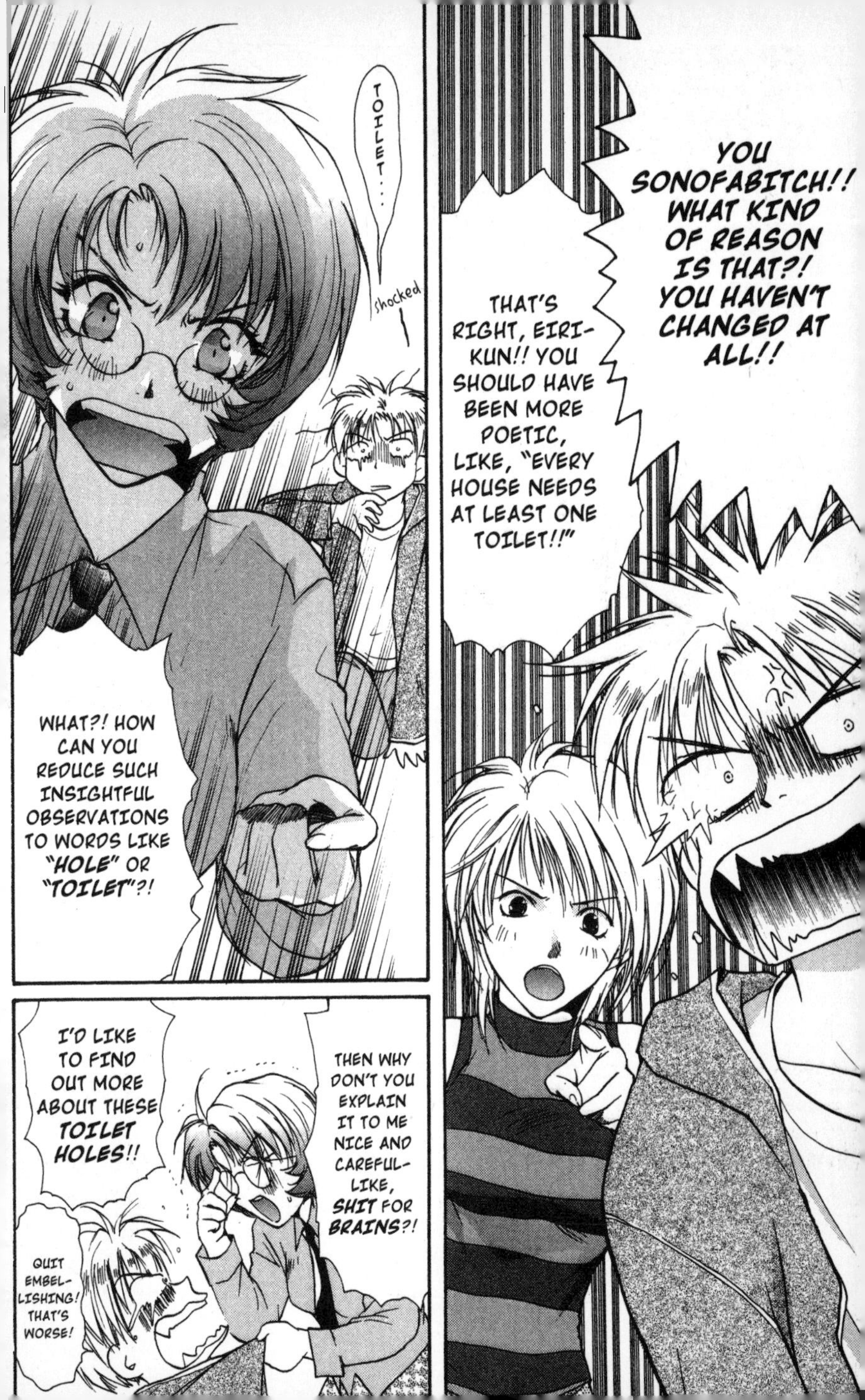
YOU SONOFABITCH!! WHAT KIND OF REASON IS THAT?! YOU HAVEN'T CHANGED AT ALL!!
THAT'S RIGHT, EIRI-KUN!! YOU SHOULD HAVE BEEN MORE POETIC, LIKE, "EVERY HOUSE NEEDS AT LEAST ONE TOILET!!"
TOILET...
shocked
WHAT?! HOW CAN YOU REDUCE SUCH INSIGHTFUL OBSERVATIONS TO WORDS LIKE "HOLE" OR "TOILET"?!
THEN WHY DON'T YOU EXPLAIN IT TO ME NICE AND CAREFUL-LIKE, SHIT FOR BRAINS?!
I'D LIKE TO FIND OUT MORE ABOUT THESE TOILET HOLES!!
QUIT EMBEL-LISHING! THAT'S WORSE!

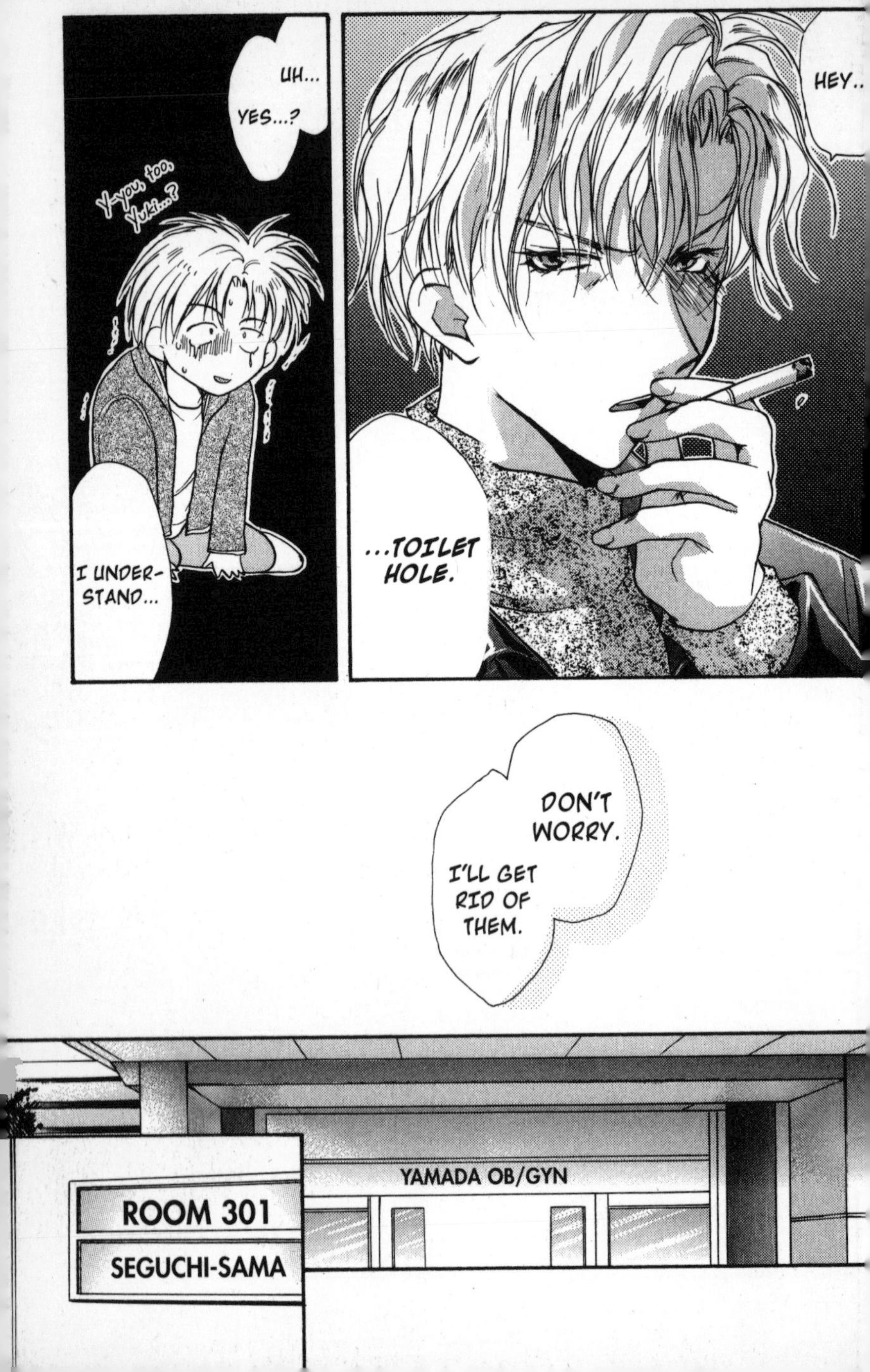
HEY...
...TOILET HOLE.
UH...
YES...?
Y-you, too, Yuki...?
I UNDER-STAND...
DON'T WORRY.
I'LL GET RID OF THEM.
YAMADA OB/GYN
ROOM 301
SEGUCHI-SAMA

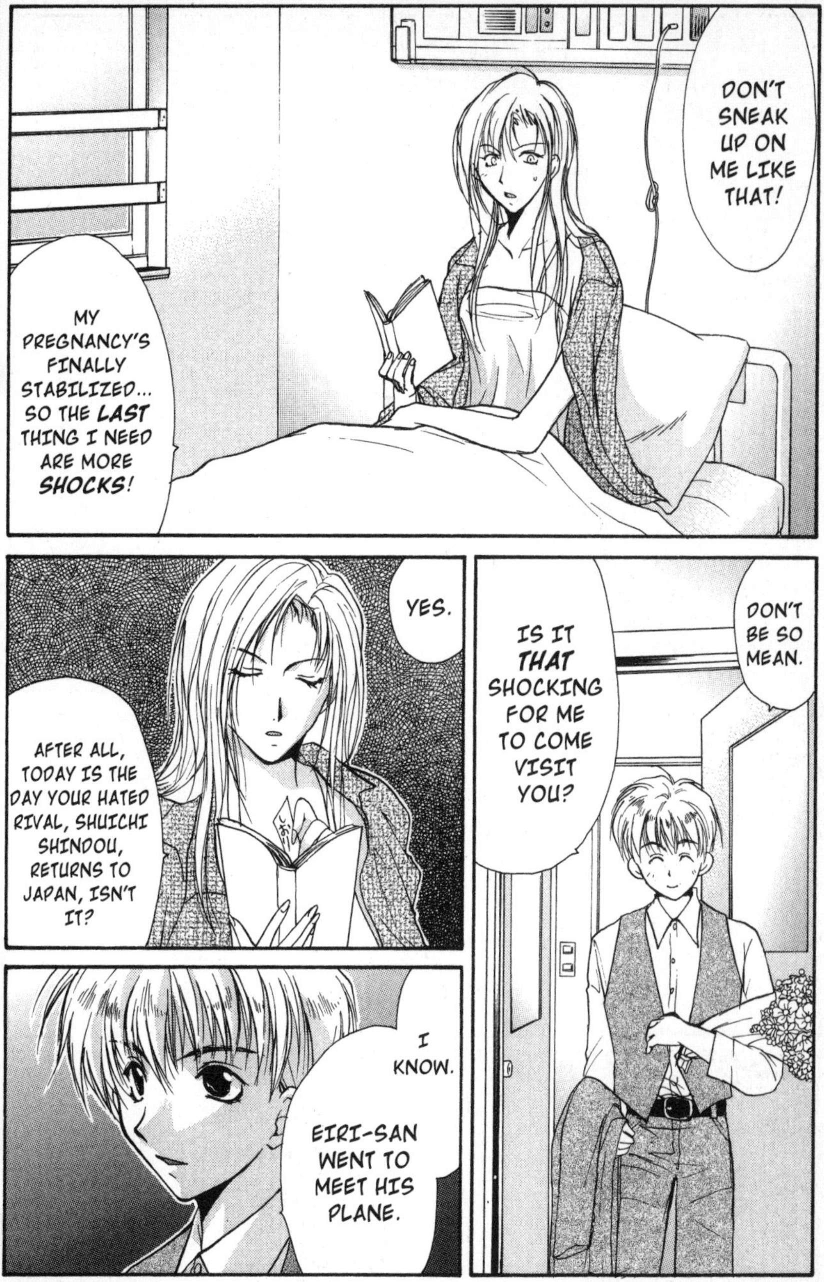
DON'T SNEAK UP ON ME LIKE THAT!
MY PREGNANCY'S FINALLY STABILIZED... SO THE LAST THING I NEED ARE MORE SHOCKS!
DON'T BE SO MEAN.
IS IT THAT SHOCKING FOR ME TO COME VISIT YOU?
YES.
AFTER ALL, TODAY IS THE DAY YOUR HATED RIVAL, SHUICHI SHINDOU, RETURNS TO JAPAN, ISN'T IT?
I KNOW.
EIRI-SAN WENT TO MEET HIS PLANE.

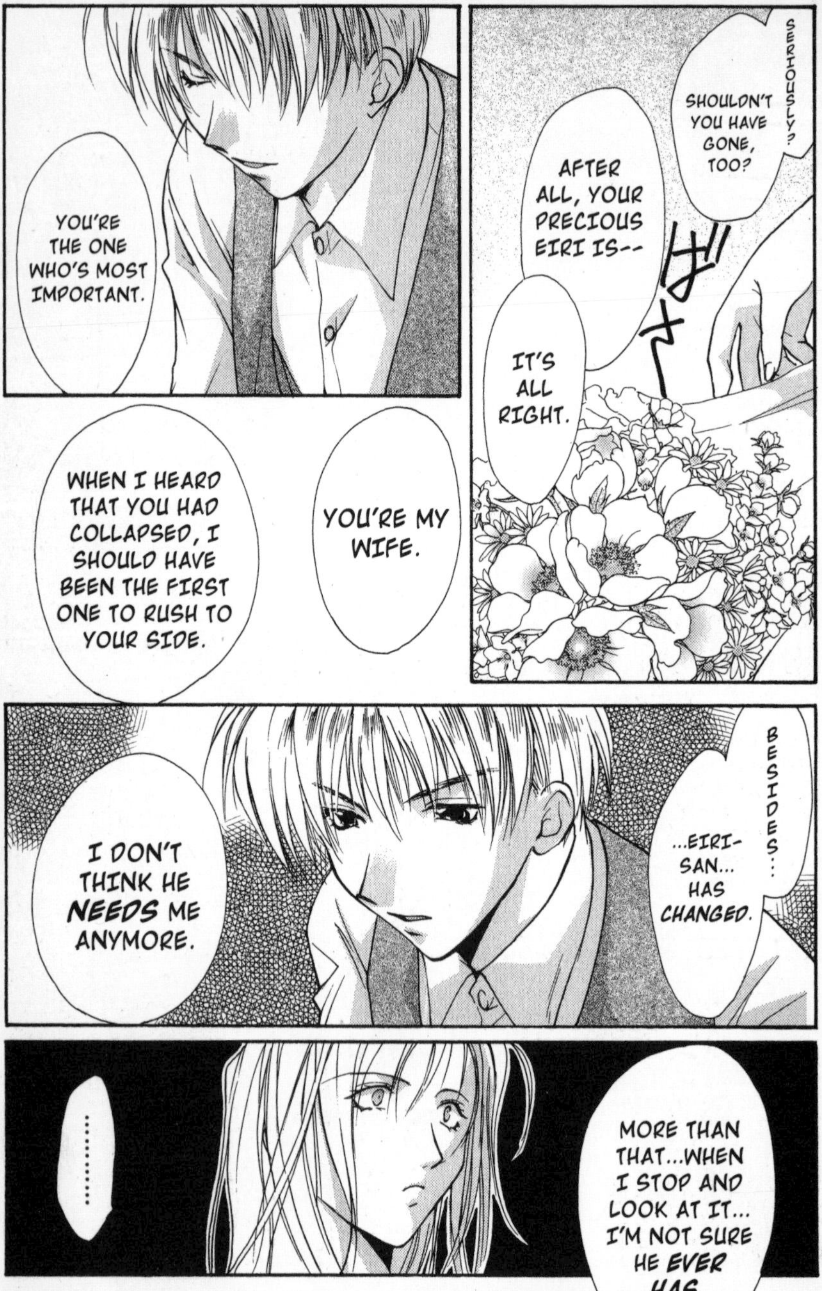
SERIOUSLY?
SHOULDN'T YOU HAVE GONE, TOO?
AFTER ALL, YOUR PRECIOUS EIRI IS--
ばさ
IT'S ALL RIGHT.
YOU'RE THE ONE WHO'S MOST IMPORTANT.
YOU'RE MY WIFE.
WHEN I HEARD THAT YOU HAD COLLAPSED, I SHOULD HAVE BEEN THE FIRST ONE TO RUSH TO YOUR SIDE.
BESIDES...
...EIRI-SAN... HAS CHANGED.
I DON'T THINK HE NEEDS ME ANYMORE.
MORE THAN THAT...WHEN I STOP AND LOOK AT IT... I'M NOT SURE HE EVER HAS.
....

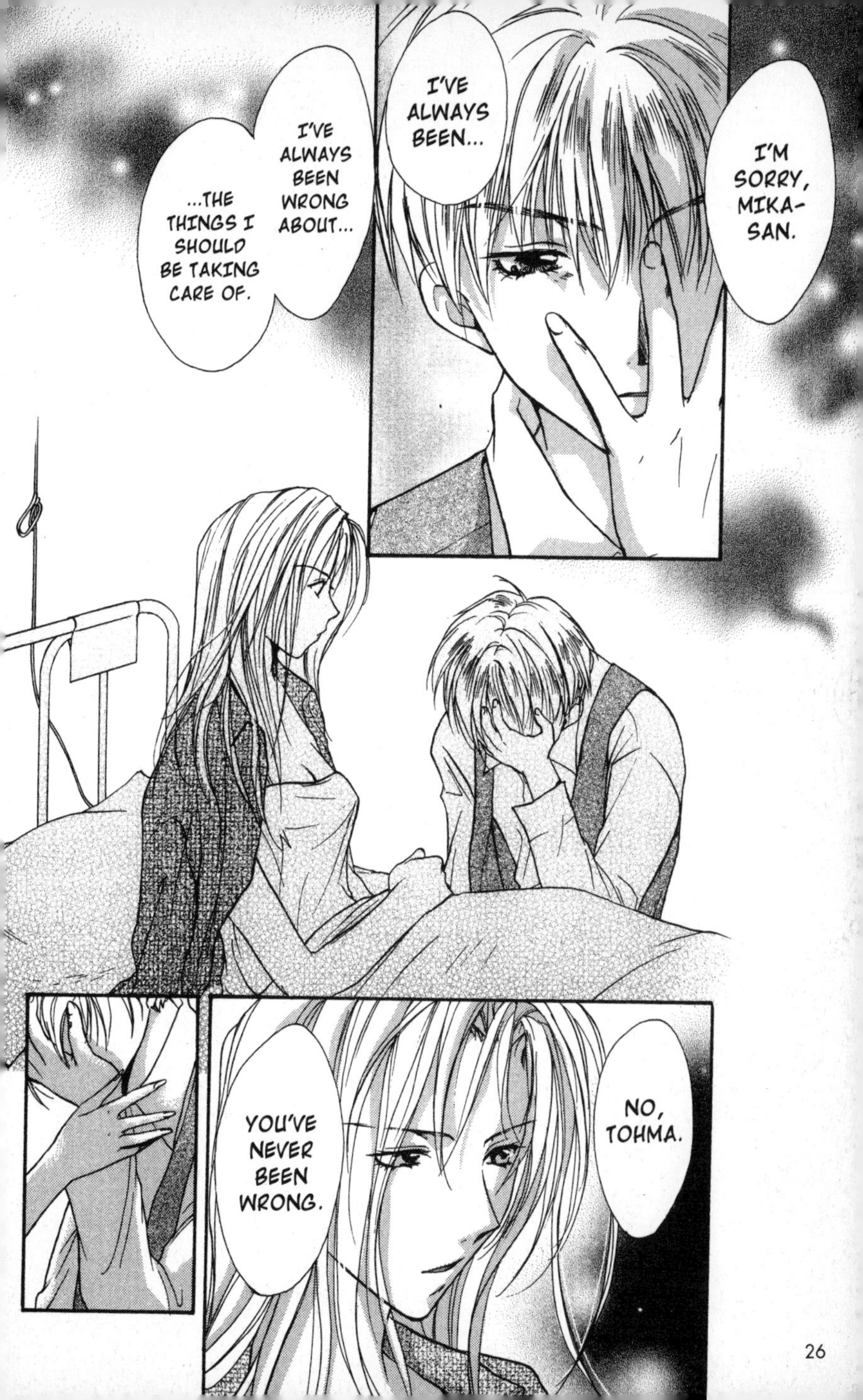
I'M SORRY, MIKA-SAN.
I'VE ALWAYS BEEN...
I'VE ALWAYS BEEN WRONG ABOUT...
...THE THINGS I SHOULD BE TAKING CARE OF.
NO, TOHMA.
YOU'VE NEVER BEEN WRONG.

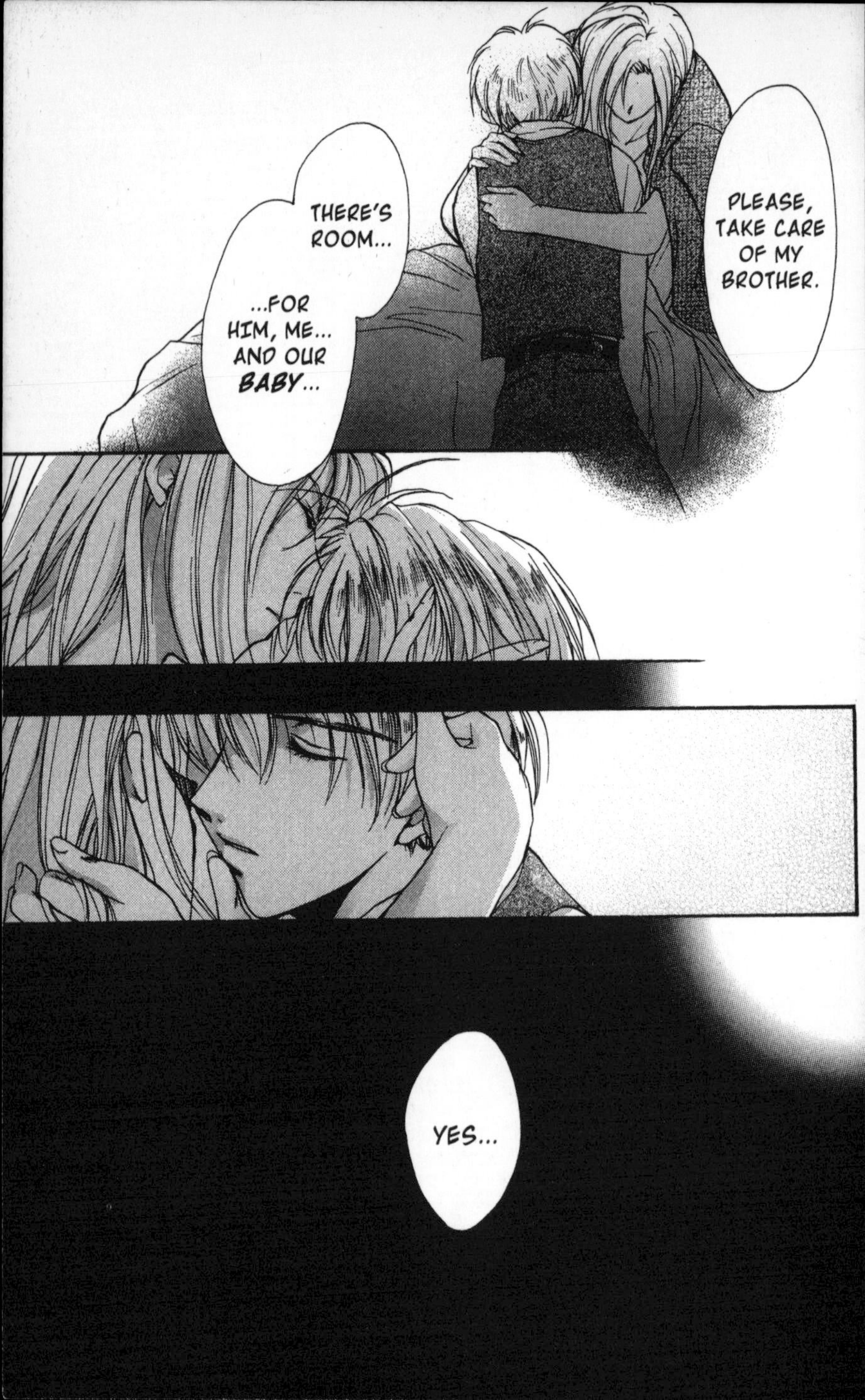
PLEASE, TAKE CARE OF MY BROTHER.
THERE'S ROOM...
...FOR HIM, ME... AND OUR *BABY*...
YES...

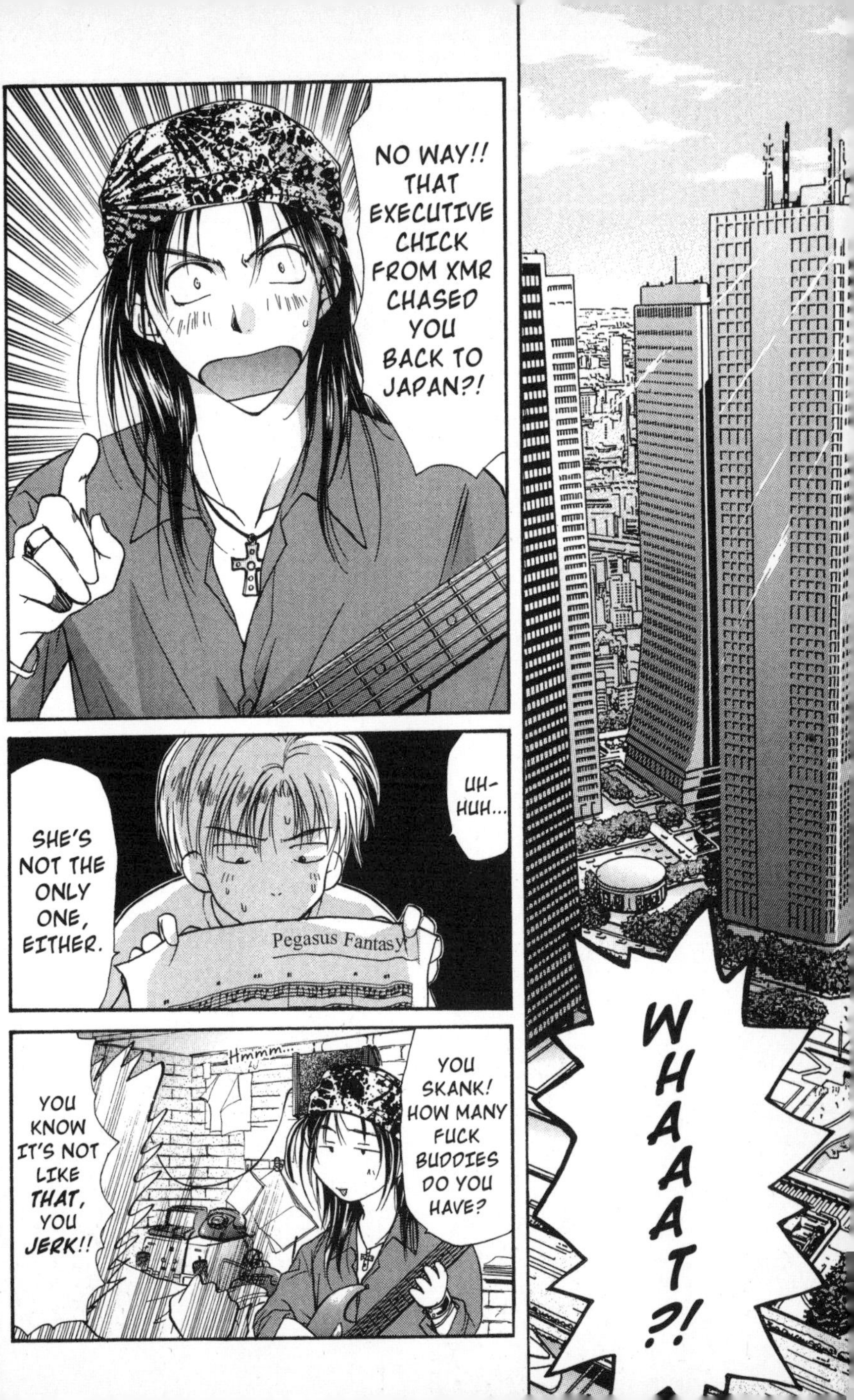
WHAAAT?!
NO WAY!! THAT EXECUTIVE CHICK FROM XMR CHASED YOU BACK TO JAPAN?!
UH-HUH...
SHE'S NOT THE ONLY ONE, EITHER.
Pegasus Fantasy
YOU SKANK! HOW MANY FUCK BUDDIES DO YOU HAVE?
Hmmm...
YOU KNOW IT'S NOT LIKE THAT, YOU JERK!!

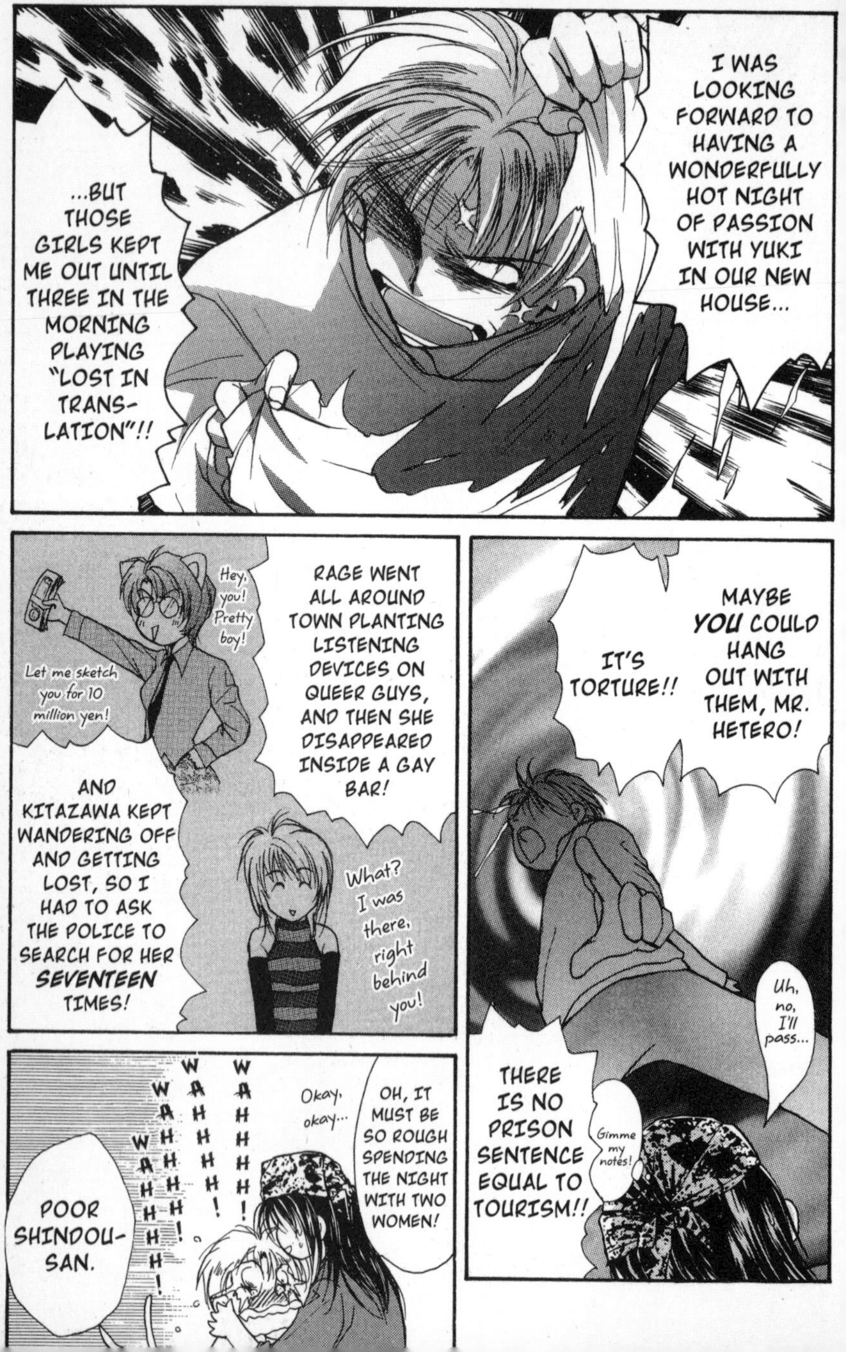
I WAS LOOKING FORWARD TO HAVING A WONDERFULLY HOT NIGHT OF PASSION WITH YUKI IN OUR NEW HOUSE...
...BUT THOSE GIRLS KEPT ME OUT UNTIL THREE IN THE MORNING PLAYING "LOST IN TRANS-LATION"!!
IT'S TORTURE!!
MAYBE YOU COULD HANG OUT WITH THEM, MR. HETERO!
Uh, no, I'll pass...
THERE IS NO PRISON SENTENCE EQUAL TO TOURISM!!
Gimme my notes!
RAGE WENT ALL AROUND TOWN PLANTING LISTENING DEVICES ON QUEER GUYS, AND THEN SHE DISAPPEARED INSIDE A GAY BAR!
Hey, you! Pretty boy!
Let me sketch you for 10 million yen!
AND KITAZAWA KEPT WANDERING OFF AND GETTING LOST, SO I HAD TO ASK THE POLICE TO SEARCH FOR HER SEVENTEEN TIMES!
What? I was there, right behind you!
OH, IT MUST BE SO ROUGH SPENDING THE NIGHT WITH TWO WOMEN!
Okay, okay...
WAHHHHH!
WAHHHHH!
WAHHHHH!
WAHHHHH!
POOR SHINDOU-SAN.

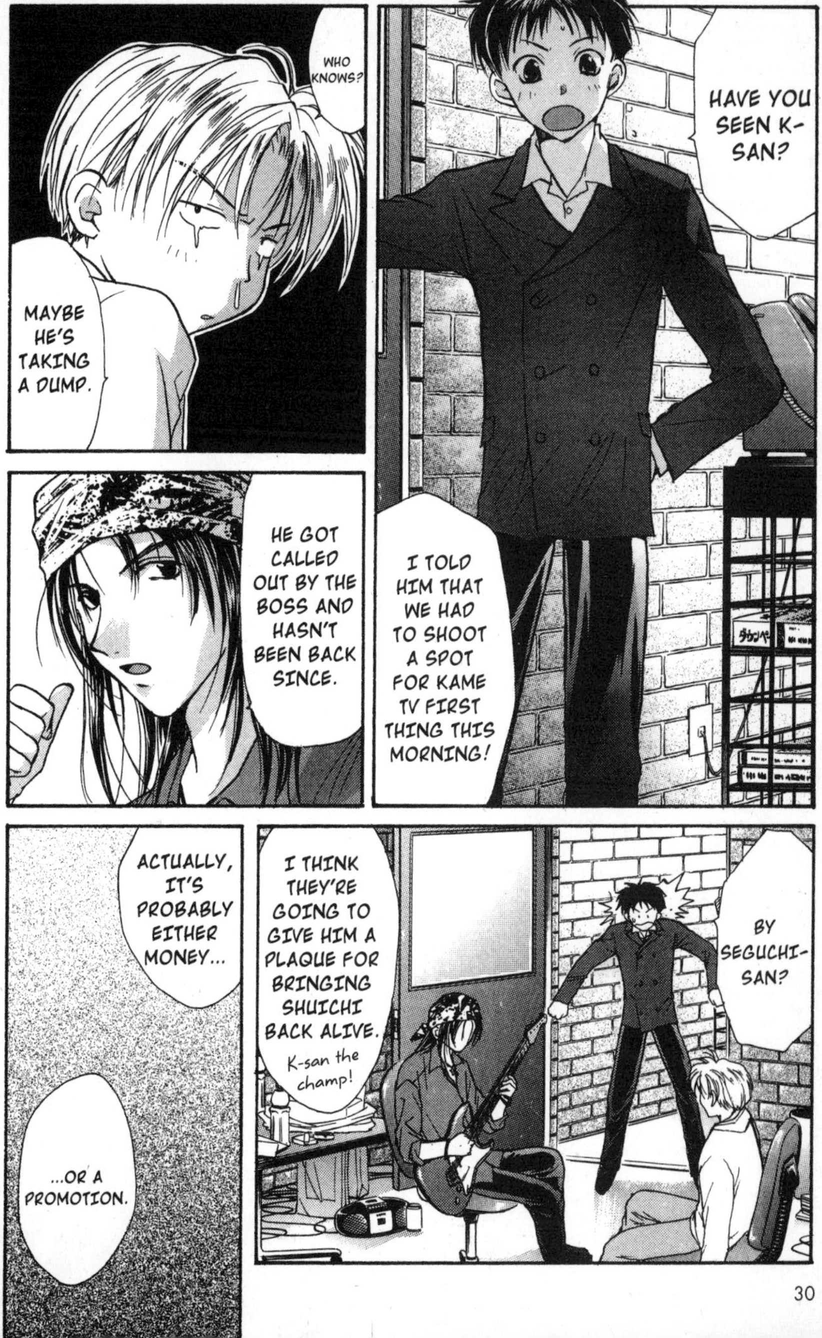
HAVE YOU SEEN K-SAN?
I TOLD HIM THAT WE HAD TO SHOOT A SPOT FOR KAME TV FIRST THING THIS MORNING!
WHO KNOWS?
MAYBE HE'S TAKING A DUMP.
HE GOT CALLED OUT BY THE BOSS AND HASN'T BEEN BACK SINCE.
BY SEGUCHI-SAN?
I THINK THEY'RE GOING TO GIVE HIM A PLAQUE FOR BRINGING SHUICHI BACK ALIVE.
K-san the champ!
ACTUALLY, IT'S PROBABLY EITHER MONEY...
...OR A PROMOTION.

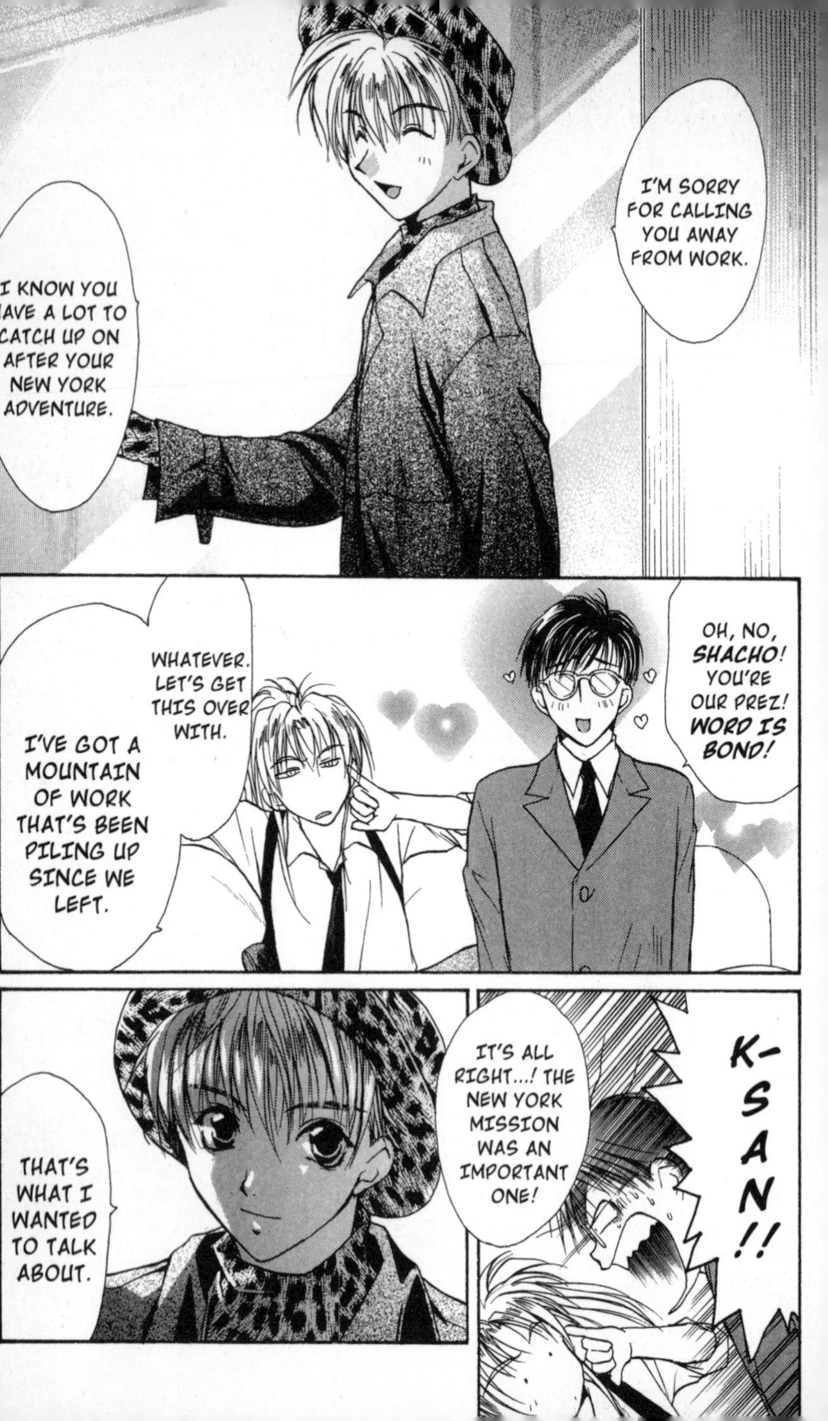
I'M SORRY FOR CALLING YOU AWAY FROM WORK.
I KNOW YOU HAVE A LOT TO CATCH UP ON AFTER YOUR NEW YORK ADVENTURE.
OH, NO, **SHACHO**! YOU'RE OUR PREZ! **WORD IS BOND!**
WHATEVER. LET'S GET THIS OVER WITH.
I'VE GOT A MOUNTAIN OF WORK THAT'S BEEN PILING UP SINCE WE LEFT.
K-SAN!!
IT'S ALL RIGHT...! THE NEW YORK MISSION WAS AN IMPORTANT ONE!
THAT'S WHAT I WANTED TO TALK ABOUT.

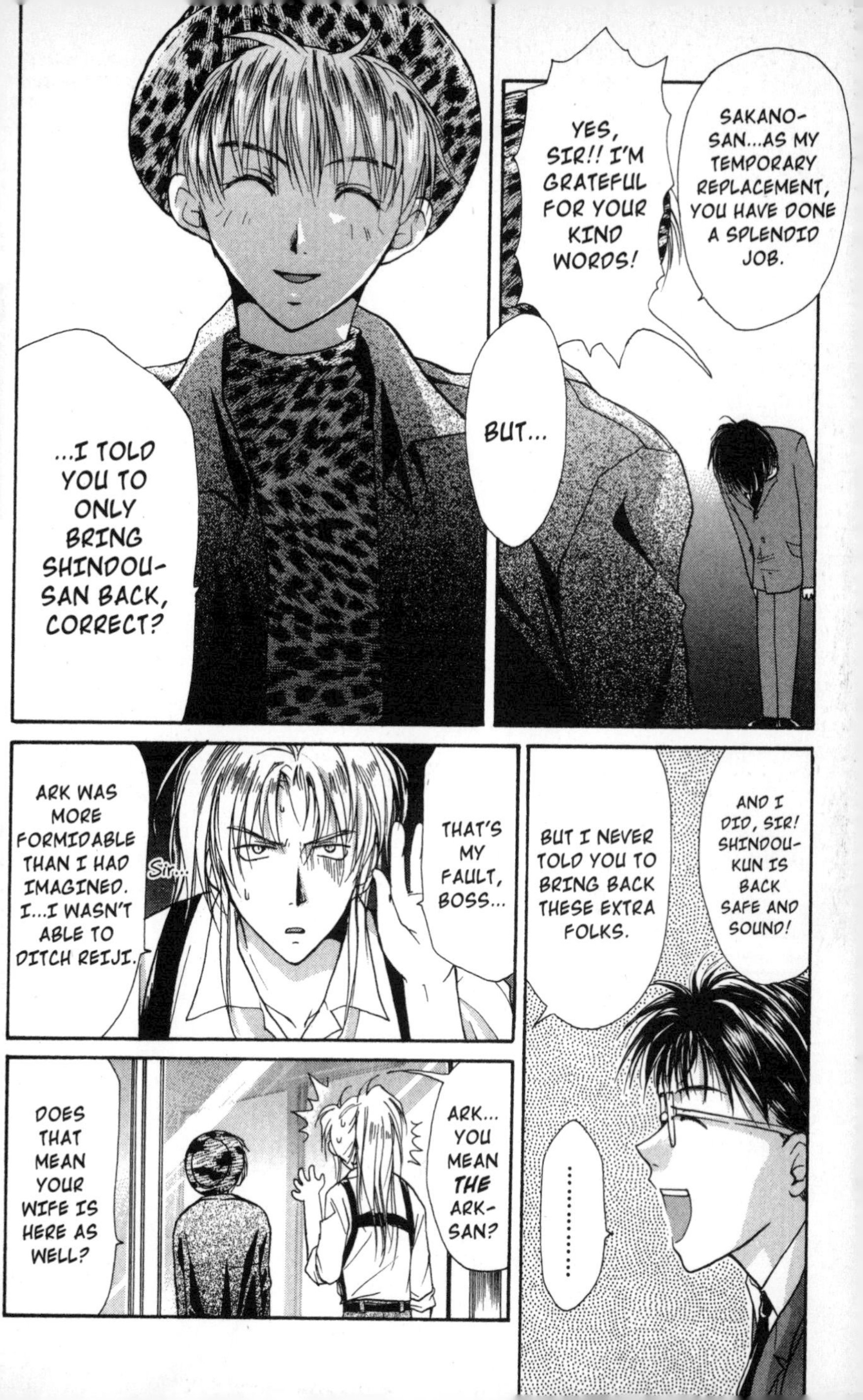
SAKANO-SAN...AS MY TEMPORARY REPLACEMENT, YOU HAVE DONE A SPLENDID JOB.
YES, SIR!! I'M GRATEFUL FOR YOUR KIND WORDS!
BUT...
...I TOLD YOU TO ONLY BRING SHINDOU-SAN BACK, CORRECT?
AND I DID, SIR! SHINDOU-KUN IS BACK SAFE AND SOUND!
BUT I NEVER TOLD YOU TO BRING BACK THESE EXTRA FOLKS.
......
THAT'S MY FAULT, BOSS...
Sir...
ARK WAS MORE FORMIDABLE THAN I HAD IMAGINED. I...I WASN'T ABLE TO DITCH REIJI.
ARK... YOU MEAN *THE* ARK-SAN?
DOES THAT MEAN YOUR WIFE IS HERE AS WELL?

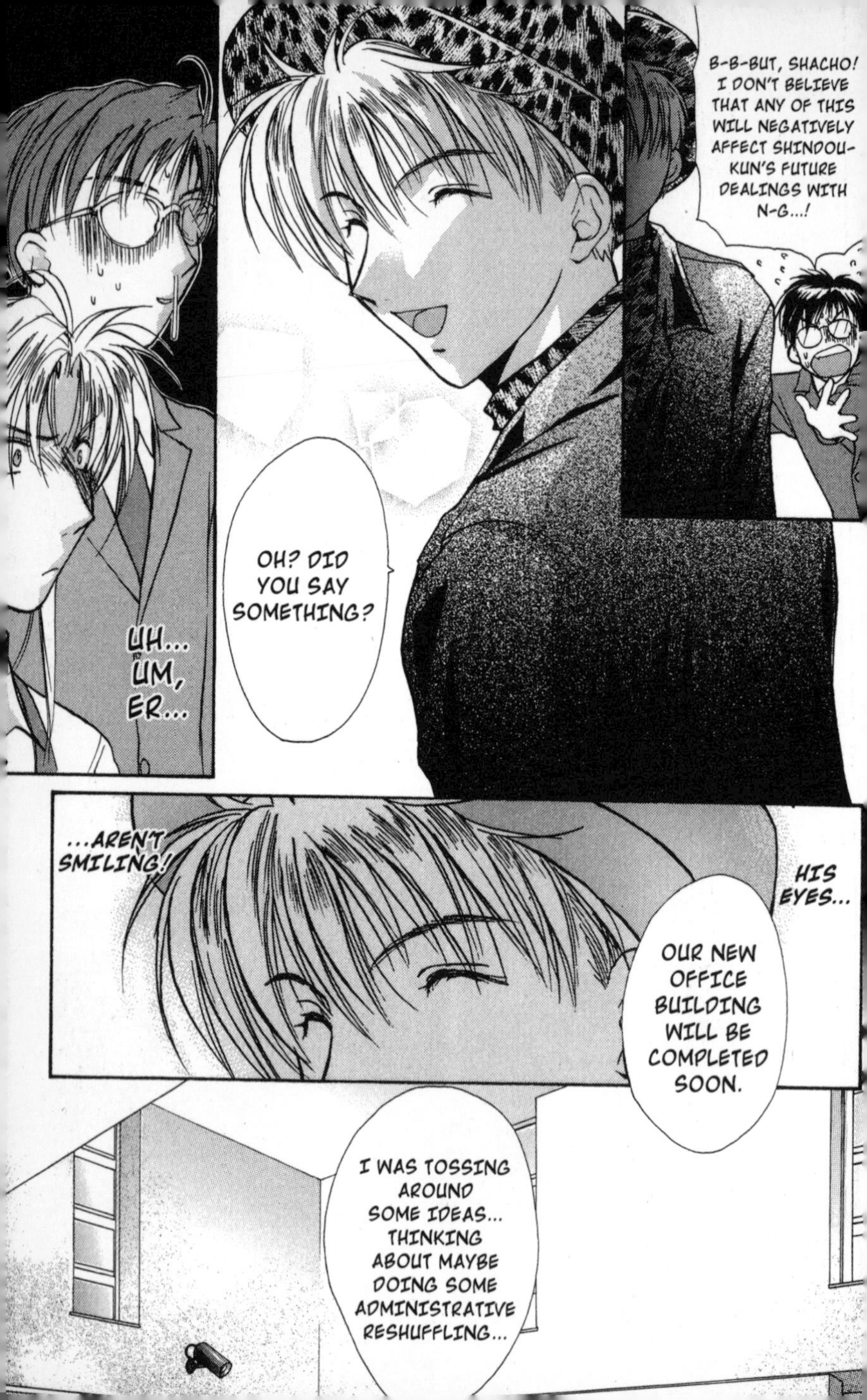
B-B-BUT, SHACHO! I DON'T BELIEVE THAT ANY OF THIS WILL NEGATIVELY AFFECT SHINDOU-KUN'S FUTURE DEALINGS WITH N-G...!
OH? DID YOU SAY SOMETHING?
UH... UM, ER...
HIS EYES...
...AREN'T SMILING!
OUR NEW OFFICE BUILDING WILL BE COMPLETED SOON.
I WAS TOSSING AROUND SOME IDEAS... THINKING ABOUT MAYBE DOING SOME ADMINISTRATIVE RESHUFFLING...

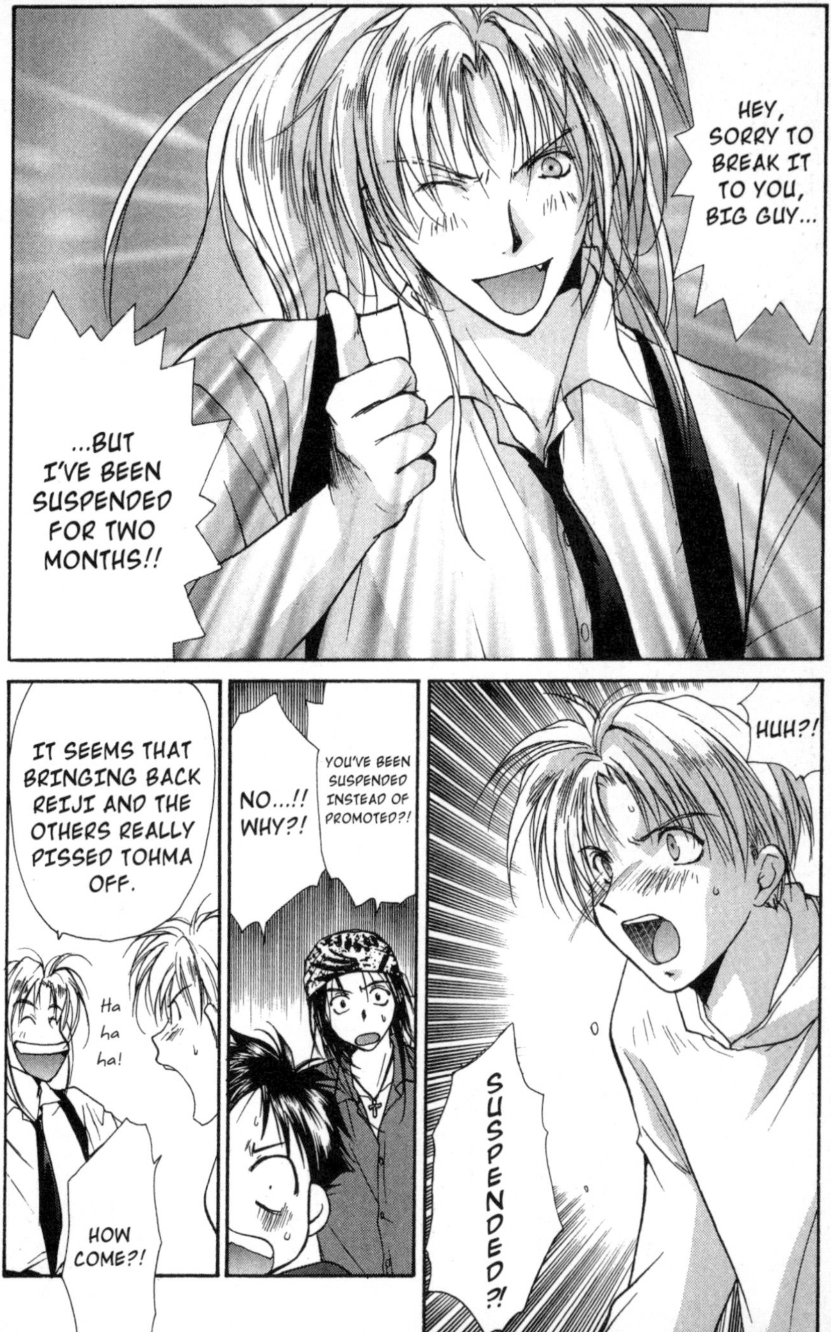
HEY, SORRY TO BREAK IT TO YOU, BIG GUY...
...BUT I'VE BEEN SUSPENDED FOR TWO MONTHS!!
HUH?!
SUSPENDED?!
YOU'VE BEEN SUSPENDED INSTEAD OF PROMOTED?!
NO...!! WHY?!
IT SEEMS THAT BRINGING BACK REIJI AND THE OTHERS REALLY PISSED TOHMA OFF.
Ha ha ha!
HOW COME?!

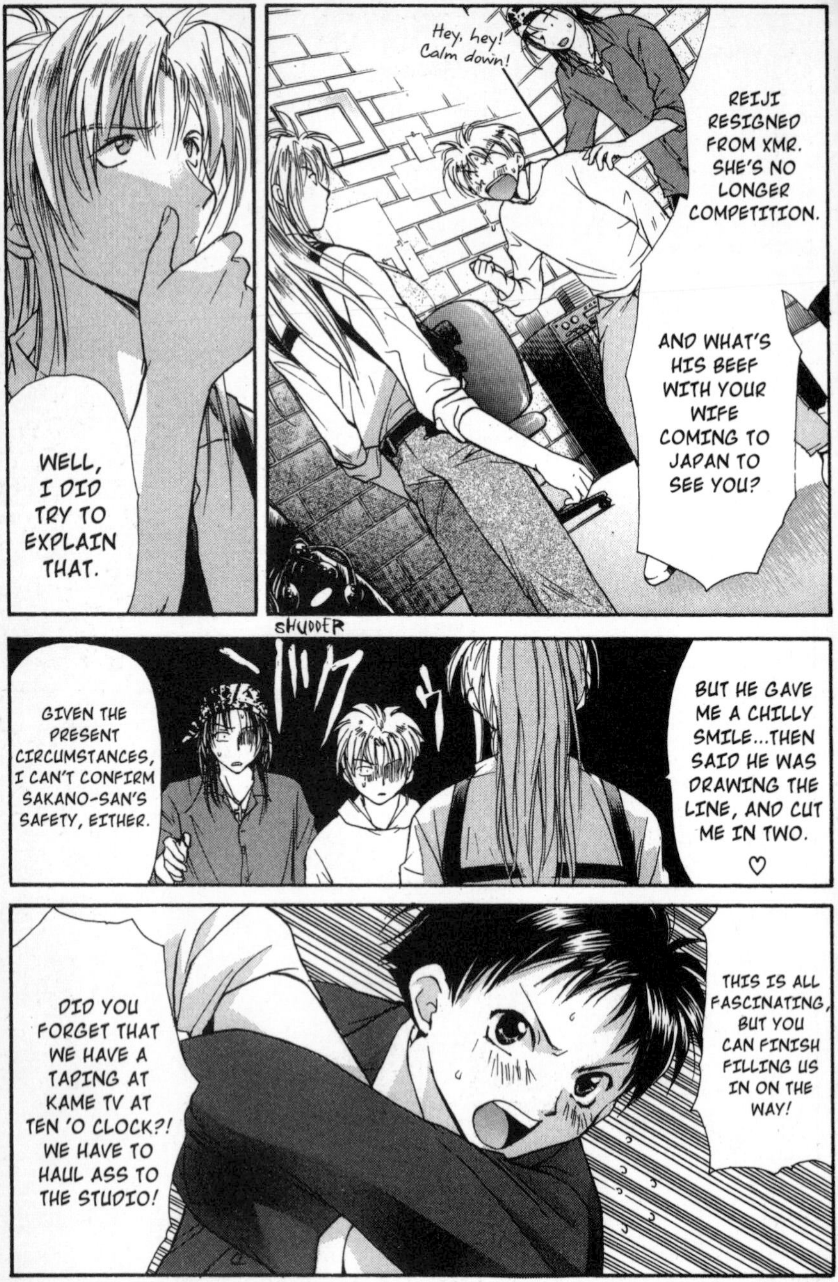
REIJI RESIGNED FROM XMR. SHE'S NO LONGER COMPETITION.
AND WHAT'S HIS BEEF WITH YOUR WIFE COMING TO JAPAN TO SEE YOU?
Hey, hey! Calm down!
WELL, I DID TRY TO EXPLAIN THAT.
SHUDDER
BUT HE GAVE ME A CHILLY SMILE...THEN SAID HE WAS DRAWING THE LINE, AND CUT ME IN TWO. ♡
GIVEN THE PRESENT CIRCUMSTANCES, I CAN'T CONFIRM SAKANO-SAN'S SAFETY, EITHER.
THIS IS ALL FASCINATING, BUT YOU CAN FINISH FILLING US IN ON THE WAY!
DID YOU FORGET THAT WE HAVE A TAPING AT KAME TV AT TEN 'O CLOCK?! WE HAVE TO HAUL ASS TO THE STUDIO!

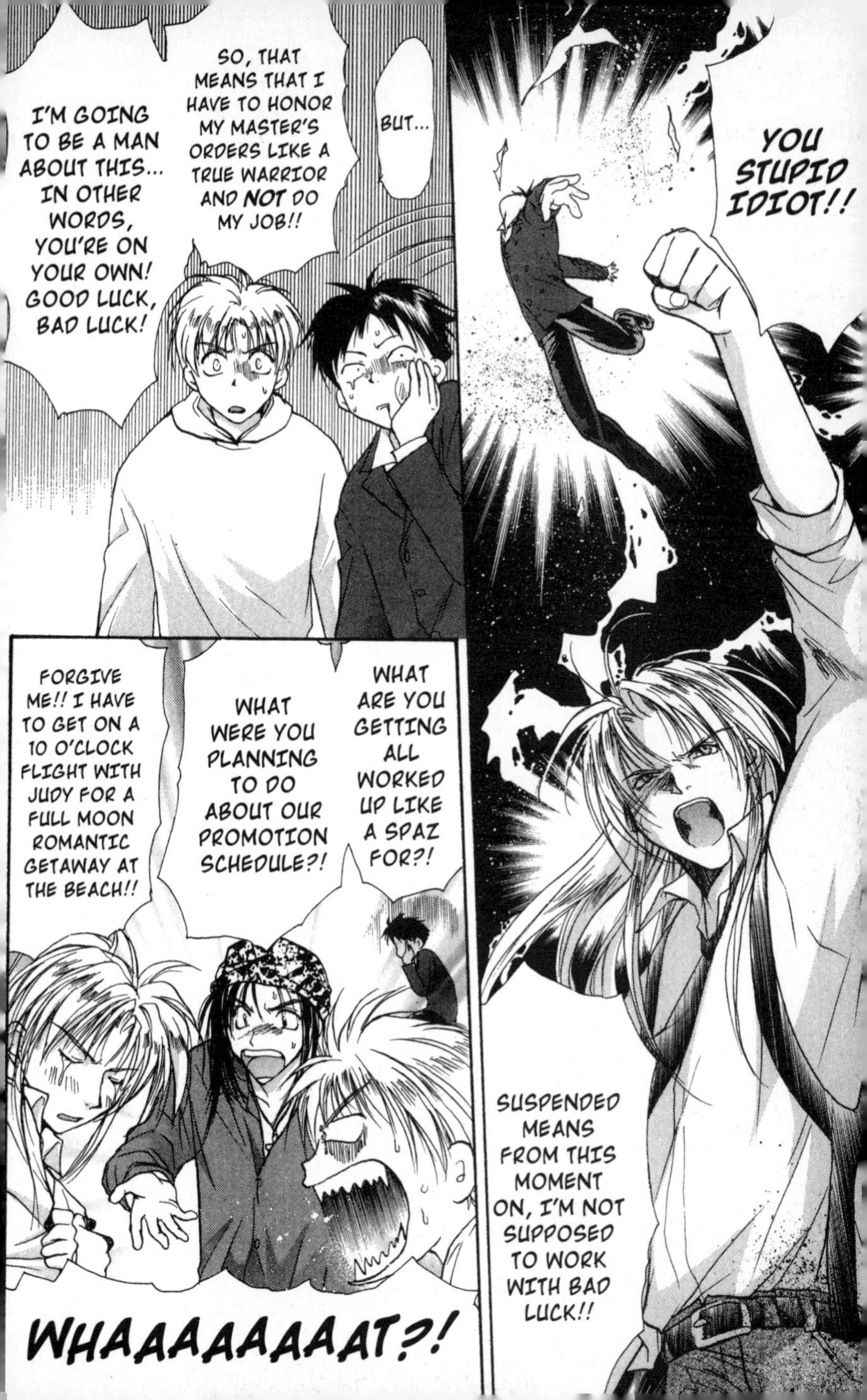
YOU STUPID IDIOT!!
SUSPENDED MEANS FROM THIS MOMENT ON, I'M NOT SUPPOSED TO WORK WITH BAD LUCK!!
BUT...
SO, THAT MEANS THAT I HAVE TO HONOR MY MASTER'S ORDERS LIKE A TRUE WARRIOR AND **NOT** DO MY JOB!!
I'M GOING TO BE A MAN ABOUT THIS... IN OTHER WORDS, YOU'RE ON YOUR OWN! GOOD LUCK, BAD LUCK!
WHAT ARE YOU GETTING ALL WORKED UP LIKE A SPAZ FOR?!
WHAT WERE YOU PLANNING TO DO ABOUT OUR PROMOTION SCHEDULE?!
FORGIVE ME!! I HAVE TO GET ON A 10 O'CLOCK FLIGHT WITH JUDY FOR A FULL MOON ROMANTIC GETAWAY AT THE BEACH!!
WHAAAAAAAAT?!

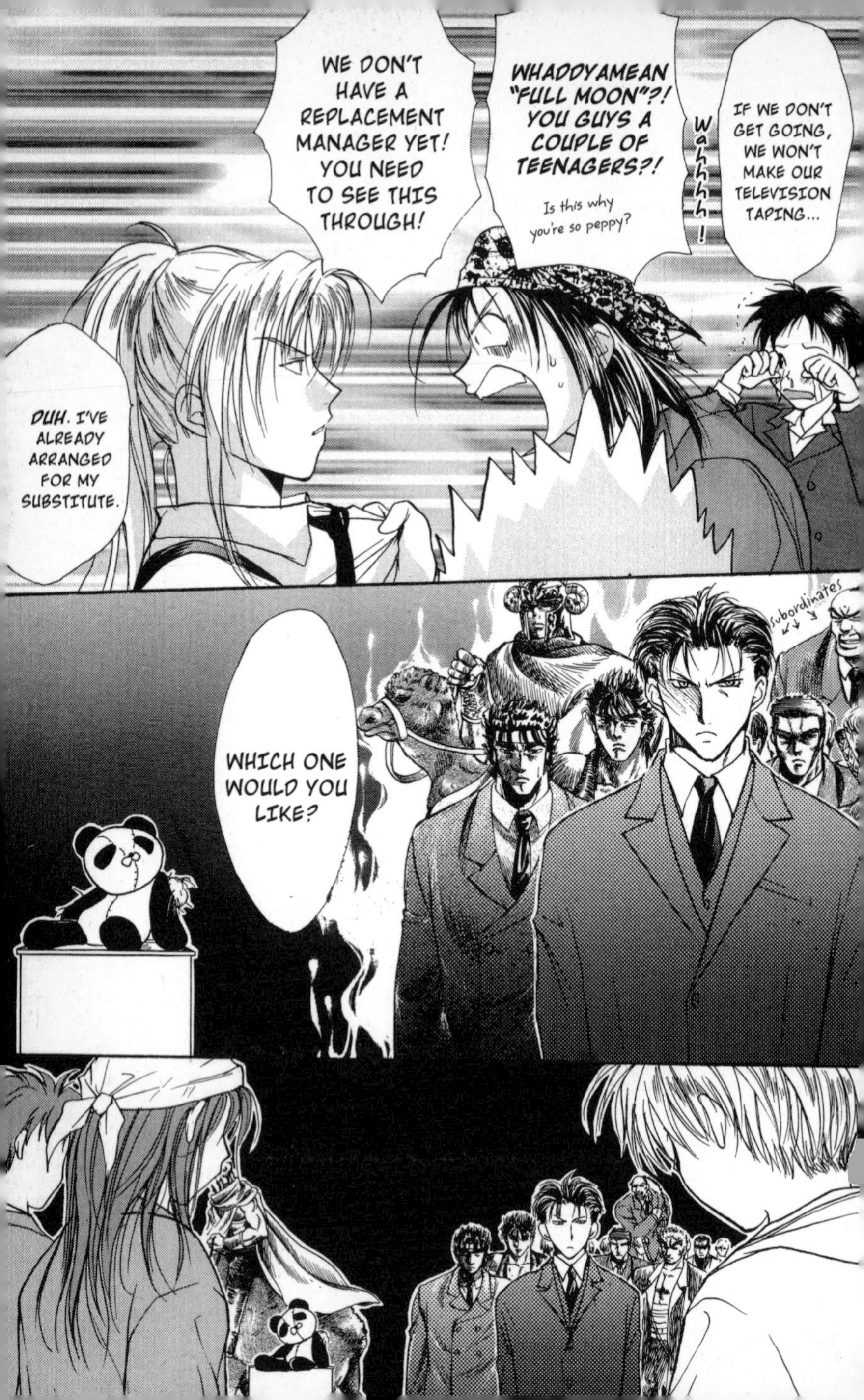
IF WE DON'T GET GOING, WE WON'T MAKE OUR TELEVISION TAPING...
Wahhhh!
WHADDYAMEAN "FULL MOON"?! YOU GUYS A COUPLE OF TEENAGERS?!
Is this why you're so peppy?
WE DON'T HAVE A REPLACEMENT MANAGER YET! YOU NEED TO SEE THIS THROUGH!
DUH. I'VE ALREADY ARRANGED FOR MY SUBSTITUTE.
subordinates
WHICH ONE WOULD YOU LIKE?

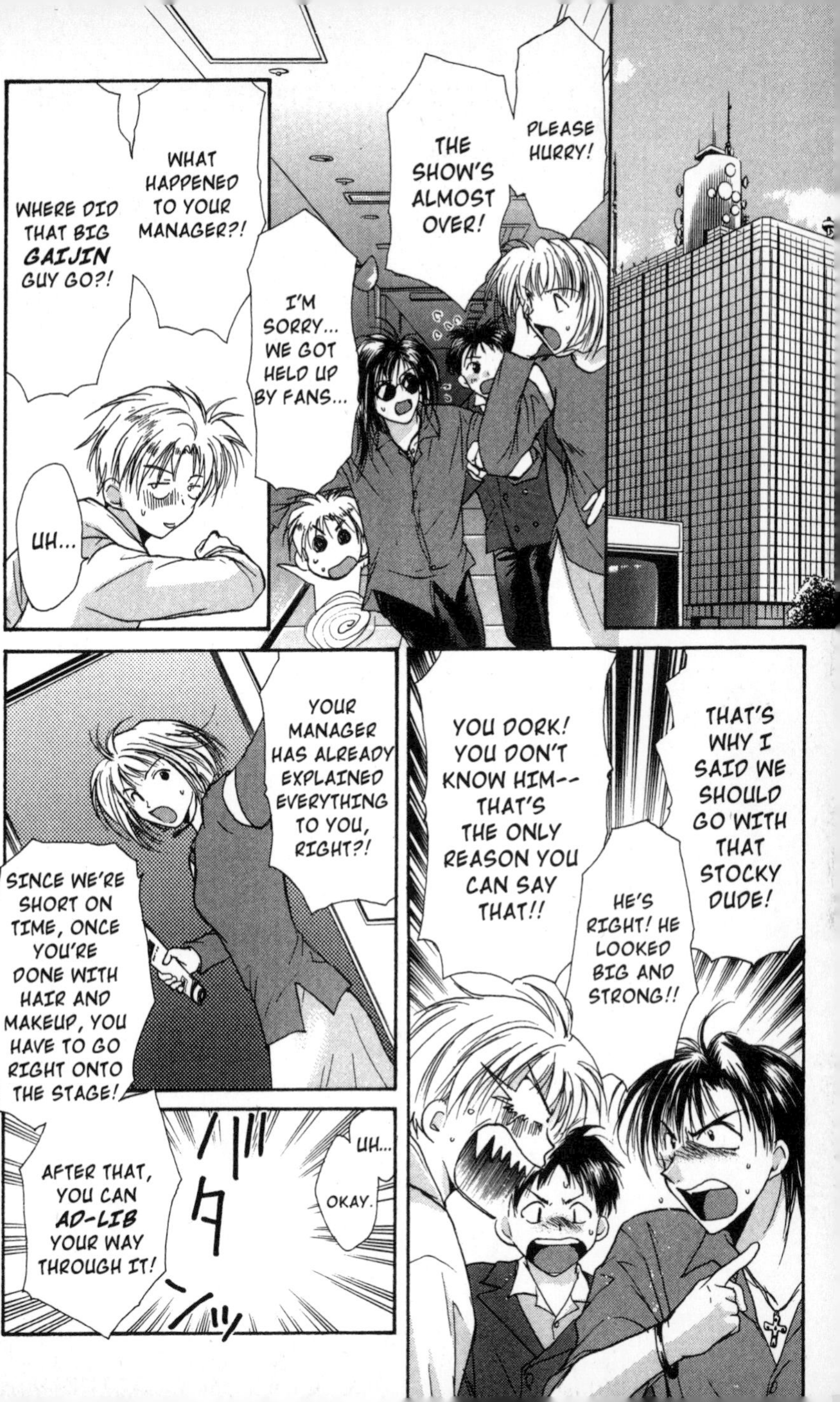
PLEASE HURRY!
THE SHOW'S ALMOST OVER!
I'M SORRY... WE GOT HELD UP BY FANS...
WHAT HAPPENED TO YOUR MANAGER?!
WHERE DID THAT BIG *GAIJIN* GUY GO?!
UH...
THAT'S WHY I SAID WE SHOULD GO WITH THAT STOCKY DUDE!
YOU DORK! YOU DON'T KNOW HIM--THAT'S THE ONLY REASON YOU CAN SAY THAT!!
HE'S RIGHT! HE LOOKED BIG AND STRONG!!
YOUR MANAGER HAS ALREADY EXPLAINED EVERYTHING TO YOU, RIGHT?!
SINCE WE'RE SHORT ON TIME, ONCE YOU'RE DONE WITH HAIR AND MAKEUP, YOU HAVE TO GO RIGHT ONTO THE STAGE!
UH...
OKAY.
バタンッ
AFTER THAT, YOU CAN *AD-LIB* YOUR WAY THROUGH IT!

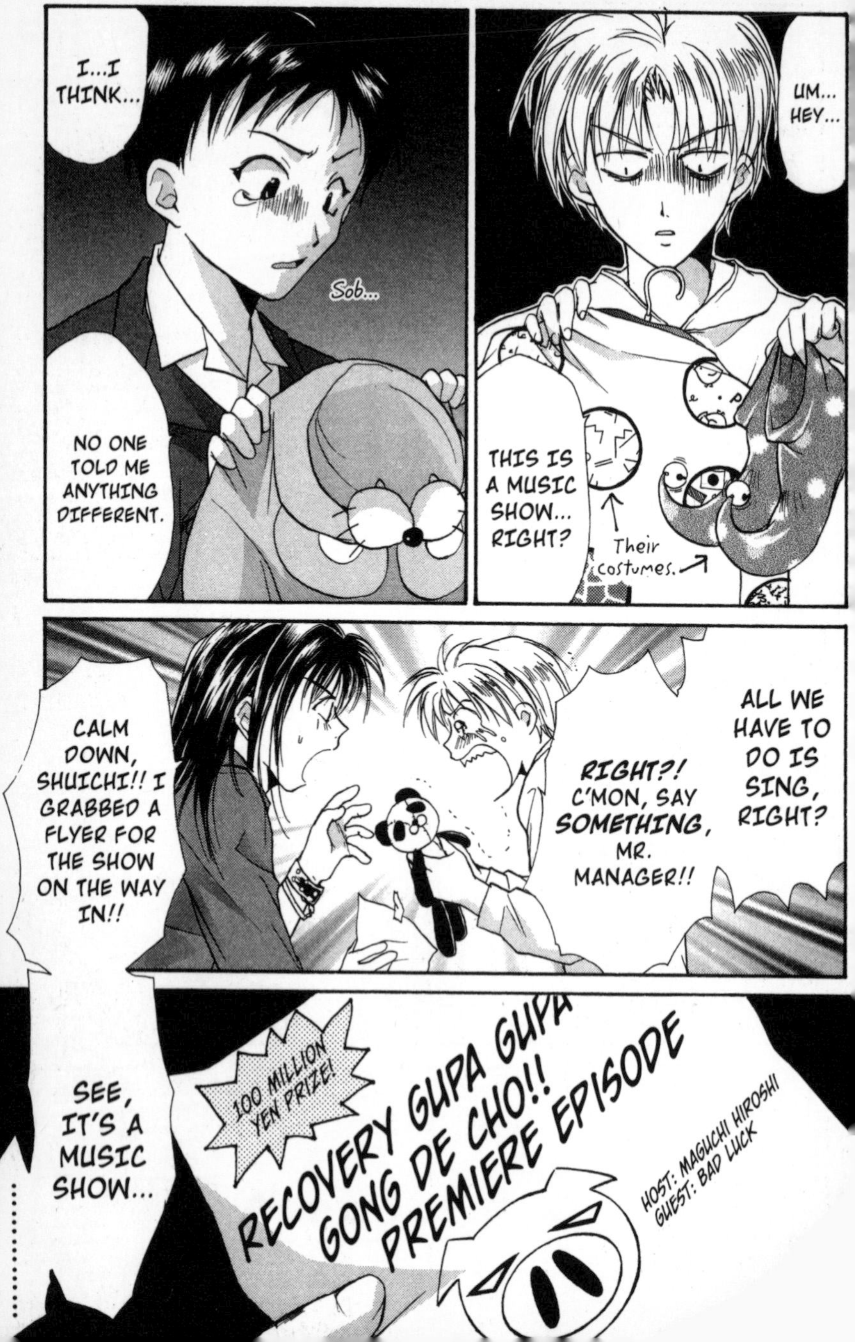
UM... HEY...
THIS IS A MUSIC SHOW... RIGHT?
Their costumes.
I...I THINK...
Sob...
NO ONE TOLD ME ANYTHING DIFFERENT.
ALL WE HAVE TO DO IS SING, RIGHT?
RIGHT?! C'MON, SAY SOMETHING, MR. MANAGER!!
CALM DOWN, SHUICHI!! I GRABBED A FLYER FOR THE SHOW ON THE WAY IN!!
HOST: MAGUCHI HIROSHI
GUEST: BAD LUCK
RECOVERY GUPA GUPA GONG DE CHO!! PREMIERE EPISODE
100 MILLION YEN PRIZE!
SEE, IT'S A MUSIC SHOW...

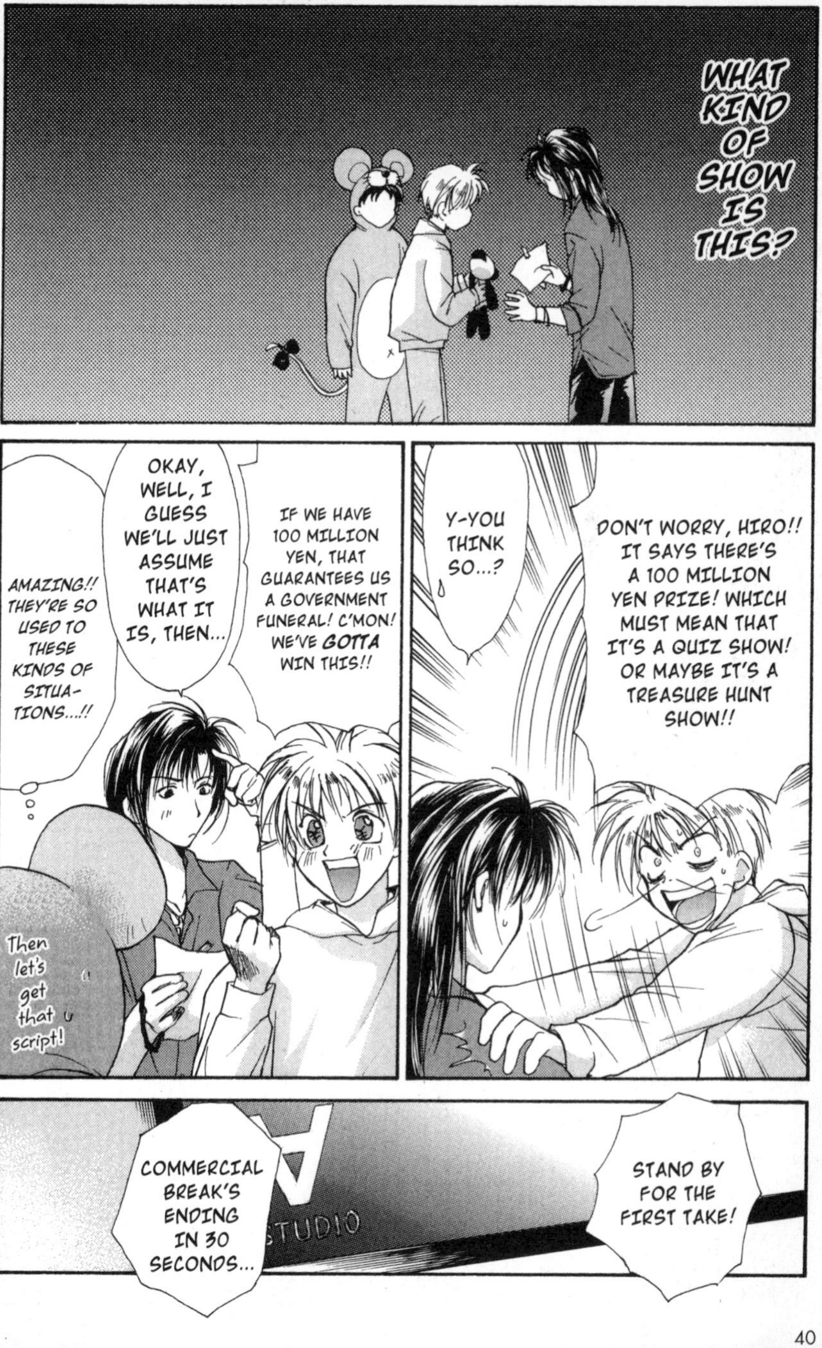
WHAT KIND OF SHOW IS THIS?
DON'T WORRY, HIRO!! IT SAYS THERE'S A 100 MILLION YEN PRIZE! WHICH MUST MEAN THAT IT'S A QUIZ SHOW! OR MAYBE IT'S A TREASURE HUNT SHOW!!
Y-YOU THINK SO...?
IF WE HAVE 100 MILLION YEN, THAT GUARANTEES US A GOVERNMENT FUNERAL! C'MON! WE'VE GOTTA WIN THIS!!
OKAY, WELL, I GUESS WE'LL JUST ASSUME THAT'S WHAT IT IS, THEN...
AMAZING!! THEY'RE SO USED TO THESE KINDS OF SITUA-TIONS...!!
Then let's get that script!
STAND BY FOR THE FIRST TAKE!
COMMERCIAL BREAK'S ENDING IN 30 SECONDS...
STUDIO

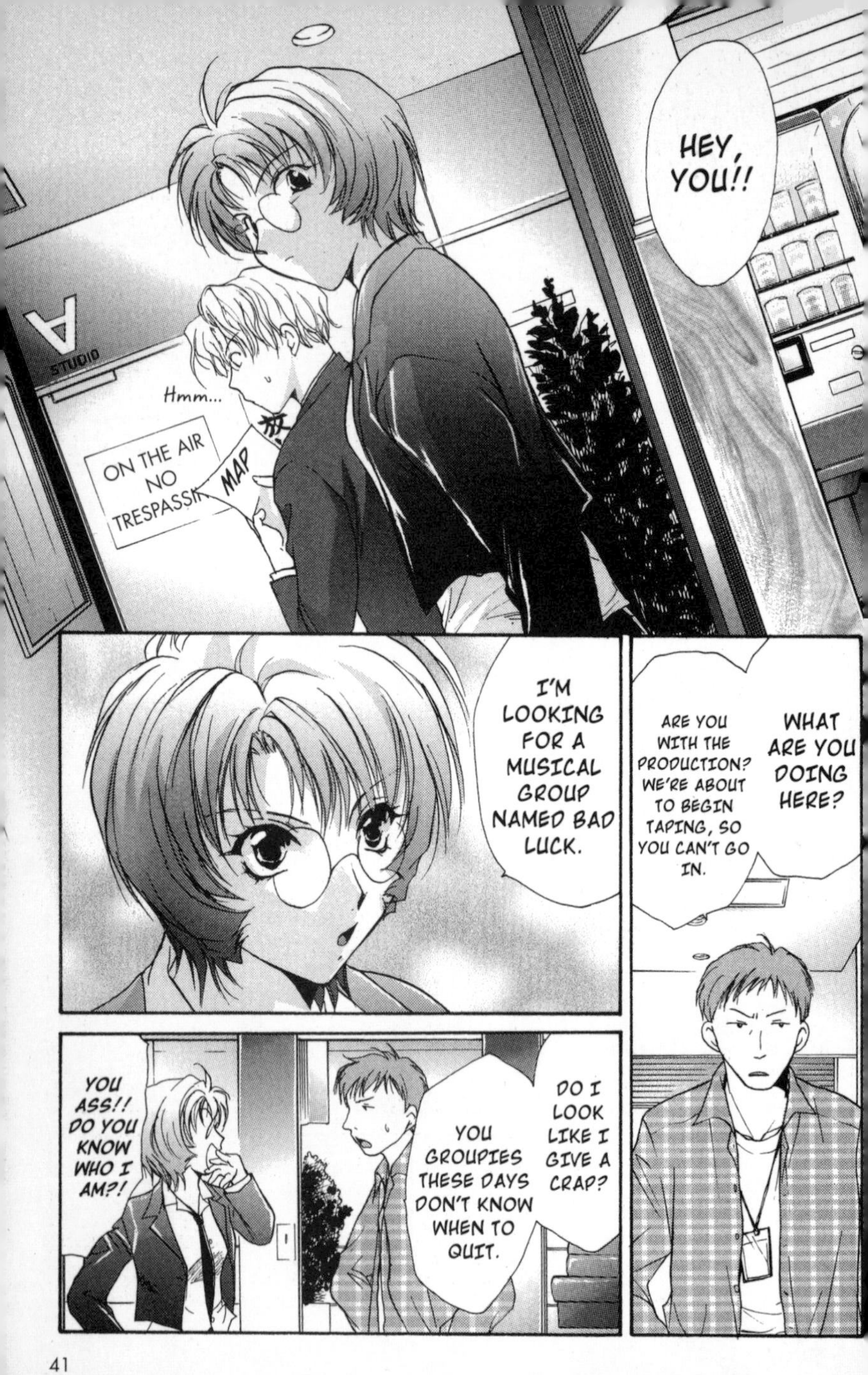
HEY, YOU!!
A STUDIO
Hmm...
ON THE AIR NO TRESPASSI
MAP
WHAT ARE YOU DOING HERE?
ARE YOU WITH THE PRODUCTION? WE'RE ABOUT TO BEGIN TAPING, SO YOU CAN'T GO IN.
I'M LOOKING FOR A MUSICAL GROUP NAMED BAD LUCK.
DO I LOOK LIKE I GIVE A CRAP?
YOU GROUPIES THESE DAYS DON'T KNOW WHEN TO QUIT.
YOU ASS!! DO YOU KNOW WHO I AM?!

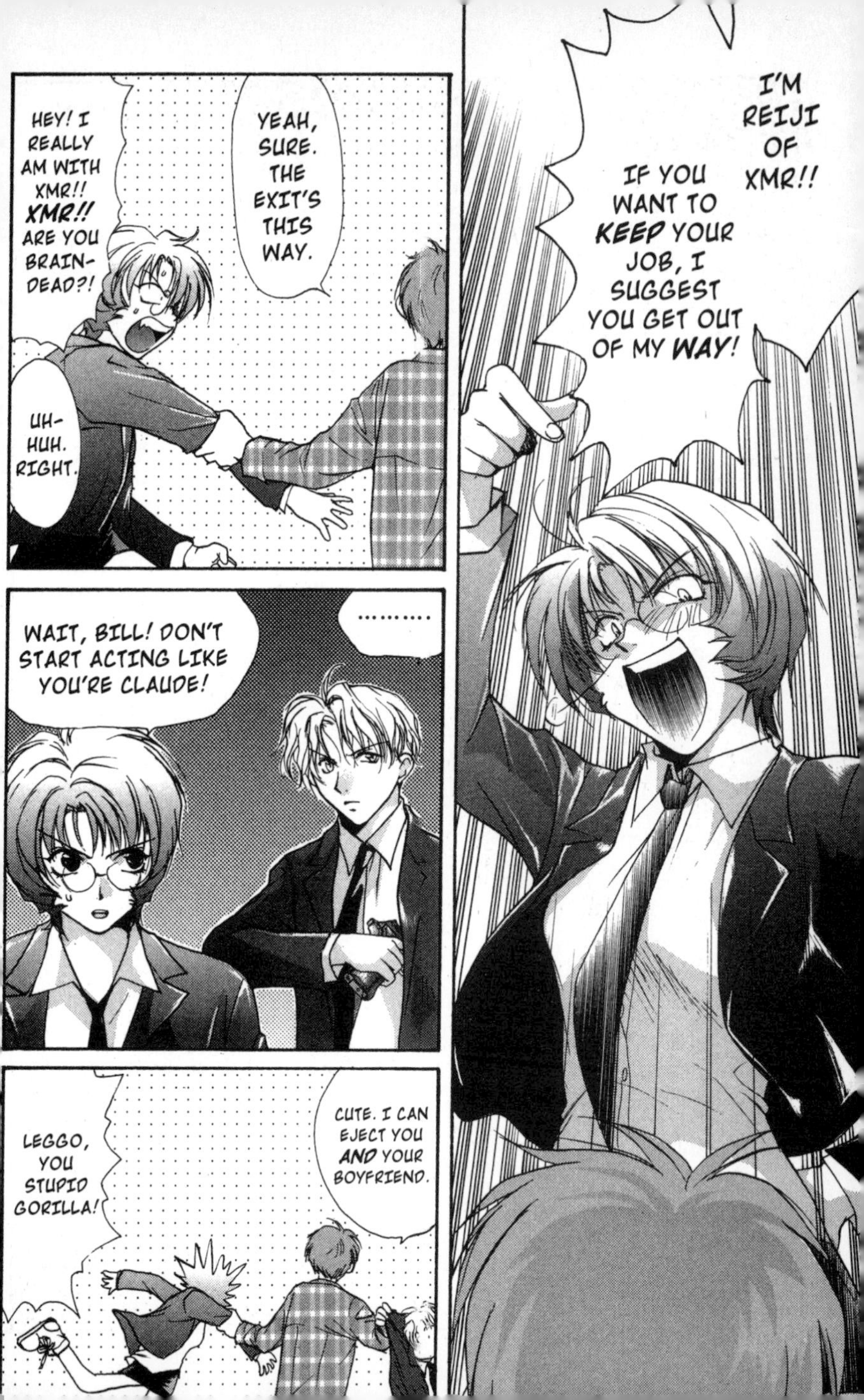
I'M REIJI OF XMR!!
IF YOU WANT TO **KEEP** YOUR JOB, I SUGGEST YOU GET OUT OF MY **WAY**!
YEAH, SURE. THE EXIT'S THIS WAY.
HEY! I REALLY AM WITH XMR!! **XMR!!** ARE YOU BRAIN-DEAD?!
UH-HUH. RIGHT.
....
WAIT, BILL! DON'T START ACTING LIKE YOU'RE CLAUDE!
CUTE. I CAN EJECT YOU **AND** YOUR BOYFRIEND.
LEGGO, YOU STUPID GORILLA!

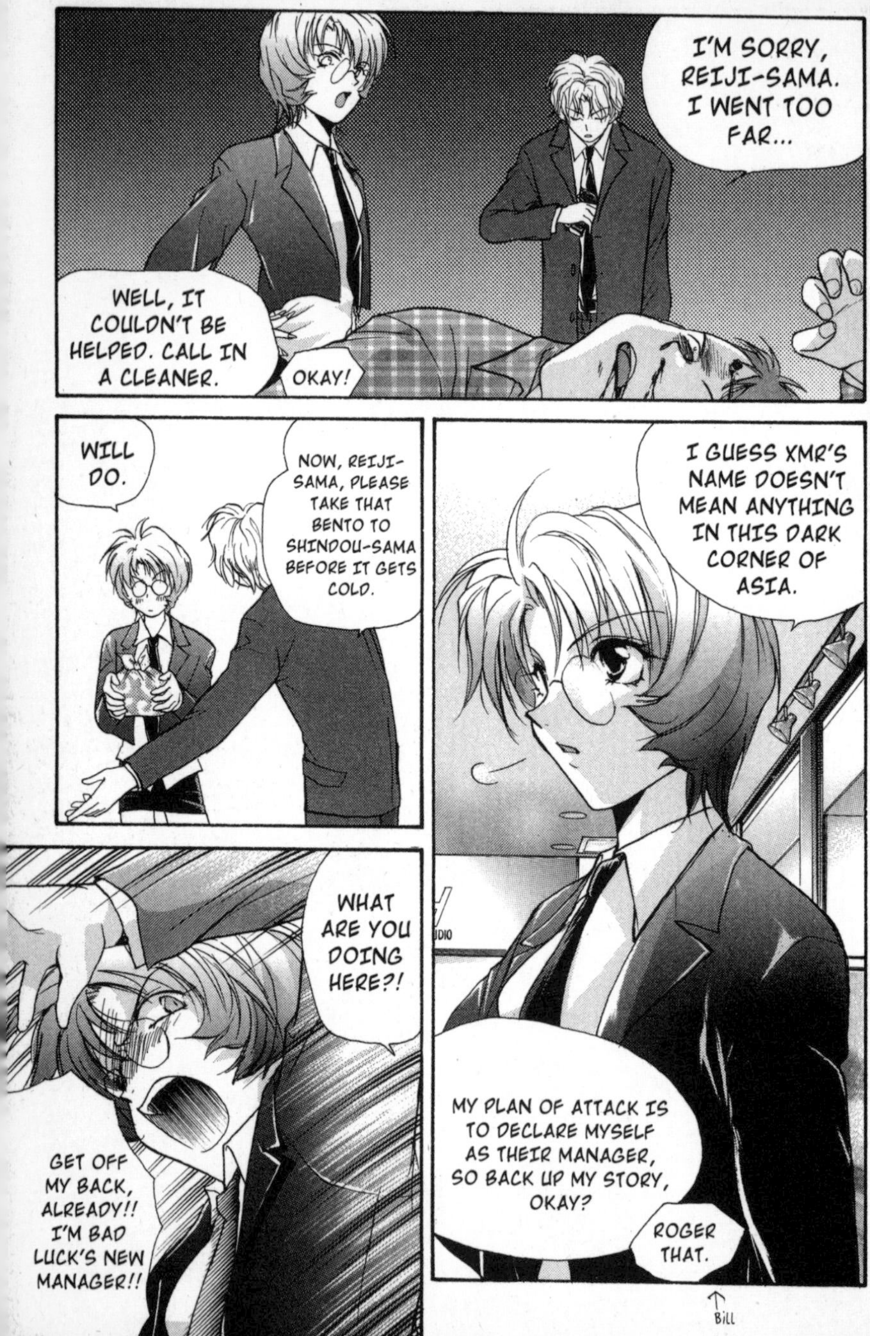
I'M SORRY, REIJI-SAMA. I WENT TOO FAR...
WELL, IT COULDN'T BE HELPED. CALL IN A CLEANER.
OKAY!
I GUESS XMR'S NAME DOESN'T MEAN ANYTHING IN THIS DARK CORNER OF ASIA.
MY PLAN OF ATTACK IS TO DECLARE MYSELF AS THEIR MANAGER, SO BACK UP MY STORY, OKAY?
ROGER THAT.
↑ Bill
NOW, REIJI-SAMA, PLEASE TAKE THAT BENTO TO SHINDOU-SAMA BEFORE IT GETS COLD.
WILL DO.
WHAT ARE YOU DOING HERE?!
GET OFF MY BACK, ALREADY!! I'M BAD LUCK'S NEW MANAGER!!

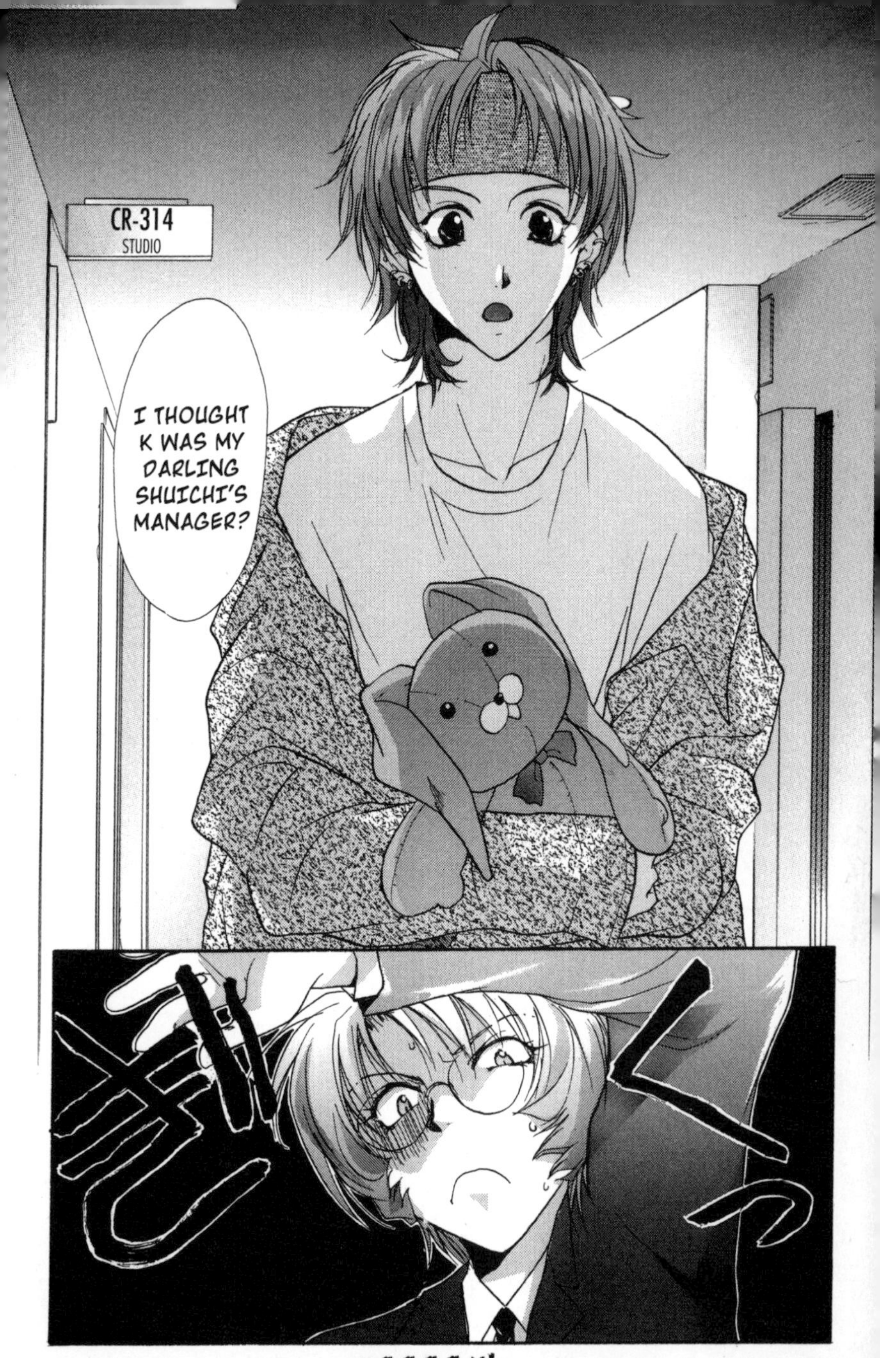
CR-314
STUDIO
I THOUGHT K WAS MY DARLING SHUICHI'S MANAGER?
GAAAAH!

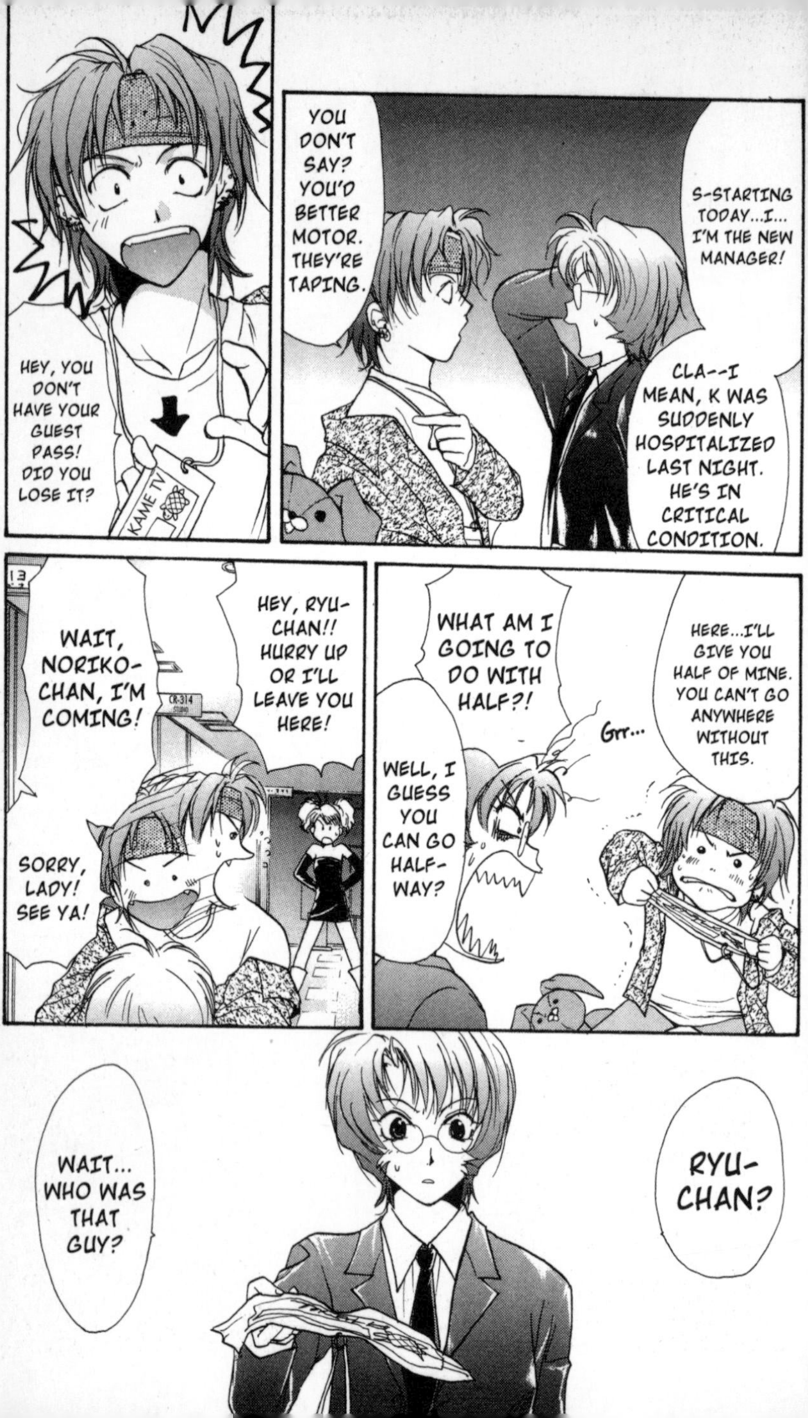
S-STARTING TODAY...I... I'M THE NEW MANAGER!
YOU DON'T SAY? YOU'D BETTER MOTOR. THEY'RE TAPING.
CLA--I MEAN, K WAS SUDDENLY HOSPITALIZED LAST NIGHT. HE'S IN CRITICAL CONDITION.
HEY, YOU DON'T HAVE YOUR GUEST PASS! DID YOU LOSE IT?
KAME TV
HERE...I'LL GIVE YOU HALF OF MINE. YOU CAN'T GO ANYWHERE WITHOUT THIS.
WHAT AM I GOING TO DO WITH HALF?!
Grr...
WELL, I GUESS YOU CAN GO HALF-WAY?
HEY, RYU-CHAN!! HURRY UP OR I'LL LEAVE YOU HERE!
WAIT, NORIKO-CHAN, I'M COMING!
SORRY, LADY! SEE YA!
RYU-CHAN?
WAIT... WHO WAS THAT GUY?

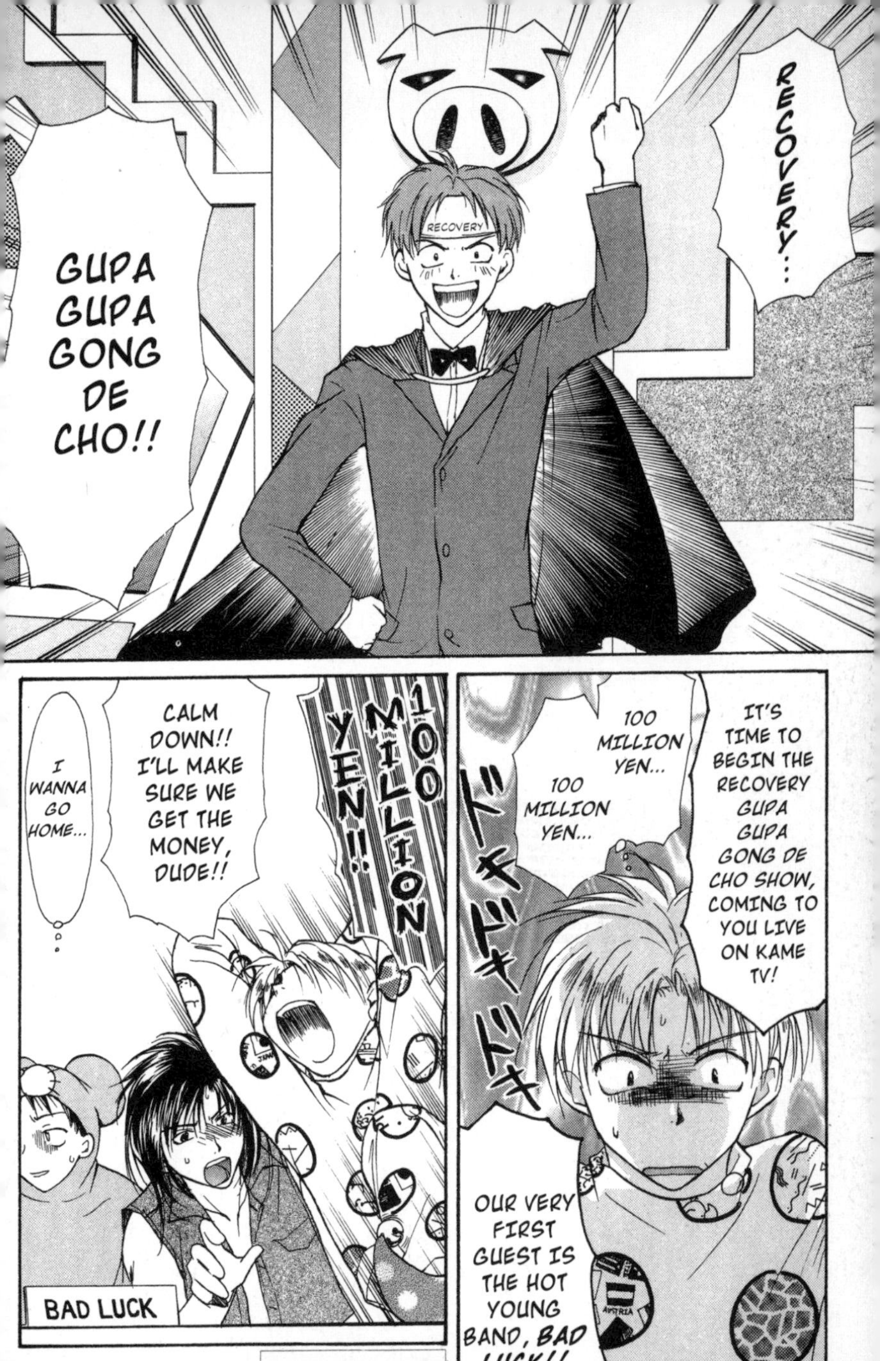
RECOVERY
RECOVERY...
GUPA GUPA GONG DE CHO!!
IT'S TIME TO BEGIN THE RECOVERY GUPA GUPA GONG DE CHO SHOW, COMING TO YOU LIVE ON KAME TV!
100 MILLION YEN...
100 MILLION YEN...
ドキドキドキ
OUR VERY FIRST GUEST IS THE HOT YOUNG BAND, *BAD LUCK!!*
100 MILLION YEN!!
CALM DOWN!! I'LL MAKE SURE WE GET THE MONEY, DUDE!!
I WANNA GO HOME...
BAD LUCK

track42 END

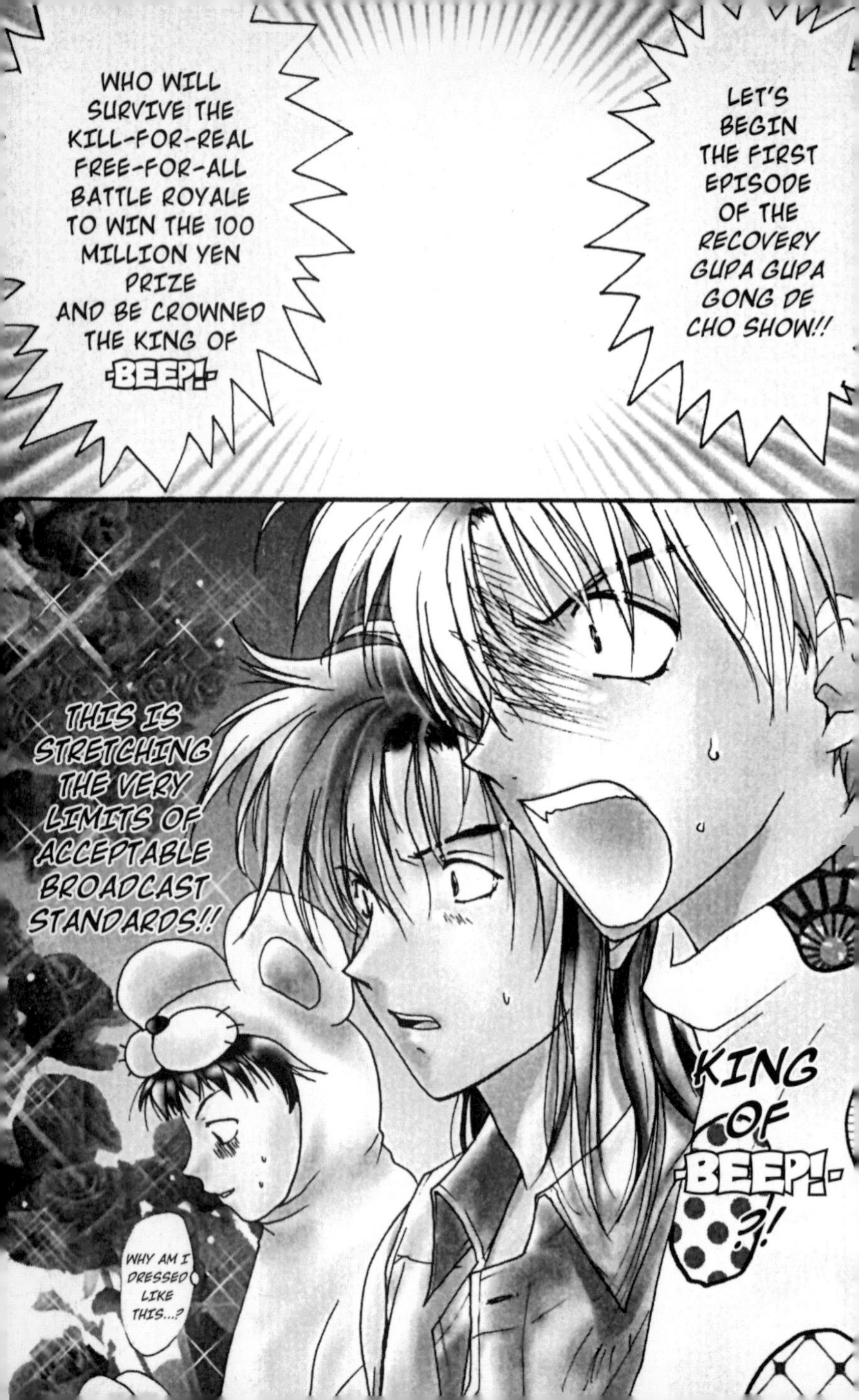
LET'S BEGIN THE FIRST EPISODE OF THE RECOVERY GUPA GUPA GONG DE CHO SHOW!!
WHO WILL SURVIVE THE KILL-FOR-REAL FREE-FOR-ALL BATTLE ROYALE TO WIN THE 100 MILLION YEN PRIZE AND BE CROWNED THE KING OF -BEEP!-
KING OF -BEEP!- ?!
THIS IS STRETCHING THE VERY LIMITS OF ACCEPTABLE BROADCAST STANDARDS!!
WHY AM I DRESSED LIKE THIS...?

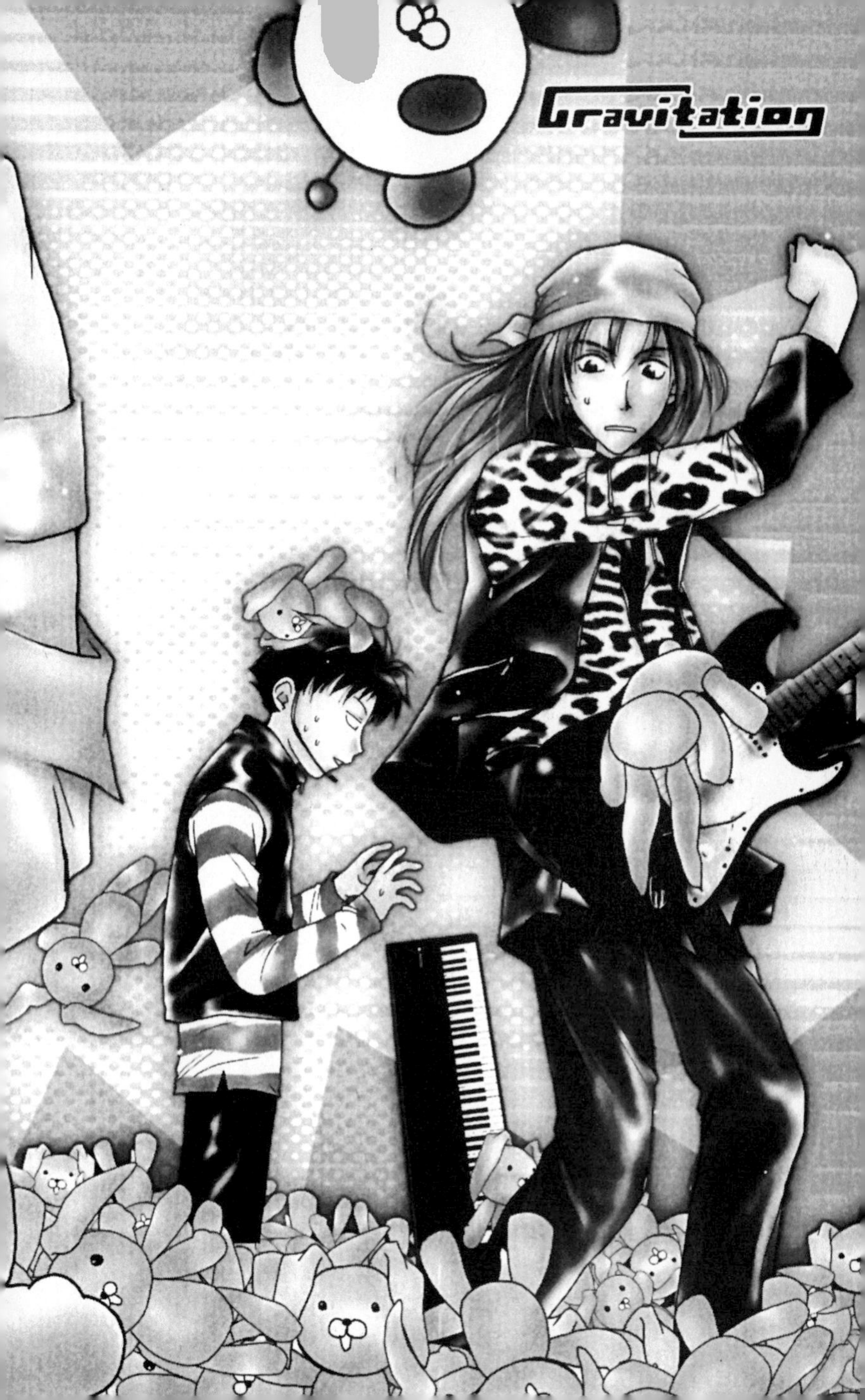
Gravitation

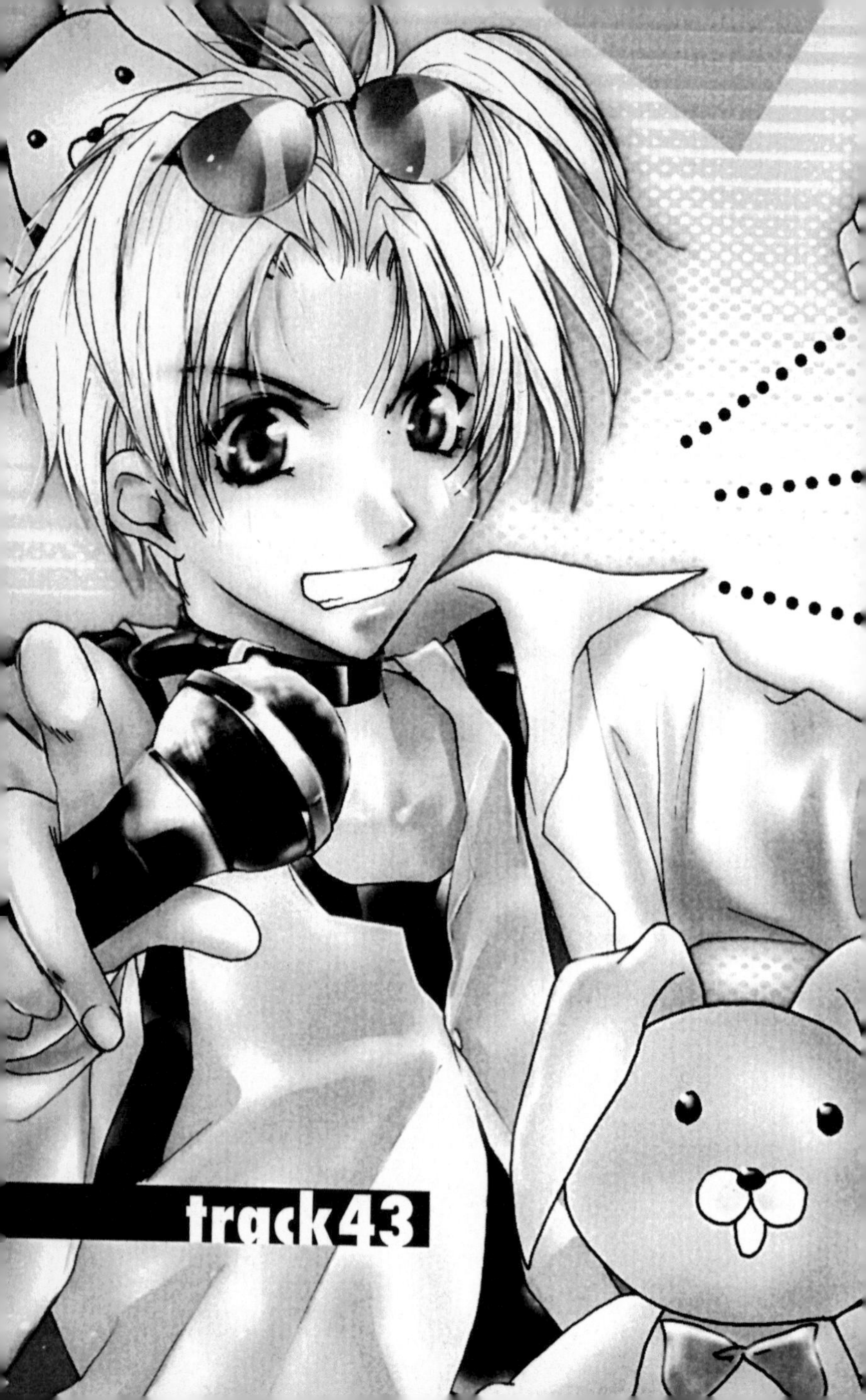
track43

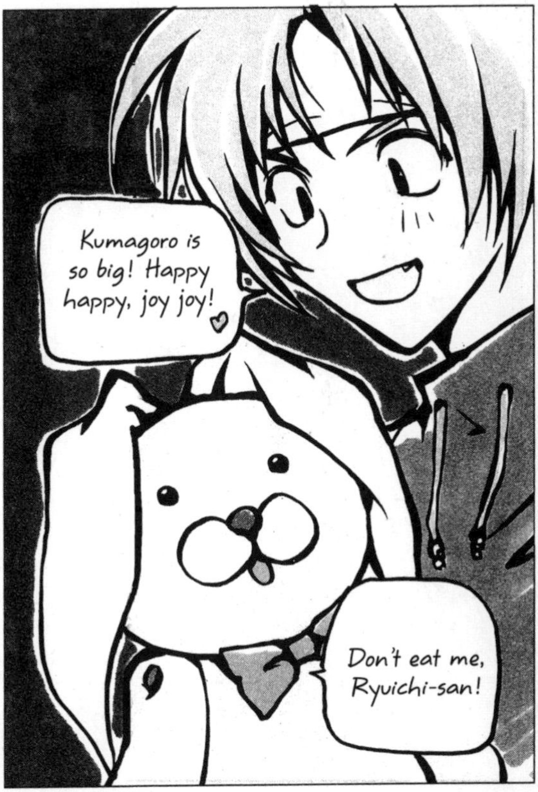
Kumagoro is so big! Happy happy, joy joy!
Don't eat me, Ryuichi-san!

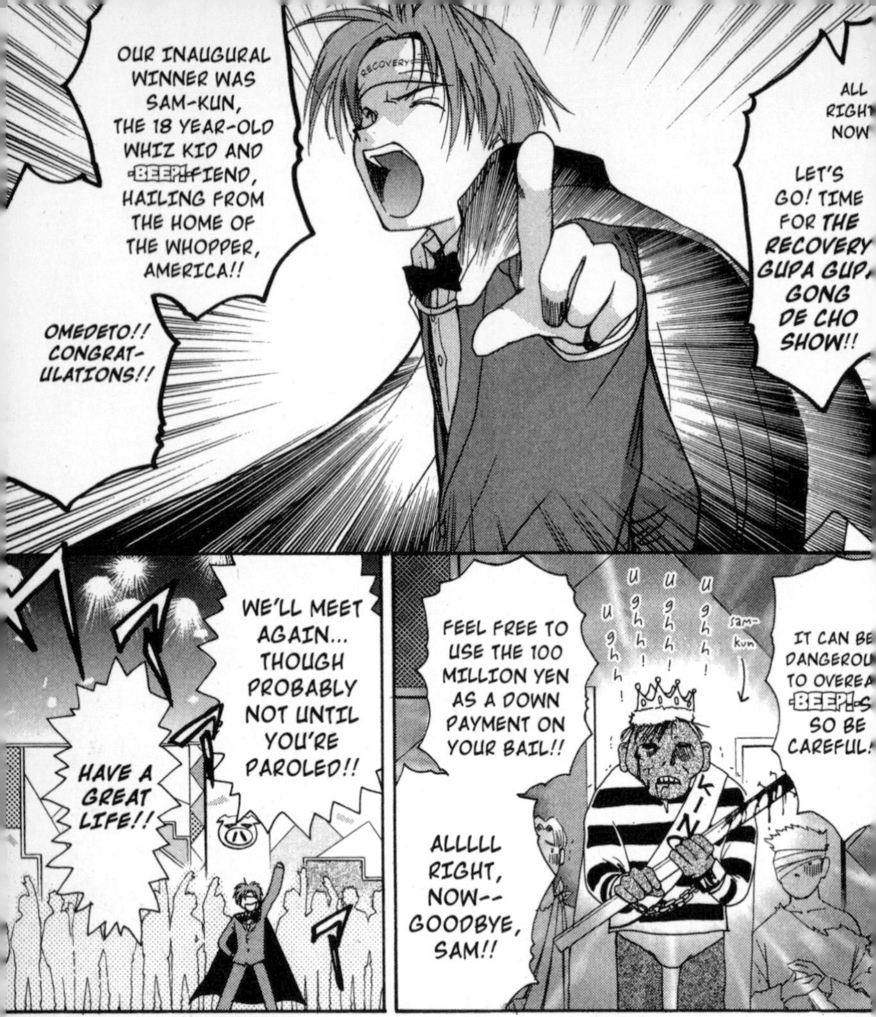
ALL RIGHT NOW
LET'S GO! TIME FOR THE RECOVERY GUPA GUP GONG DE CHO SHOW!!
RECOVERY
OUR INAUGURAL WINNER WAS SAM-KUN, THE 18 YEAR-OLD WHIZ KID AND -BEEP!- FIEND, HAILING FROM THE HOME OF THE WHOPPER, AMERICA!!
OMEDETO!! CONGRATULATIONS!!
IT CAN BE DANGEROU TO OVEREA -BEEP!-S SO BE CAREFUL
sam-kun
ughh! ughh! ughh! ughh!
FEEL FREE TO USE THE 100 MILLION YEN AS A DOWN PAYMENT ON YOUR BAIL!!
KING
ALLLLL RIGHT, NOW--GOODBYE, SAM!!
WE'LL MEET AGAIN... THOUGH PROBABLY NOT UNTIL YOU'RE PAROLED!!
HAVE A GREAT LIFE!!
Yahhhhhh!!

ABOUT GRAVITATION TRACK 42

Regarding Killing Machine King Sam-kun, his dialogue is almost all grunts. And The *Recovery Gupa Gupa Gong De Cho Show* scenes only take up two pages!! But even from that, you can probably tell what kind of show it is. I guess writing everything with beeps and grunts makes everything seem more dangerous, y'know? The host of this show was the same guy who hosted *Quiz de Pon!* a long time ago. Oh--and he's not Hiro's older brother. (I just thought of that one.)

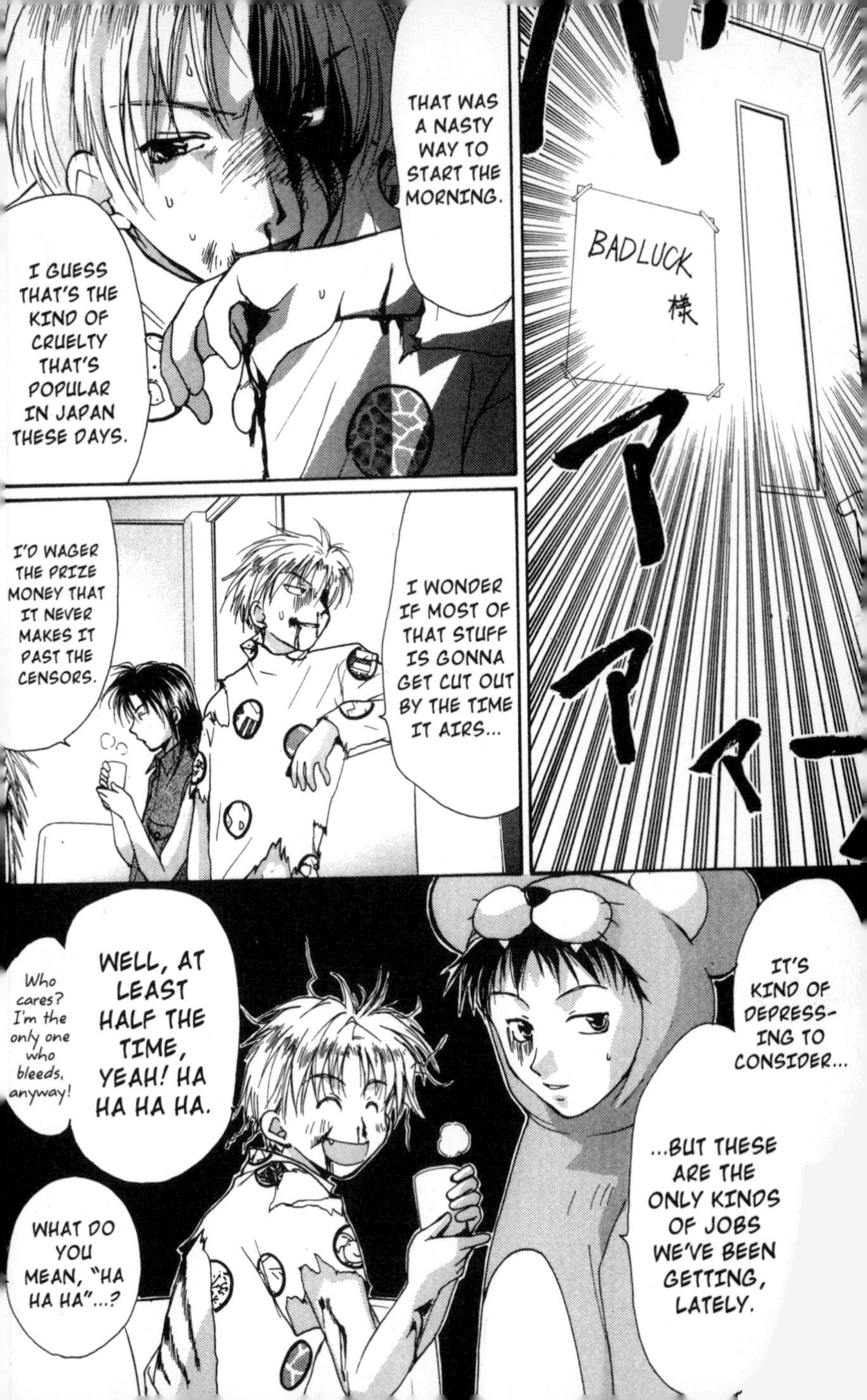
BADLUCK 様
THAT WAS A NASTY WAY TO START THE MORNING.
I GUESS THAT'S THE KIND OF CRUELTY THAT'S POPULAR IN JAPAN THESE DAYS.
I WONDER IF MOST OF THAT STUFF IS GONNA GET CUT OUT BY THE TIME IT AIRS...
I'D WAGER THE PRIZE MONEY THAT IT NEVER MAKES IT PAST THE CENSORS.
IT'S KIND OF DEPRESS-ING TO CONSIDER...
...BUT THESE ARE THE ONLY KINDS OF JOBS WE'VE BEEN GETTING, LATELY.
WELL, AT LEAST HALF THE TIME, YEAH! HA HA HA HA.
Who cares? I'm the only one who bleeds, anyway!
WHAT DO YOU MEAN, "HA HA HA"...?

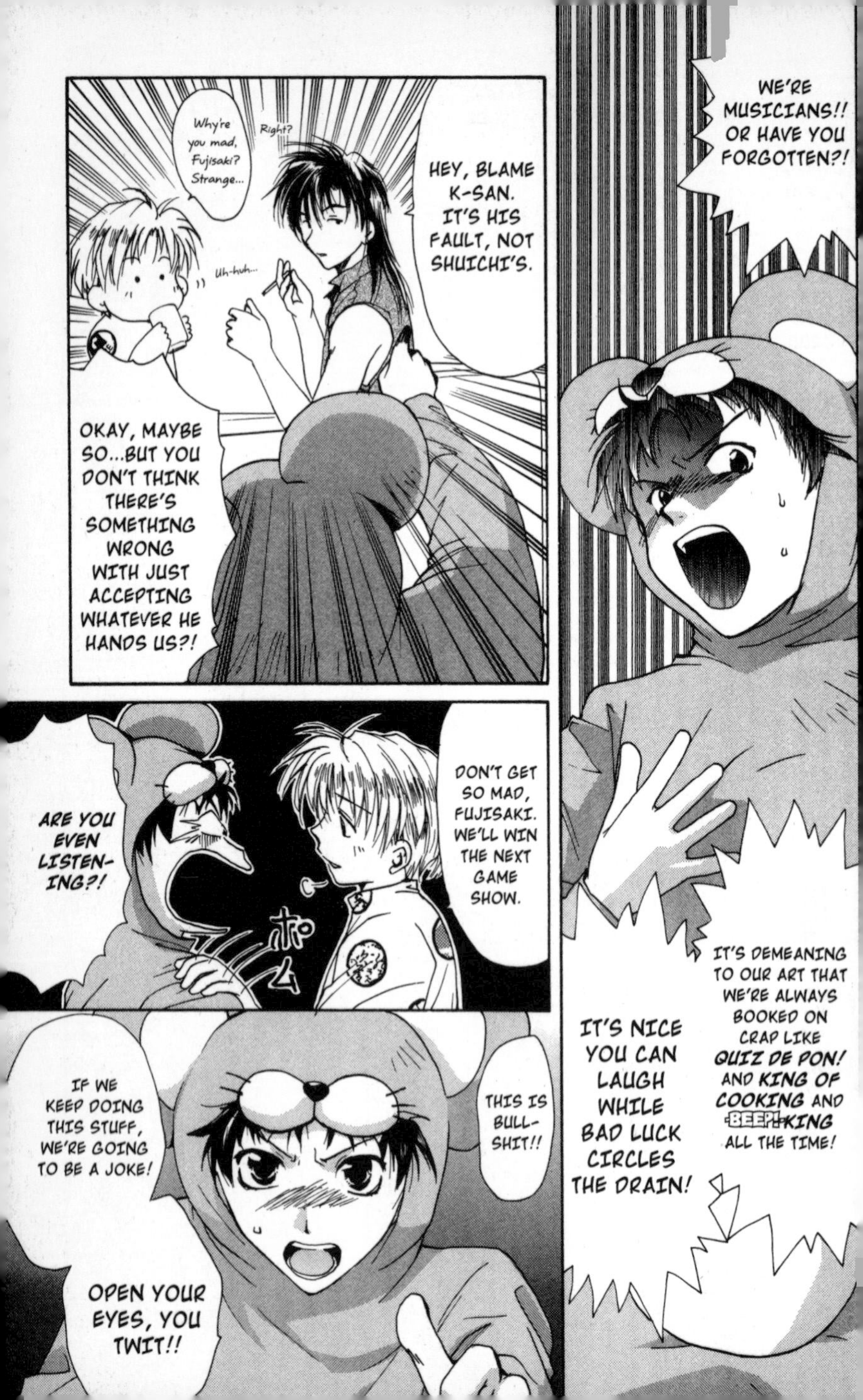

WE'RE MUSICIANS!! OR HAVE YOU FORGOTTEN?!
IT'S DEMEANING TO OUR ART THAT WE'RE ALWAYS BOOKED ON CRAP LIKE QUIZ DE PON! AND KING OF COOKING AND -BEEP!-KING ALL THE TIME!
IT'S NICE YOU CAN LAUGH WHILE BAD LUCK CIRCLES THE DRAIN!
HEY, BLAME K-SAN. IT'S HIS FAULT, NOT SHUICHI'S.
Right?
Why're you mad, Fujisaki? Strange...
Uh-huh...
OKAY, MAYBE SO...BUT YOU DON'T THINK THERE'S SOMETHING WRONG WITH JUST ACCEPTING WHATEVER HE HANDS US?!
DON'T GET SO MAD, FUJISAKI. WE'LL WIN THE NEXT GAME SHOW.
ポム
ARE YOU EVEN LISTENING?!
THIS IS BULLSHIT!!
IF WE KEEP DOING THIS STUFF, WE'RE GOING TO BE A JOKE!
OPEN YOUR EYES, YOU TWIT!!

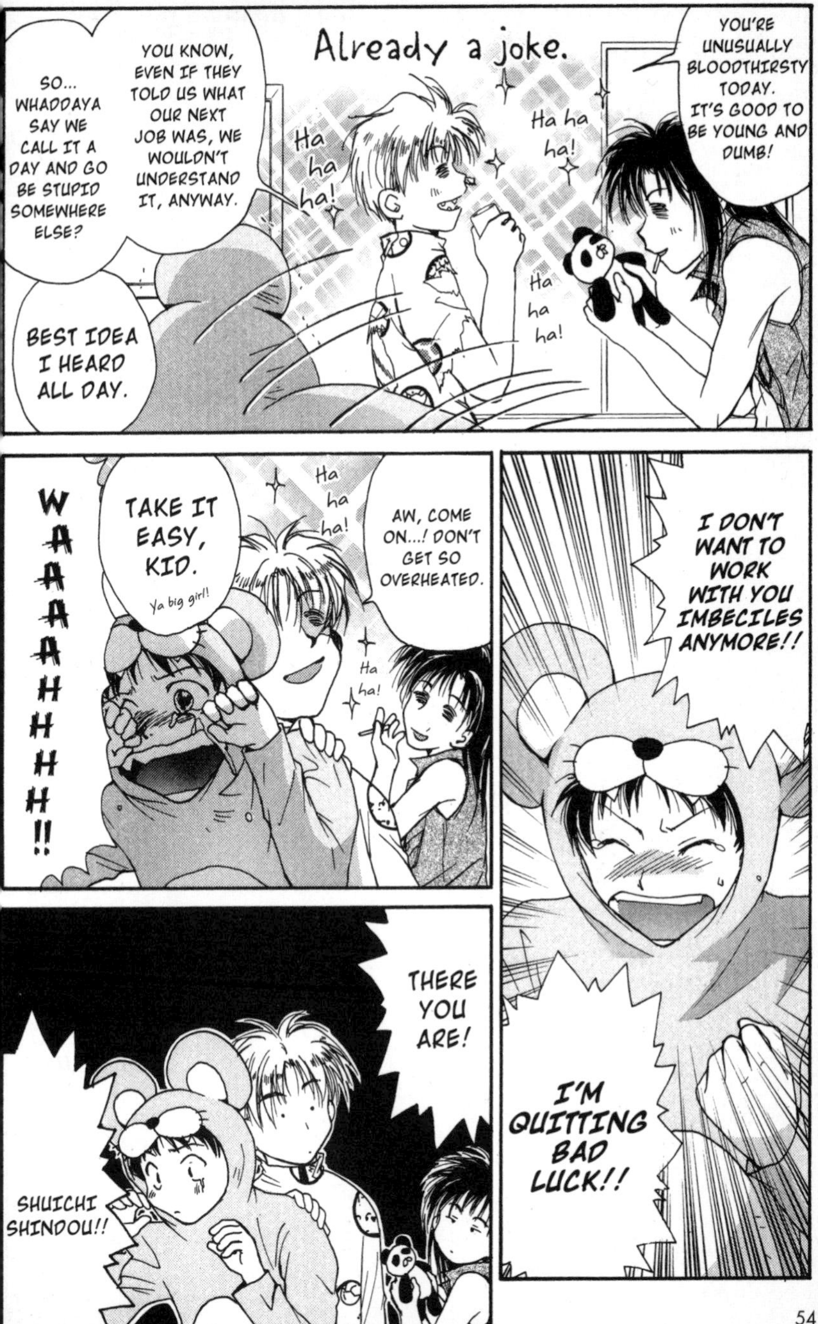
YOU'RE UNUSUALLY BLOODTHIRSTY TODAY. IT'S GOOD TO BE YOUNG AND DUMB!
Already a joke.
Ha ha ha!
Ha ha ha!
YOU KNOW, EVEN IF THEY TOLD US WHAT OUR NEXT JOB WAS, WE WOULDN'T UNDERSTAND IT, ANYWAY.
SO... WHADDAYA SAY WE CALL IT A DAY AND GO BE STUPID SOMEWHERE ELSE?
Ha ha ha!
BEST IDEA I HEARD ALL DAY.
I DON'T WANT TO WORK WITH YOU IMBECILES ANYMORE!!
I'M QUITTING BAD LUCK!!
AW, COME ON...! DON'T GET SO OVERHEATED.
Ha ha ha!
Ha ha!
TAKE IT EASY, KID.
Ya big girl!
WAAAAAAHHHHH!!
THERE YOU ARE!
SHUICHI SHINDOU!!

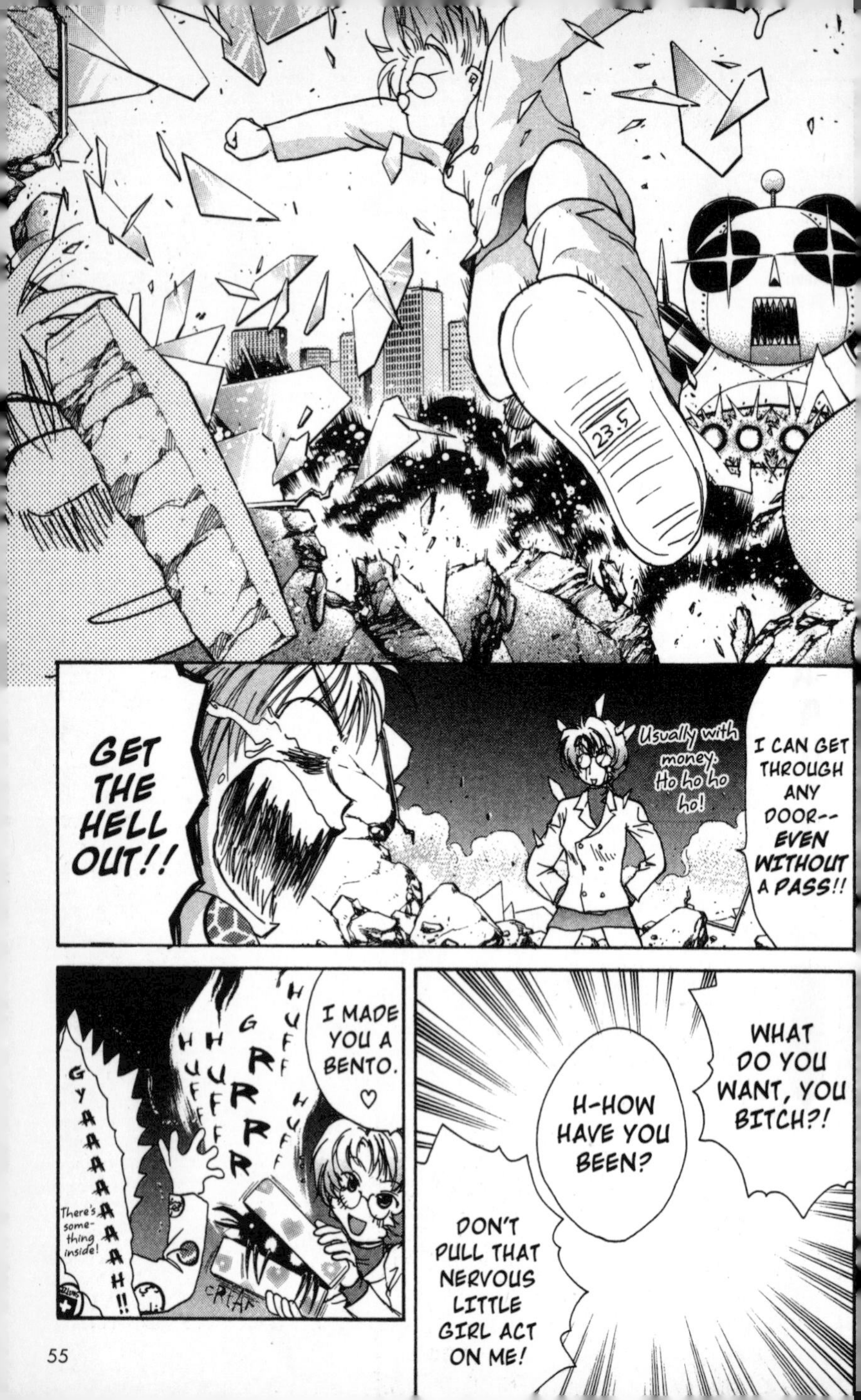
23.5
I CAN GET THROUGH ANY DOOR-- EVEN WITHOUT A PASS!!
Usually with money. Ho ho ho ho!
GET THE HELL OUT!!
WHAT DO YOU WANT, YOU BITCH?!
H-HOW HAVE YOU BEEN?
DON'T PULL THAT NERVOUS LITTLE GIRL ACT ON ME!
I MADE YOU A BENTO. ♥
HUFF HUFF
GRRRR
HUFF
HUFF
GYAAAAAAAAH!!
There's something inside!

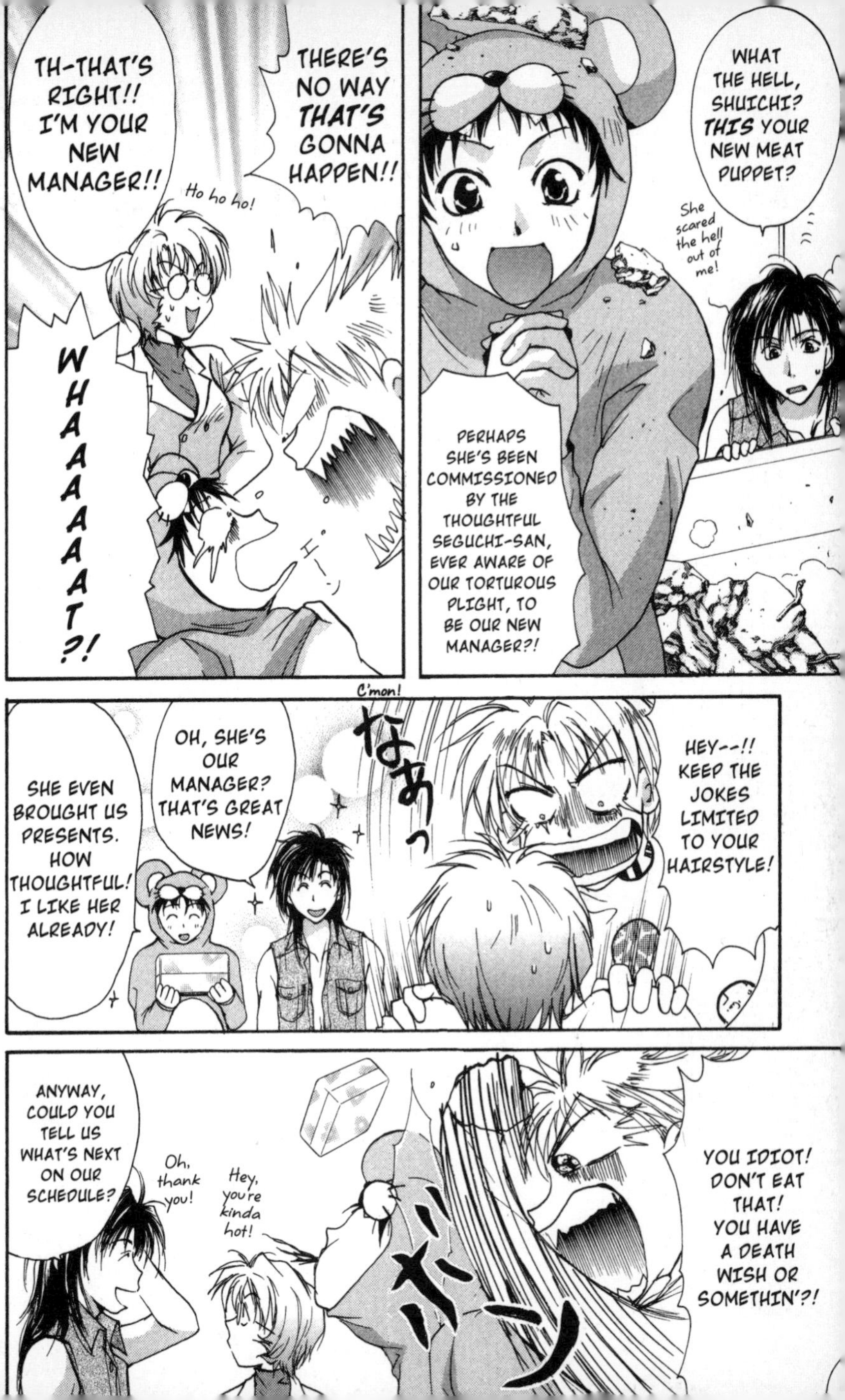

WHAT THE HELL, SHUICHI? THIS YOUR NEW MEAT PUPPET?
She scared the hell out of me!
PERHAPS SHE'S BEEN COMMISSIONED BY THE THOUGHTFUL SEGUCHI-SAN, EVER AWARE OF OUR TORTUROUS PLIGHT, TO BE OUR NEW MANAGER?!
THERE'S NO WAY THAT'S GONNA HAPPEN!!
TH-THAT'S RIGHT!! I'M YOUR NEW MANAGER!!
Ho ho ho!
WHAAAAAAAAAT?!
C'mon!
HEY--!! KEEP THE JOKES LIMITED TO YOUR HAIRSTYLE!
なあっ
OH, SHE'S OUR MANAGER? THAT'S GREAT NEWS!
SHE EVEN BROUGHT US PRESENTS. HOW THOUGHTFUL! I LIKE HER ALREADY!
YOU IDIOT! DON'T EAT THAT! YOU HAVE A DEATH WISH OR SOMETHIN'?!
Hey, you're kinda hot!
Oh, thank you!
ANYWAY, COULD YOU TELL US WHAT'S NEXT ON OUR SCHEDULE?

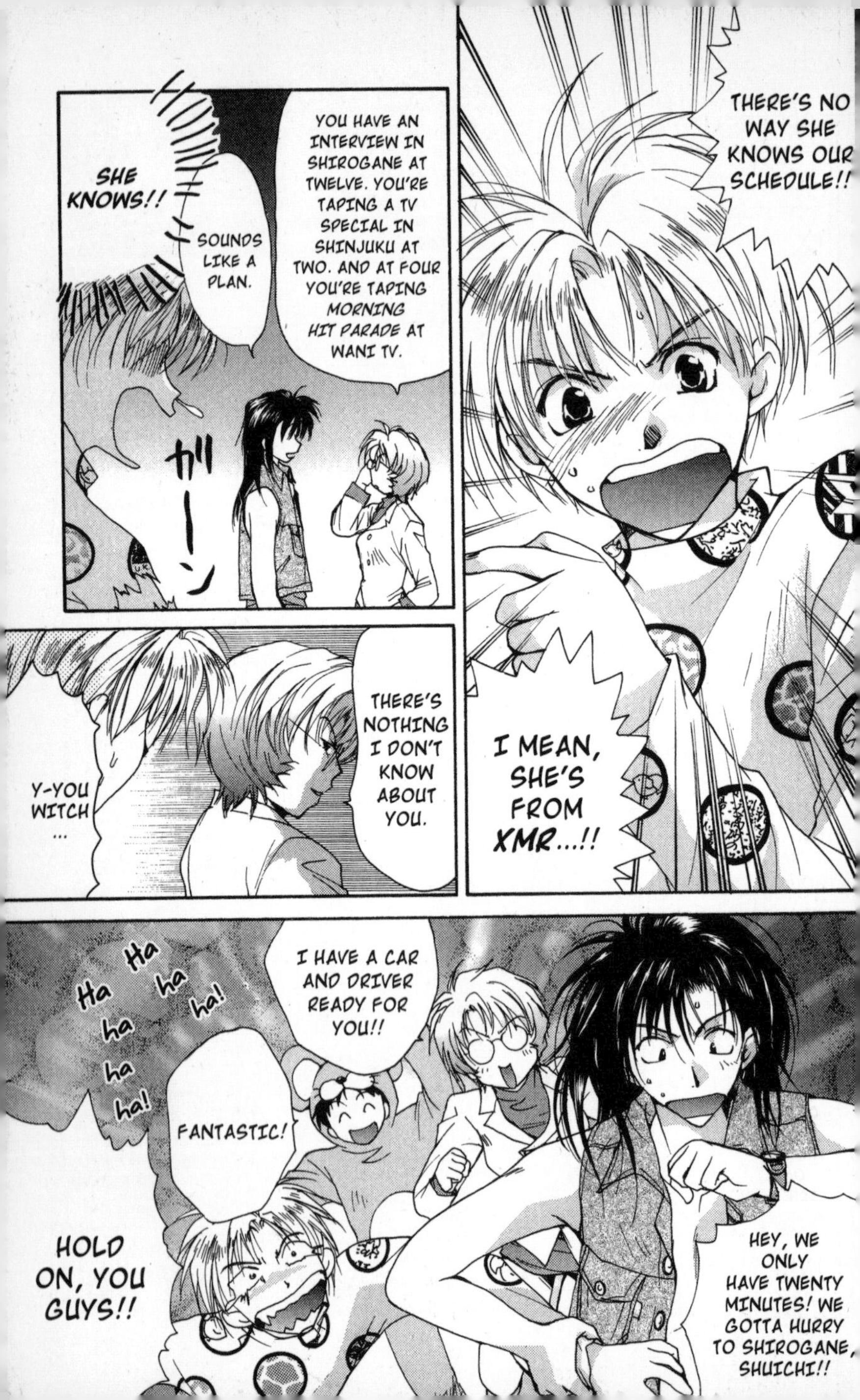
THERE'S NO WAY SHE KNOWS OUR SCHEDULE!!
I MEAN, SHE'S FROM XMR...!!
YOU HAVE AN INTERVIEW IN SHIROGANE AT TWELVE. YOU'RE TAPING A TV SPECIAL IN SHINJUKU AT TWO. AND AT FOUR YOU'RE TAPING MORNING HIT PARADE AT WANI TV.
SOUNDS LIKE A PLAN.
SHE KNOWS!!
ガーン
THERE'S NOTHING I DON'T KNOW ABOUT YOU.
Y-YOU WITCH...
I HAVE A CAR AND DRIVER READY FOR YOU!!
Ha Ha ha ha! ha ha ha!
FANTASTIC!
HEY, WE ONLY HAVE TWENTY MINUTES! WE GOTTA HURRY TO SHIROGANE, SHUICHI!!
HOLD ON, YOU GUYS!!

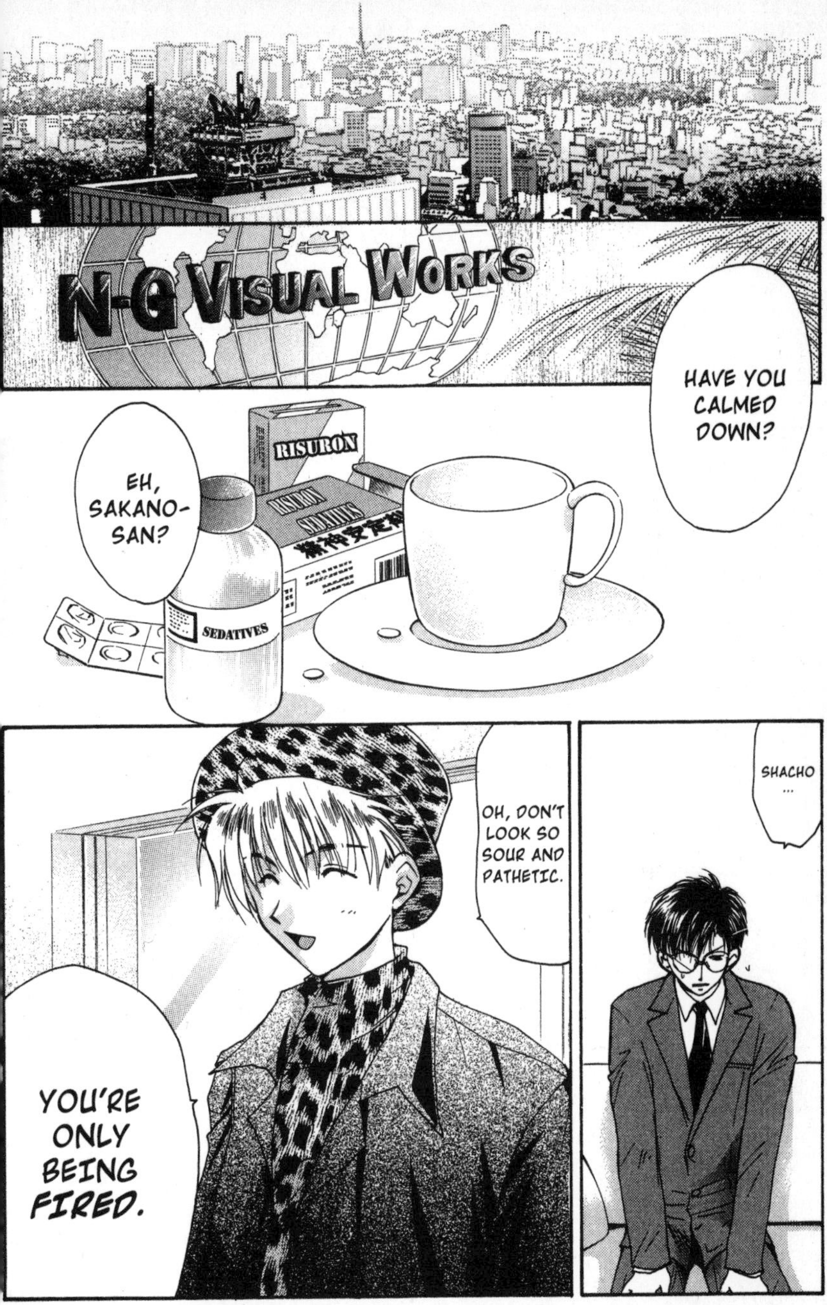
N-G VISUAL WORKS
HAVE YOU CALMED DOWN?
EH, SAKANO-SAN?
RISURON
SEDATIVES
SHACHO ...
OH, DON'T LOOK SO SOUR AND PATHETIC.
YOU'RE ONLY BEING FIRED.

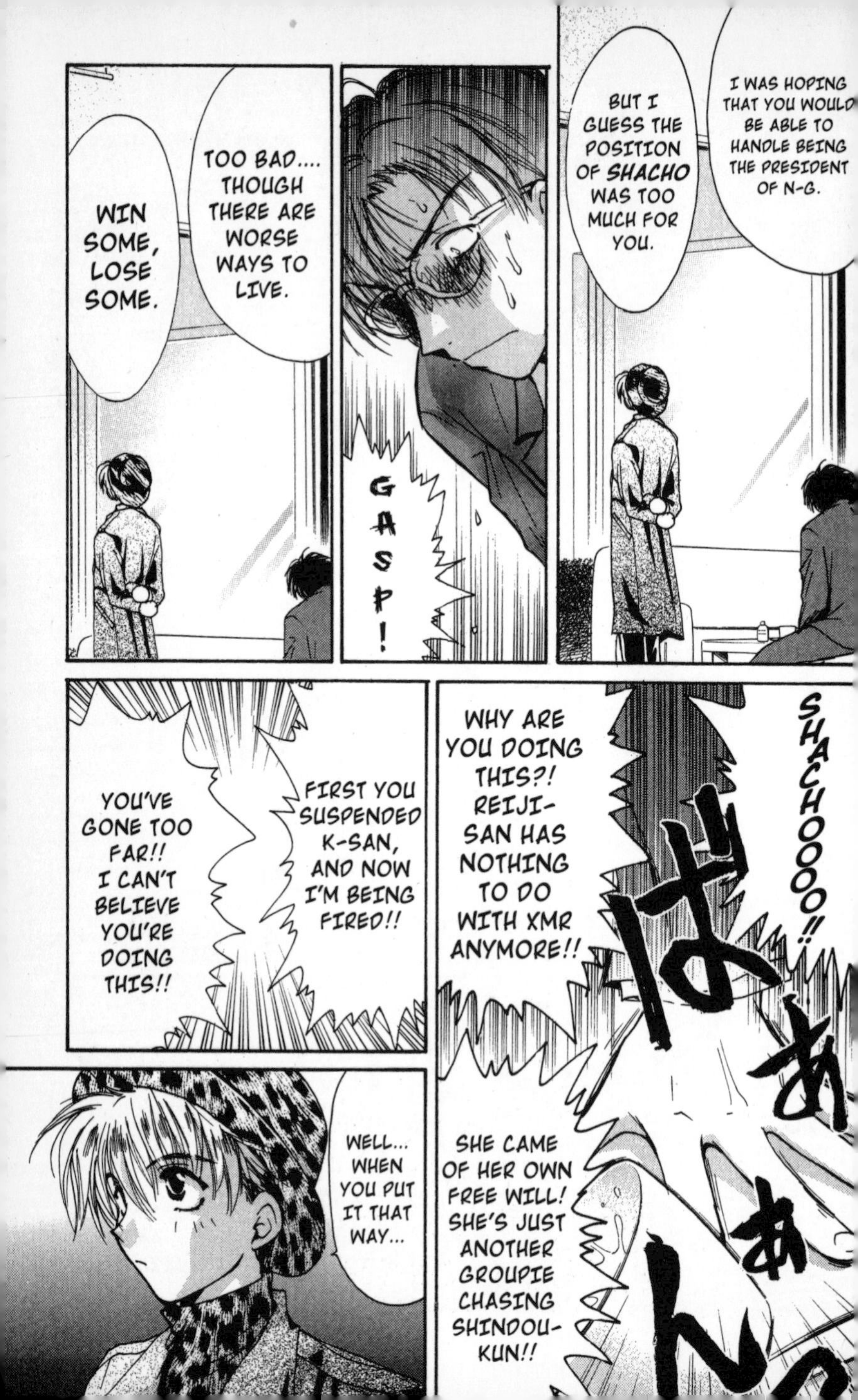
I WAS HOPING THAT YOU WOULD BE ABLE TO HANDLE BEING THE PRESIDENT OF N-G.
BUT I GUESS THE POSITION OF SHACHO WAS TOO MUCH FOR YOU.
GASP!
TOO BAD.... THOUGH THERE ARE WORSE WAYS TO LIVE.
WIN SOME, LOSE SOME.
SHACHOOOOO!!
ばあん
WHY ARE YOU DOING THIS?! REIJI-SAN HAS NOTHING TO DO WITH XMR ANYMORE!!
SHE CAME OF HER OWN FREE WILL! SHE'S JUST ANOTHER GROUPIE CHASING SHINDOU-KUN!!
FIRST YOU SUSPENDED K-SAN, AND NOW I'M BEING FIRED!!
YOU'VE GONE TOO FAR!! I CAN'T BELIEVE YOU'RE DOING THIS!!
WELL... WHEN YOU PUT IT THAT WAY...

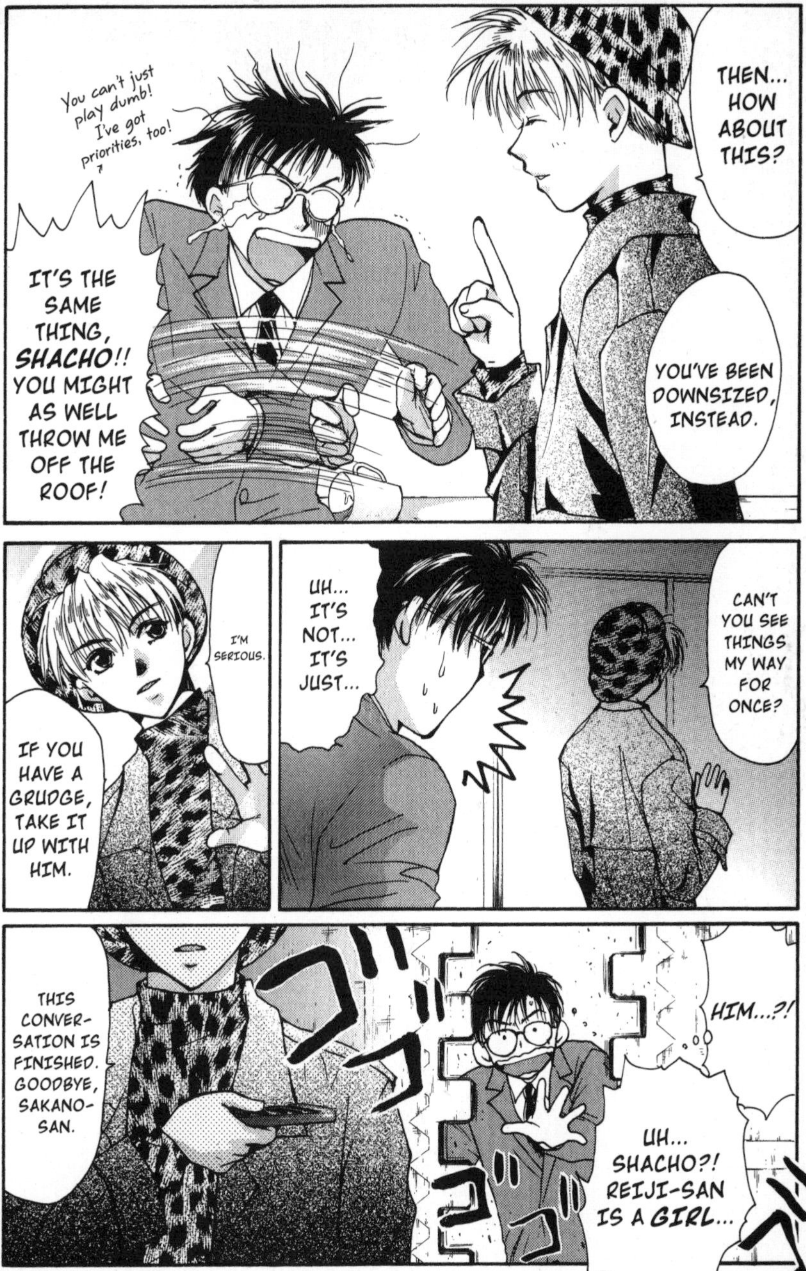
THEN... HOW ABOUT THIS?
YOU'VE BEEN DOWNSIZED, INSTEAD.
You can't just play dumb! I've got priorities, too!
IT'S THE SAME THING, **SHACHO**!! YOU MIGHT AS WELL THROW ME OFF THE ROOF!
CAN'T YOU SEE THINGS MY WAY FOR ONCE?
UH... IT'S NOT... IT'S JUST...
I'M SERIOUS.
IF YOU HAVE A GRUDGE, TAKE IT UP WITH HIM.
HIM...?!
UH... SHACHO?! REIJI-SAN IS A **GIRL**...
THIS CONVER-SATION IS FINISHED. GOODBYE, SAKANO-SAN.

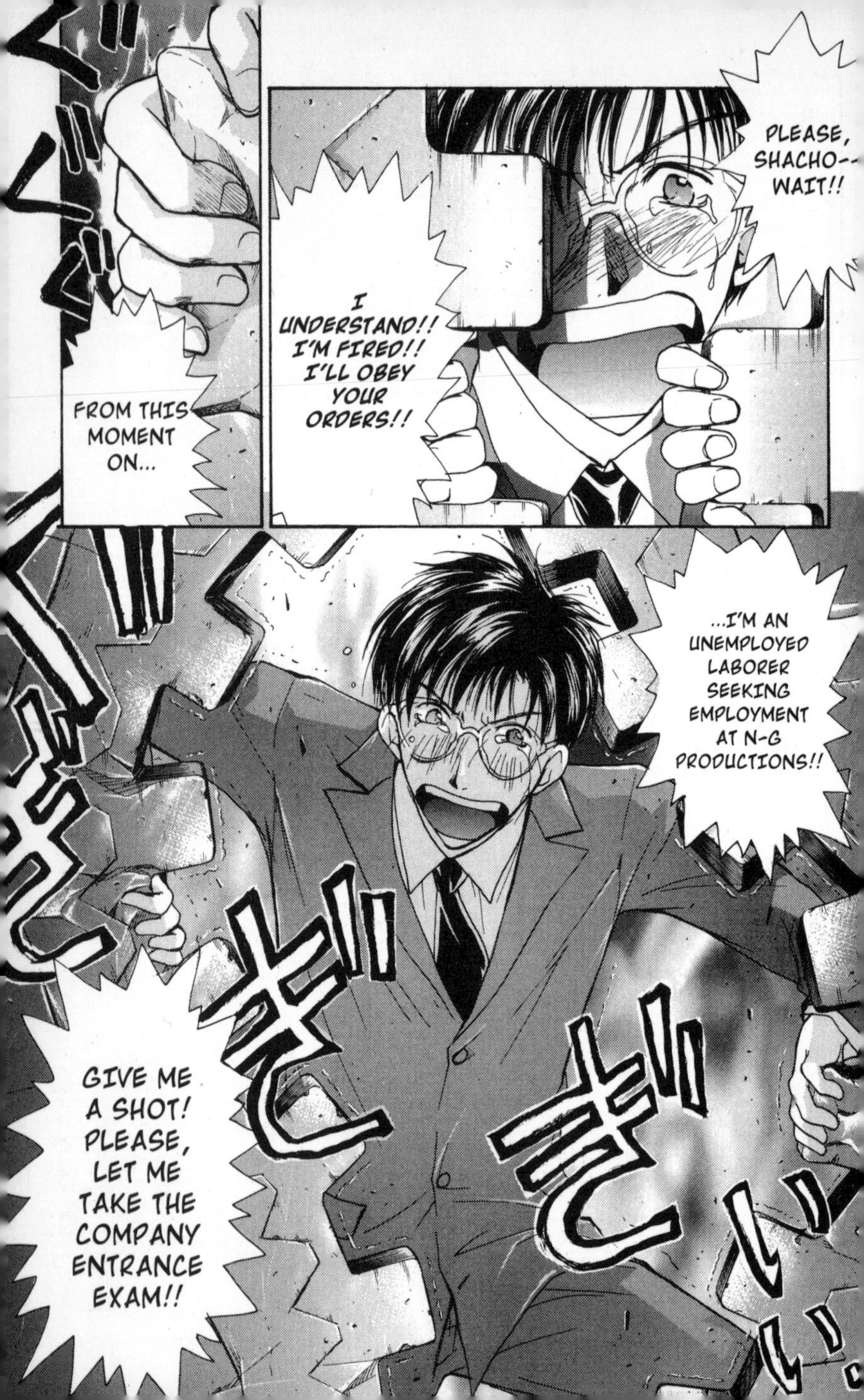
PLEASE, SHACHO-- WAIT!!
I UNDERSTAND!! I'M FIRED!! I'LL OBEY YOUR ORDERS!!
FROM THIS MOMENT ON...
...I'M AN UNEMPLOYED LABORER SEEKING EMPLOYMENT AT N-G PRODUCTIONS!!
GIVE ME A SHOT! PLEASE, LET ME TAKE THE COMPANY ENTRANCE EXAM!!

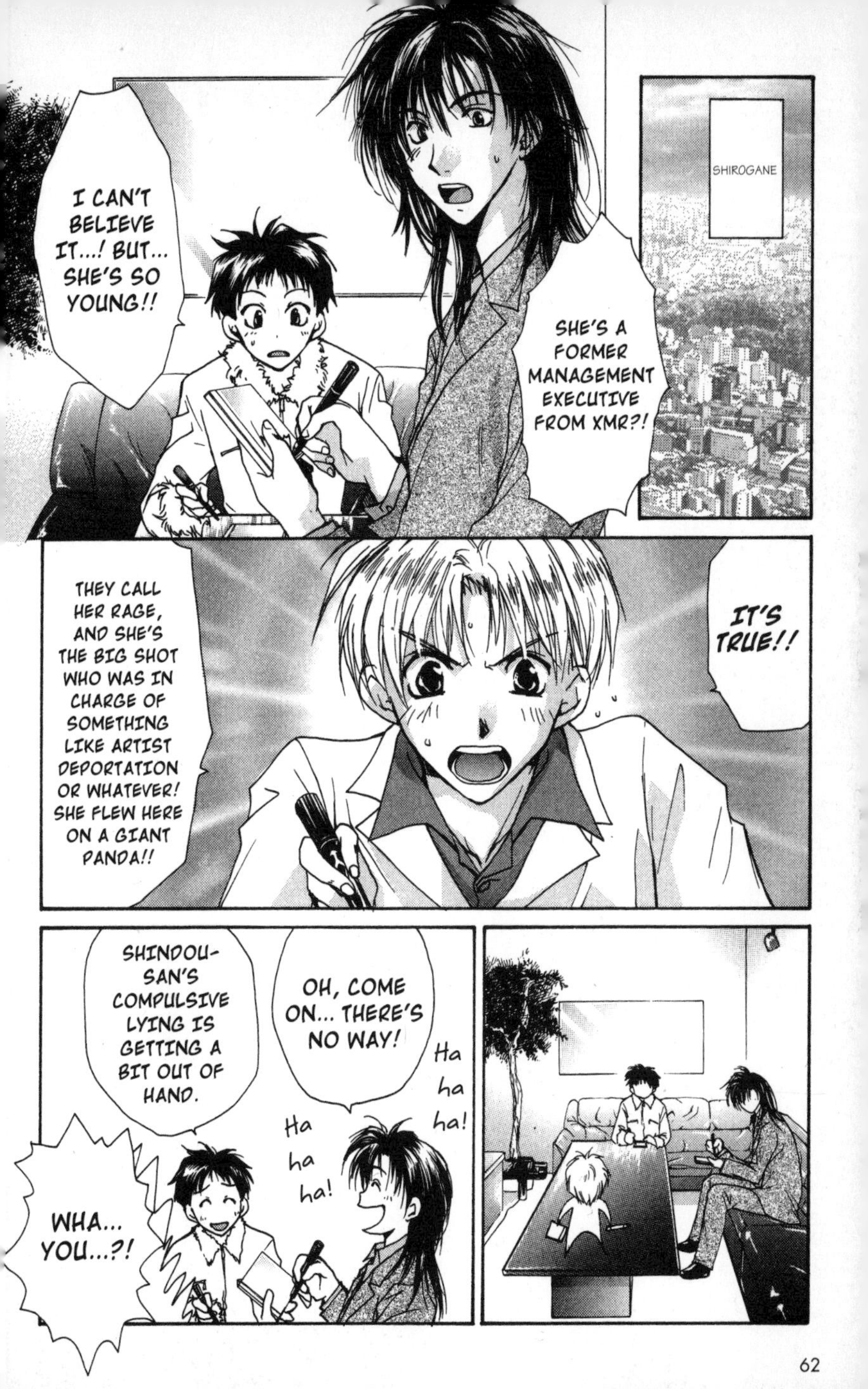

SHIROGANE
SHE'S A FORMER MANAGEMENT EXECUTIVE FROM XMR?!
I CAN'T BELIEVE IT....! BUT... SHE'S SO YOUNG!!
IT'S TRUE!!
THEY CALL HER RAGE, AND SHE'S THE BIG SHOT WHO WAS IN CHARGE OF SOMETHING LIKE ARTIST DEPORTATION OR WHATEVER! SHE FLEW HERE ON A GIANT PANDA!!
OH, COME ON... THERE'S NO WAY!
Ha ha ha!
SHINDOU-SAN'S COMPULSIVE LYING IS GETTING A BIT OUT OF HAND.
Ha ha ha!
WHA... YOU...?!

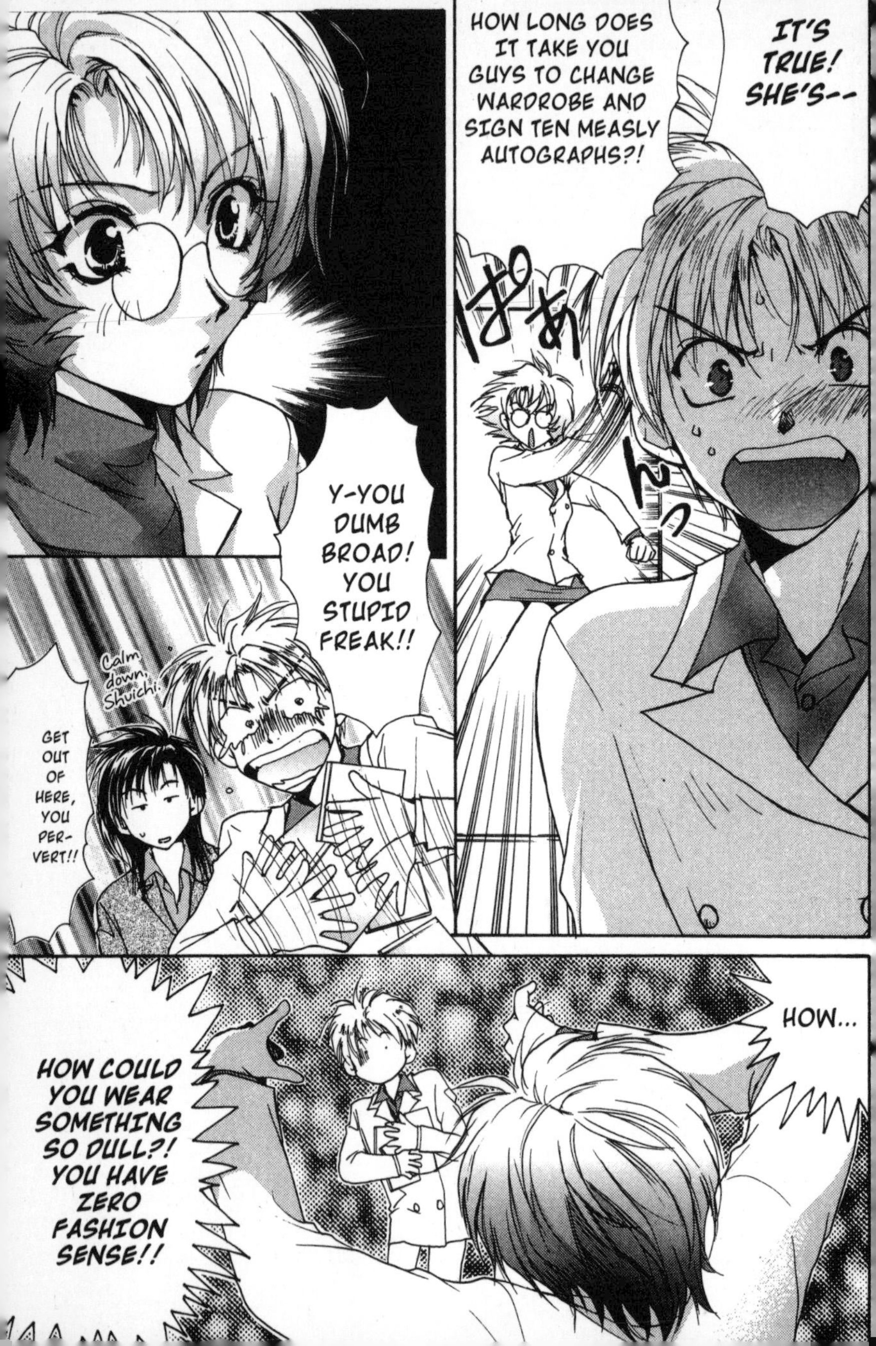
IT'S TRUE! SHE'S--
HOW LONG DOES IT TAKE YOU GUYS TO CHANGE WARDROBE AND SIGN TEN MEASLY AUTOGRAPHS?!
ぱあんっ
Y-YOU DUMB BROAD! YOU STUPID FREAK!!
Calm down, Shuichi.
GET OUT OF HERE, YOU PER-VERT!!
HOW...
HOW COULD YOU WEAR SOMETHING SO DULL?! YOU HAVE ZERO FASHION SENSE!!

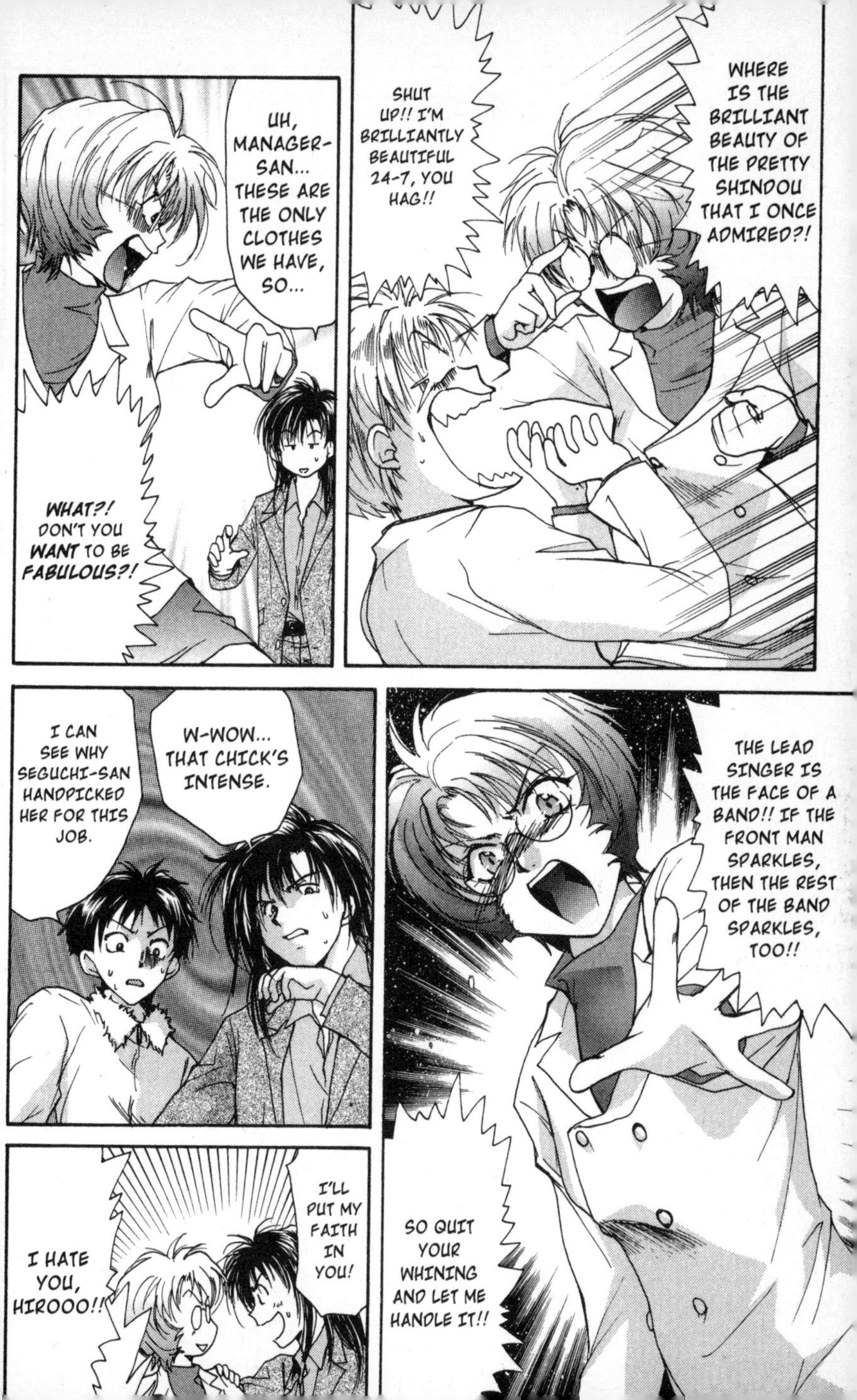
WHERE IS THE BRILLIANT BEAUTY OF THE PRETTY SHINDOU THAT I ONCE ADMIRED?!
SHUT UP!! I'M BRILLIANTLY BEAUTIFUL 24-7, YOU HAG!!
UH, MANAGER-SAN... THESE ARE THE ONLY CLOTHES WE HAVE, SO...
WHAT?! DON'T YOU WANT TO BE FABULOUS?!
THE LEAD SINGER IS THE FACE OF A BAND!! IF THE FRONT MAN SPARKLES, THEN THE REST OF THE BAND SPARKLES, TOO!!
SO QUIT YOUR WHINING AND LET ME HANDLE IT!!
W-WOW... THAT CHICK'S INTENSE.
I CAN SEE WHY SEGUCHI-SAN HANDPICKED HER FOR THIS JOB.
I'LL PUT MY FAITH IN YOU!
I HATE YOU, HIROOO!!

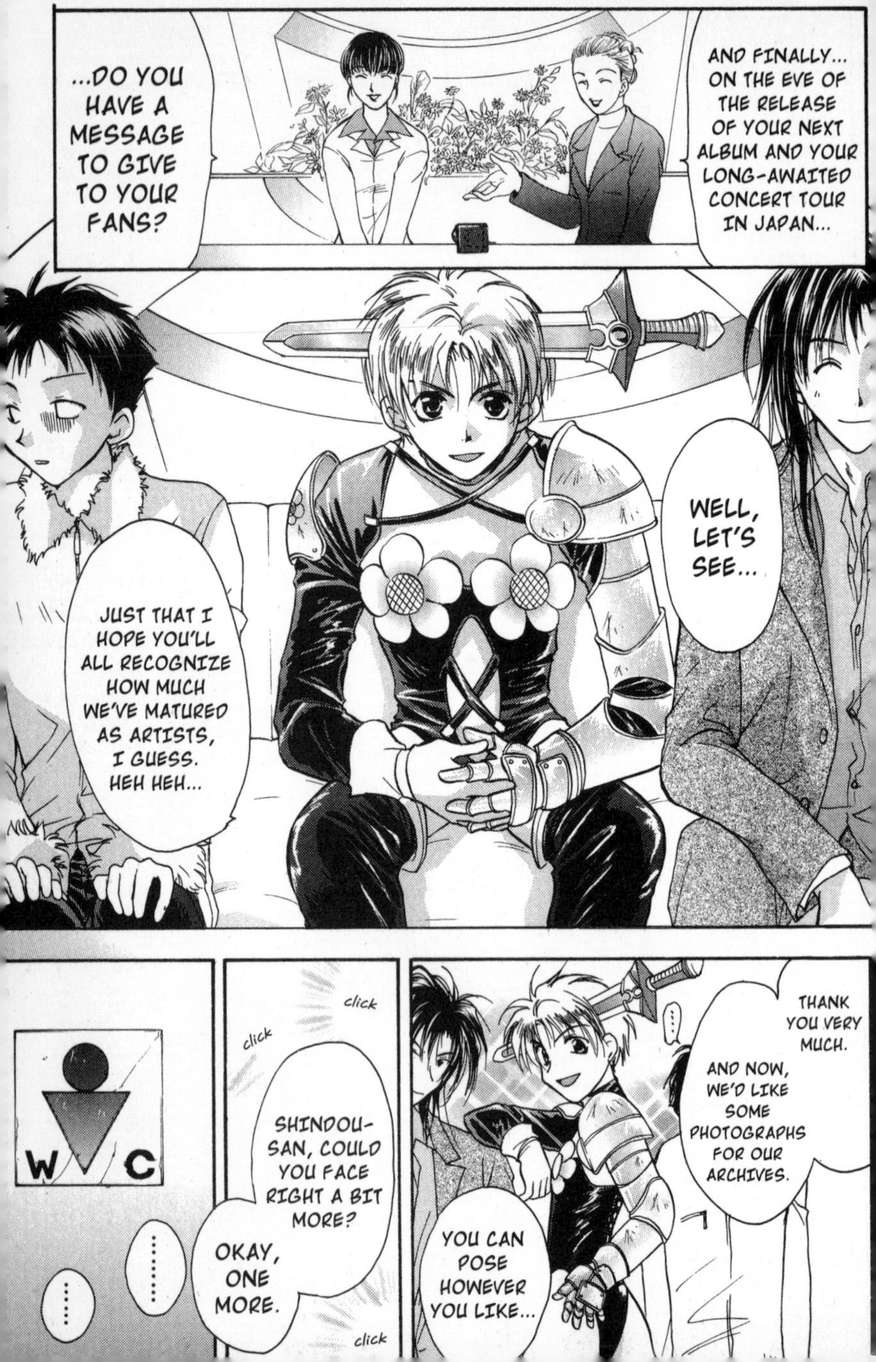

AND FINALLY... ON THE EVE OF THE RELEASE OF YOUR NEXT ALBUM AND YOUR LONG-AWAITED CONCERT TOUR IN JAPAN...
...DO YOU HAVE A MESSAGE TO GIVE TO YOUR FANS?
WELL, LET'S SEE...
JUST THAT I HOPE YOU'LL ALL RECOGNIZE HOW MUCH WE'VE MATURED AS ARTISTS, I GUESS. HEH HEH...
....
THANK YOU VERY MUCH.
AND NOW, WE'D LIKE SOME PHOTOGRAPHS FOR OUR ARCHIVES.
YOU CAN POSE HOWEVER YOU LIKE...
click
click
SHINDOU-SAN, COULD YOU FACE RIGHT A BIT MORE?
OKAY, ONE MORE.
click
W C
......
......

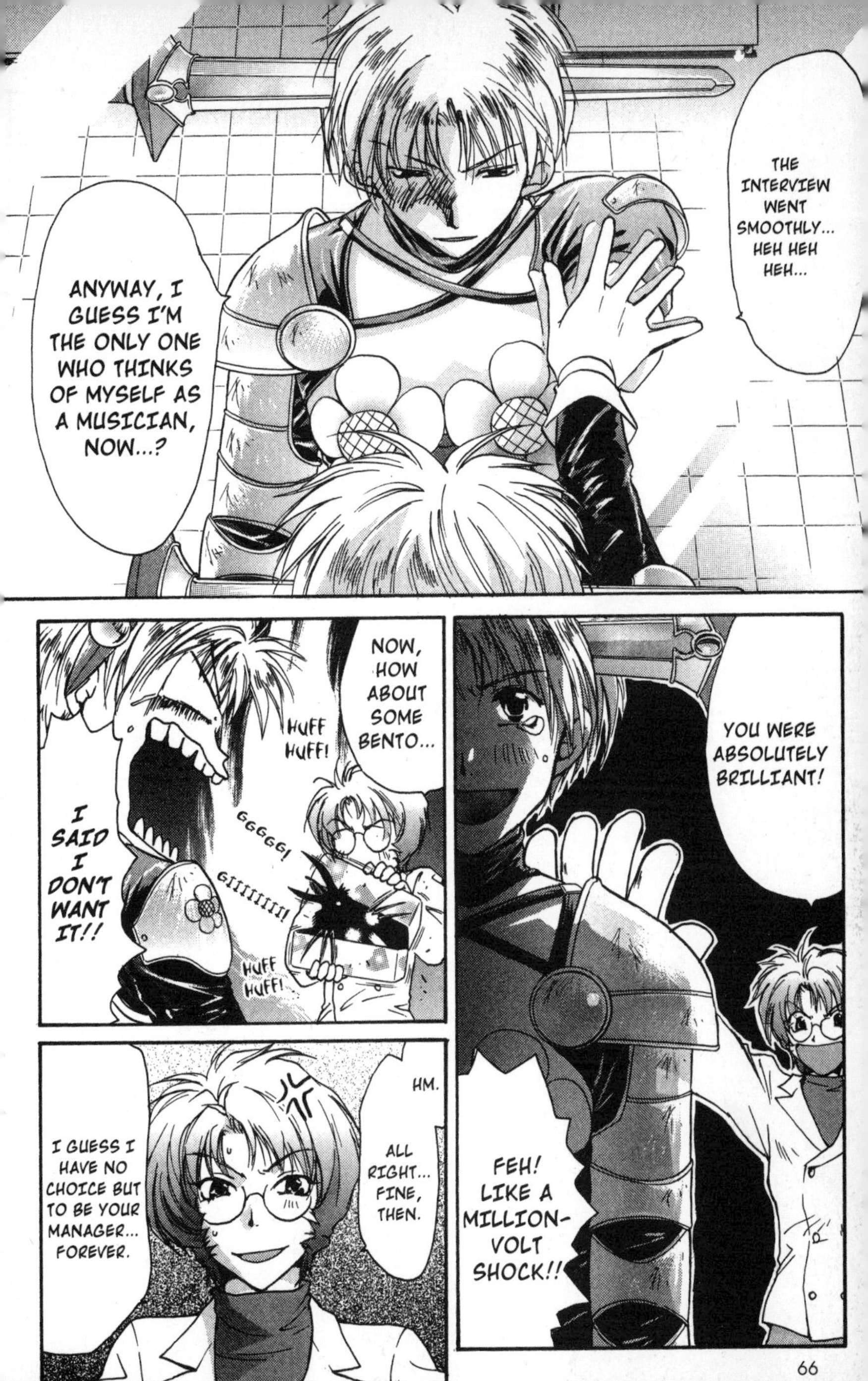
THE INTERVIEW WENT SMOOTHLY... HEH HEH HEH...
ANYWAY, I GUESS I'M THE ONLY ONE WHO THINKS OF MYSELF AS A MUSICIAN, NOW...?
YOU WERE ABSOLUTELY BRILLIANT!
FEH! LIKE A MILLION-VOLT SHOCK!!
NOW, HOW ABOUT SOME BENTO...
HUFF HUFF!
GGGGG!
GIIIIIIII!
I SAID I DON'T WANT IT!!
HUFF HUFF!
HM.
ALL RIGHT... FINE, THEN.
I GUESS I HAVE NO CHOICE BUT TO BE YOUR MANAGER... FOREVER.

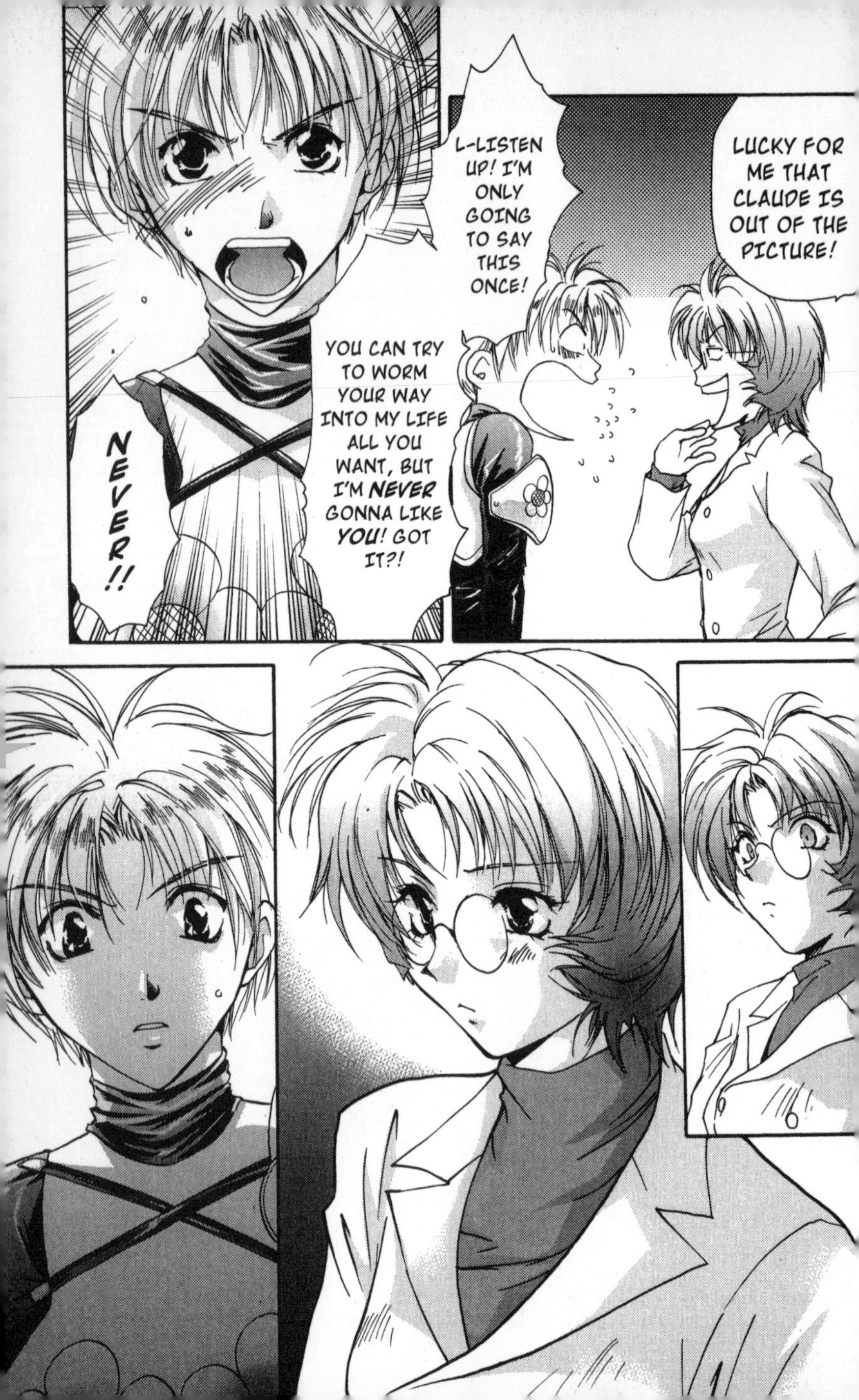
LUCKY FOR ME THAT CLAUDE IS OUT OF THE PICTURE!
L-LISTEN UP! I'M ONLY GOING TO SAY THIS ONCE!
YOU CAN TRY TO WORM YOUR WAY INTO MY LIFE ALL YOU WANT, BUT I'M **NEVER** GONNA LIKE **YOU**! GOT IT?!
NEVER!!

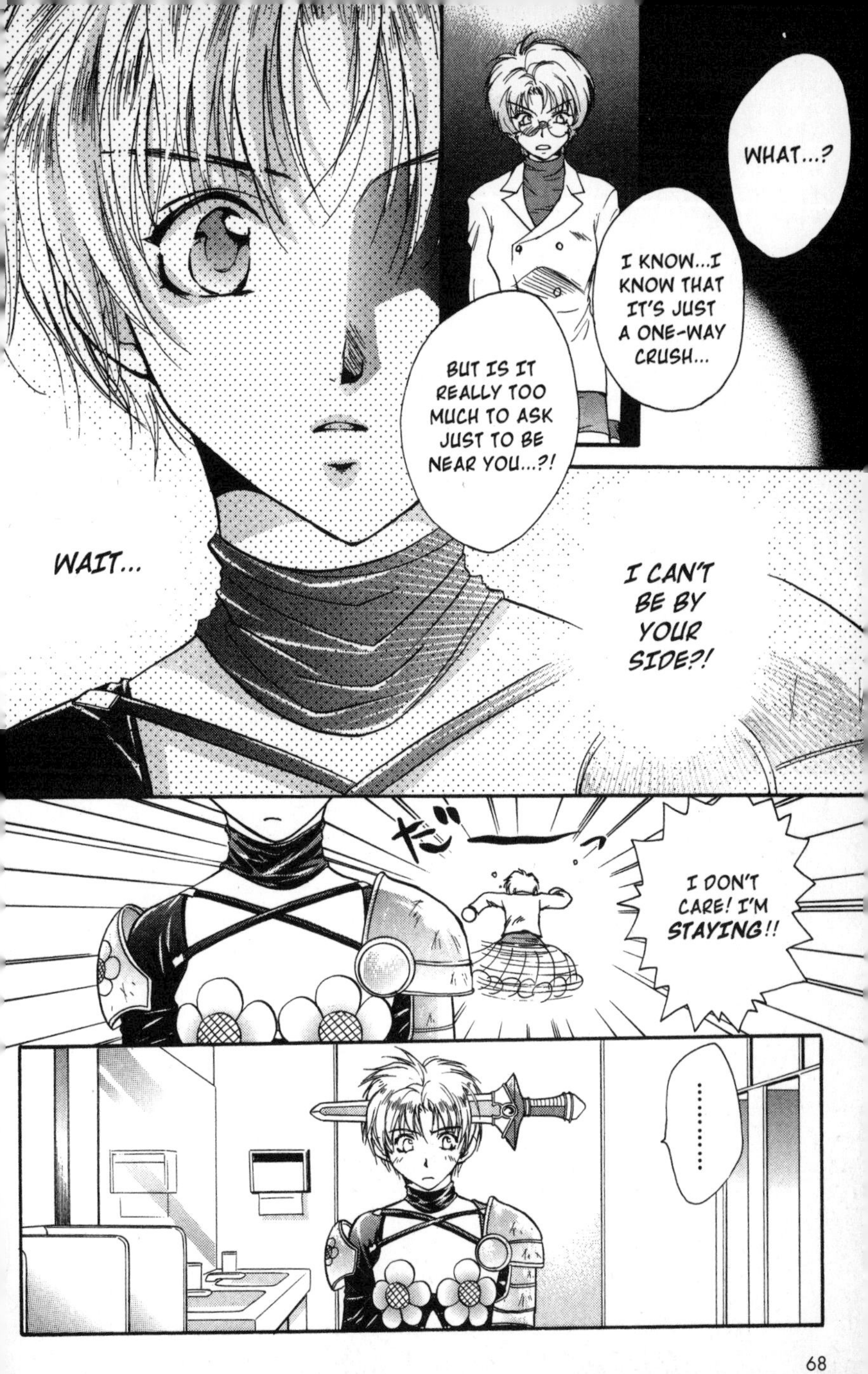
WHAT...?
I KNOW...I KNOW THAT IT'S JUST A ONE-WAY CRUSH...
BUT IS IT REALLY TOO MUCH TO ASK JUST TO BE NEAR YOU...?!
I CAN'T BE BY YOUR SIDE?!
WAIT...
だーーっ
I DON'T CARE! I'M STAYING!!
......

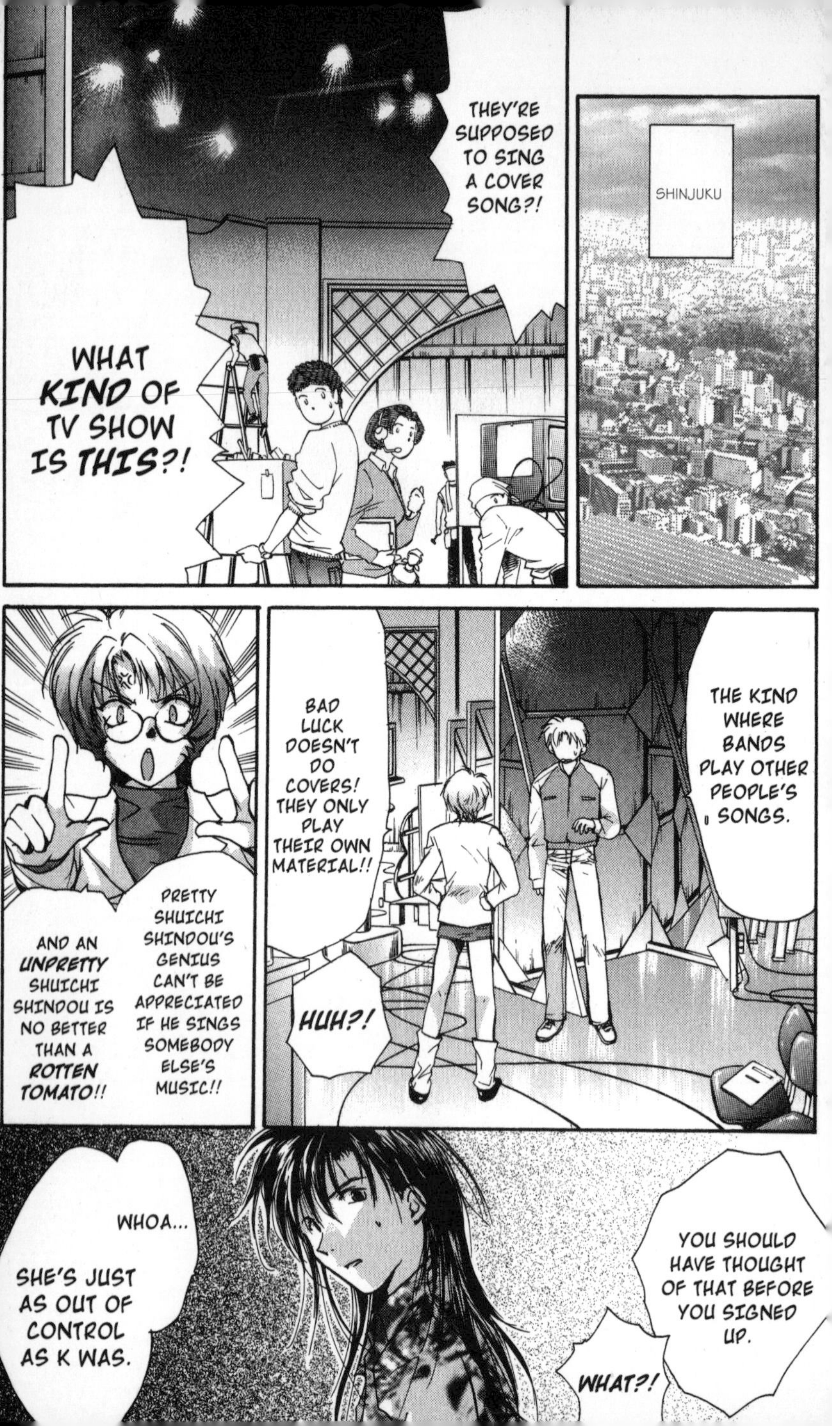
SHINJUKU
THEY'RE SUPPOSED TO SING A COVER SONG?!
WHAT KIND OF TV SHOW IS THIS?!
THE KIND WHERE BANDS PLAY OTHER PEOPLE'S SONGS.
BAD LUCK DOESN'T DO COVERS! THEY ONLY PLAY THEIR OWN MATERIAL!!
HUH?!
PRETTY SHUICHI SHINDOU'S GENIUS CAN'T BE APPRECIATED IF HE SINGS SOMEBODY ELSE'S MUSIC!!
AND AN UNPRETTY SHUICHI SHINDOU IS NO BETTER THAN A ROTTEN TOMATO!!
YOU SHOULD HAVE THOUGHT OF THAT BEFORE YOU SIGNED UP.
WHAT?!
WHOA...
SHE'S JUST AS OUT OF CONTROL AS K WAS.

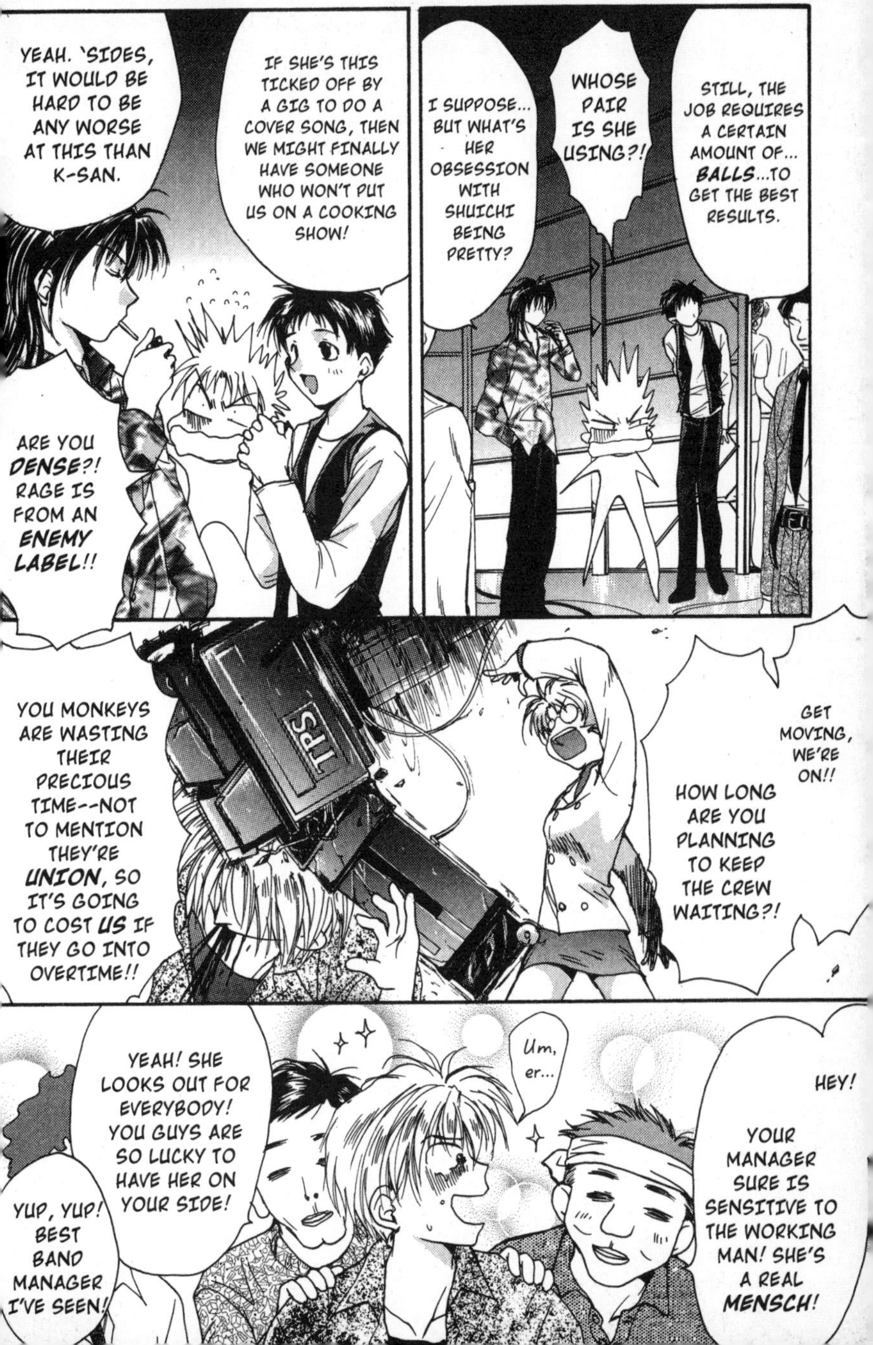
STILL, THE JOB REQUIRES A CERTAIN AMOUNT OF... BALLS...TO GET THE BEST RESULTS.
WHOSE PAIR IS SHE USING?!
I SUPPOSE... BUT WHAT'S HER OBSESSION WITH SHUICHI BEING PRETTY?
IF SHE'S THIS TICKED OFF BY A GIG TO DO A COVER SONG, THEN WE MIGHT FINALLY HAVE SOMEONE WHO WON'T PUT US ON A COOKING SHOW!
YEAH. 'SIDES, IT WOULD BE HARD TO BE ANY WORSE AT THIS THAN K-SAN.
ARE YOU DENSE?! RAGE IS FROM AN ENEMY LABEL!!
GET MOVING, WE'RE ON!!
HOW LONG ARE YOU PLANNING TO KEEP THE CREW WAITING?!
TPS
YOU MONKEYS ARE WASTING THEIR PRECIOUS TIME--NOT TO MENTION THEY'RE UNION, SO IT'S GOING TO COST US IF THEY GO INTO OVERTIME!!
HEY!
YOUR MANAGER SURE IS SENSITIVE TO THE WORKING MAN! SHE'S A REAL MENSCH!
Um, er...
YEAH! SHE LOOKS OUT FOR EVERYBODY! YOU GUYS ARE SO LUCKY TO HAVE HER ON YOUR SIDE!
YUP, YUP! BEST BAND MANAGER I'VE SEEN!

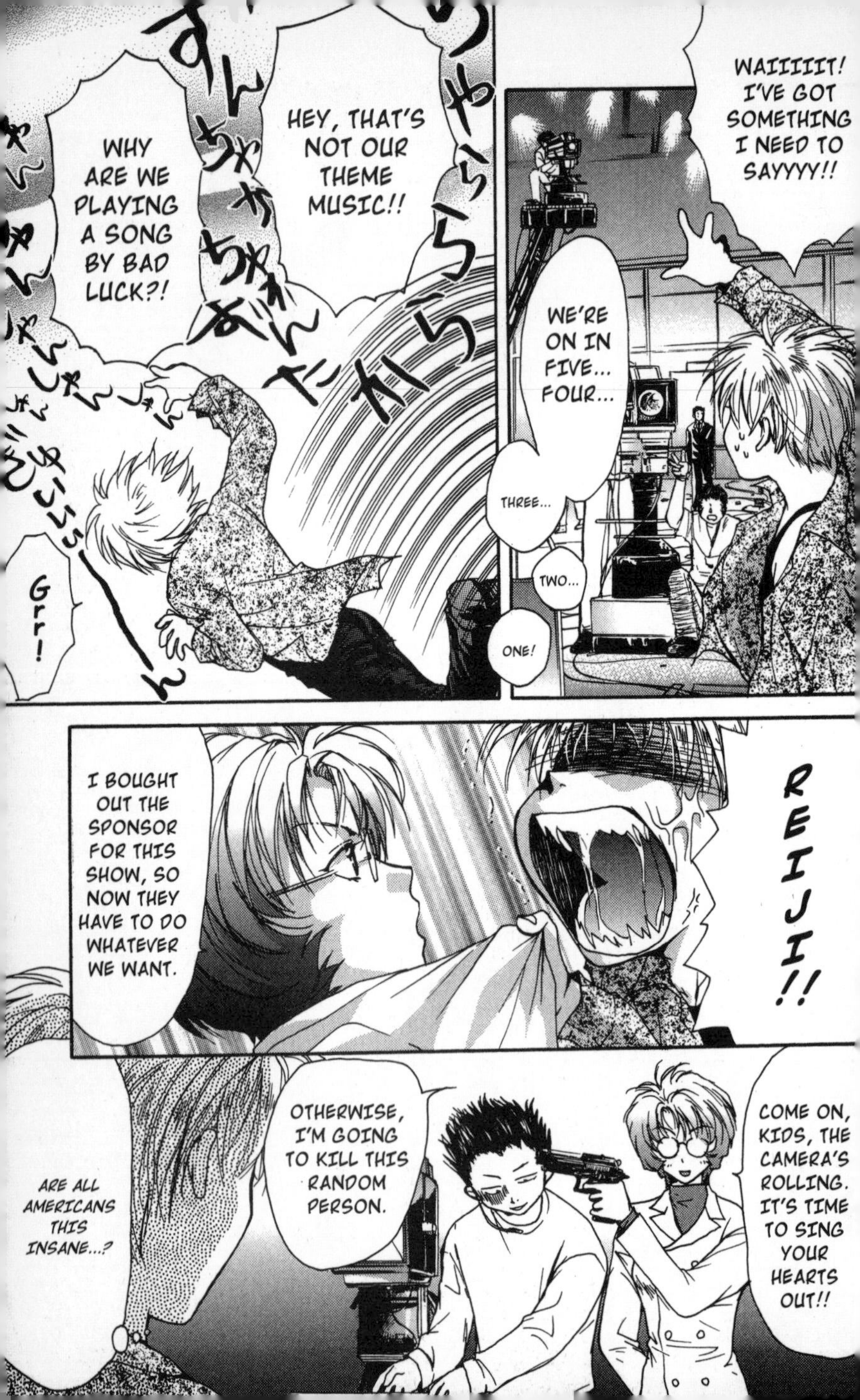
WAIIIIIT! I'VE GOT SOMETHING I NEED TO SAYYYY!!
WE'RE ON IN FIVE... FOUR...
THREE...
TWO...
ONE!
HEY, THAT'S NOT OUR THEME MUSIC!!
WHY ARE WE PLAYING A SONG BY BAD LUCK?!
Grr!
REIJI!!
I BOUGHT OUT THE SPONSOR FOR THIS SHOW, SO NOW THEY HAVE TO DO WHATEVER WE WANT.
COME ON, KIDS, THE CAMERA'S ROLLING. IT'S TIME TO SING YOUR HEARTS OUT!!
OTHERWISE, I'M GOING TO KILL THIS RANDOM PERSON.
ARE ALL AMERICANS THIS INSANE...?

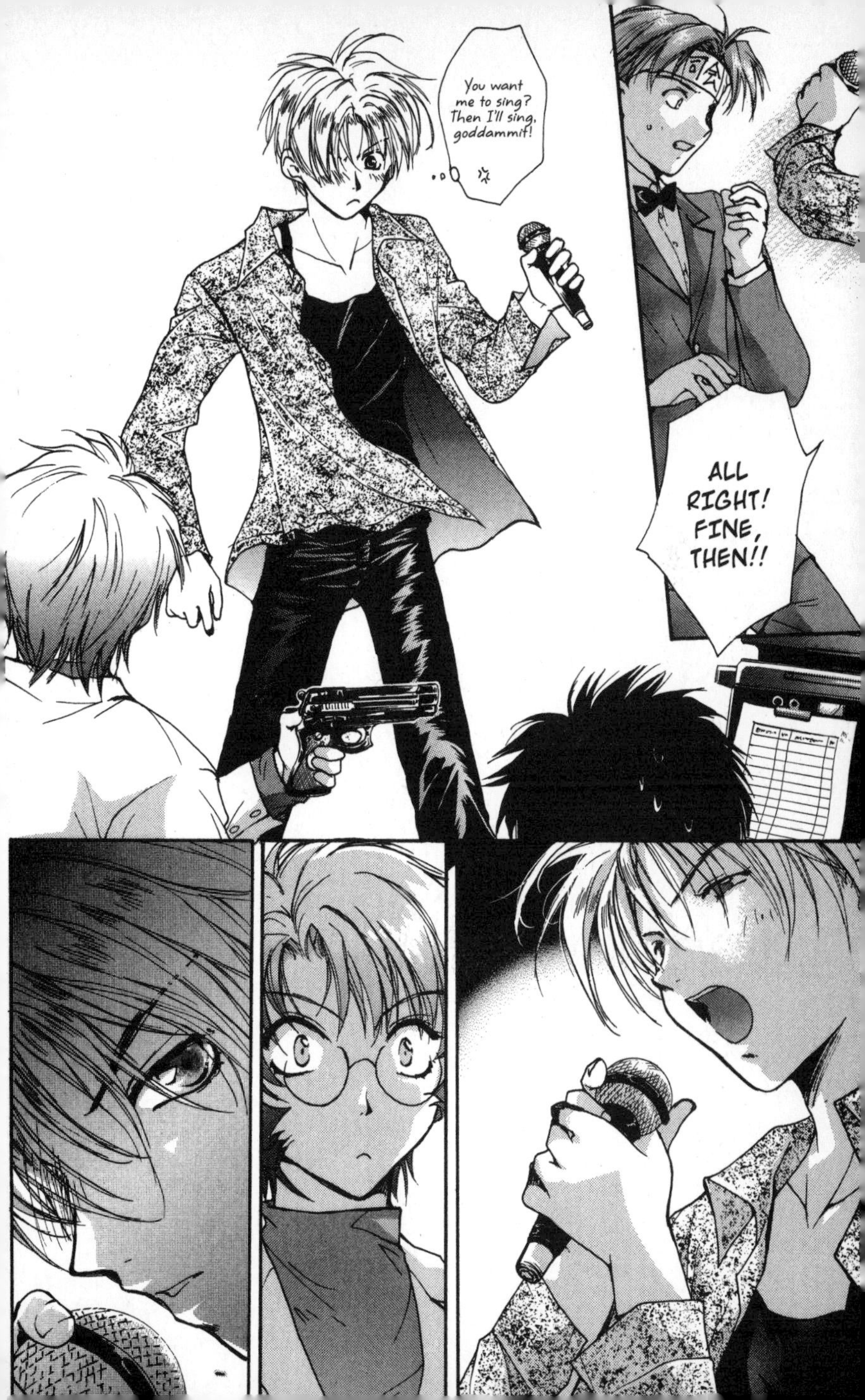
ALL RIGHT! FINE, THEN!!
You want me to sing? Then I'll sing, goddammit!

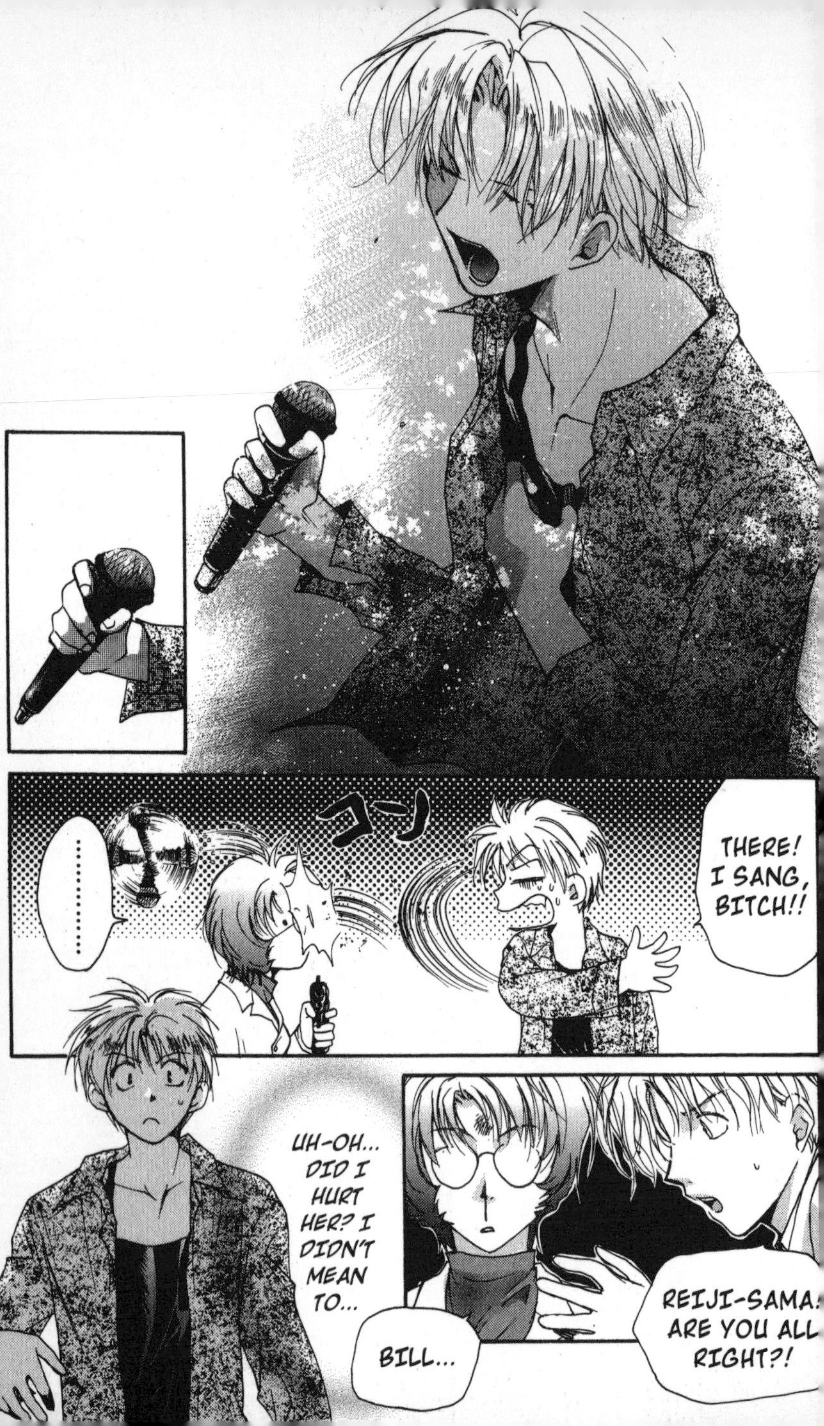
THERE! I SANG, BITCH!!
....
REIJI-SAMA! ARE YOU ALL RIGHT?!
BILL...
UH-OH... DID I HURT HER? I DIDN'T MEAN TO...

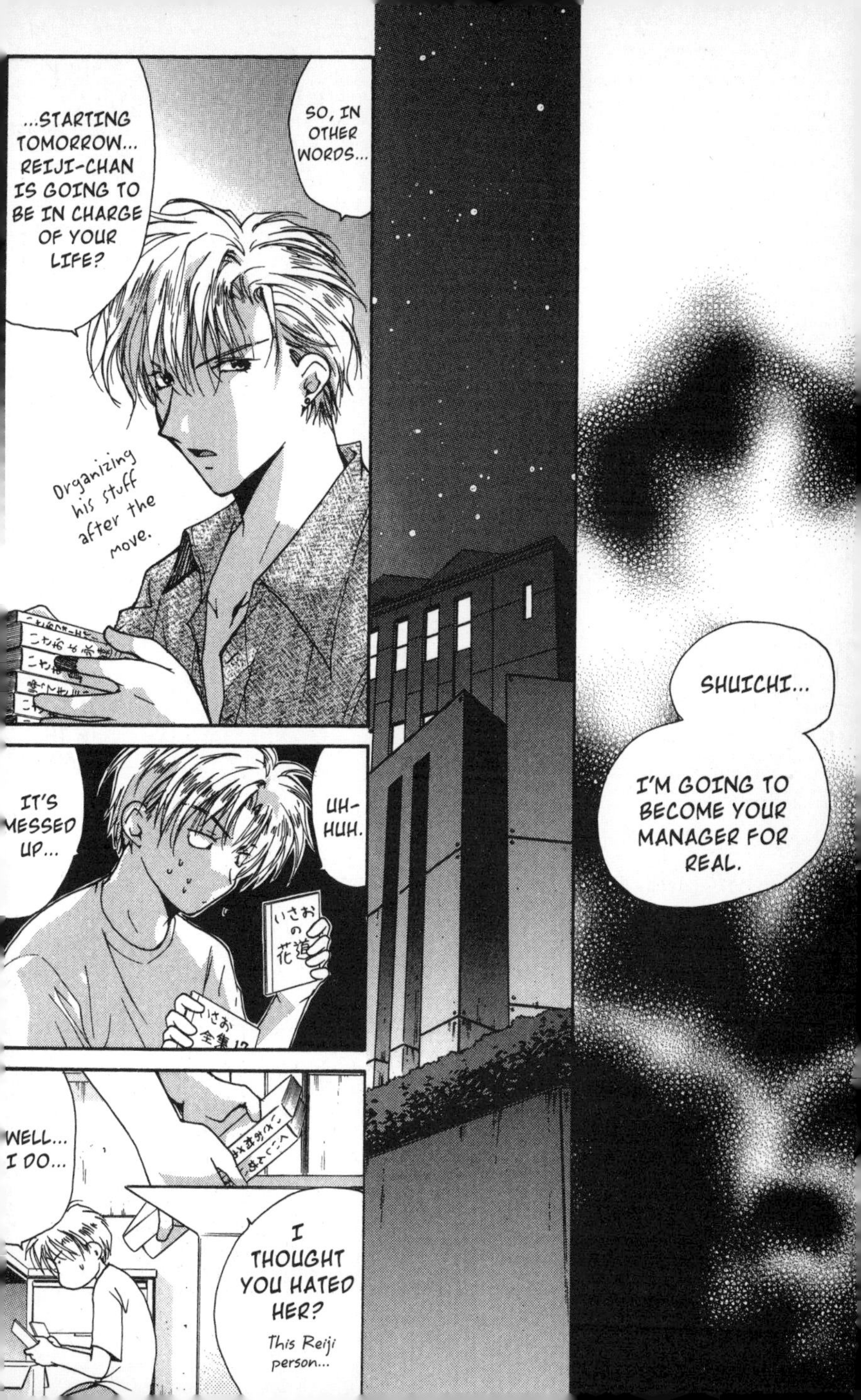
SHUICHI...
I'M GOING TO BECOME YOUR MANAGER FOR REAL.
SO, IN OTHER WORDS...
...STARTING TOMORROW... REIJI-CHAN IS GOING TO BE IN CHARGE OF YOUR LIFE?
Organizing his stuff after the move.
UH-HUH.
IT'S MESSED UP...
いさおの花道
I THOUGHT YOU HATED HER?
This Reiji person...
WELL... I DO...

ABOUT GRAVITATION TRACK 43

Jealous Rage and Shuichi... Oh, my, this is such the young girl's manga, you know? (Though this is a boy-on-boy comic.) Although the bespectacled Rage was a stop-gap character, I had no idea she would become this prominent. And I've finally gotten used to drawing that bulb-head hairstyle of hers. I'm planning to have Rage work a little harder in the future. Thanks to her, all hell's breaking loose. I can't let her go home until she takes responsibility for this situation she's created...

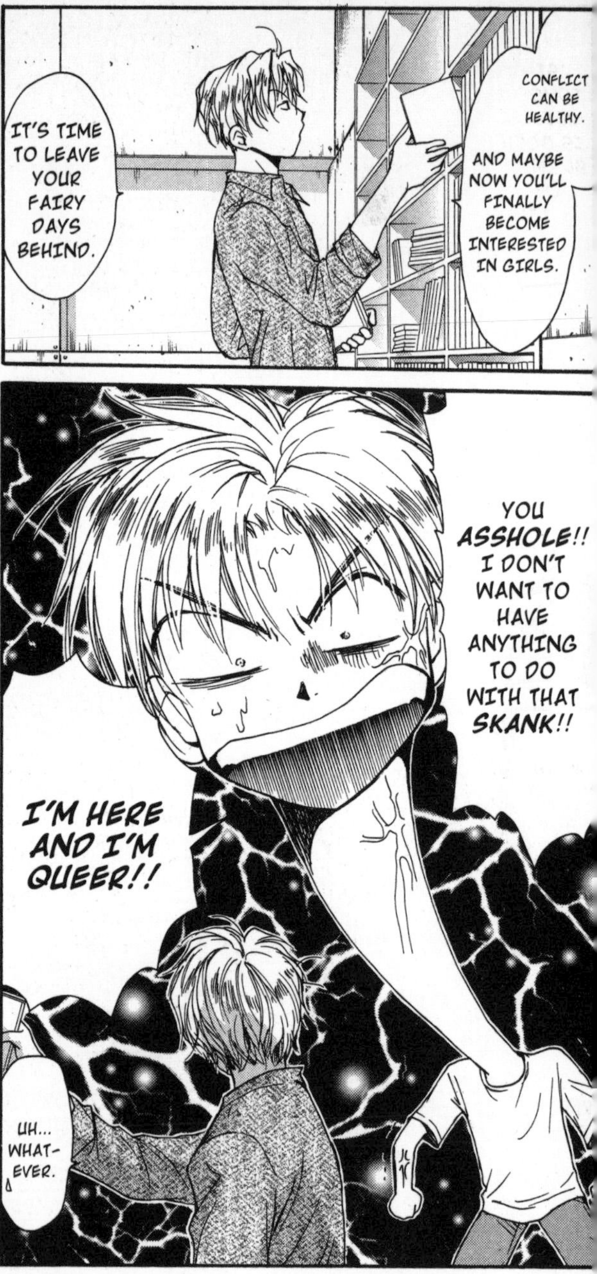
CONFLICT CAN BE HEALTHY.
AND MAYBE NOW YOU'LL FINALLY BECOME INTERESTED IN GIRLS.
IT'S TIME TO LEAVE YOUR FAIRY DAYS BEHIND.
YOU ASSHOLE!! I DON'T WANT TO HAVE ANYTHING TO DO WITH THAT SKANK!!
I'M HERE AND I'M QUEER!!
UH... WHAT-EVER.

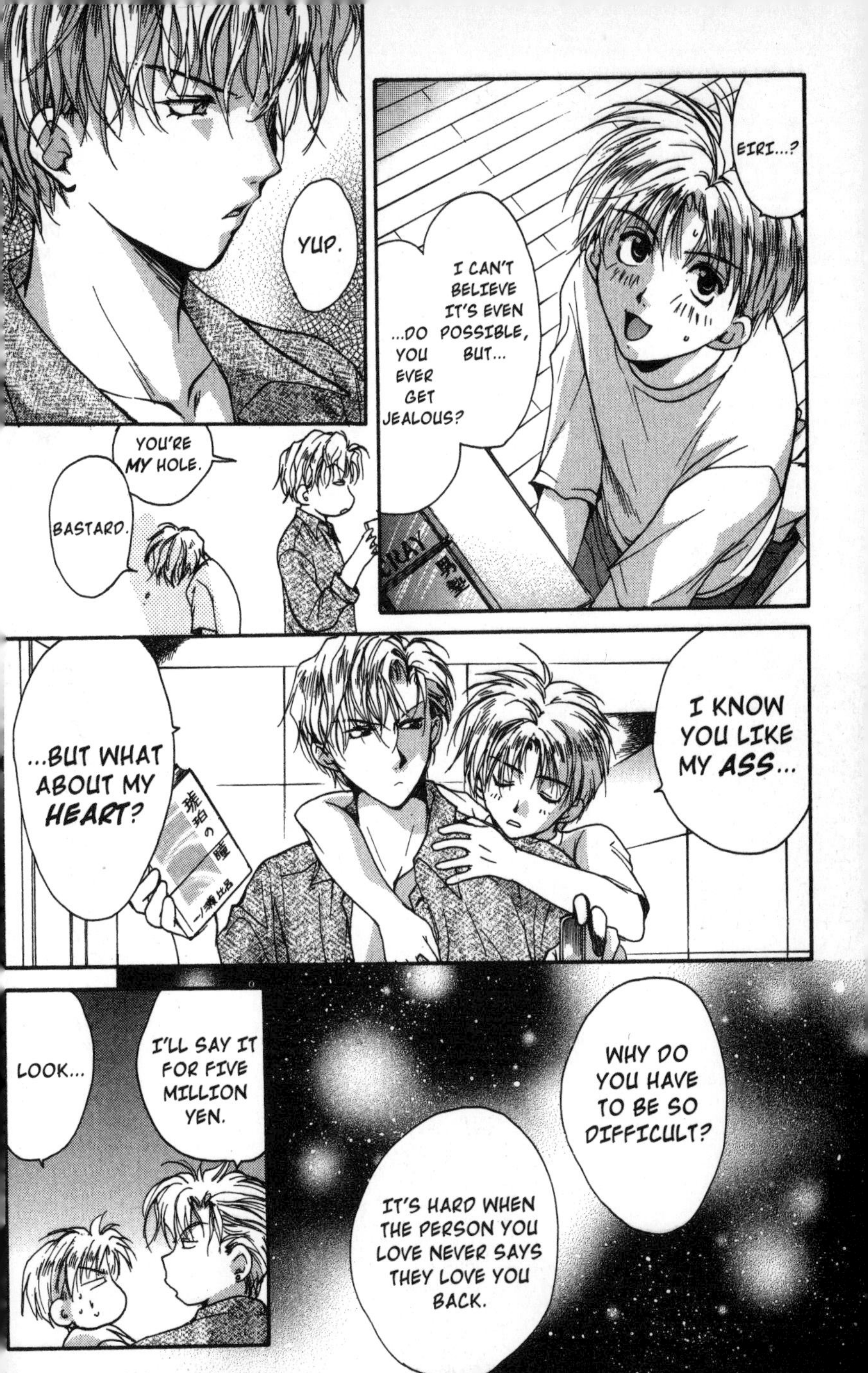
EIRI...?
I CAN'T BELIEVE IT'S EVEN POSSIBLE, BUT...
...DO YOU EVER GET JEALOUS?
YUP.
YOU'RE MY HOLE.
BASTARD.
I KNOW YOU LIKE MY ASS...
...BUT WHAT ABOUT MY HEART?
WHY DO YOU HAVE TO BE SO DIFFICULT?
IT'S HARD WHEN THE PERSON YOU LOVE NEVER SAYS THEY LOVE YOU BACK.
I'LL SAY IT FOR FIVE MILLION YEN.
LOOK...

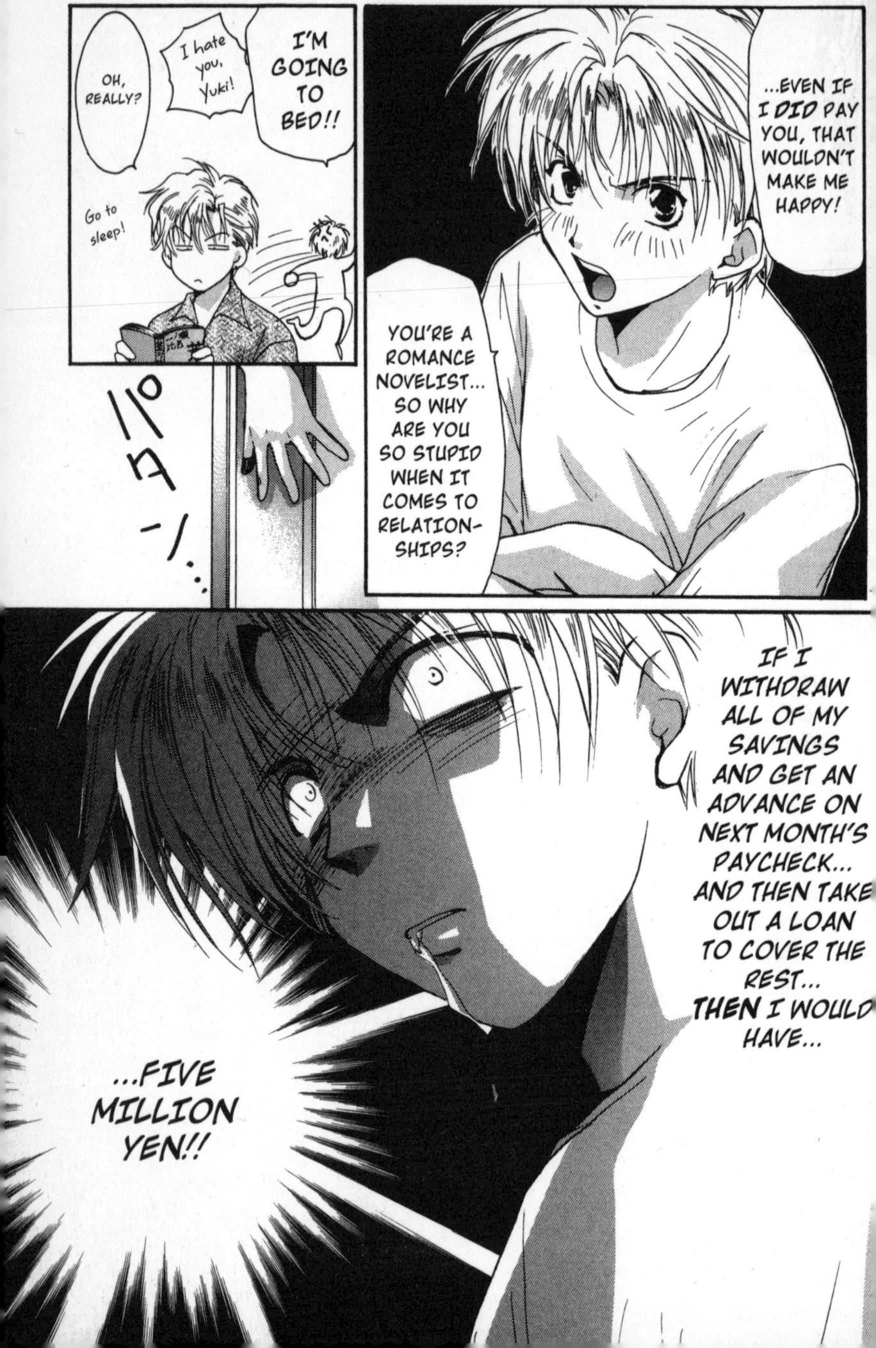
...EVEN IF I DID PAY YOU, THAT WOULDN'T MAKE ME HAPPY!
YOU'RE A ROMANCE NOVELIST... SO WHY ARE YOU SO STUPID WHEN IT COMES TO RELATIONSHIPS?
I'M GOING TO BED!!
I hate you, Yuki!
OH, REALLY?
Go to sleep!
IF I WITHDRAW ALL OF MY SAVINGS AND GET AN ADVANCE ON NEXT MONTH'S PAYCHECK... AND THEN TAKE OUT A LOAN TO COVER THE REST... THEN I WOULD HAVE...
...FIVE MILLION YEN!!

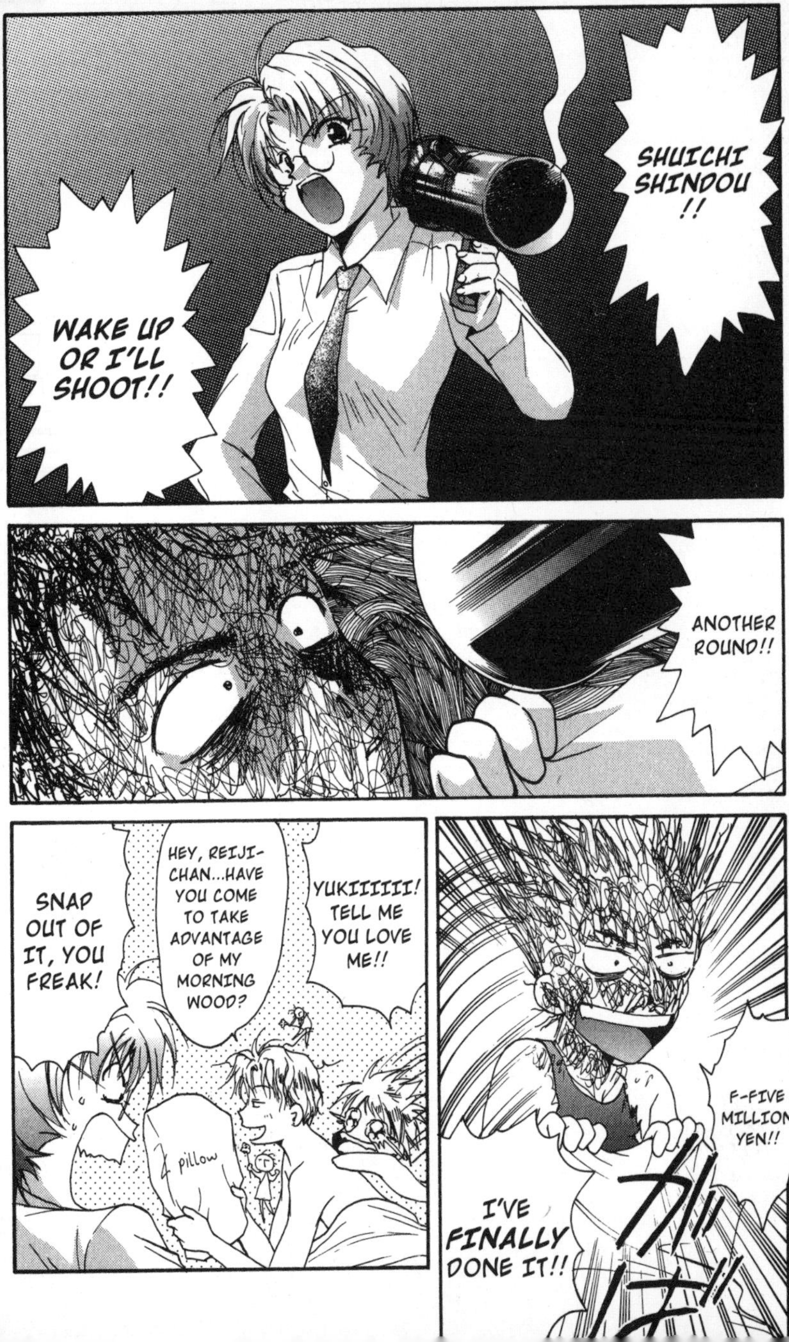
SHUICHI SHINDOU!!
WAKE UP OR I'LL SHOOT!!
ANOTHER ROUND!!
F-FIVE MILLION YEN!!
I'VE FINALLY DONE IT!!
YUKIIIIII! TELL ME YOU LOVE ME!!
HEY, REIJI-CHAN...HAVE YOU COME TO TAKE ADVANTAGE OF MY MORNING WOOD?
SNAP OUT OF IT, YOU FREAK!
pillow

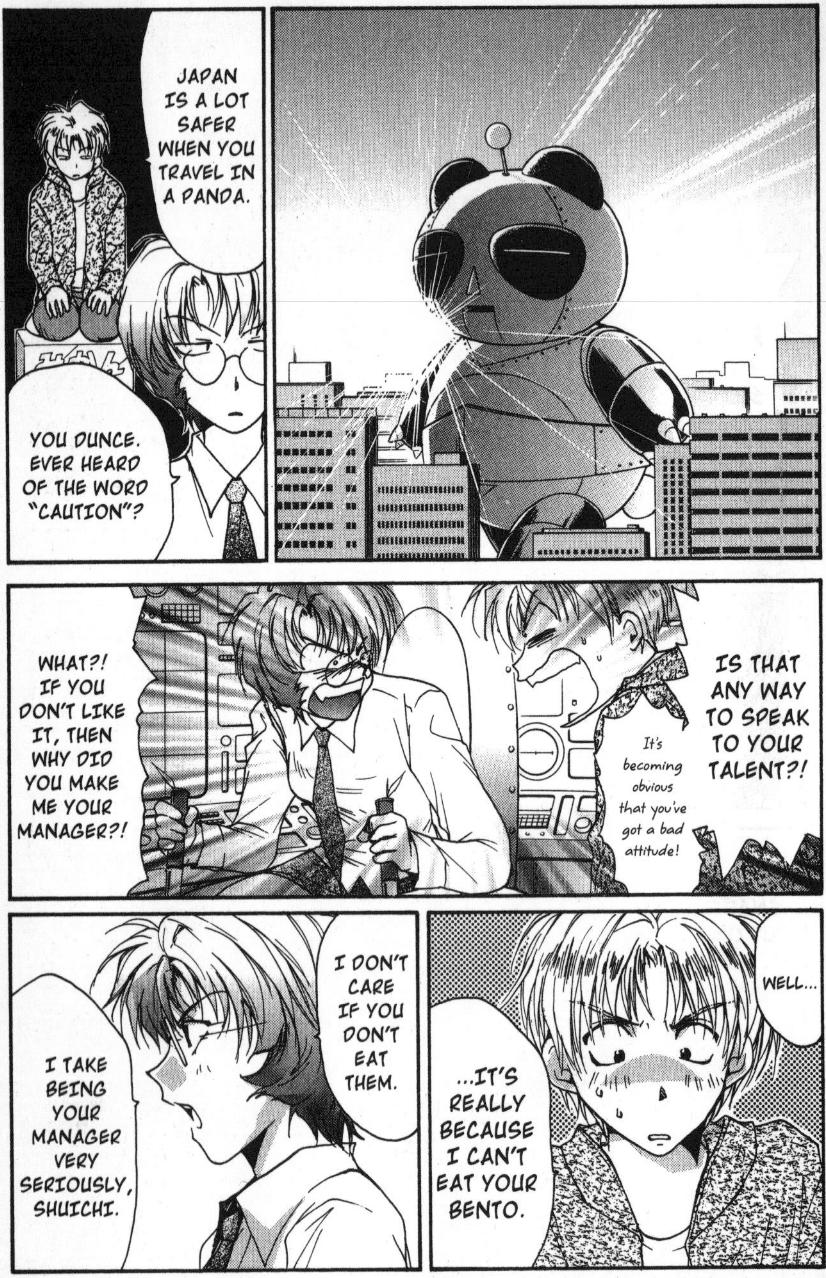
JAPAN IS A LOT SAFER WHEN YOU TRAVEL IN A PANDA.
YOU DUNCE. EVER HEARD OF THE WORD "CAUTION"?
IS THAT ANY WAY TO SPEAK TO YOUR TALENT?!
It's becoming obvious that you've got a bad attitude!
WHAT?! IF YOU DON'T LIKE IT, THEN WHY DID YOU MAKE ME YOUR MANAGER?!
WELL...
...IT'S REALLY BECAUSE I CAN'T EAT YOUR BENTO.
I DON'T CARE IF YOU DON'T EAT THEM.
I TAKE BEING YOUR MANAGER VERY SERIOUSLY, SHUICHI.

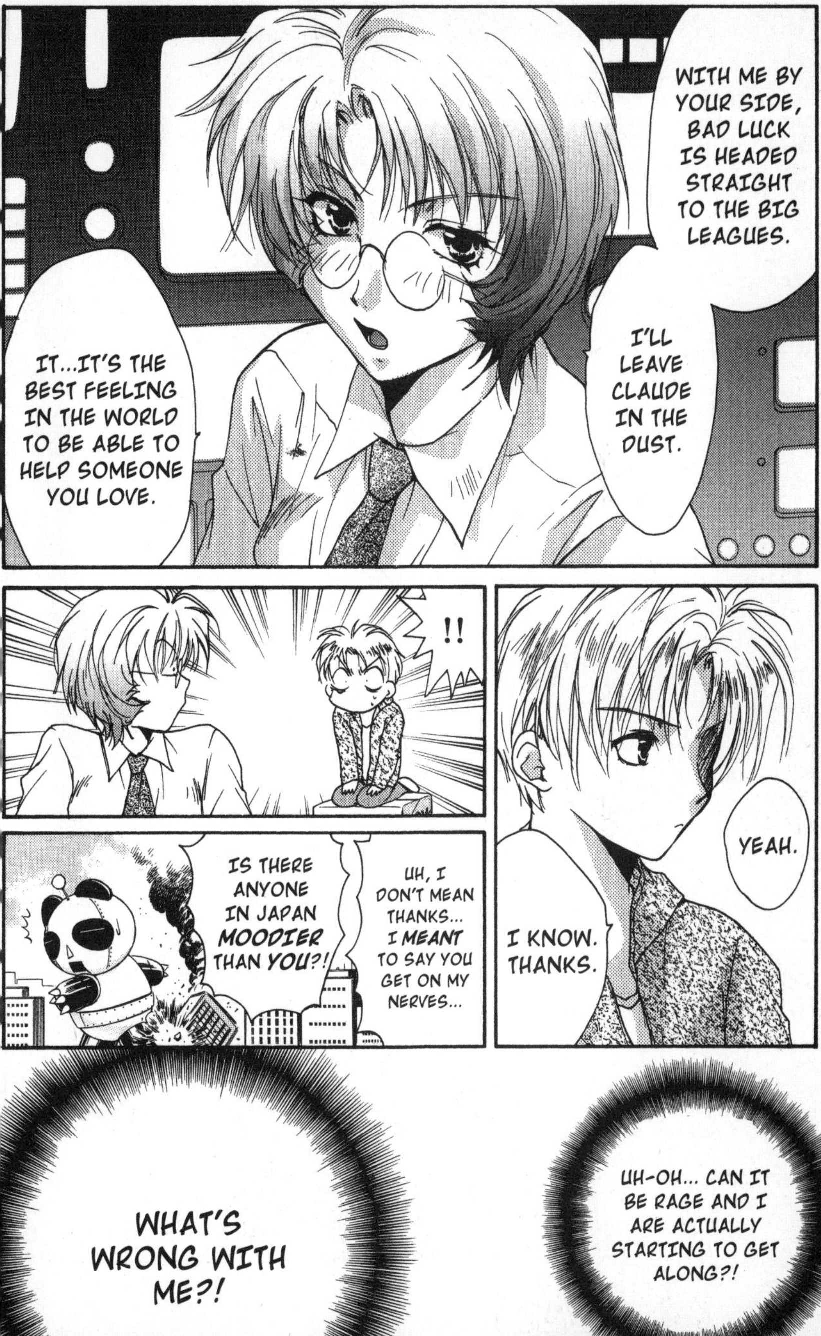
WITH ME BY YOUR SIDE, BAD LUCK IS HEADED STRAIGHT TO THE BIG LEAGUES.
I'LL LEAVE CLAUDE IN THE DUST.
IT...IT'S THE BEST FEELING IN THE WORLD TO BE ABLE TO HELP SOMEONE YOU LOVE.
YEAH.
I KNOW. THANKS.
!!
UH, I DON'T MEAN THANKS... I *MEANT* TO SAY YOU GET ON MY NERVES...
IS THERE ANYONE IN JAPAN *MOODIER* THAN *YOU*?!
UH-OH... CAN IT BE RAGE AND I ARE ACTUALLY STARTING TO GET ALONG?!
WHAT'S WRONG WITH ME?!

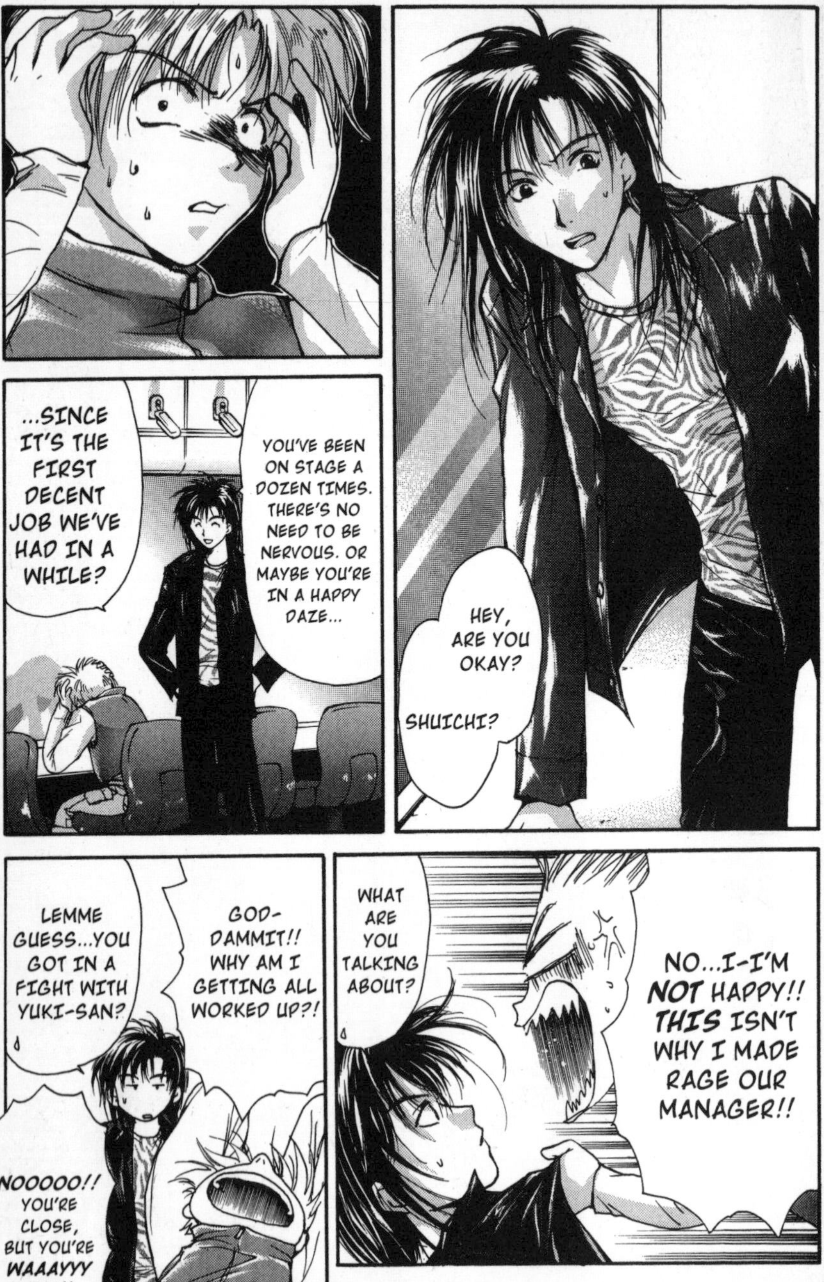
HEY, ARE YOU OKAY?
SHUICHI?
YOU'VE BEEN ON STAGE A DOZEN TIMES. THERE'S NO NEED TO BE NERVOUS. OR MAYBE YOU'RE IN A HAPPY DAZE...
...SINCE IT'S THE FIRST DECENT JOB WE'VE HAD IN A WHILE?
NO...I-I'M **NOT** HAPPY!! **THIS** ISN'T WHY I MADE RAGE OUR MANAGER!!
WHAT ARE YOU TALKING ABOUT?
GOD-DAMMIT!! WHY AM I GETTING ALL WORKED UP?!
LEMME GUESS...YOU GOT IN A FIGHT WITH YUKI-SAN?
NOOOOO!! YOU'RE CLOSE, BUT YOU'RE **WAAAYYY** OFF!!

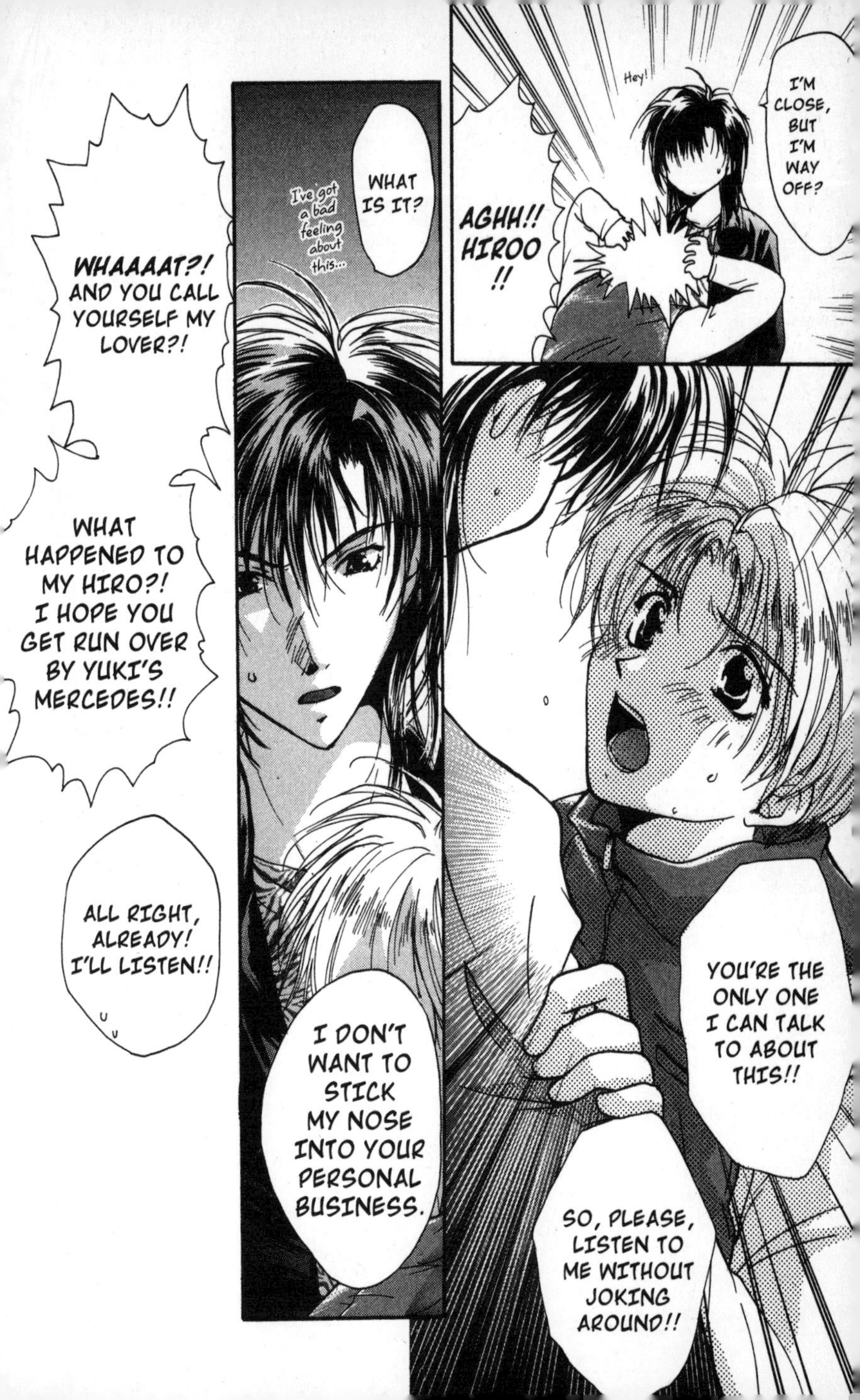
I'M CLOSE, BUT I'M WAY OFF?
Hey!
AGHH!! HIROO!!
YOU'RE THE ONLY ONE I CAN TALK TO ABOUT THIS!!
SO, PLEASE, LISTEN TO ME WITHOUT JOKING AROUND!!
WHAT IS IT?
I've got a bad feeling about this...
I DON'T WANT TO STICK MY NOSE INTO YOUR PERSONAL BUSINESS.
WHAAAAT?! AND YOU CALL YOURSELF MY LOVER?!
WHAT HAPPENED TO MY HIRO?! I HOPE YOU GET RUN OVER BY YUKI'S MERCEDES!!
ALL RIGHT, ALREADY! I'LL LISTEN!!

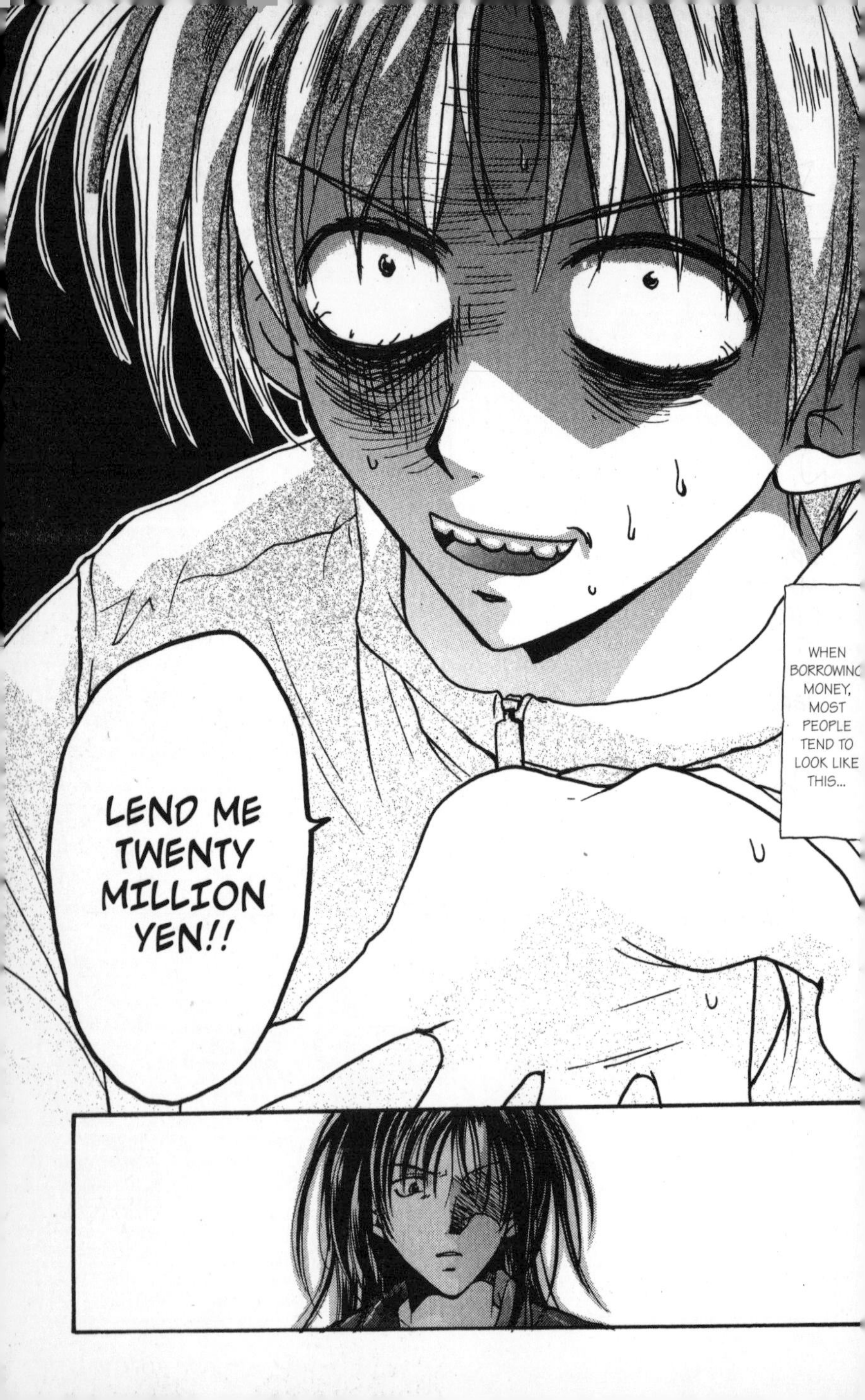
WHEN BORROWING MONEY, MOST PEOPLE TEND TO LOOK LIKE THIS...
LEND ME TWENTY MILLION YEN!!

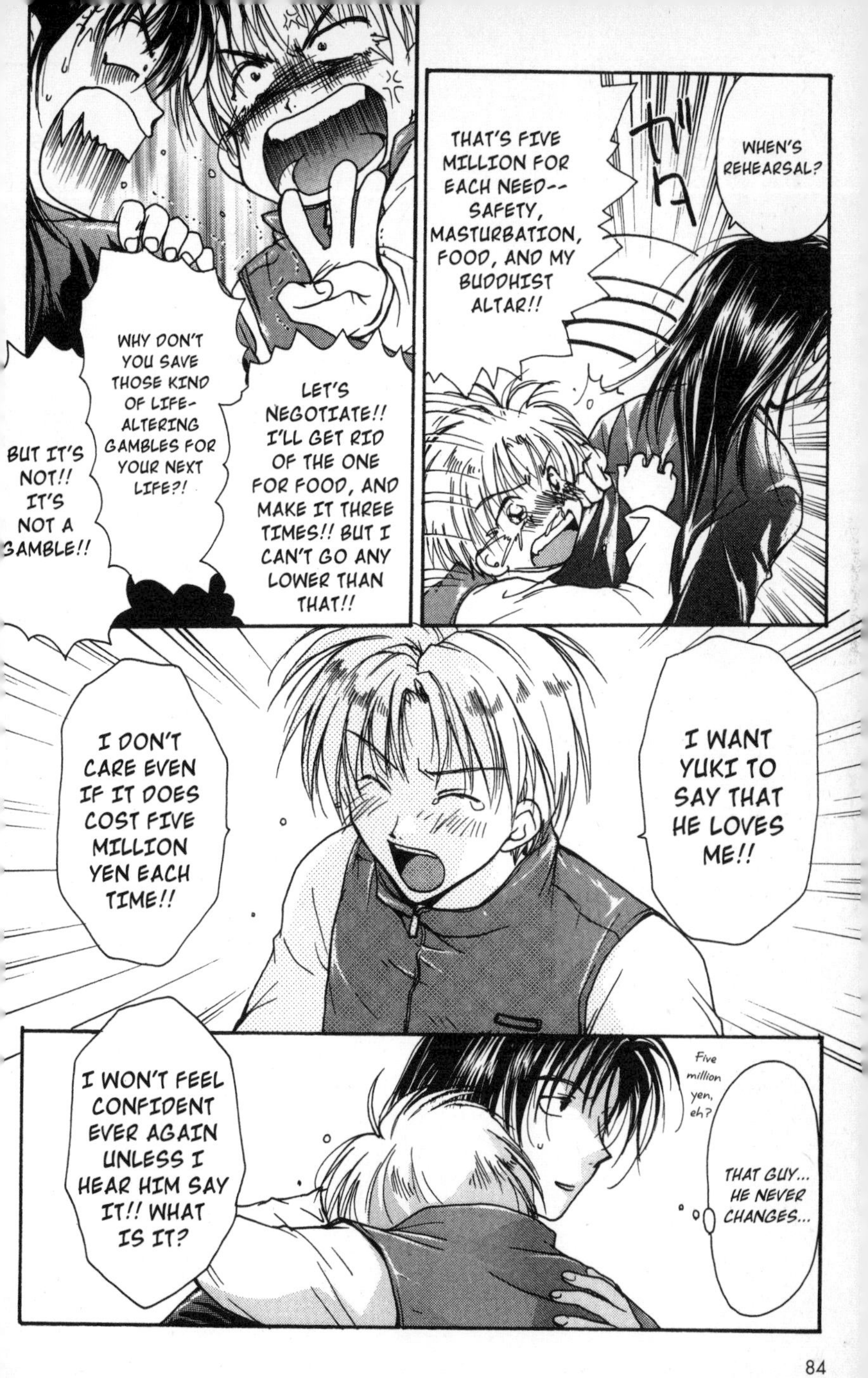
WHEN'S REHEARSAL?
THAT'S FIVE MILLION FOR EACH NEED--SAFETY, MASTURBATION, FOOD, AND MY BUDDHIST ALTAR!!
LET'S NEGOTIATE!! I'LL GET RID OF THE ONE FOR FOOD, AND MAKE IT THREE TIMES!! BUT I CAN'T GO ANY LOWER THAN THAT!!
WHY DON'T YOU SAVE THOSE KIND OF LIFE-ALTERING GAMBLES FOR YOUR NEXT LIFE?!
BUT IT'S NOT!! IT'S NOT A GAMBLE!!
I WANT YUKI TO SAY THAT HE LOVES ME!!
I DON'T CARE EVEN IF IT DOES COST FIVE MILLION YEN EACH TIME!!
Five million yen, eh?
THAT GUY... HE NEVER CHANGES...
I WON'T FEEL CONFIDENT EVER AGAIN UNLESS I HEAR HIM SAY IT!! WHAT IS IT?

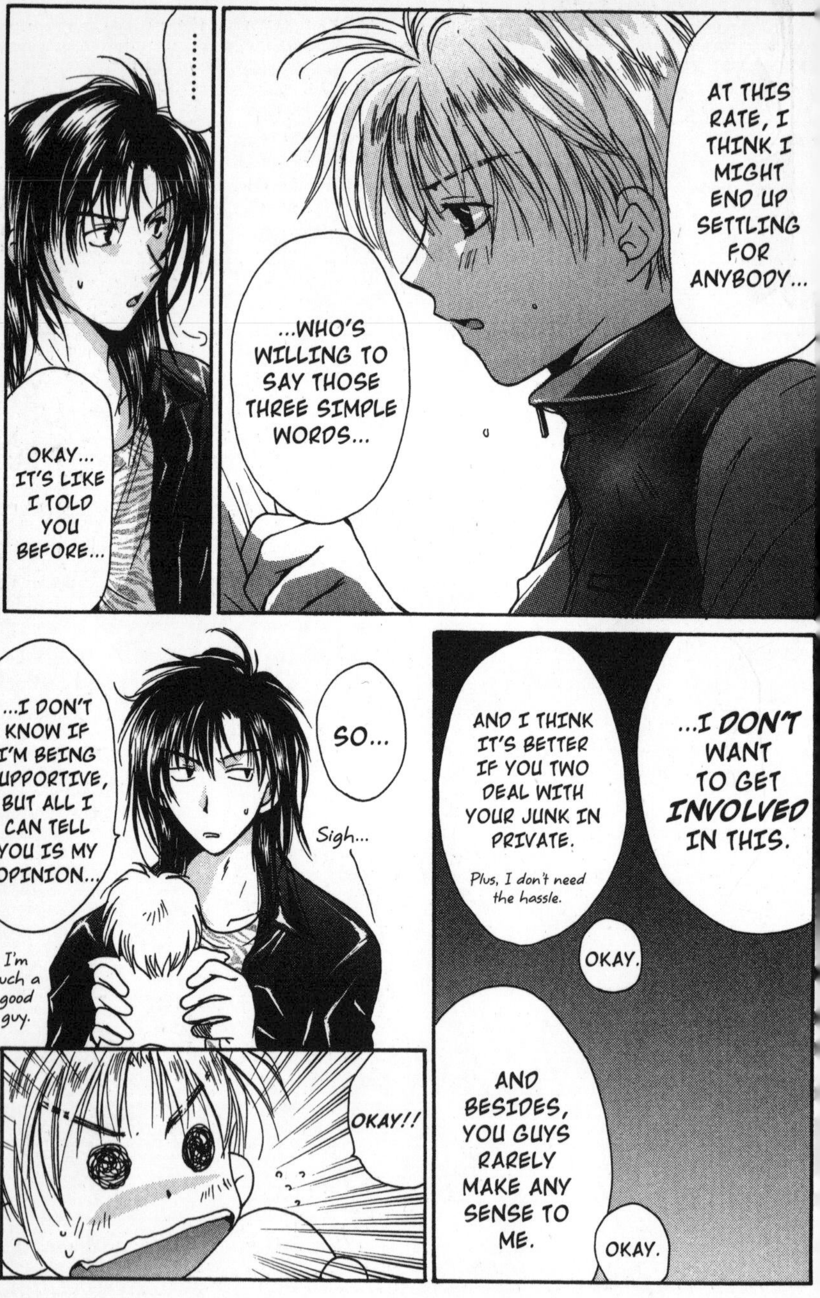
AT THIS RATE, I THINK I MIGHT END UP SETTLING FOR ANYBODY...
...WHO'S WILLING TO SAY THOSE THREE SIMPLE WORDS...
......
OKAY... IT'S LIKE I TOLD YOU BEFORE...
...I *DON'T* WANT TO GET *INVOLVED* IN THIS.
AND I THINK IT'S BETTER IF YOU TWO DEAL WITH YOUR JUNK IN PRIVATE.
Plus, I don't need the hassle.
OKAY.
AND BESIDES, YOU GUYS RARELY MAKE ANY SENSE TO ME.
OKAY.
SO...
...I DON'T KNOW IF I'M BEING SUPPORTIVE, BUT ALL I CAN TELL YOU IS MY OPINION...
Sigh...
I'm such a good guy.
OKAY!!

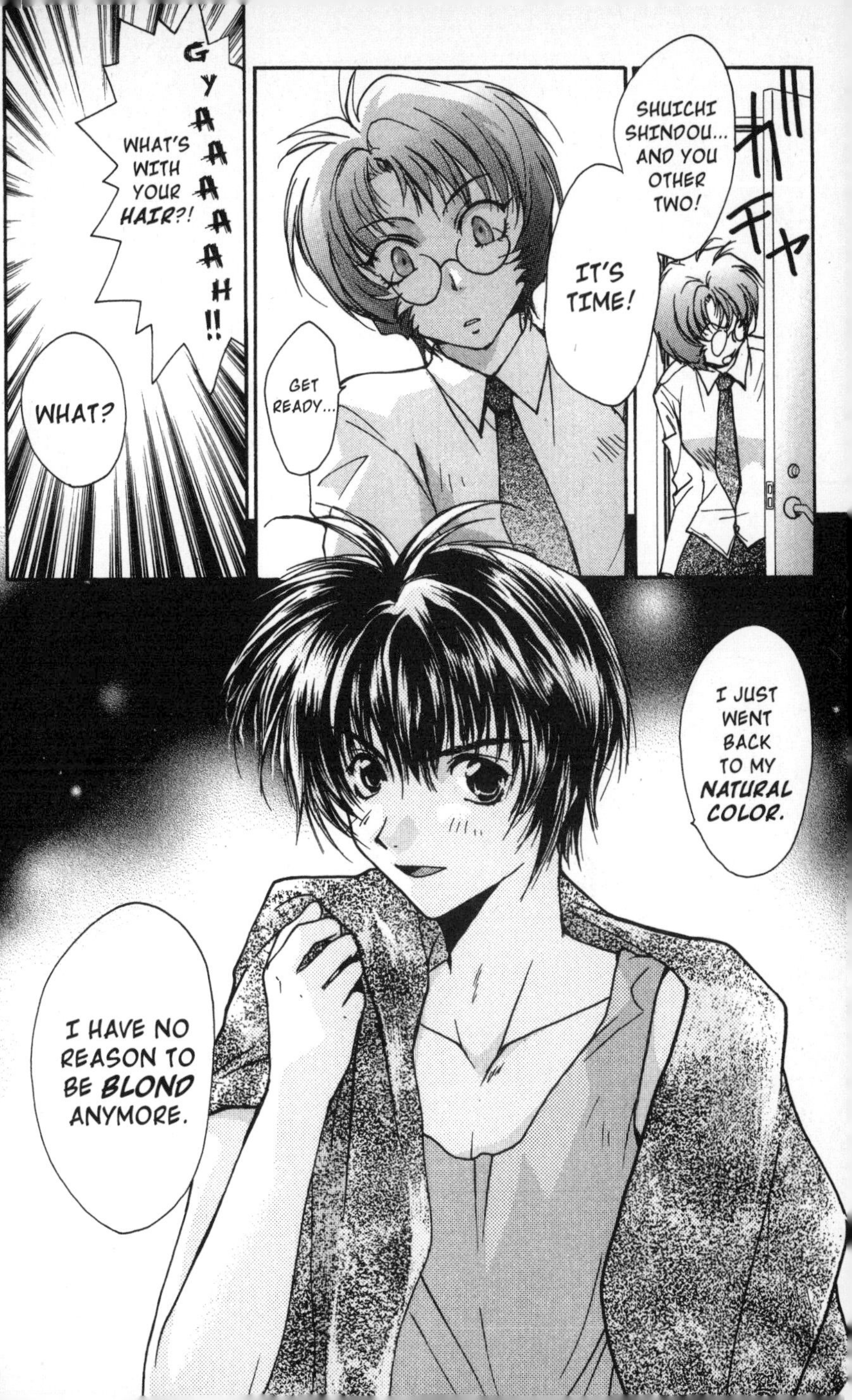
ガチャ
SHUICHI SHINDOU... AND YOU OTHER TWO!
IT'S TIME!
GET READY...
GYAAAAAH!!
WHAT'S WITH YOUR HAIR?!
WHAT?
I JUST WENT BACK TO MY NATURAL COLOR.
I HAVE NO REASON TO BE BLOND ANYMORE.

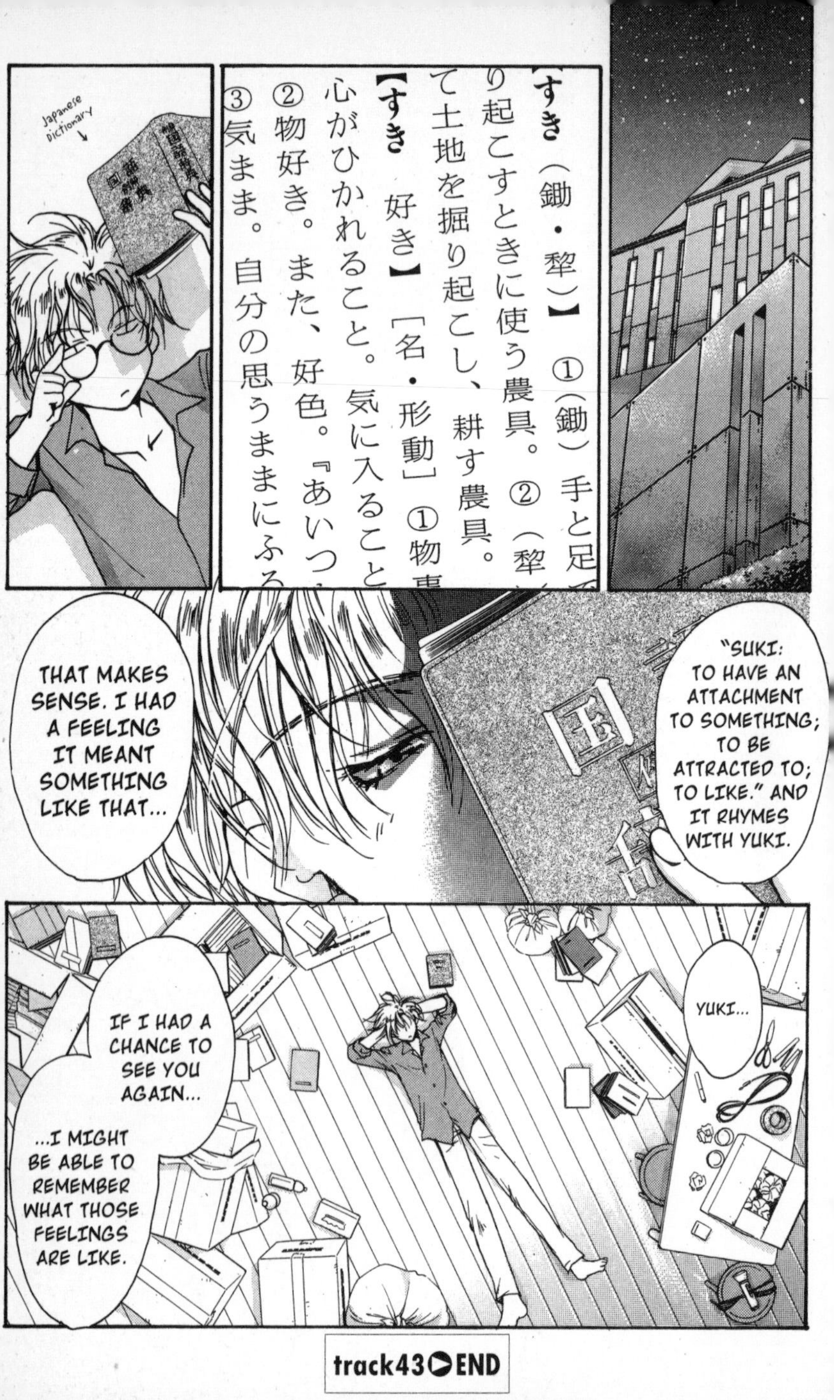
【すき（鋤・犂）】①（鋤）手と足
り起こすときに使う農具。②（犂
て土地を掘り起こし、耕す農具。
【すき　好き】［名・形動］①物
心がひかれること。気に入ること
②物好き。また、好色。『あいつ
③気まま。自分の思うままにふる
Japanese Dictionary
"SUKI: TO HAVE AN ATTACHMENT TO SOMETHING; TO BE ATTRACTED TO; TO LIKE." AND IT RHYMES WITH YUKI.
THAT MAKES SENSE. I HAD A FEELING IT MEANT SOMETHING LIKE THAT...
YUKI...
IF I HAD A CHANCE TO SEE YOU AGAIN...
...I MIGHT BE ABLE TO REMEMBER WHAT THOSE FEELINGS ARE LIKE.

track43 ▶ END

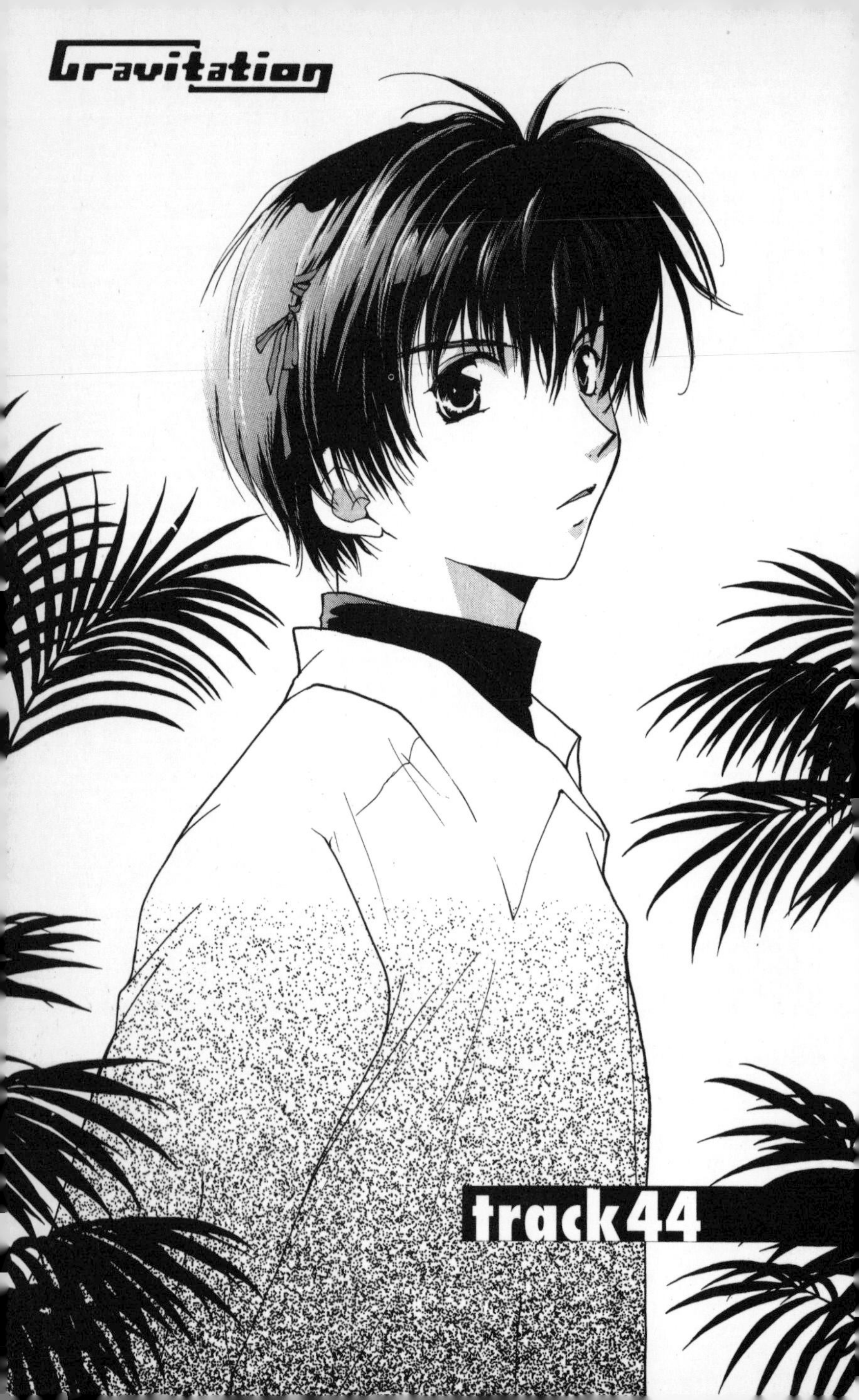
Gravitation
track 44

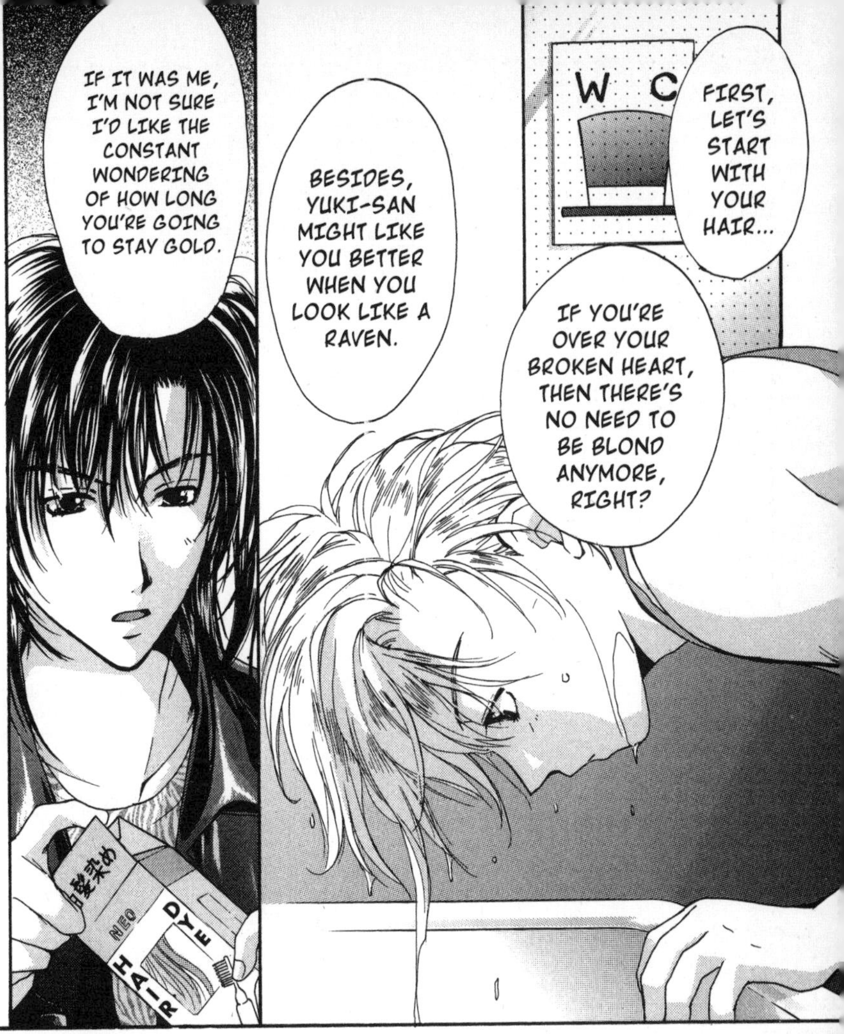
FIRST, LET'S START WITH YOUR HAIR...
IF YOU'RE OVER YOUR BROKEN HEART, THEN THERE'S NO NEED TO BE BLOND ANYMORE, RIGHT?
BESIDES, YUKI-SAN MIGHT LIKE YOU BETTER WHEN YOU LOOK LIKE A RAVEN.
IF IT WAS ME, I'M NOT SURE I'D LIKE THE CONSTANT WONDERING OF HOW LONG YOU'RE GOING TO STAY GOLD.
HAIR DYE

ABOUT GRAVITATION TRACK 44

TITS

When I first started drawing Yoshiki's tits, I thought I had made them pretty big, but now they're gone. Also, Eiri's coat totally changes into something different in Track 45...!! It was tough. Also, even though it's the same day, different scene, Rage's clothes have changed, too. It was really tough. And I haven't fixed anything.

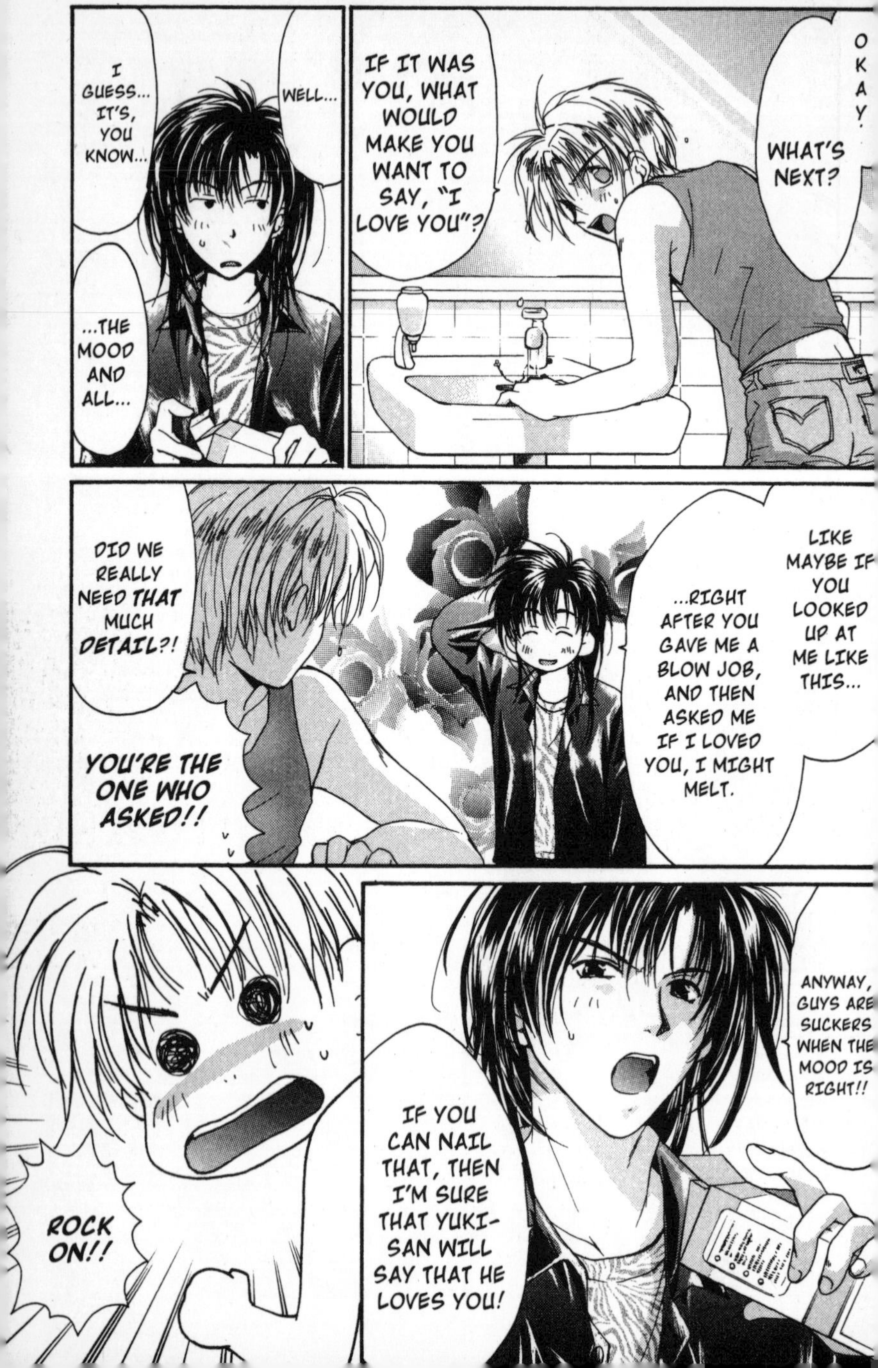
OKAY. WHAT'S NEXT?
IF IT WAS YOU, WHAT WOULD MAKE YOU WANT TO SAY, "I LOVE YOU"?
WELL...
I GUESS... IT'S, YOU KNOW...
...THE MOOD AND ALL...
LIKE MAYBE IF YOU LOOKED UP AT ME LIKE THIS...
...RIGHT AFTER YOU GAVE ME A BLOW JOB, AND THEN ASKED ME IF I LOVED YOU, I MIGHT MELT.
DID WE REALLY NEED THAT MUCH DETAIL?!
YOU'RE THE ONE WHO ASKED!!
ANYWAY, GUYS ARE SUCKERS WHEN THE MOOD IS RIGHT!!
IF YOU CAN NAIL THAT, THEN I'M SURE THAT YUKI-SAN WILL SAY THAT HE LOVES YOU!
ROCK ON!!

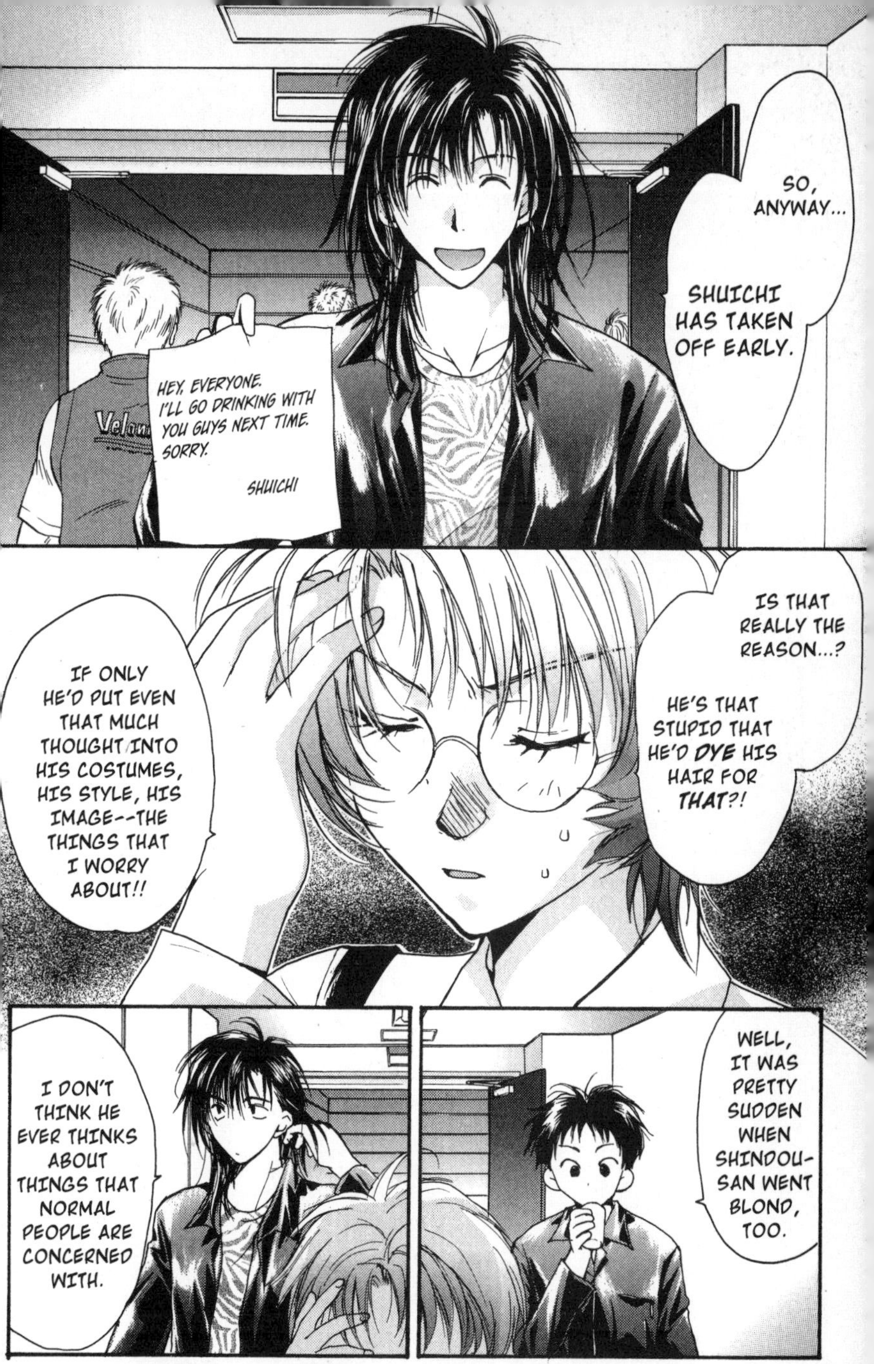
SO, ANYWAY...
SHUICHI HAS TAKEN OFF EARLY.
HEY, EVERYONE. I'LL GO DRINKING WITH YOU GUYS NEXT TIME. SORRY.
SHUICHI
IS THAT REALLY THE REASON...?
HE'S THAT STUPID THAT HE'D ***DYE*** HIS HAIR FOR ***THAT***?!
IF ONLY HE'D PUT EVEN THAT MUCH THOUGHT INTO HIS COSTUMES, HIS STYLE, HIS IMAGE--THE THINGS THAT I WORRY ABOUT!!
WELL, IT WAS PRETTY SUDDEN WHEN SHINDOU-SAN WENT BLOND, TOO.
I DON'T THINK HE EVER THINKS ABOUT THINGS THAT NORMAL PEOPLE ARE CONCERNED WITH.

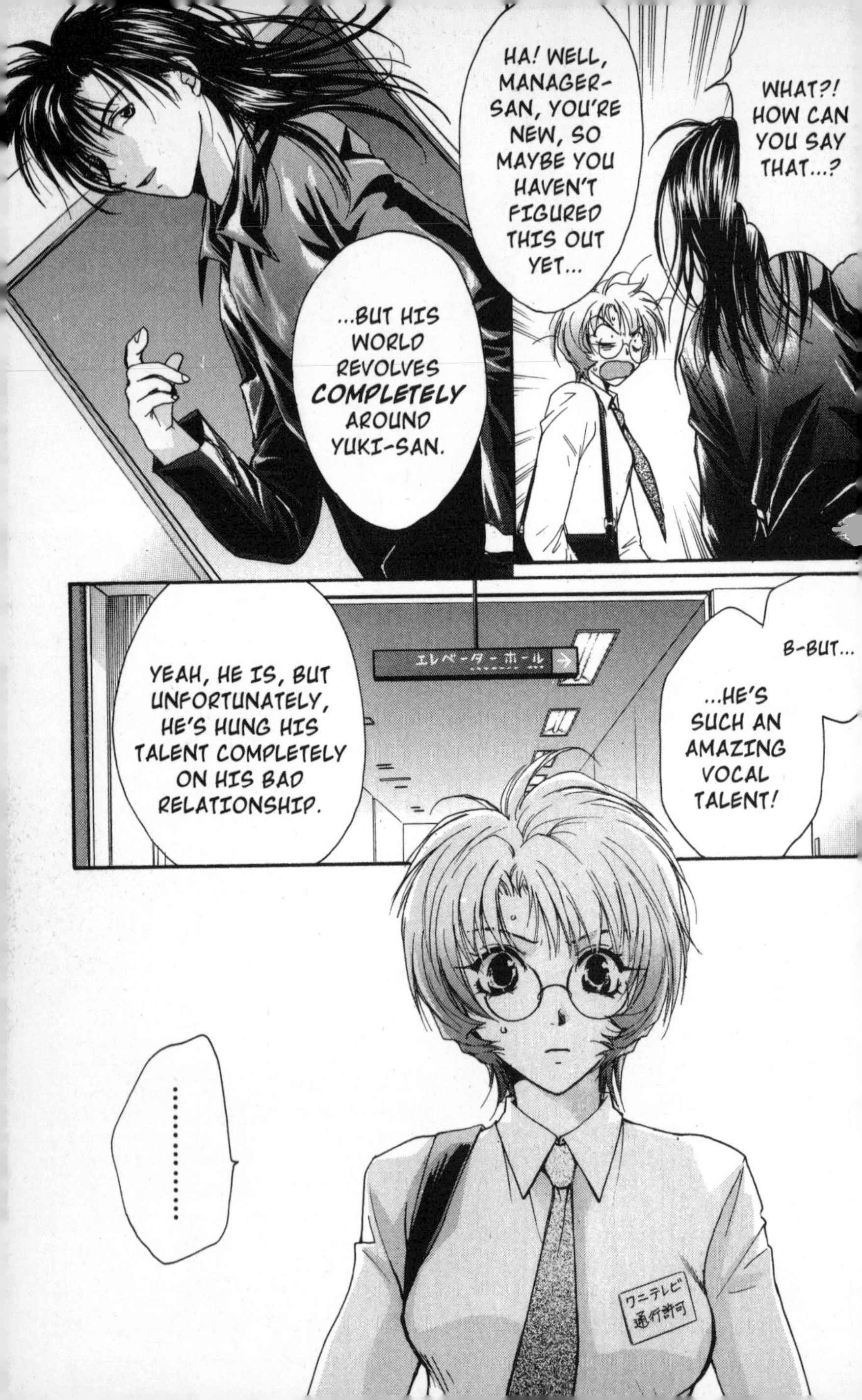
WHAT?! HOW CAN YOU SAY THAT...?
HA! WELL, MANAGER-SAN, YOU'RE NEW, SO MAYBE YOU HAVEN'T FIGURED THIS OUT YET...
...BUT HIS WORLD REVOLVES **COMPLETELY** AROUND YUKI-SAN.
B-BUT...
...HE'S SUCH AN AMAZING VOCAL TALENT!
エレベーターホール
YEAH, HE IS, BUT UNFORTUNATELY, HE'S HUNG HIS TALENT COMPLETELY ON HIS BAD RELATIONSHIP.
......
ワニテレビ 通行許可

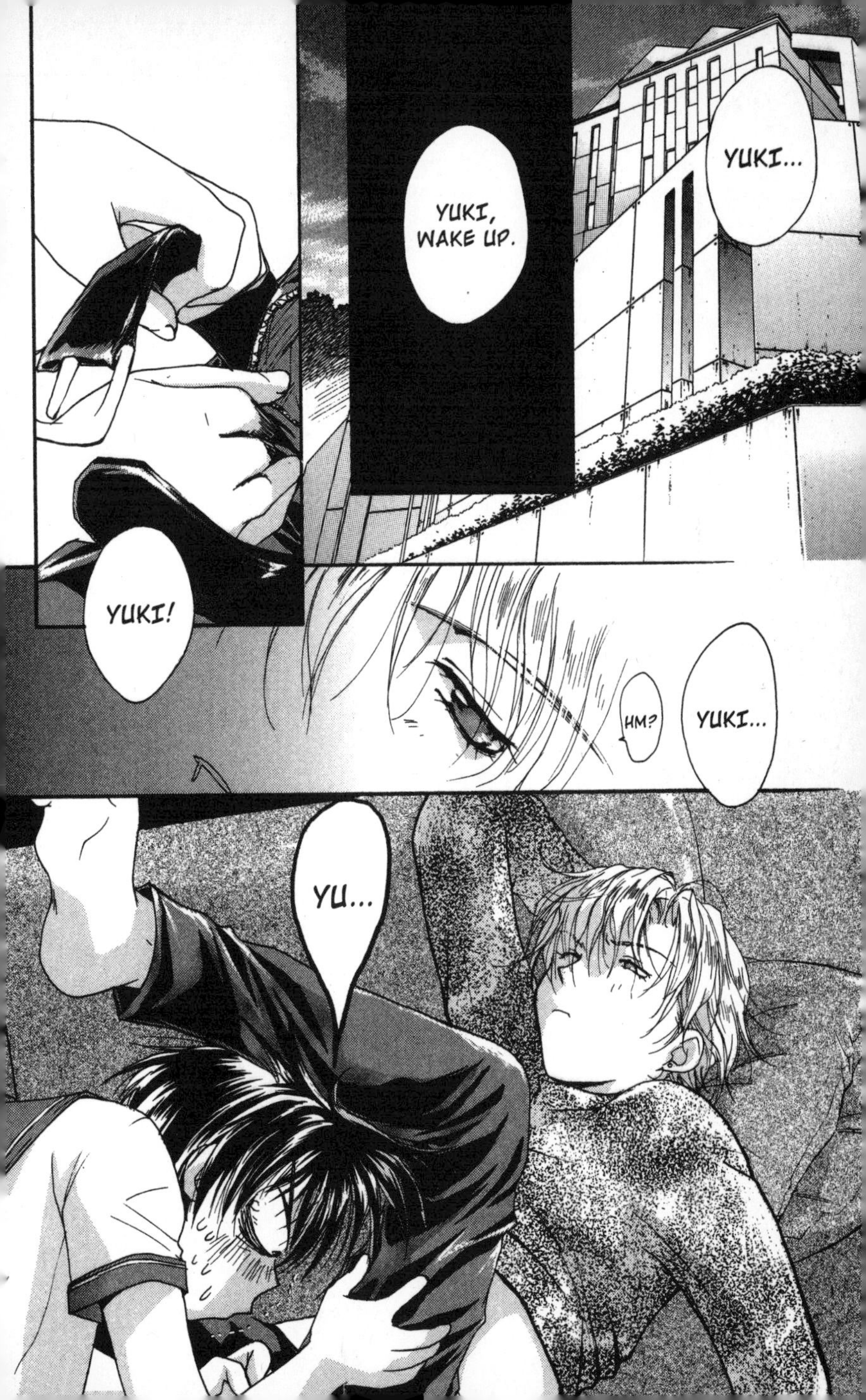
YUKI...
YUKI, WAKE UP.
YUKI!
YUKI...
HM?
YU...

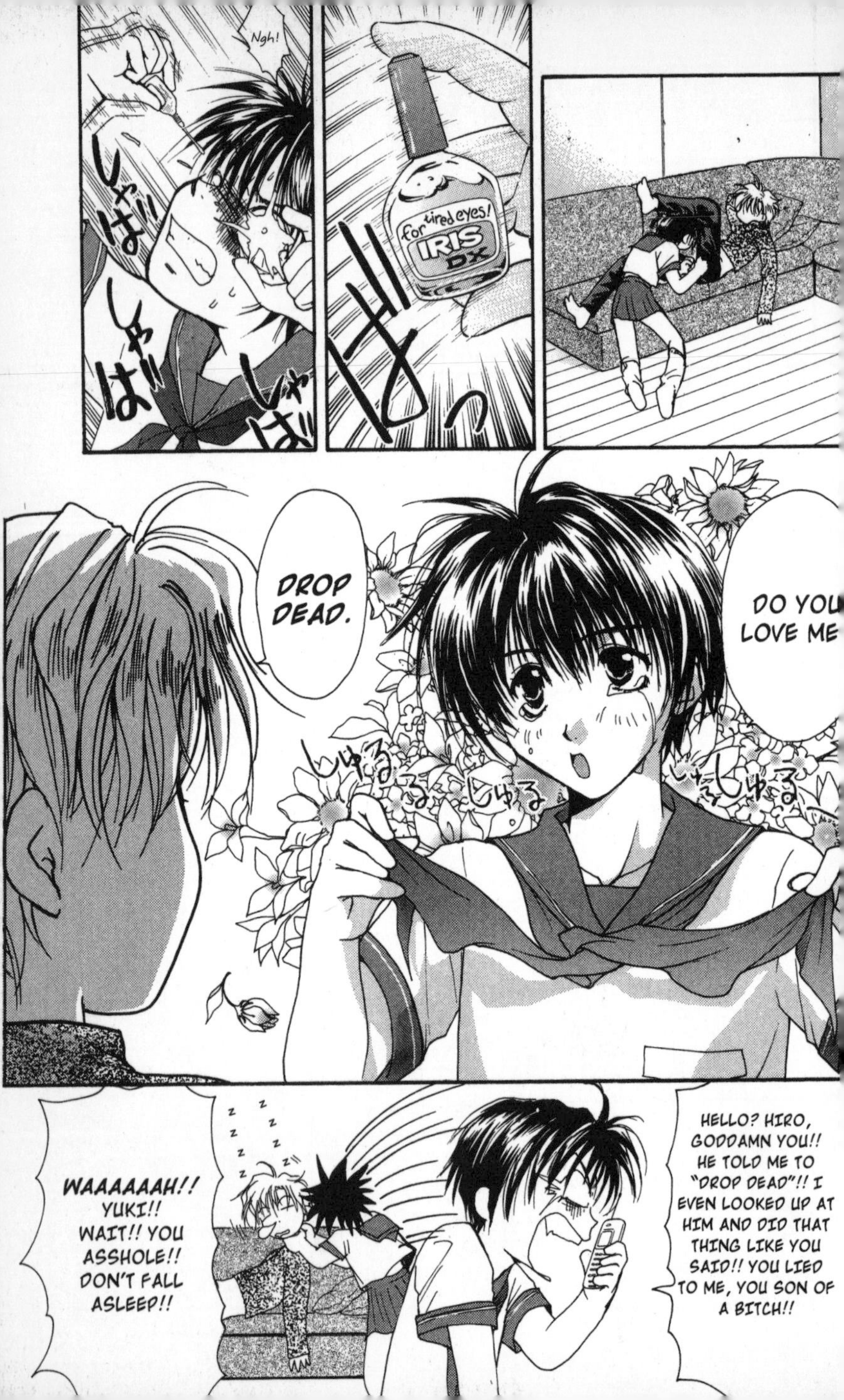
for tired eyes!
IRIS
DX
Ngh!
DO YOU LOVE ME
DROP DEAD.
HELLO? HIRO, GODDAMN YOU!! HE TOLD ME TO "DROP DEAD"!! I EVEN LOOKED UP AT HIM AND DID THAT THING LIKE YOU SAID!! YOU LIED TO ME, YOU SON OF A BITCH!!
Z Z Z Z Z Z Z Z
WAAAAAAH!! YUKI!! WAIT!! YOU ASSHOLE!! DON'T FALL ASLEEP!!

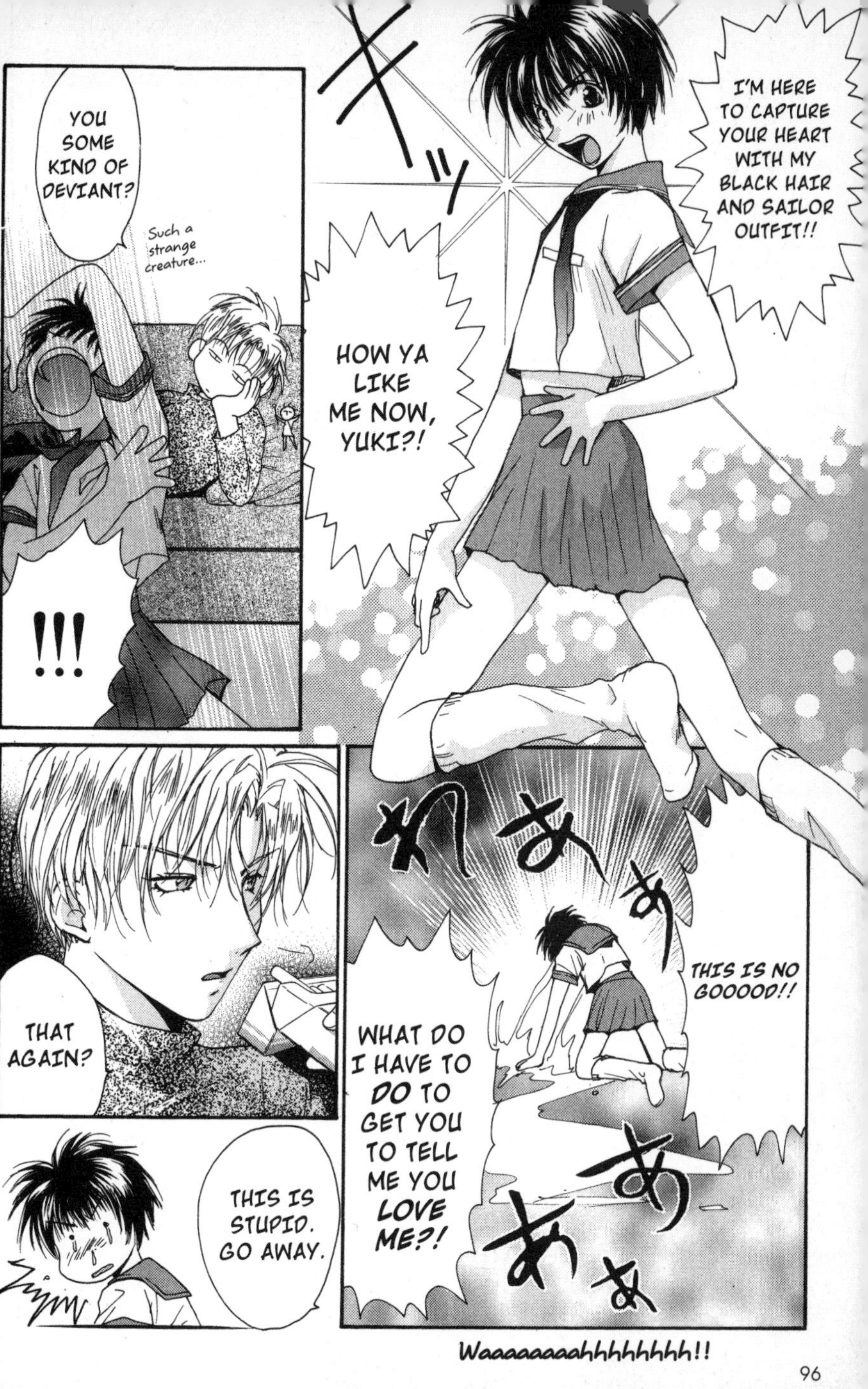
I'M HERE TO CAPTURE YOUR HEART WITH MY BLACK HAIR AND SAILOR OUTFIT!!
HOW YA LIKE ME NOW, YUKI?!
YOU SOME KIND OF DEVIANT?
Such a strange creature...
!!!
THIS IS NO GOOOOD!!
WHAT DO I HAVE TO DO TO GET YOU TO TELL ME YOU LOVE ME?!
Waaaaaaaahhhhhhhh!!
THAT AGAIN?
THIS IS STUPID. GO AWAY.

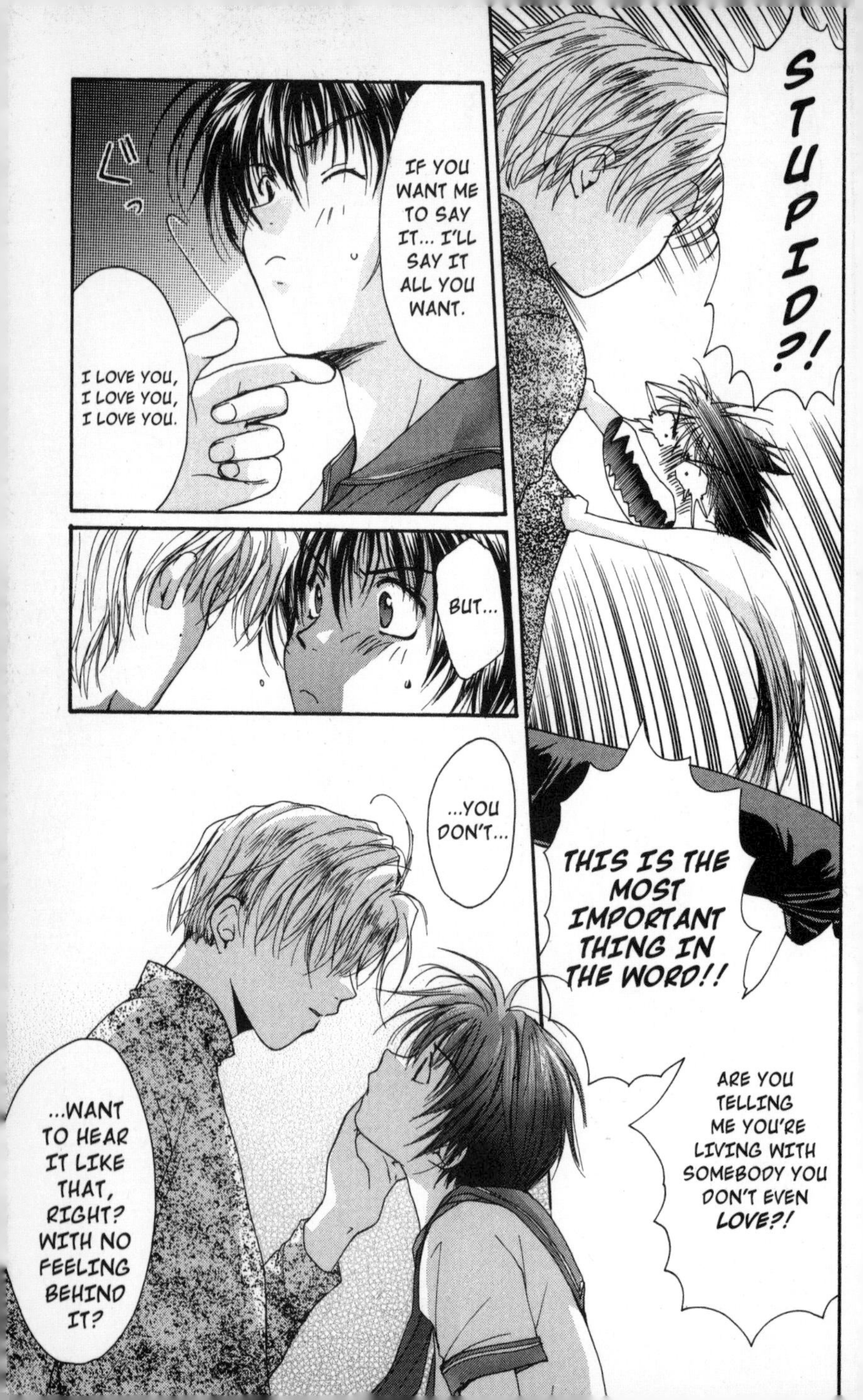

STUPID?!
THIS IS THE MOST IMPORTANT THING IN THE WORD!!
ARE YOU TELLING ME YOU'RE LIVING WITH SOMEBODY YOU DON'T EVEN *LOVE*?!
ぐっ
IF YOU WANT ME TO SAY IT... I'LL SAY IT ALL YOU WANT.
I LOVE YOU, I LOVE YOU, I LOVE YOU.
BUT...
...YOU DON'T...
...WANT TO HEAR IT LIKE THAT, RIGHT? WITH NO FEELING BEHIND IT?

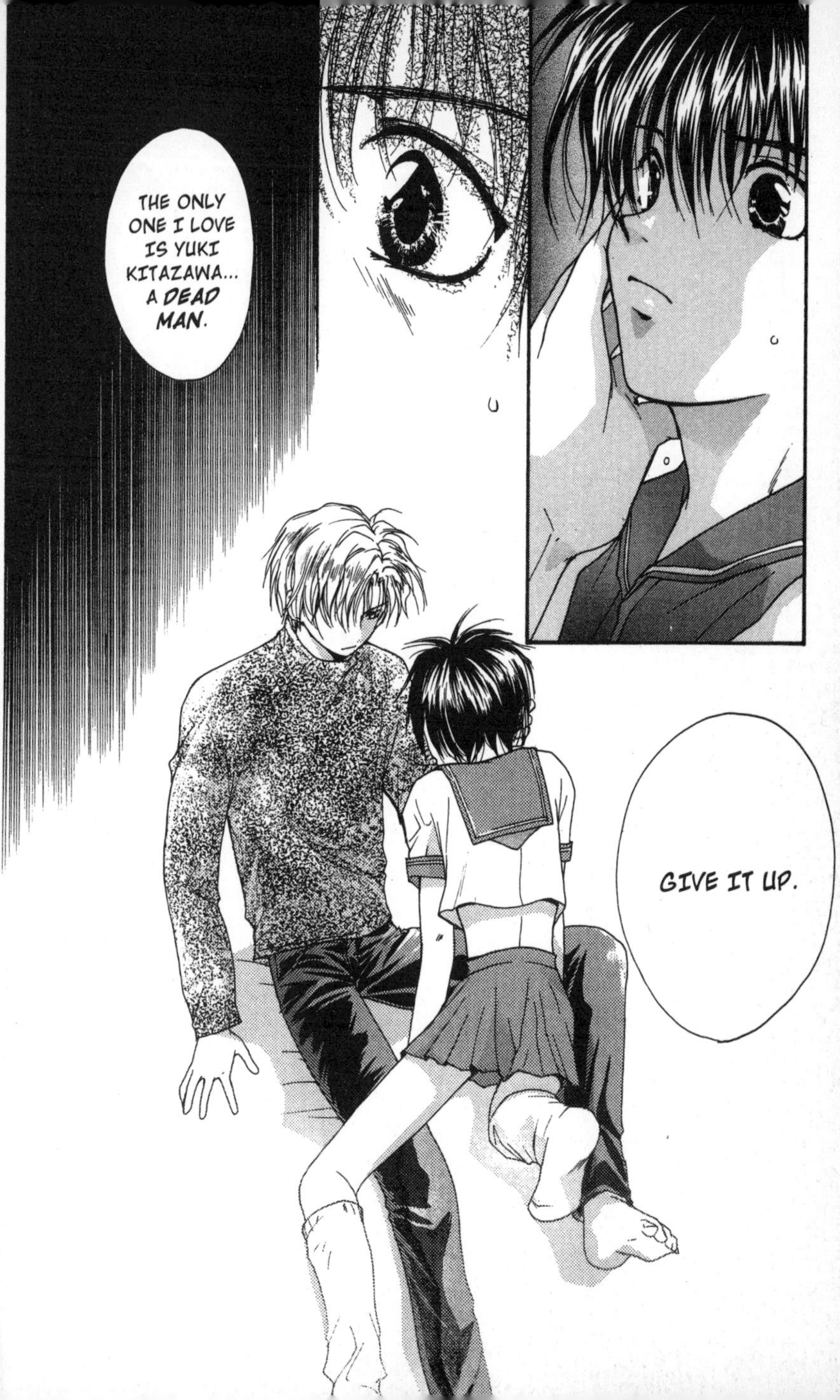
THE ONLY ONE I LOVE IS YUKI KITAZAWA... A DEAD MAN.
GIVE IT UP.

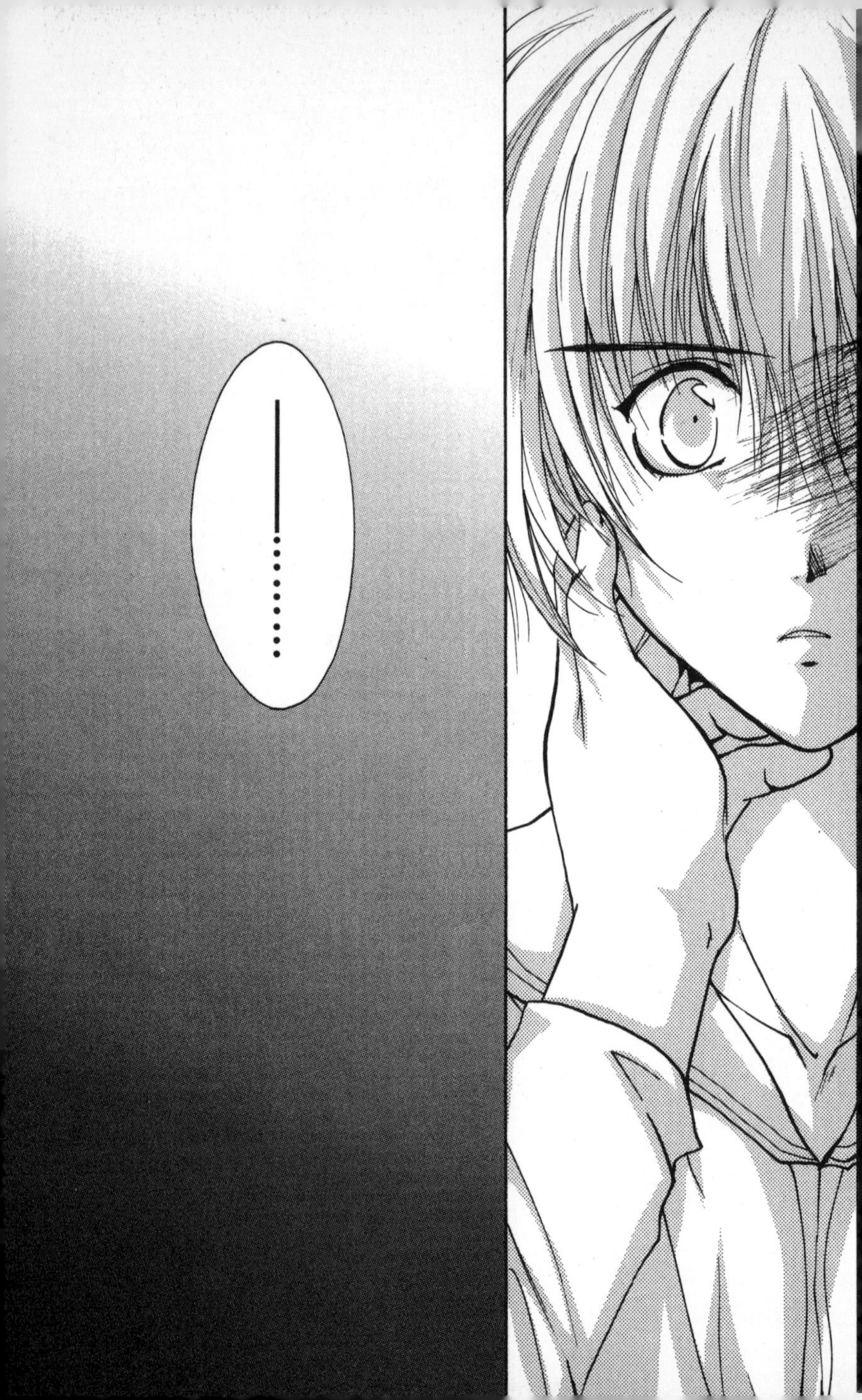
—……

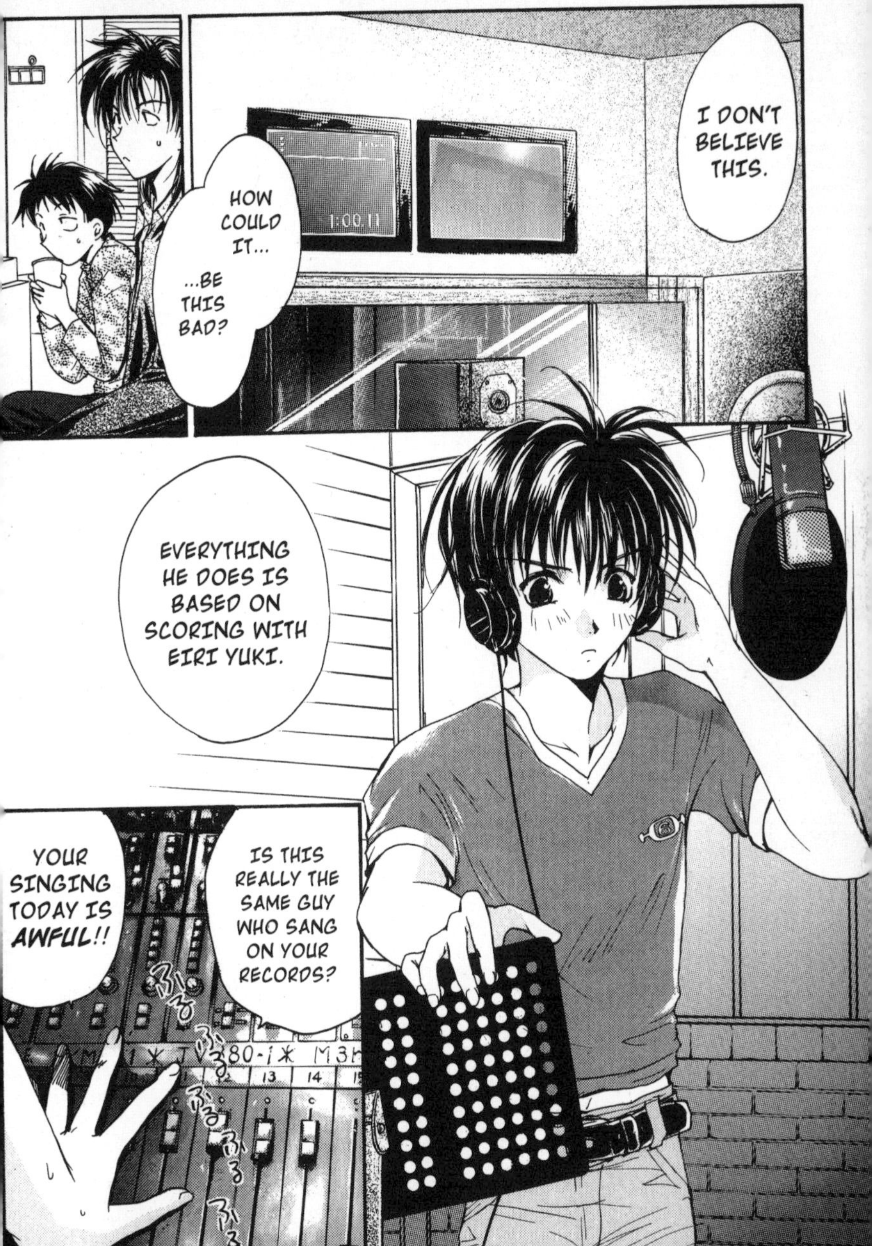
I DON'T BELIEVE THIS.
HOW COULD IT...
...BE THIS BAD?
EVERYTHING HE DOES IS BASED ON SCORING WITH EIRI YUKI.
IS THIS REALLY THE SAME GUY WHO SANG ON YOUR RECORDS?
YOUR SINGING TODAY IS **AWFUL**!!

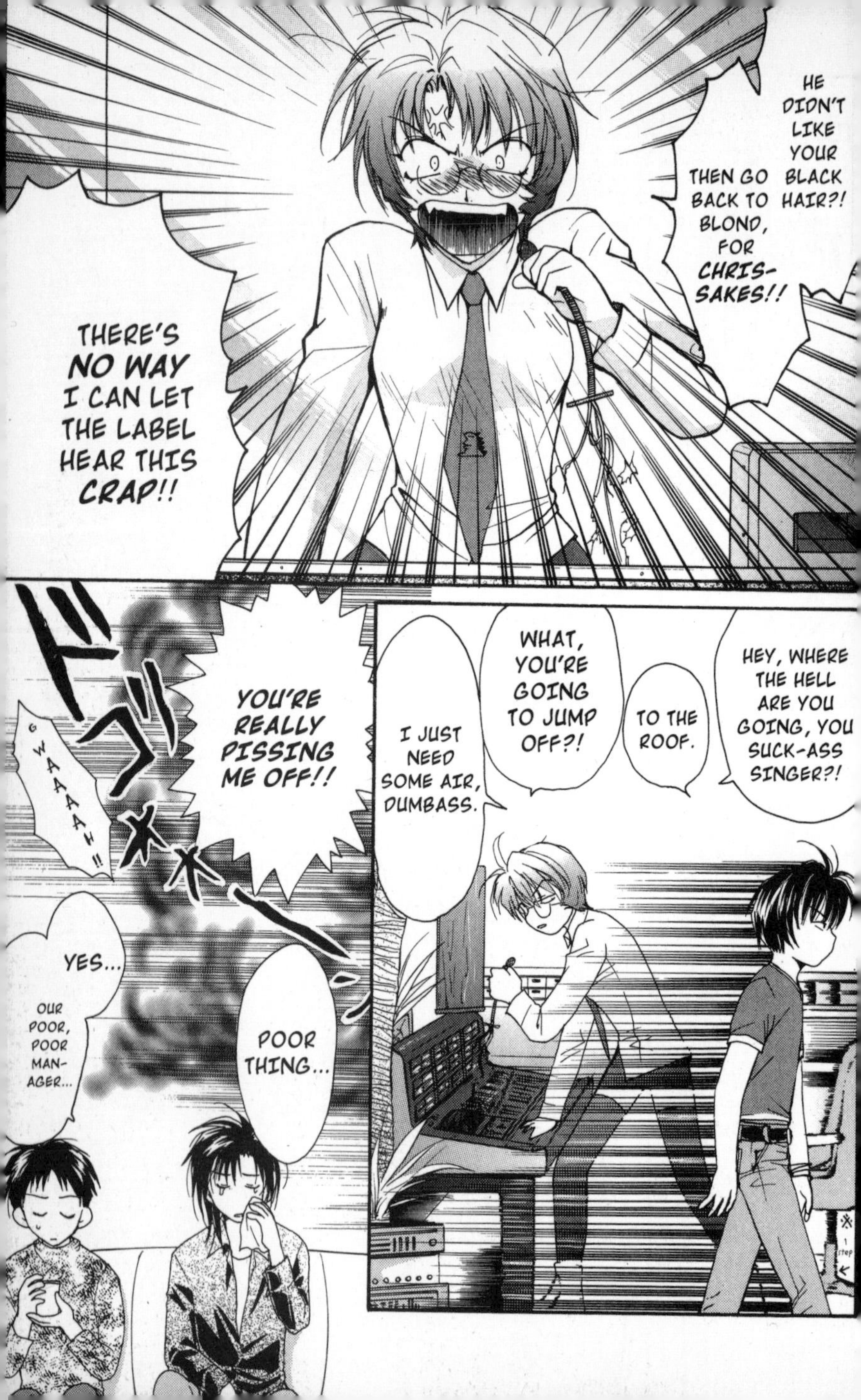
HE DIDN'T LIKE YOUR BLACK HAIR?!
THEN GO BACK TO BLOND, FOR CHRISSAKES!!
THERE'S NO WAY I CAN LET THE LABEL HEAR THIS CRAP!!
HEY, WHERE THE HELL ARE YOU GOING, YOU SUCK-ASS SINGER?!
TO THE ROOF.
WHAT, YOU'RE GOING TO JUMP OFF?!
I JUST NEED SOME AIR, DUMBASS.
1 step
YOU'RE REALLY PISSING ME OFF!!
GWAAAAAH!!
POOR THING...
YES...
OUR POOR, POOR MANAGER...

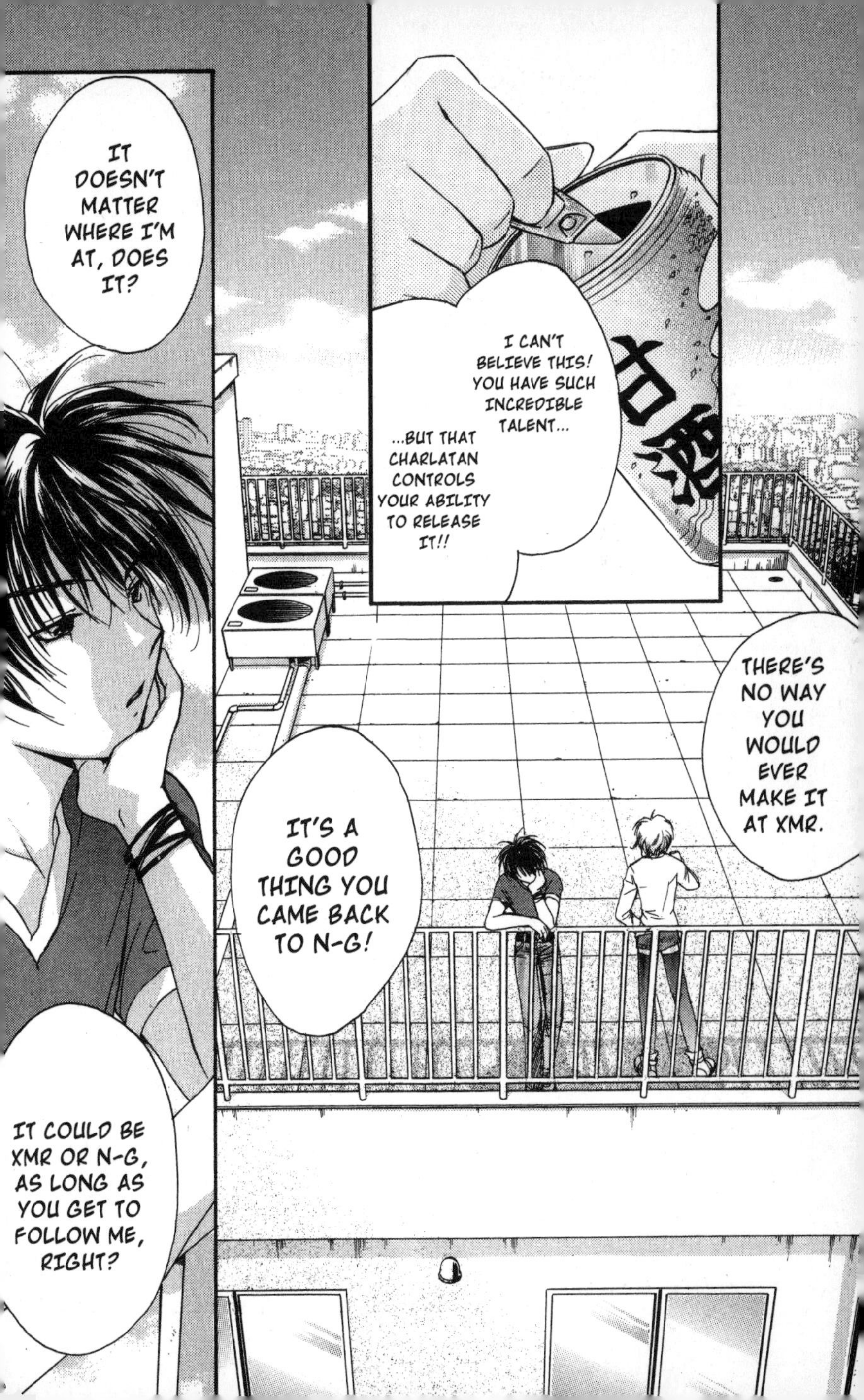
I CAN'T BELIEVE THIS! YOU HAVE SUCH INCREDIBLE TALENT...
...BUT THAT CHARLATAN CONTROLS YOUR ABILITY TO RELEASE IT!!
THERE'S NO WAY YOU WOULD EVER MAKE IT AT XMR.
IT'S A GOOD THING YOU CAME BACK TO N-G!
IT DOESN'T MATTER WHERE I'M AT, DOES IT?
IT COULD BE XMR OR N-G, AS LONG AS YOU GET TO FOLLOW ME, RIGHT?

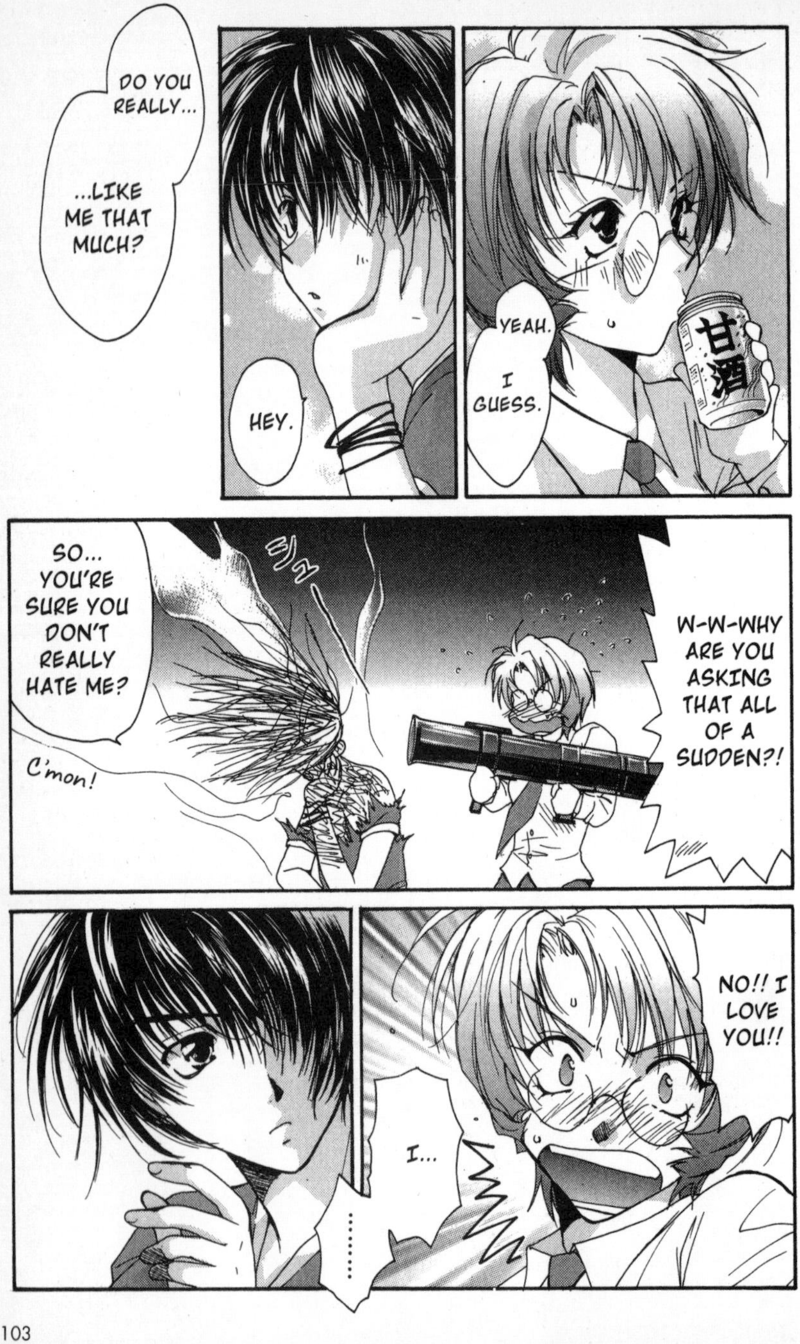
YEAH.
I GUESS.
甘酒
HEY.
DO YOU REALLY...
...LIKE ME THAT MUCH?
W-W-WHY ARE YOU ASKING THAT ALL OF A SUDDEN?!
シュー
SO... YOU'RE SURE YOU DON'T REALLY HATE ME?
C'mon!
NO!! I LOVE YOU!!
I...
......

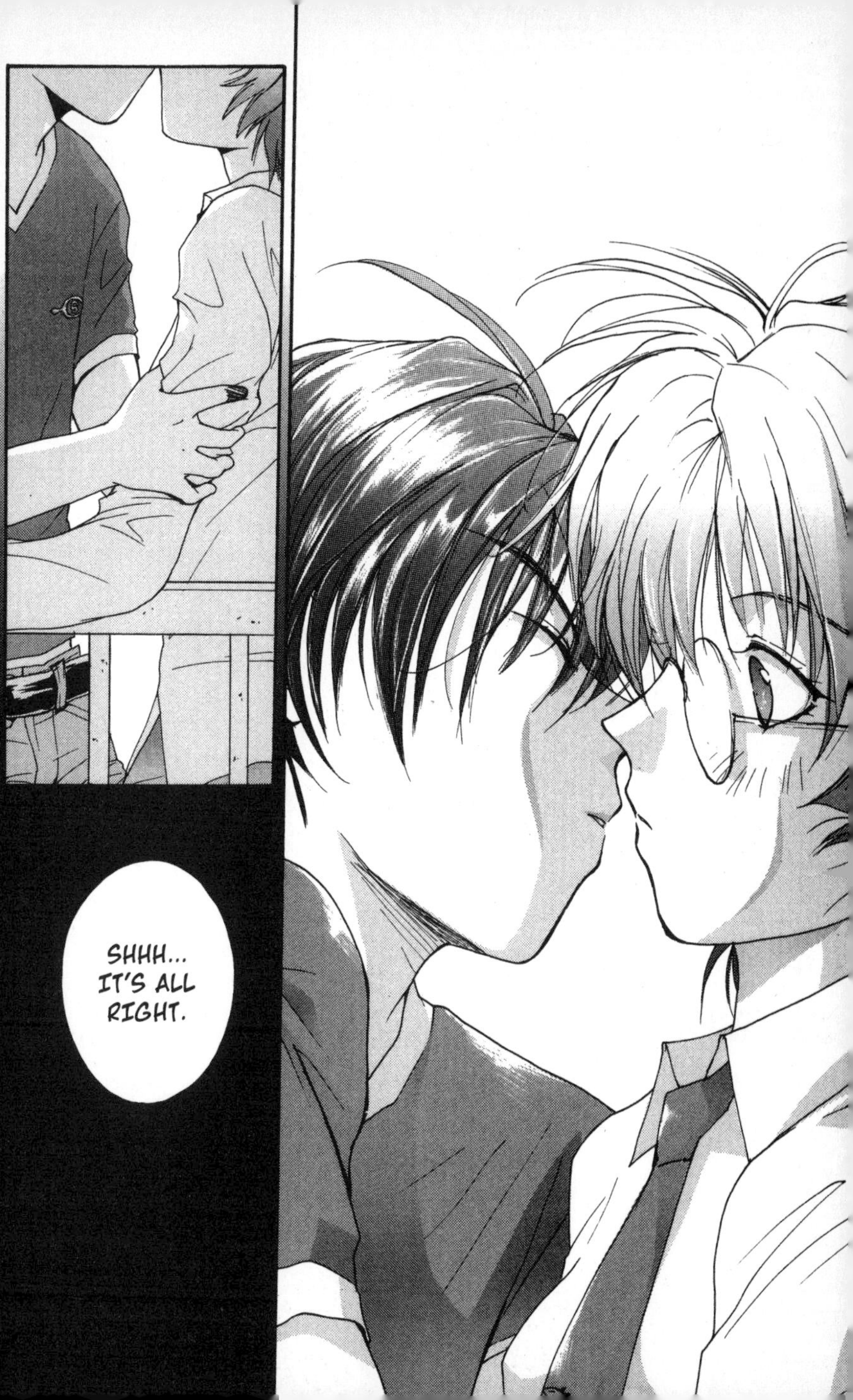
SHHH... IT'S ALL RIGHT.

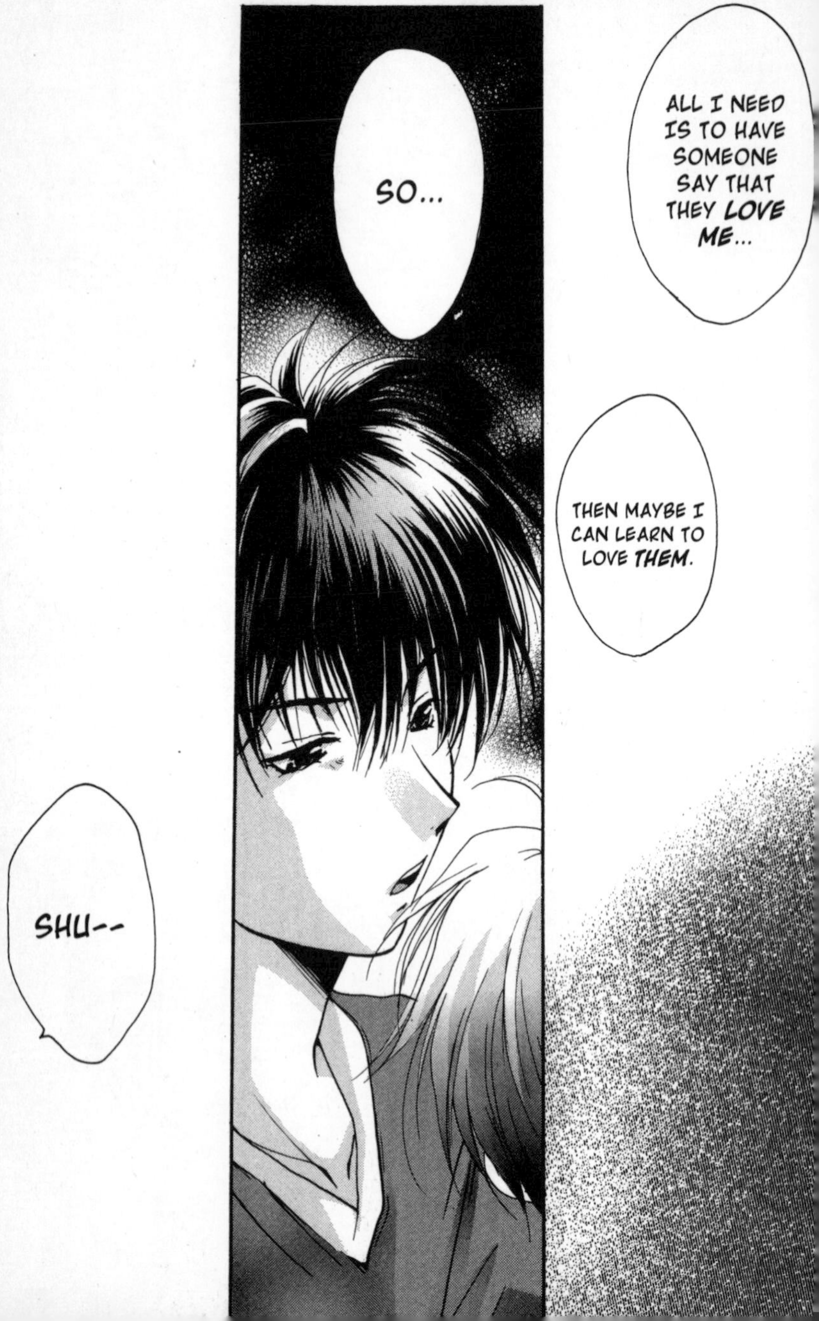
ALL I NEED IS TO HAVE SOMEONE SAY THAT THEY LOVE ME...
THEN MAYBE I CAN LEARN TO LOVE THEM.
SO...
SHU--

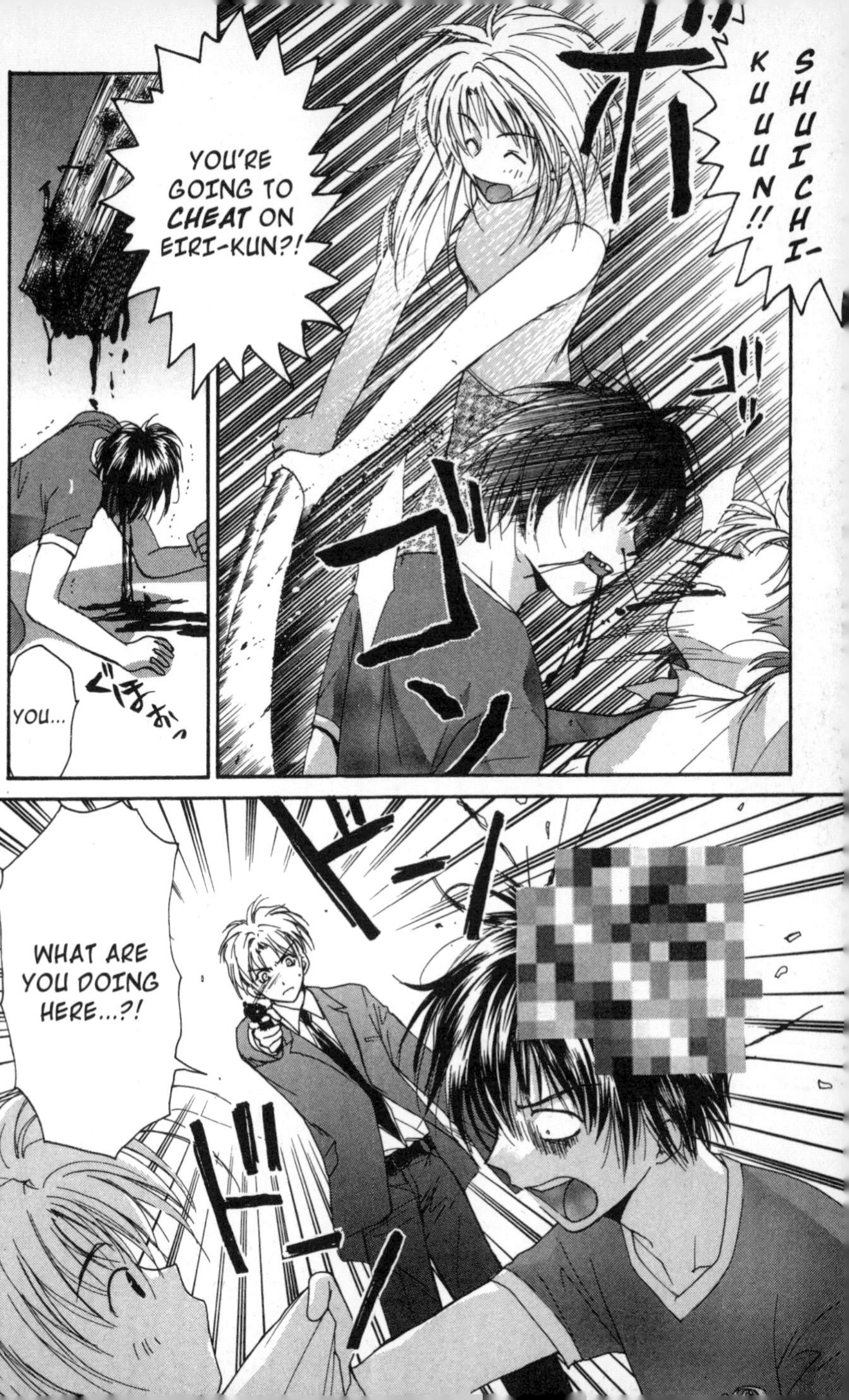
SHUICHI-
KUUUUN!!
YOU'RE GOING TO CHEAT ON EIRI-KUN?!
YOU...
WHAT ARE YOU DOING HERE...?!

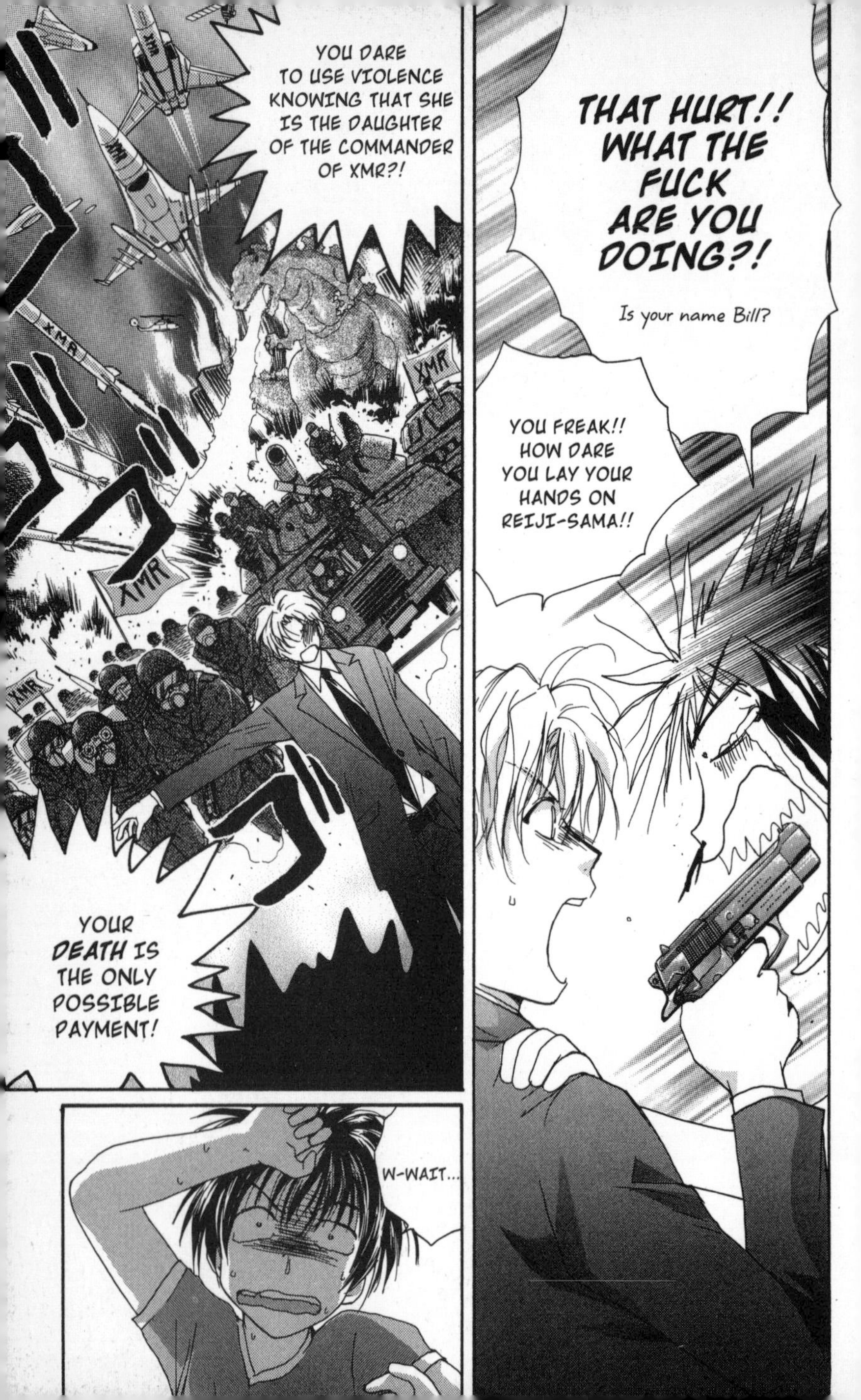
THAT HURT!! WHAT THE FUCK ARE YOU DOING?!
Is your name Bill?
YOU FREAK!! HOW DARE YOU LAY YOUR HANDS ON REIJI-SAMA!!
YOU DARE TO USE VIOLENCE KNOWING THAT SHE IS THE DAUGHTER OF THE COMMANDER OF XMR?!
YOUR DEATH IS THE ONLY POSSIBLE PAYMENT!
W-WAIT...

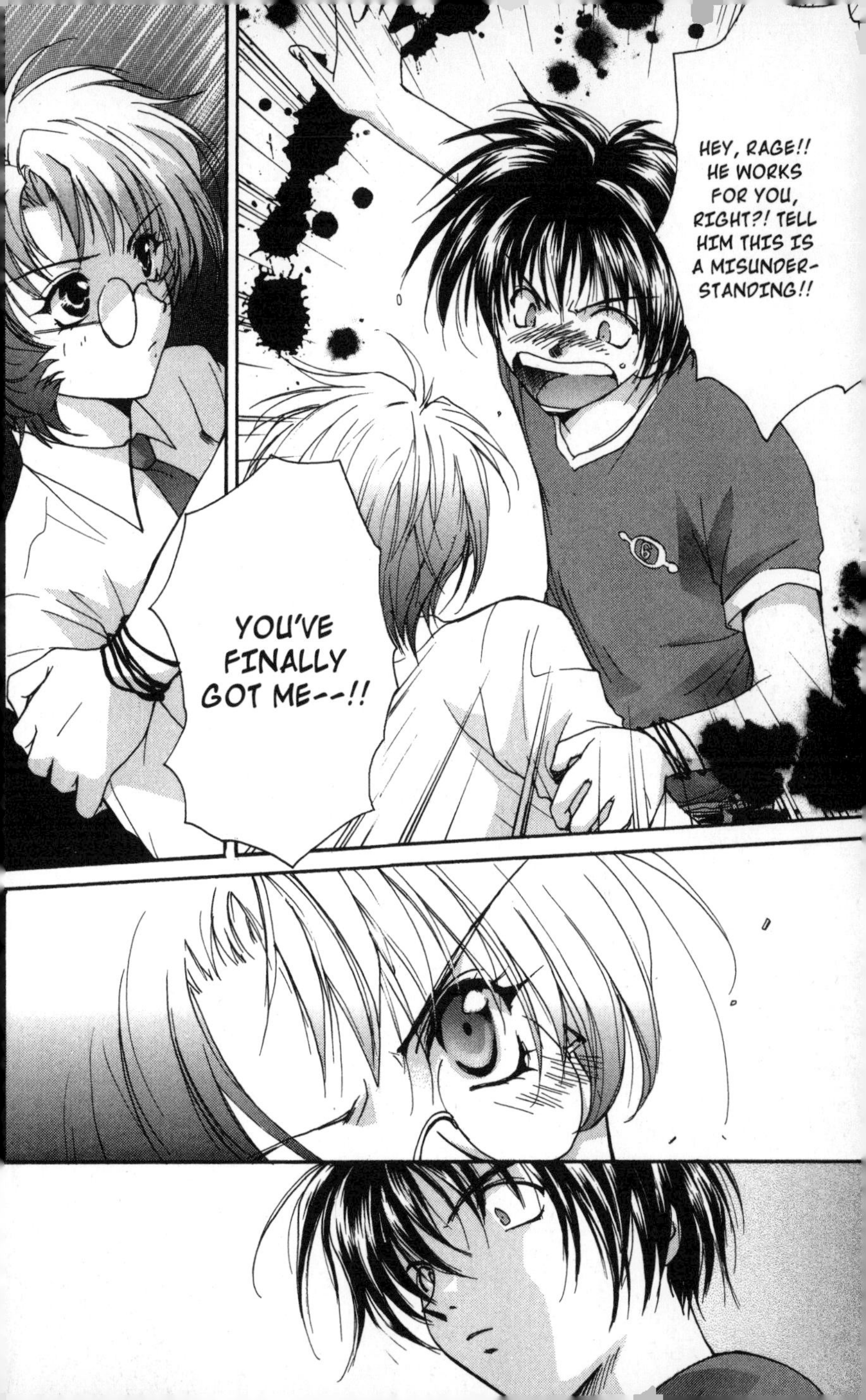
HEY, RAGE!! HE WORKS FOR YOU, RIGHT?! TELL HIM THIS IS A MISUNDER-STANDING!!
YOU'VE FINALLY GOT ME--!!

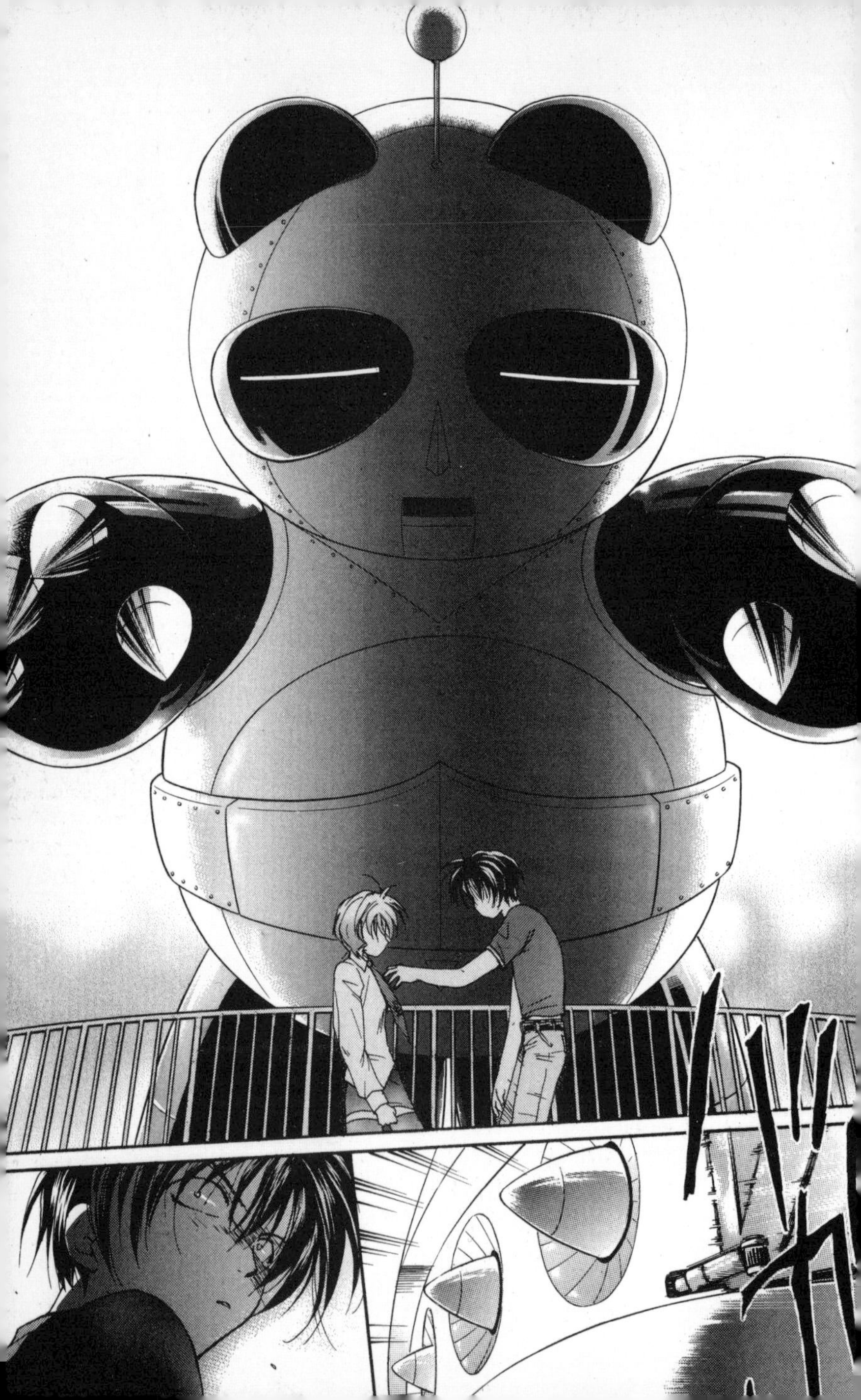

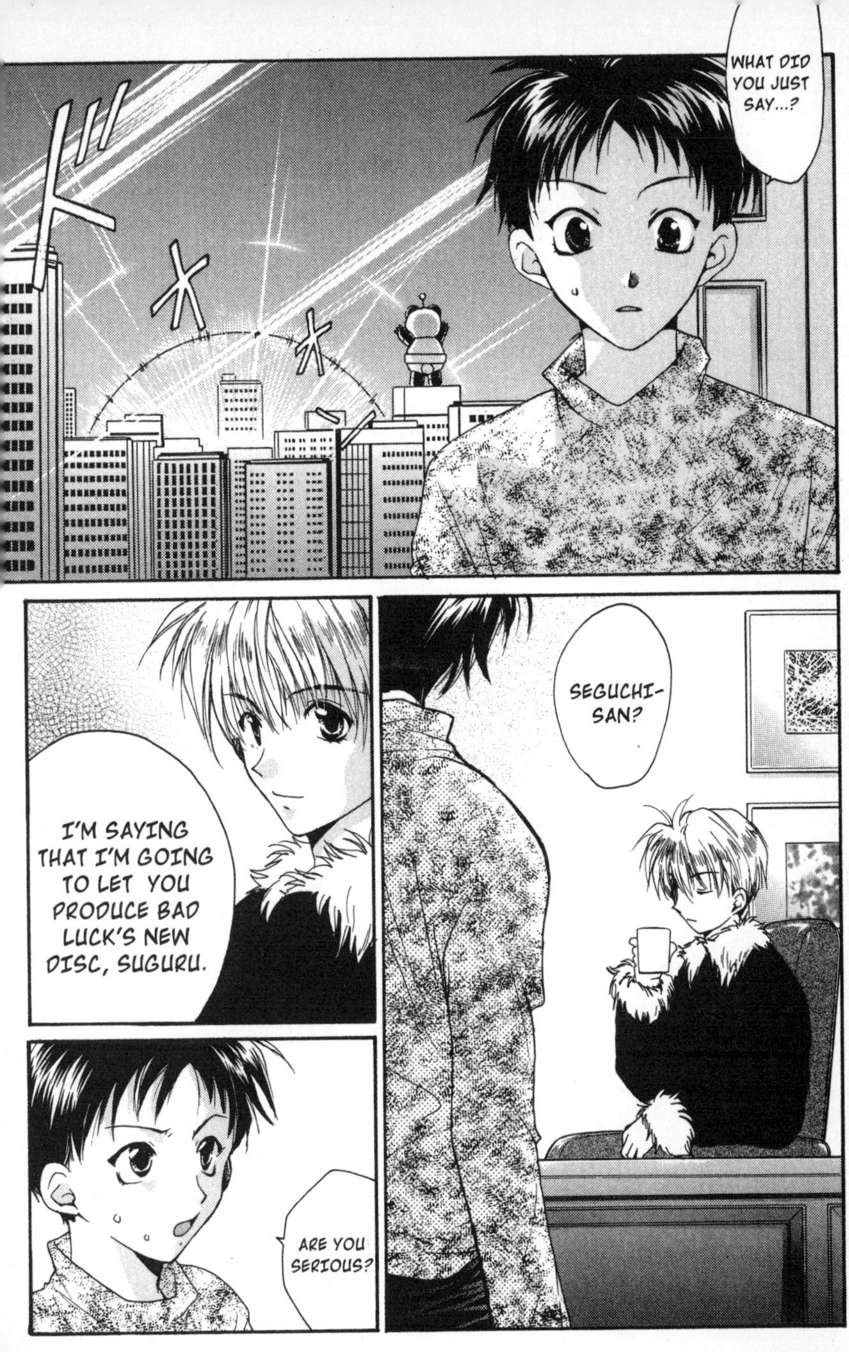
WHAT DID YOU JUST SAY...?
SEGUCHI-SAN?
I'M SAYING THAT I'M GOING TO LET YOU PRODUCE BAD LUCK'S NEW DISC, SUGURU.
ARE YOU SERIOUS?

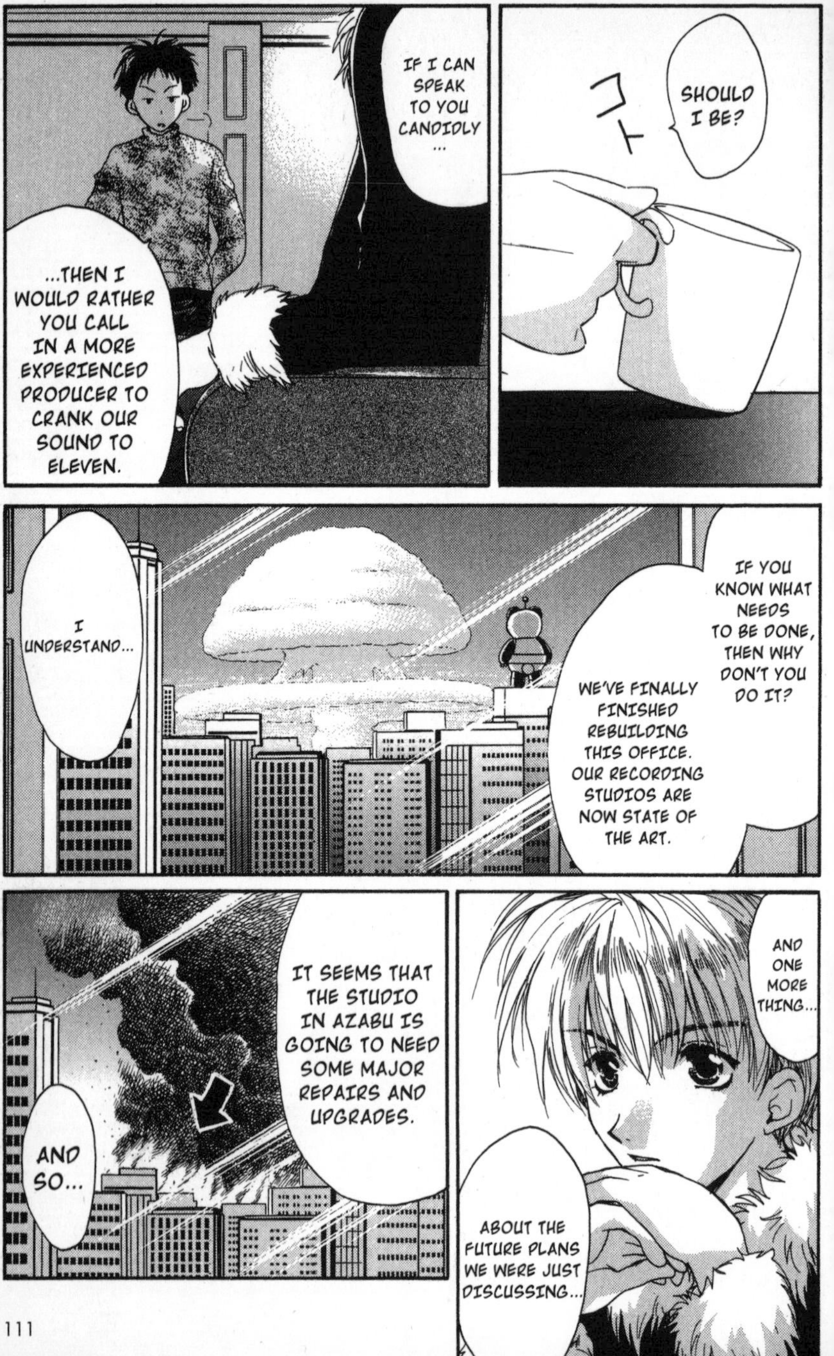
コト
SHOULD I BE?
IF I CAN SPEAK TO YOU CANDIDLY ...
...THEN I WOULD RATHER YOU CALL IN A MORE EXPERIENCED PRODUCER TO CRANK OUR SOUND TO ELEVEN.
IF YOU KNOW WHAT NEEDS TO BE DONE, THEN WHY DON'T YOU DO IT?
WE'VE FINALLY FINISHED REBUILDING THIS OFFICE. OUR RECORDING STUDIOS ARE NOW STATE OF THE ART.
I UNDERSTAND...
AND ONE MORE THING...
ABOUT THE FUTURE PLANS WE WERE JUST DISCUSSING...
IT SEEMS THAT THE STUDIO IN AZABU IS GOING TO NEED SOME MAJOR REPAIRS AND UPGRADES.
AND SO...

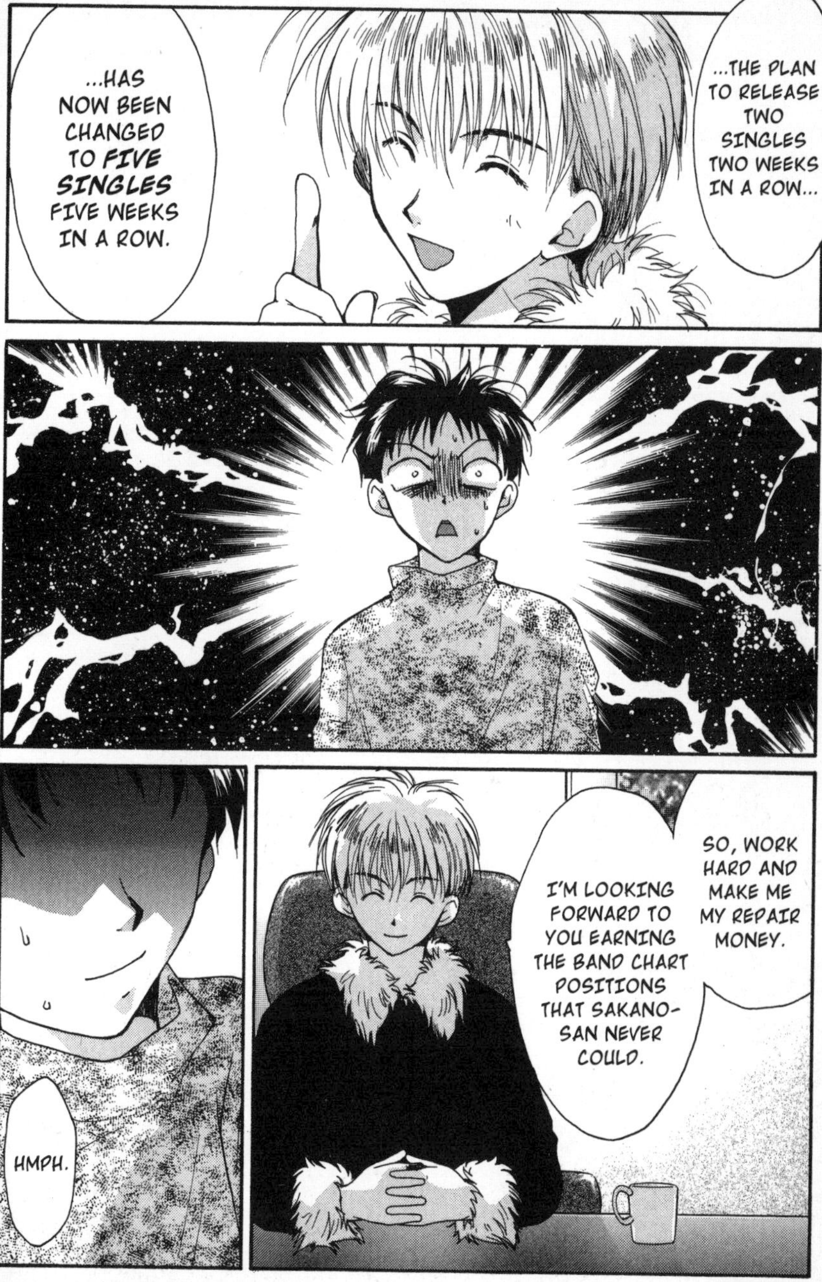
...THE PLAN TO RELEASE TWO SINGLES TWO WEEKS IN A ROW...
...HAS NOW BEEN CHANGED TO FIVE SINGLES FIVE WEEKS IN A ROW.
SO, WORK HARD AND MAKE ME MY REPAIR MONEY.
I'M LOOKING FORWARD TO YOU EARNING THE BAND CHART POSITIONS THAT SAKANO-SAN NEVER COULD.
HMPH.

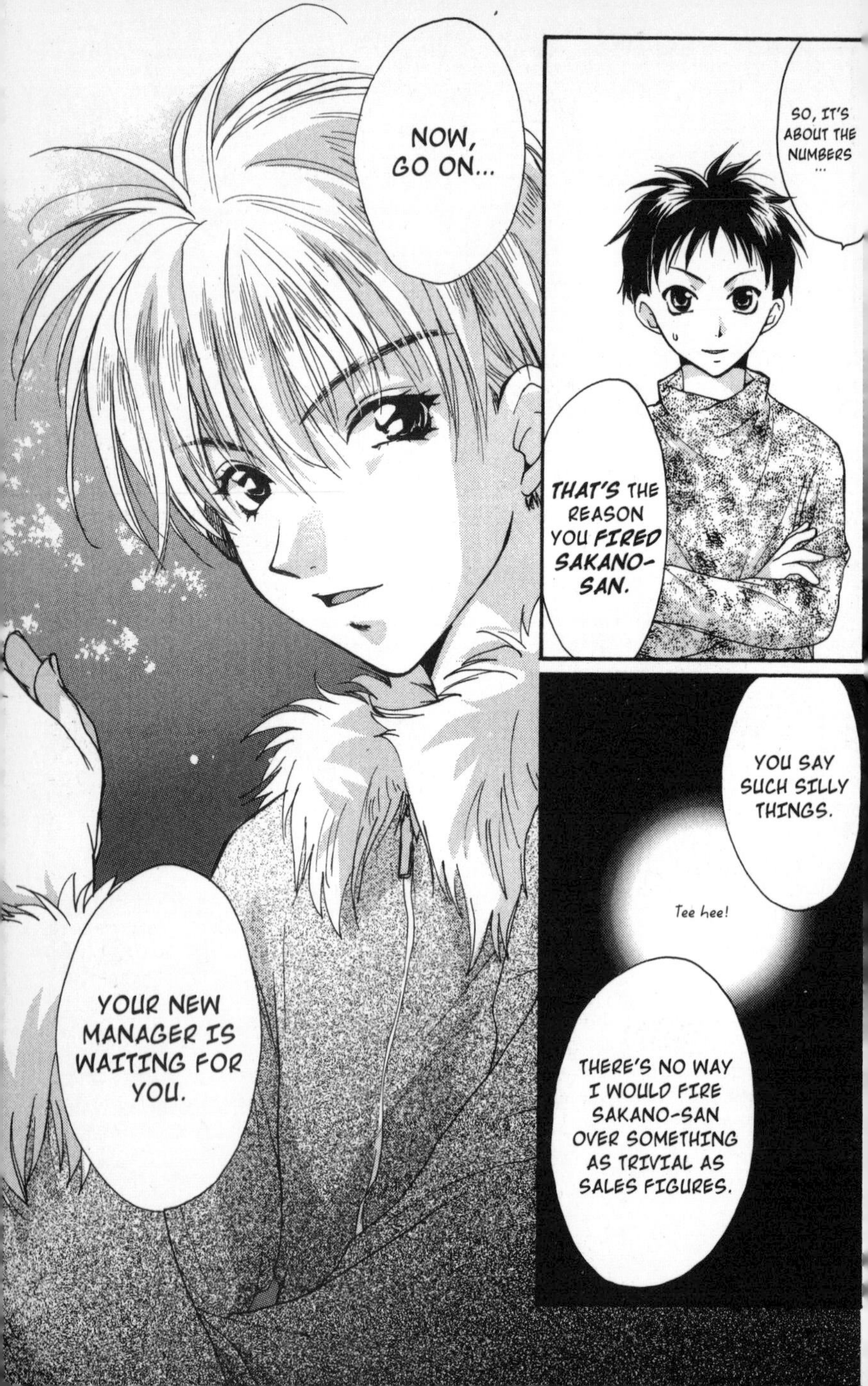

SO, IT'S ABOUT THE NUMBERS ...
THAT'S THE REASON YOU FIRED SAKANO-SAN.
YOU SAY SUCH SILLY THINGS.
Tee hee!
THERE'S NO WAY I WOULD FIRE SAKANO-SAN OVER SOMETHING AS TRIVIAL AS SALES FIGURES.
NOW, GO ON...
YOUR NEW MANAGER IS WAITING FOR YOU.

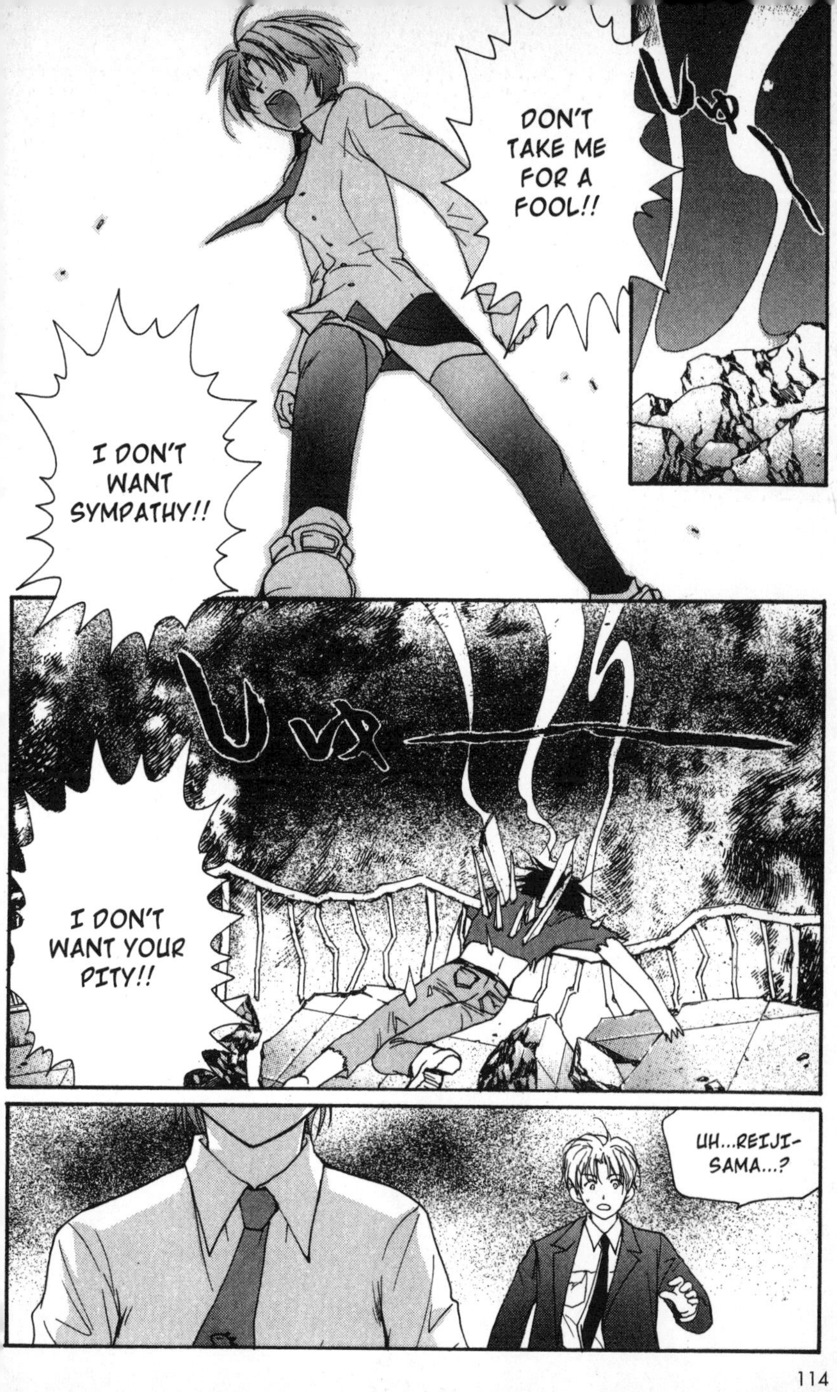
DON'T TAKE ME FOR A FOOL!!
I DON'T WANT SYMPATHY!!
I DON'T WANT YOUR PITY!!
UH...REIJI-SAMA...?

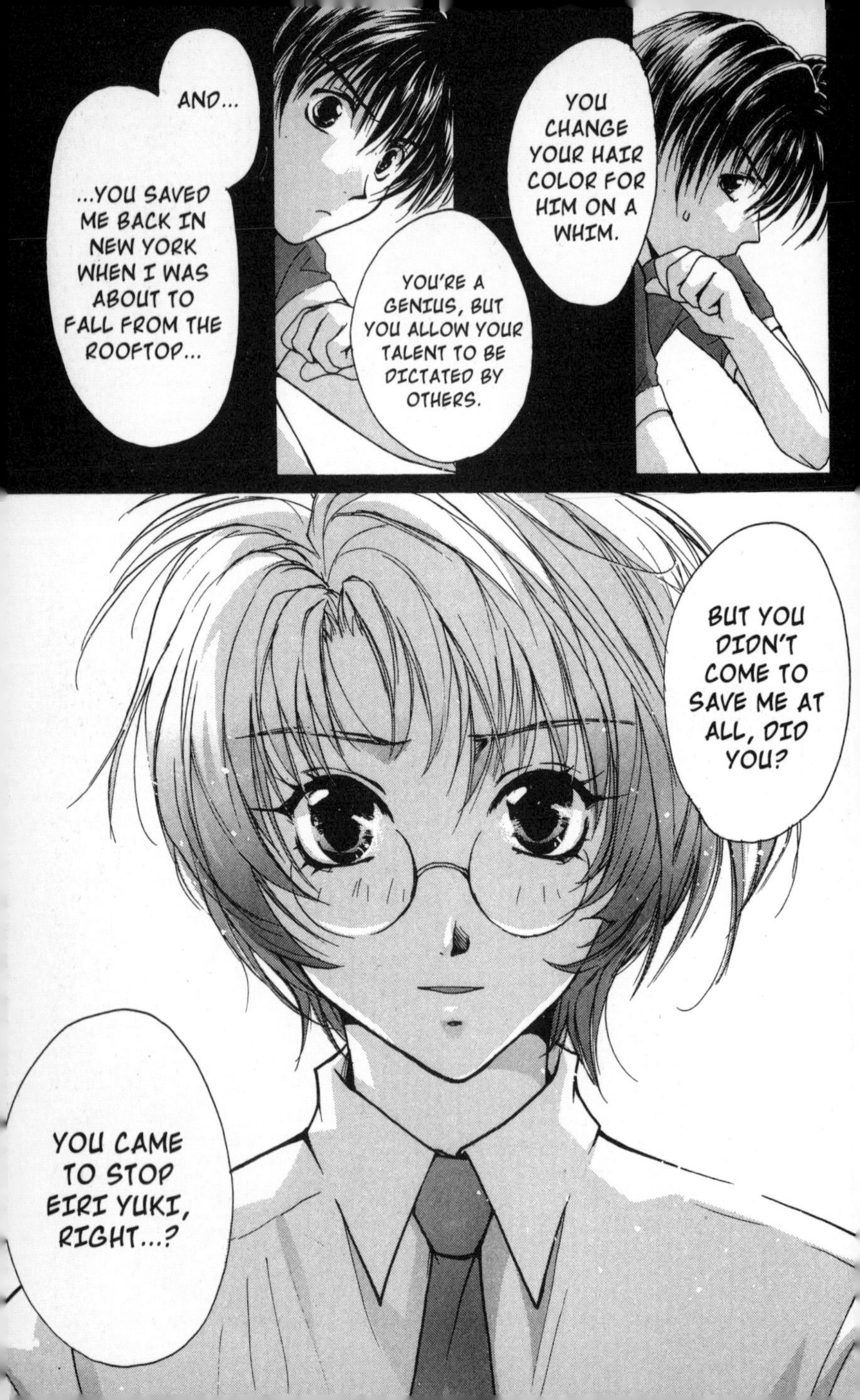
YOU CHANGE YOUR HAIR COLOR FOR HIM ON A WHIM.
YOU'RE A GENIUS, BUT YOU ALLOW YOUR TALENT TO BE DICTATED BY OTHERS.
AND...
...YOU SAVED ME BACK IN NEW YORK WHEN I WAS ABOUT TO FALL FROM THE ROOFTOP...
BUT YOU DIDN'T COME TO SAVE ME AT ALL, DID YOU?
YOU CAME TO STOP EIRI YUKI, RIGHT...?

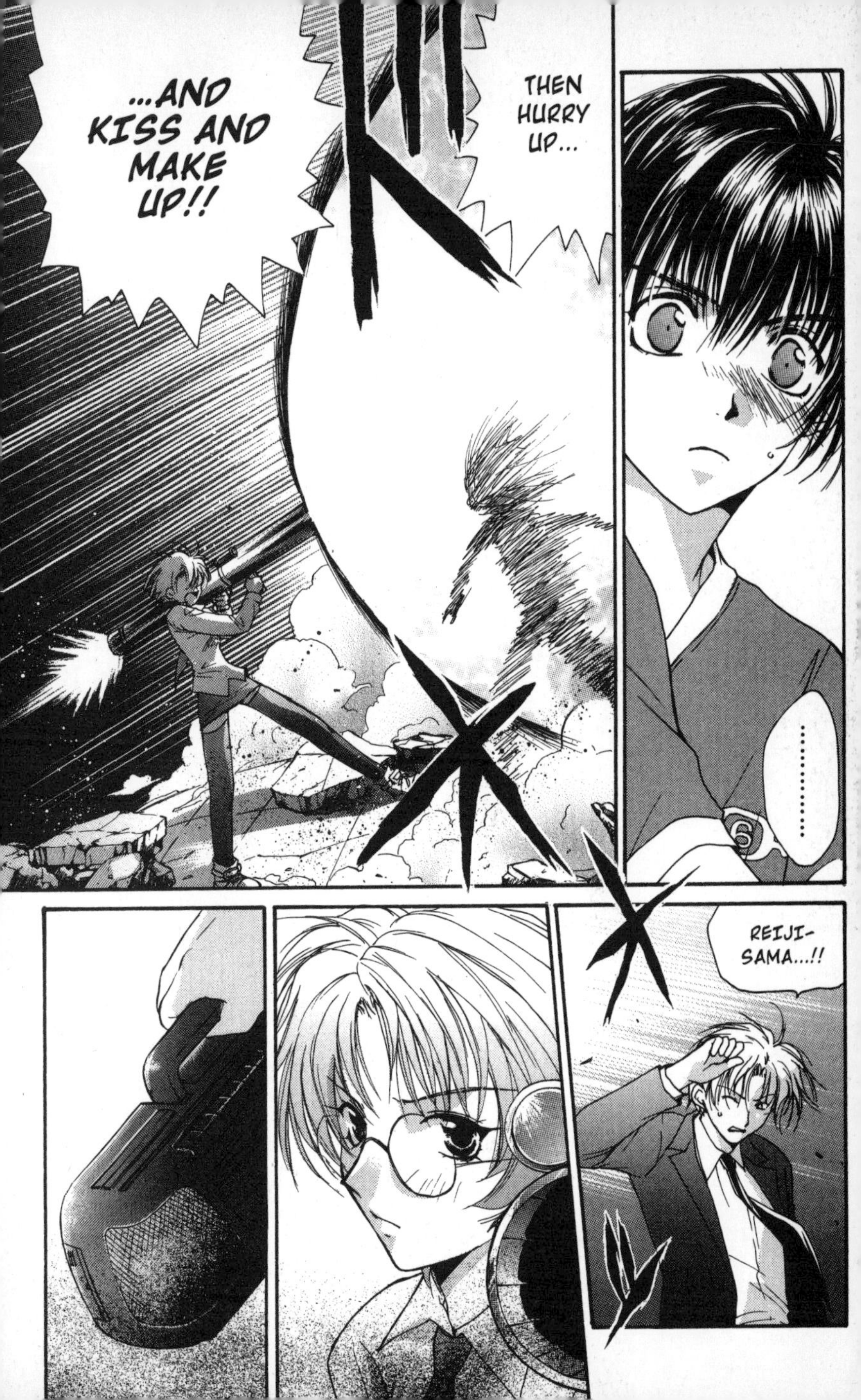

.....
THEN HURRY UP...
...AND KISS AND MAKE UP!!
REIJI-SAMA...!!

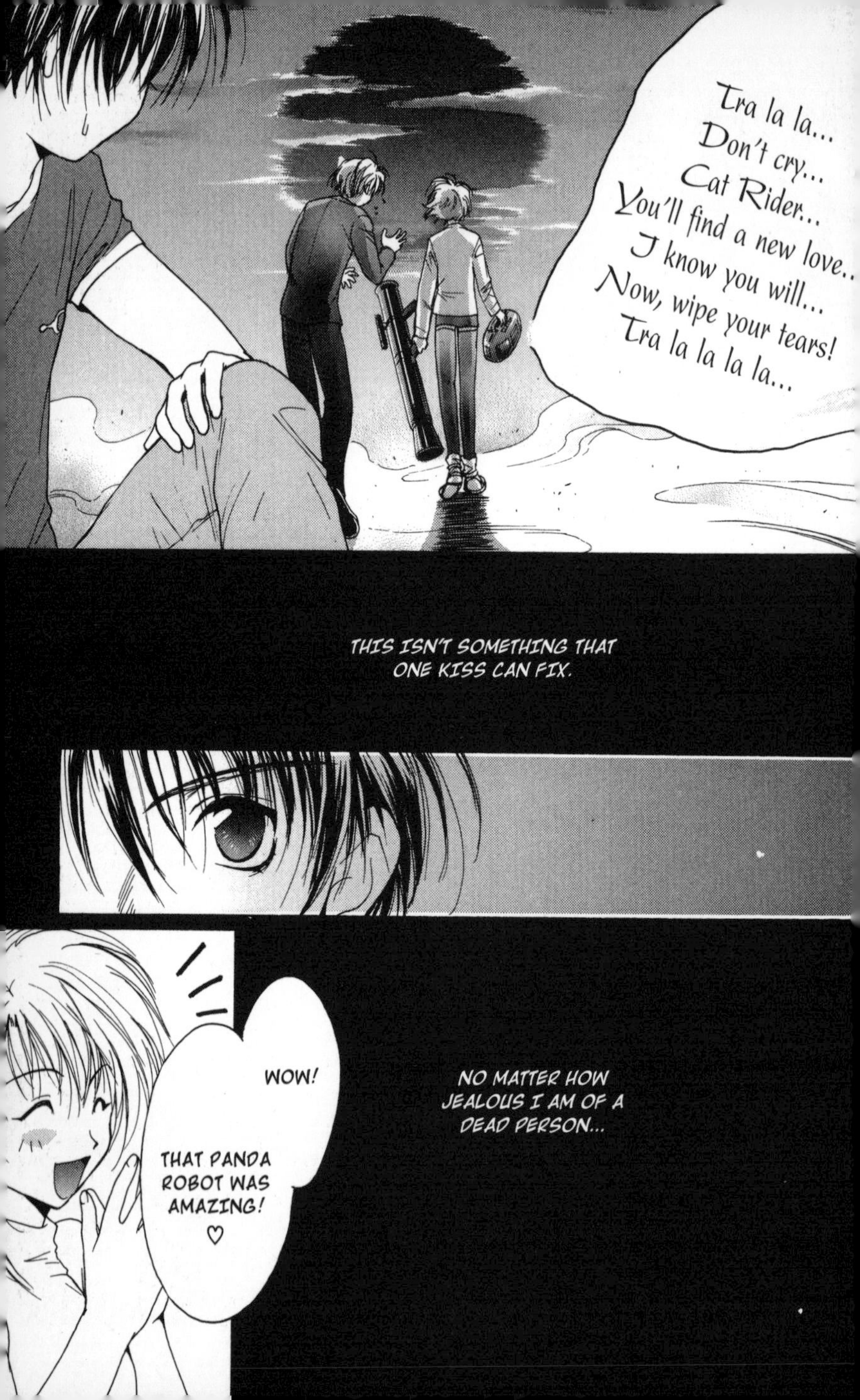
Tra la la... Don't cry... Cat Rider... You'll find a new love... I know you will... Now, wipe your tears! Tra la la la la...
THIS ISN'T SOMETHING THAT ONE KISS CAN FIX.
NO MATTER HOW JEALOUS I AM OF A DEAD PERSON...
WOW!
THAT PANDA ROBOT WAS AMAZING! ♡

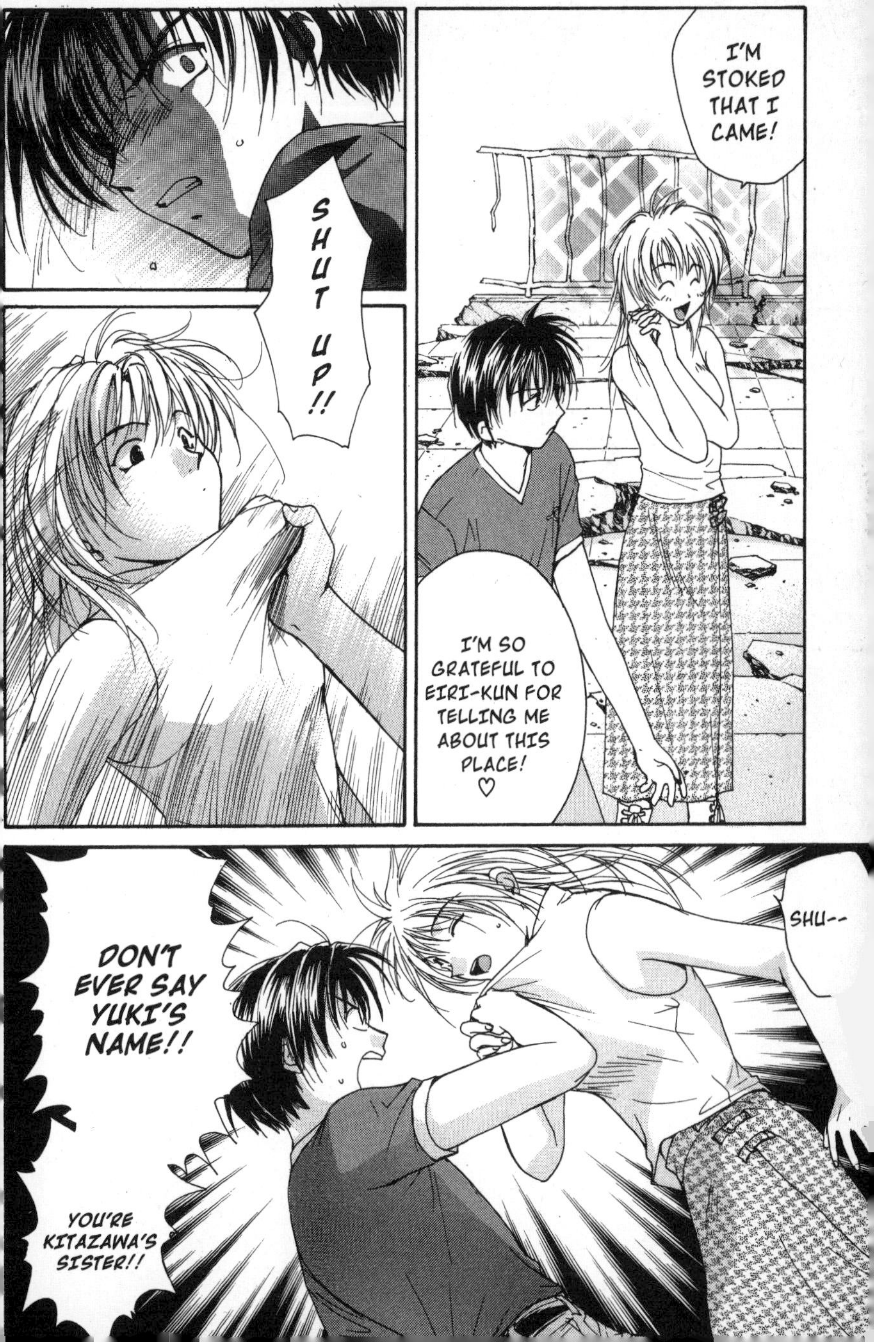
I'M STOKED THAT I CAME!
I'M SO GRATEFUL TO EIRI-KUN FOR TELLING ME ABOUT THIS PLACE! ♡
SHUT UP!!
SHU--
DON'T EVER SAY YUKI'S NAME!!
YOU'RE KITAZAWA'S SISTER!!

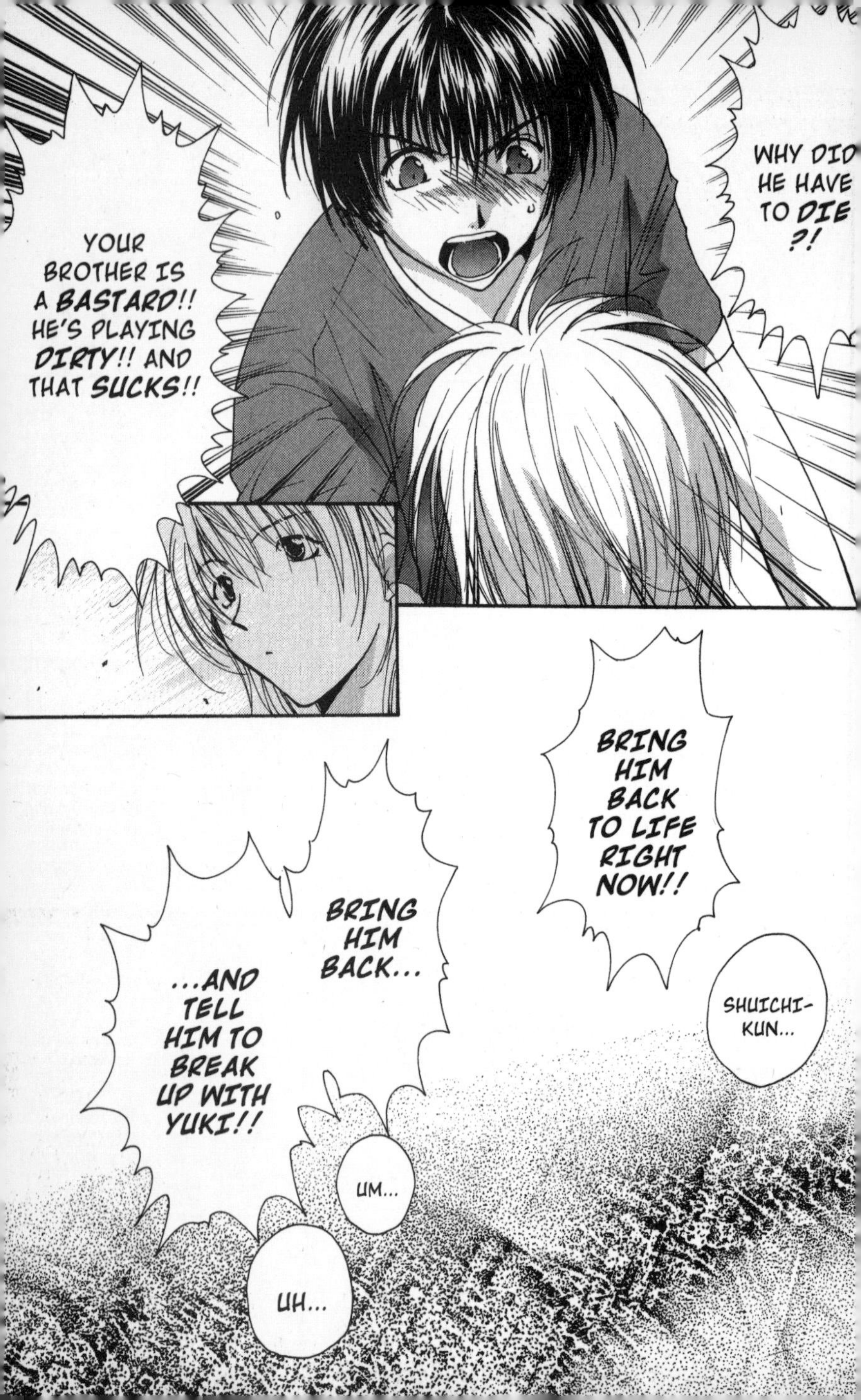
WHY DID HE HAVE TO DIE?!
YOUR BROTHER IS A BASTARD!! HE'S PLAYING DIRTY!! AND THAT SUCKS!!
BRING HIM BACK TO LIFE RIGHT NOW!!
BRING HIM BACK...
...AND TELL HIM TO BREAK UP WITH YUKI!!
SHUICHI-KUN...
UM...
UH...

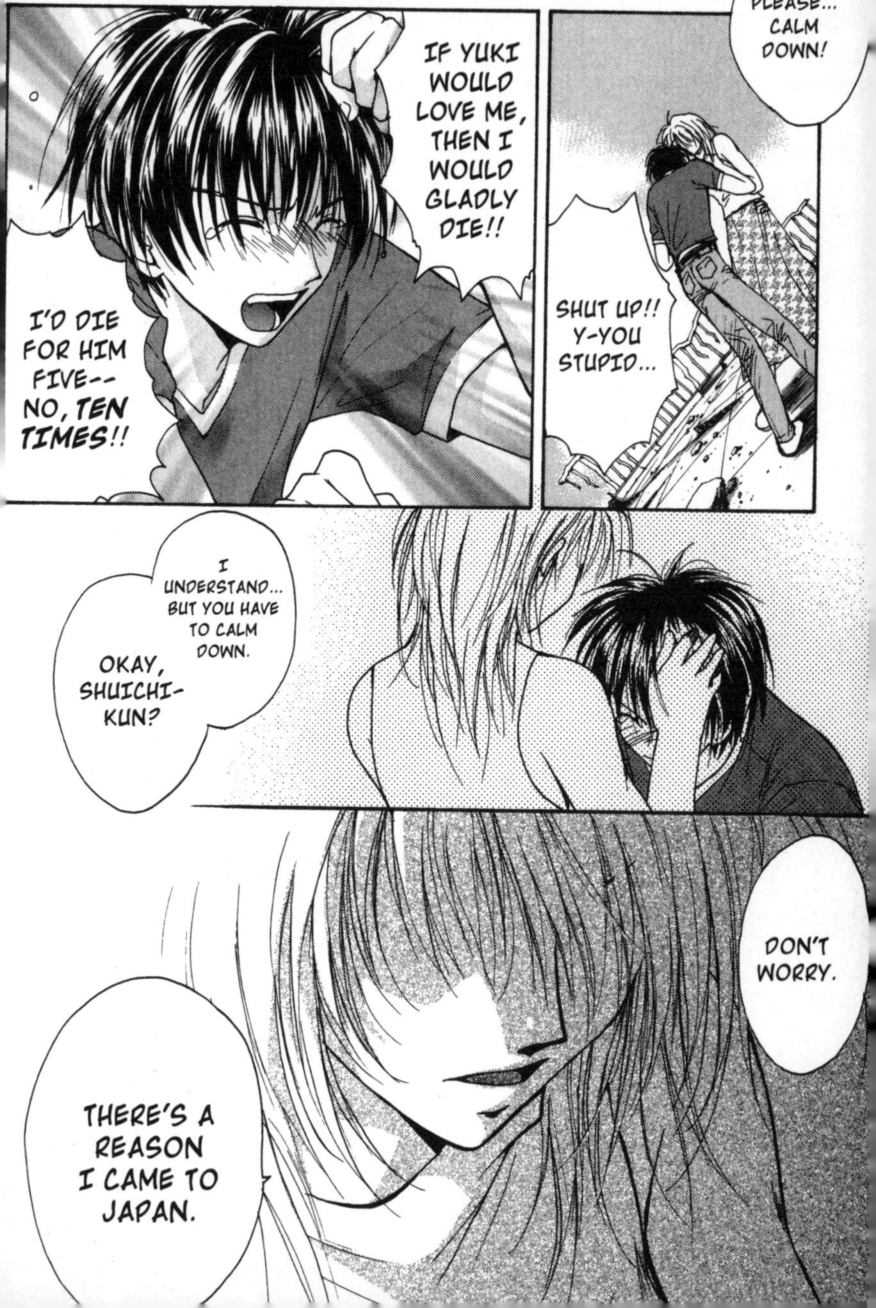
PLEASE... CALM DOWN!
SHUT UP!! Y-YOU STUPID...
IF YUKI WOULD LOVE ME, THEN I WOULD GLADLY DIE!!
I'D DIE FOR HIM FIVE-- NO, **TEN TIMES**!!
I UNDERSTAND... BUT YOU HAVE TO CALM DOWN.
OKAY, SHUICHI-KUN?
DON'T WORRY.
THERE'S A REASON I CAME TO JAPAN.

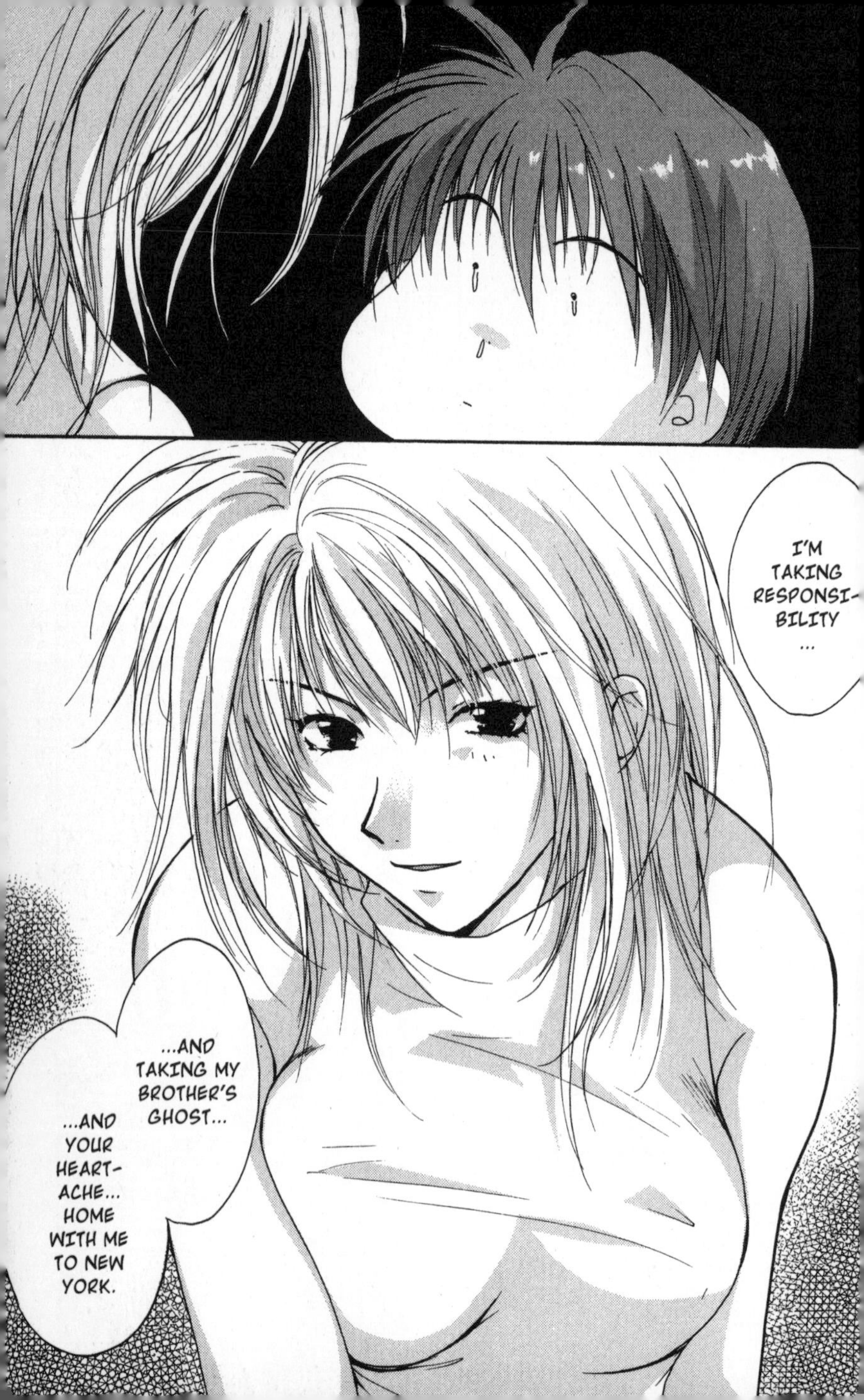
I'M TAKING RESPONSI- BILITY ...
...AND TAKING MY BROTHER'S GHOST...
...AND YOUR HEART- ACHE... HOME WITH ME TO NEW YORK.

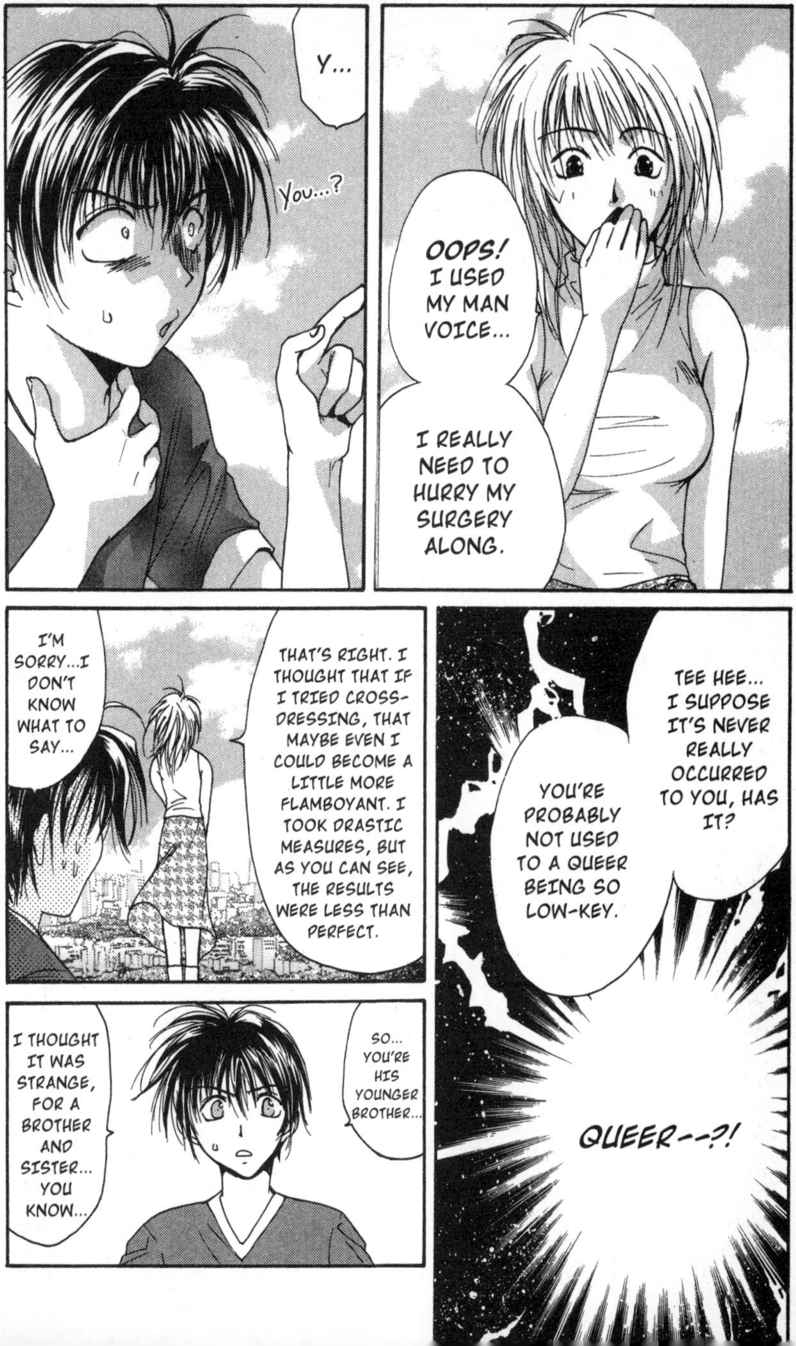
Y...
You...?
OOPS! I USED MY MAN VOICE...
I REALLY NEED TO HURRY MY SURGERY ALONG.
I'M SORRY...I DON'T KNOW WHAT TO SAY...
THAT'S RIGHT. I THOUGHT THAT IF I TRIED CROSS-DRESSING, THAT MAYBE EVEN I COULD BECOME A LITTLE MORE FLAMBOYANT. I TOOK DRASTIC MEASURES, BUT AS YOU CAN SEE, THE RESULTS WERE LESS THAN PERFECT.
I THOUGHT IT WAS STRANGE, FOR A BROTHER AND SISTER... YOU KNOW...
SO... YOU'RE HIS YOUNGER BROTHER...
TEE HEE... I SUPPOSE IT'S NEVER REALLY OCCURRED TO YOU, HAS IT?
YOU'RE PROBABLY NOT USED TO A QUEER BEING SO LOW-KEY.
QUEER--?!

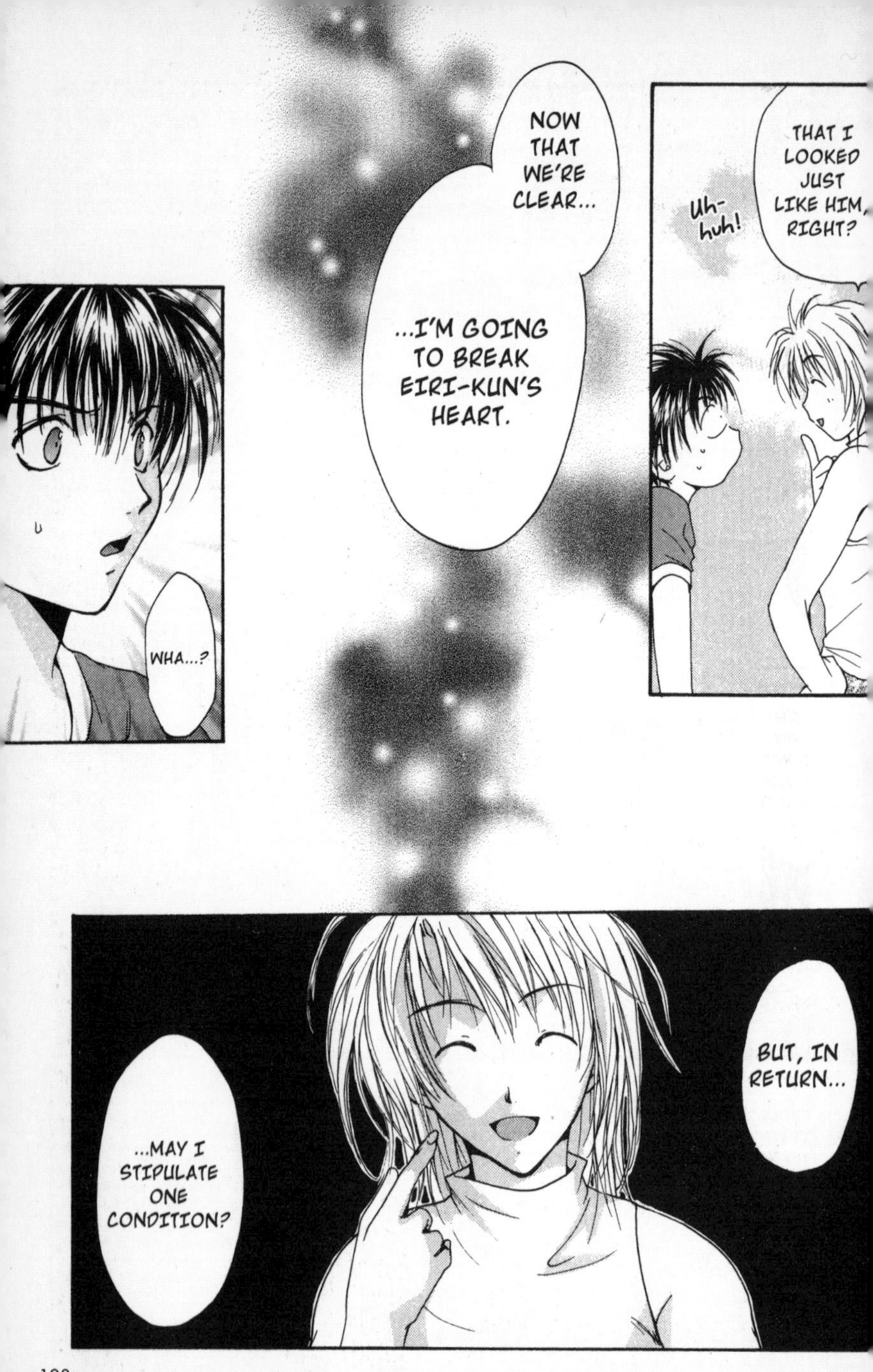
THAT I LOOKED JUST LIKE HIM, RIGHT?
Uh-huh!
NOW THAT WE'RE CLEAR...
...I'M GOING TO BREAK EIRI-KUN'S HEART.
WHA...?
BUT, IN RETURN...
...MAY I STIPULATE ONE CONDITION?

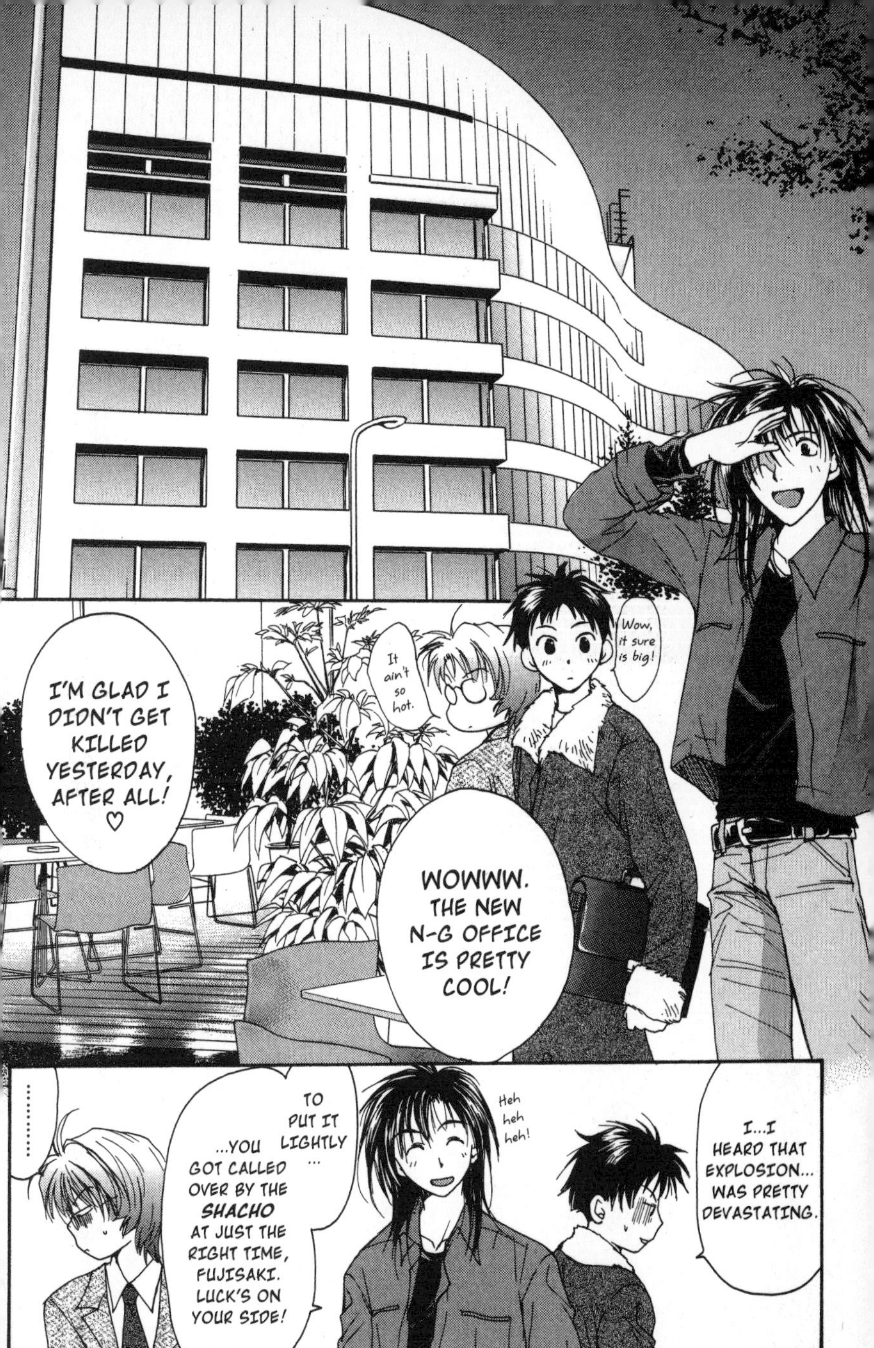
Wow, it sure is big!
It ain't so hot.
WOWWW. THE NEW N-G OFFICE IS PRETTY COOL!
I'M GLAD I DIDN'T GET KILLED YESTERDAY, AFTER ALL! ♡
I...I HEARD THAT EXPLOSION... WAS PRETTY DEVASTATING.
Heh heh heh!
TO PUT IT LIGHTLY...
...YOU GOT CALLED OVER BY THE SHACHO AT JUST THE RIGHT TIME, FUJISAKI. LUCK'S ON YOUR SIDE!
....

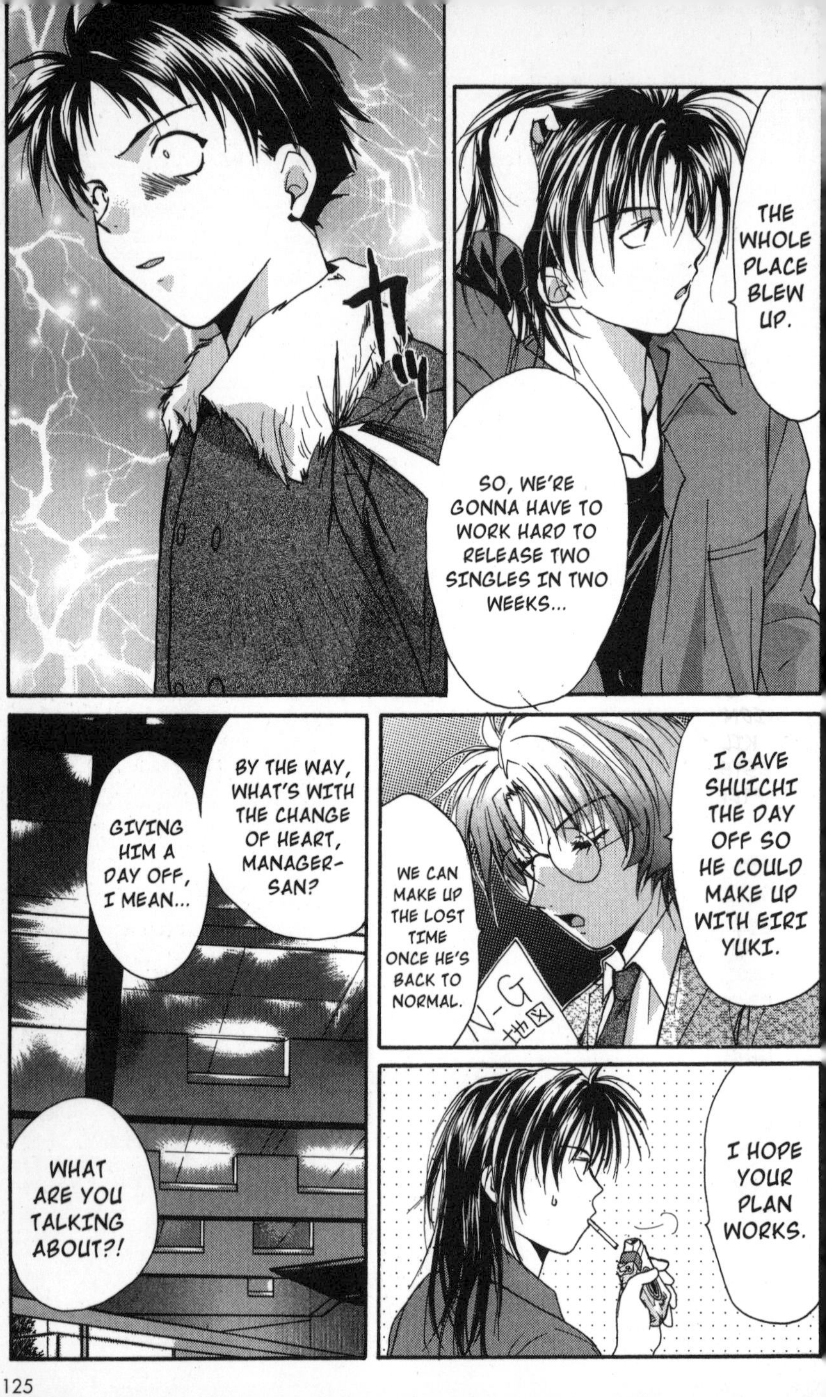
THE WHOLE PLACE BLEW UP.
SO, WE'RE GONNA HAVE TO WORK HARD TO RELEASE TWO SINGLES IN TWO WEEKS...
カッ
I GAVE SHUICHI THE DAY OFF SO HE COULD MAKE UP WITH EIRI YUKI.
WE CAN MAKE UP THE LOST TIME ONCE HE'S BACK TO NORMAL.
N-G
I HOPE YOUR PLAN WORKS.
BY THE WAY, WHAT'S WITH THE CHANGE OF HEART, MANAGER-SAN?
GIVING HIM A DAY OFF, I MEAN...
WHAT ARE YOU TALKING ABOUT?!

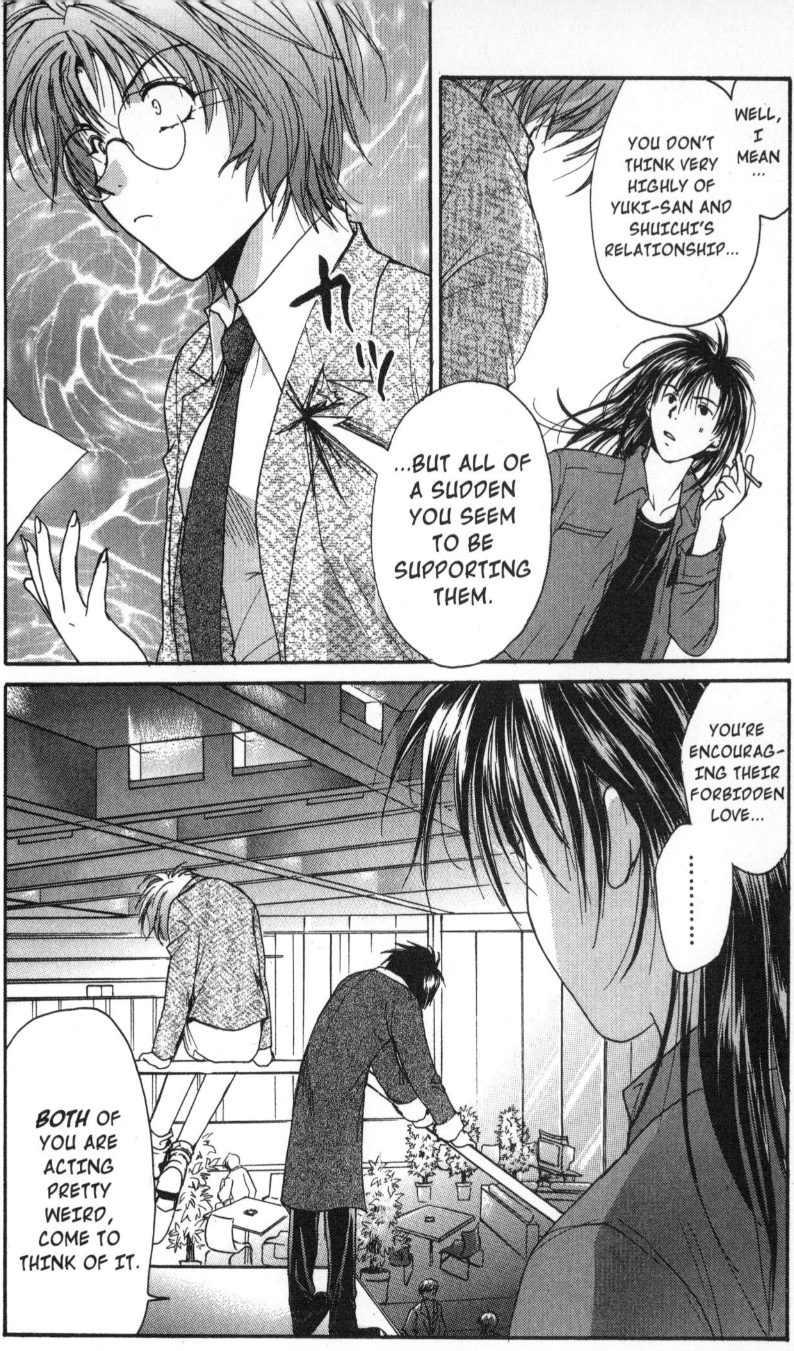
WELL, I MEAN...
YOU DON'T THINK VERY HIGHLY OF YUKI-SAN AND SHUICHI'S RELATIONSHIP...
...BUT ALL OF A SUDDEN YOU SEEM TO BE SUPPORTING THEM.
カッ
YOU'RE ENCOURAG-ING THEIR FORBIDDEN LOVE...
....
BOTH OF YOU ARE ACTING PRETTY WEIRD, COME TO THINK OF IT.

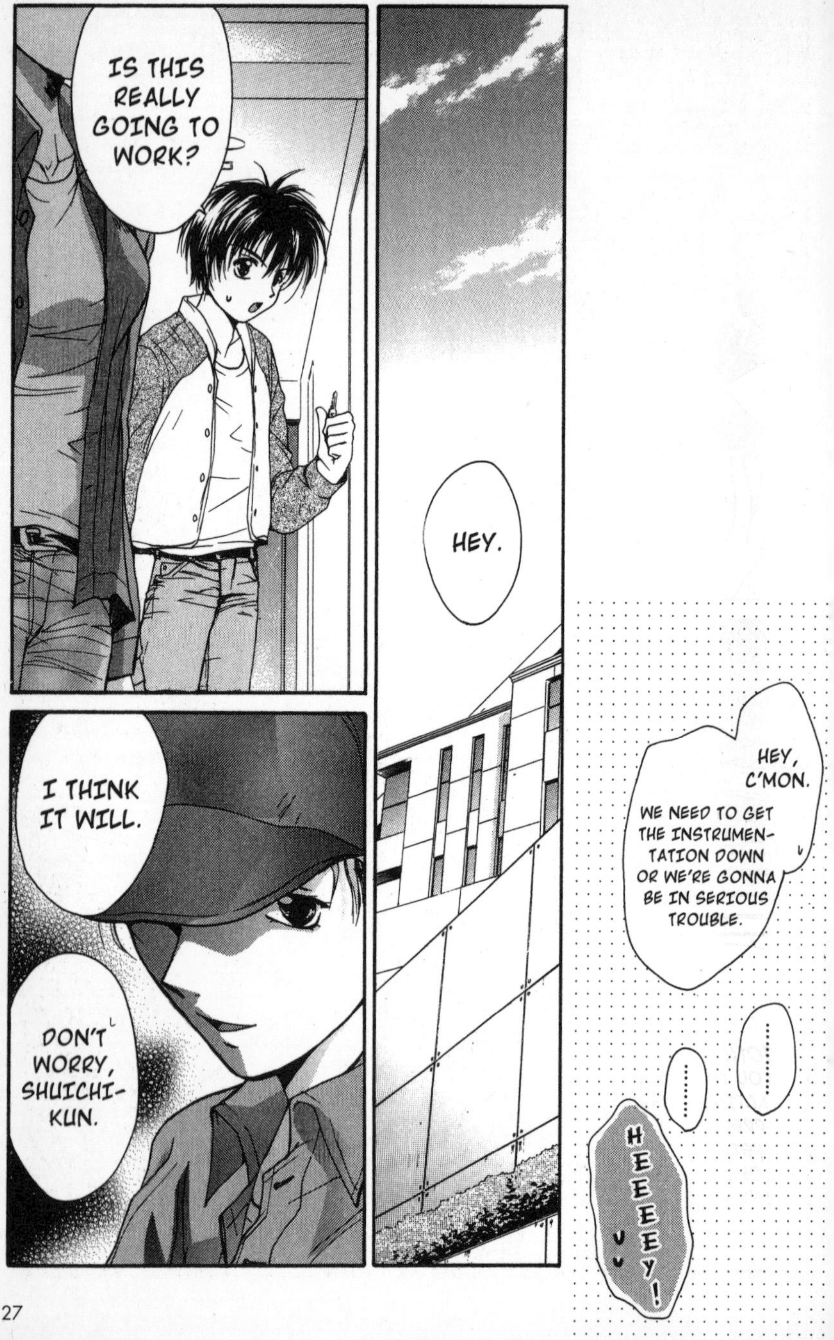
HEY.
HEY, C'MON.
WE NEED TO GET THE INSTRUMEN-TATION DOWN OR WE'RE GONNA BE IN SERIOUS TROUBLE.
......
......
HEEEEy!
IS THIS REALLY GOING TO WORK?
I THINK IT WILL.
DON'T WORRY, SHUICHI-KUN.

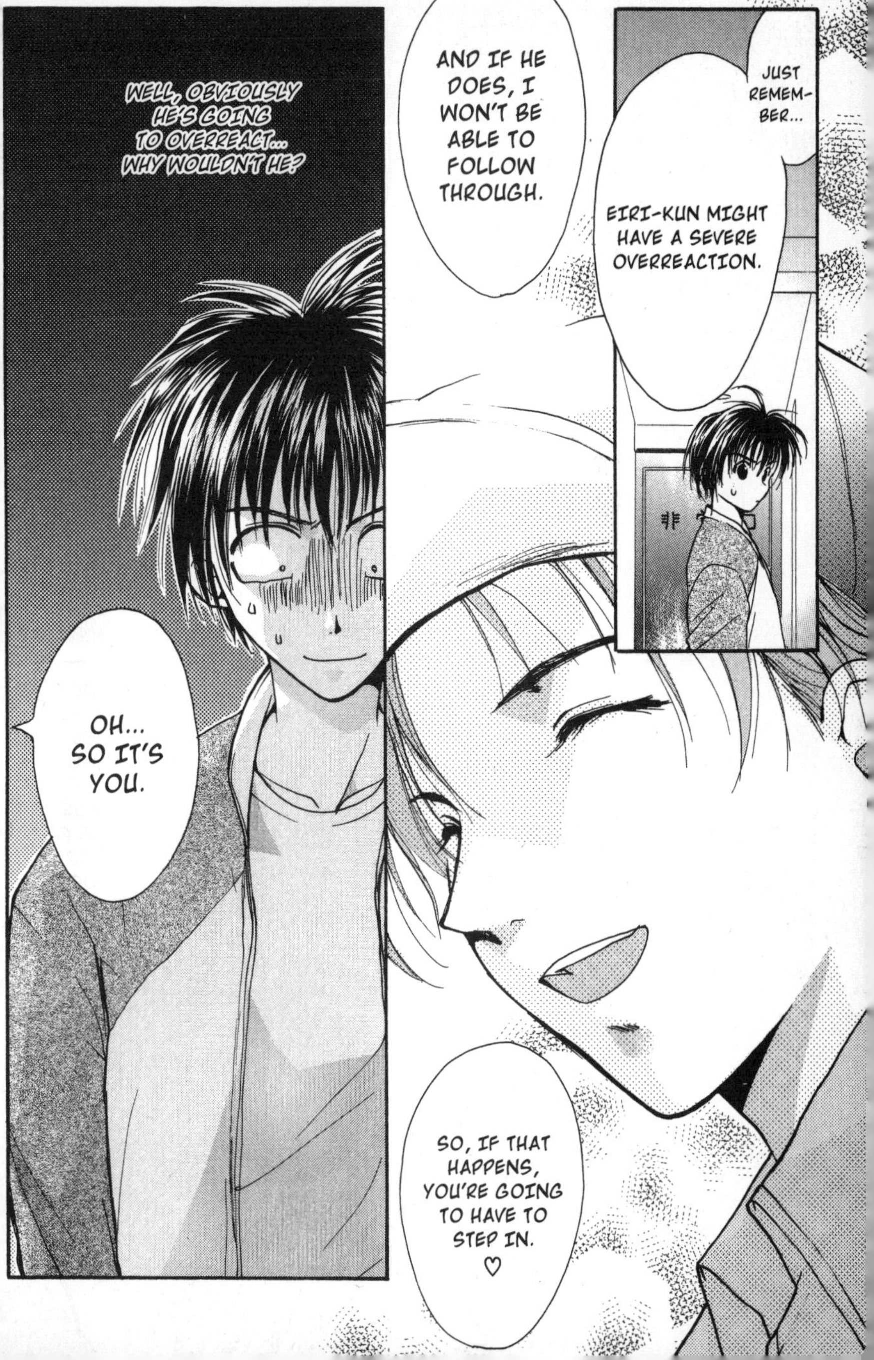
JUST REMEMBER...
EIRI-KUN MIGHT HAVE A SEVERE OVERREACTION.
AND IF HE DOES, I WON'T BE ABLE TO FOLLOW THROUGH.
SO, IF THAT HAPPENS, YOU'RE GOING TO HAVE TO STEP IN. ♡
WELL, OBVIOUSLY HE'S GOING TO OVERREACT... WHY WOULDN'T HE?
OH... SO IT'S YOU.

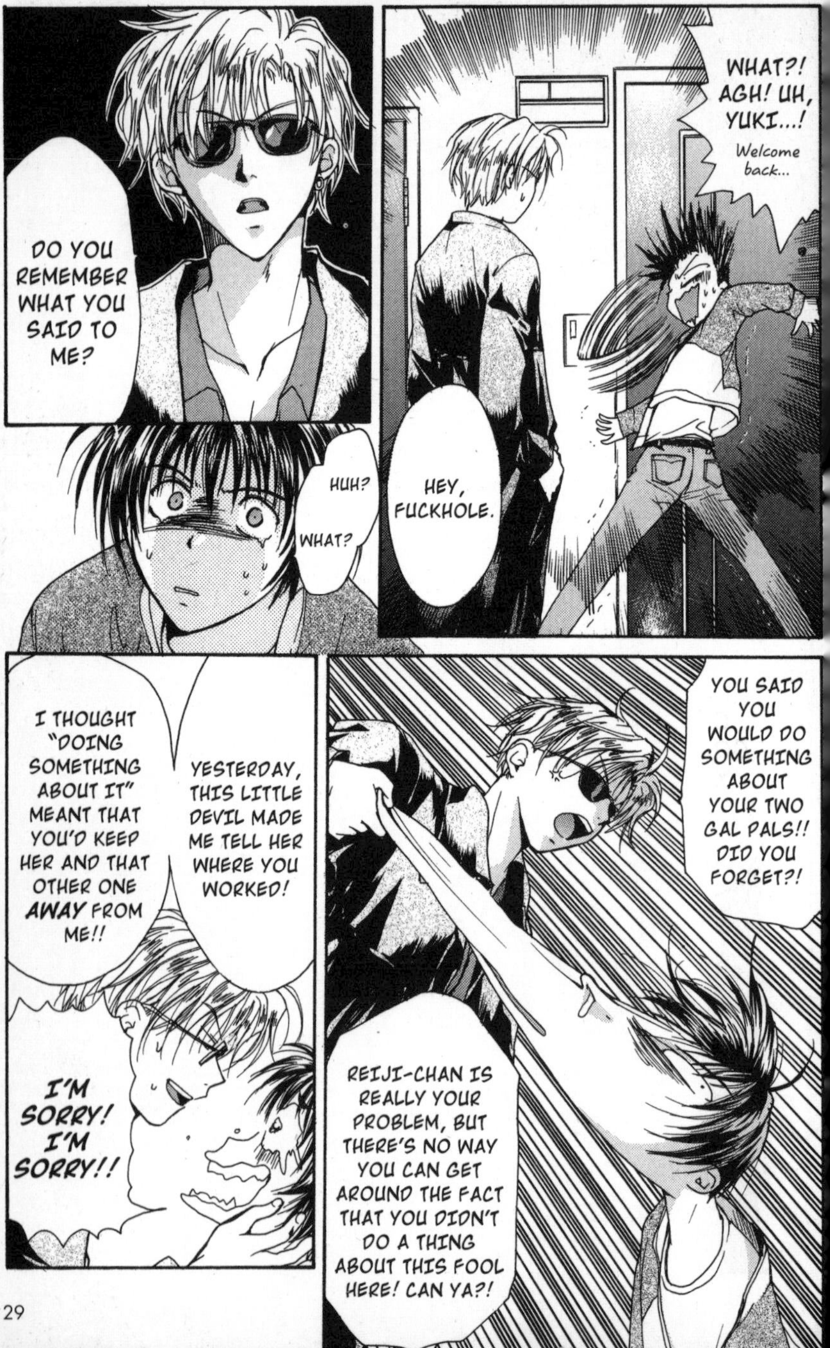
WHAT?! AGH! UH, YUKI...!
Welcome back...
HEY, FUCKHOLE.
DO YOU REMEMBER WHAT YOU SAID TO ME?
HUH?
WHAT?
YOU SAID YOU WOULD DO SOMETHING ABOUT YOUR TWO GAL PALS!! DID YOU FORGET?!
REIJI-CHAN IS REALLY YOUR PROBLEM, BUT THERE'S NO WAY YOU CAN GET AROUND THE FACT THAT YOU DIDN'T DO A THING ABOUT THIS FOOL HERE! CAN YA?!
YESTERDAY, THIS LITTLE DEVIL MADE ME TELL HER WHERE YOU WORKED!
I THOUGHT "DOING SOMETHING ABOUT IT" MEANT THAT YOU'D KEEP HER AND THAT OTHER ONE AWAY FROM ME!!
I'M SORRY! I'M SORRY!!

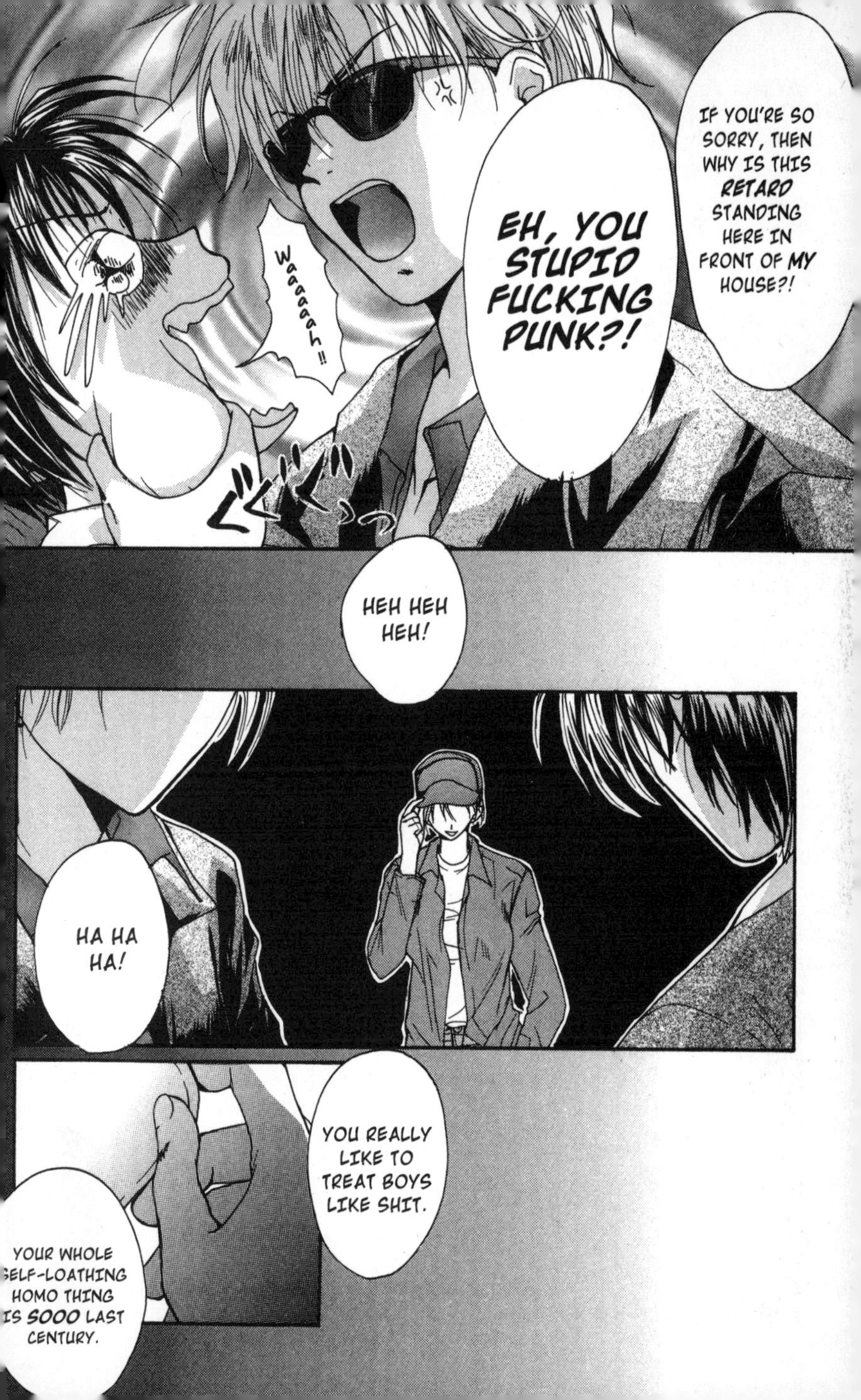
IF YOU'RE SO SORRY, THEN WHY IS THIS RETARD STANDING HERE IN FRONT OF MY HOUSE?!
EH, YOU STUPID FUCKING PUNK?!
Waaaaaah!!
HEH HEH HEH!
HA HA HA!
YOU REALLY LIKE TO TREAT BOYS LIKE SHIT.
YOUR WHOLE SELF-LOATHING HOMO THING IS SOOO LAST CENTURY.

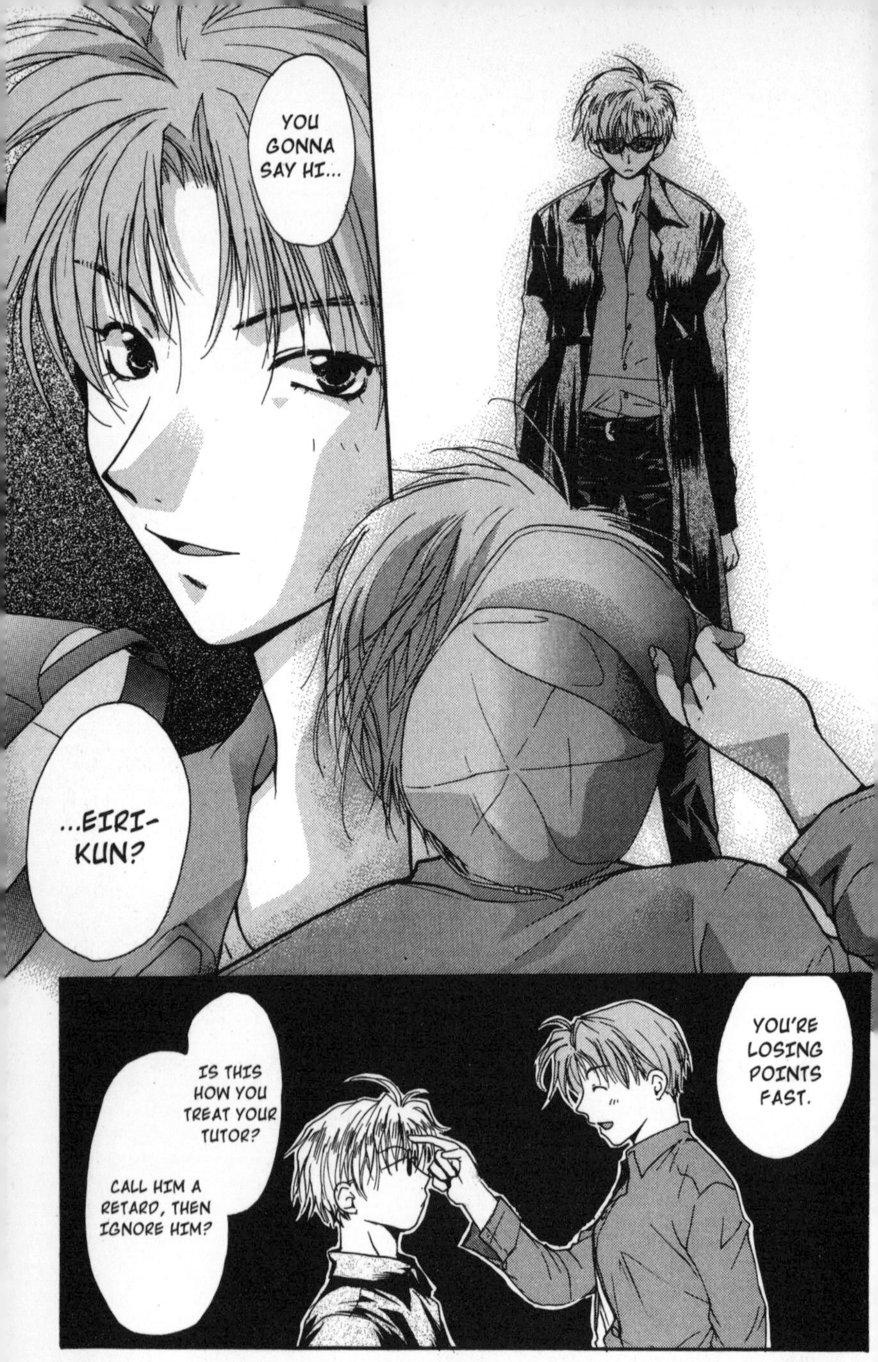
YOU GONNA SAY HI...
...EIRI-KUN?
YOU'RE LOSING POINTS FAST.
IS THIS HOW YOU TREAT YOUR TUTOR?
CALL HIM A RETARD, THEN IGNORE HIM?

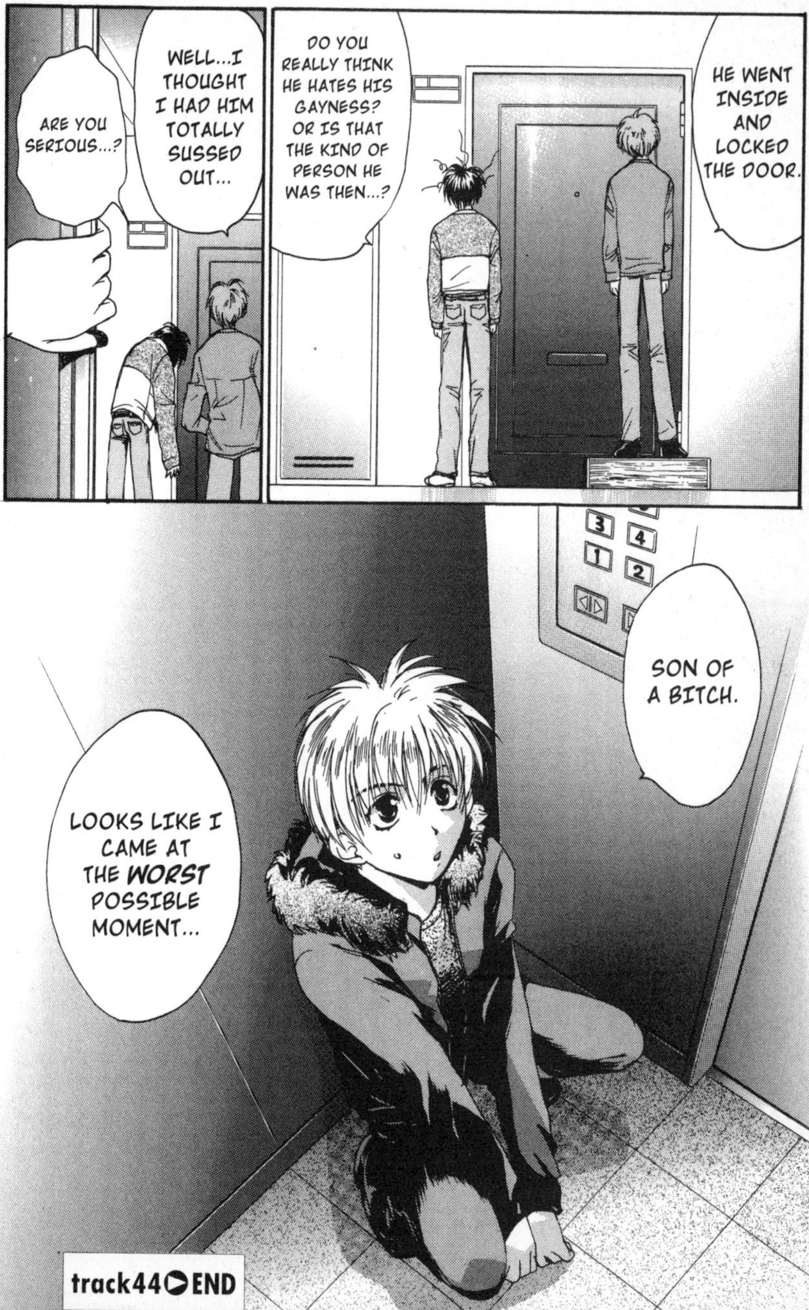
HE WENT INSIDE AND LOCKED THE DOOR.
DO YOU REALLY THINK HE HATES HIS GAYNESS? OR IS THAT THE KIND OF PERSON HE WAS THEN...?
WELL...I THOUGHT I HAD HIM TOTALLY SUSSED OUT...
ARE YOU SERIOUS...?
3 4 1 2
SON OF A BITCH.
LOOKS LIKE I CAME AT THE *WORST* POSSIBLE MOMENT...
track44 ▶ END

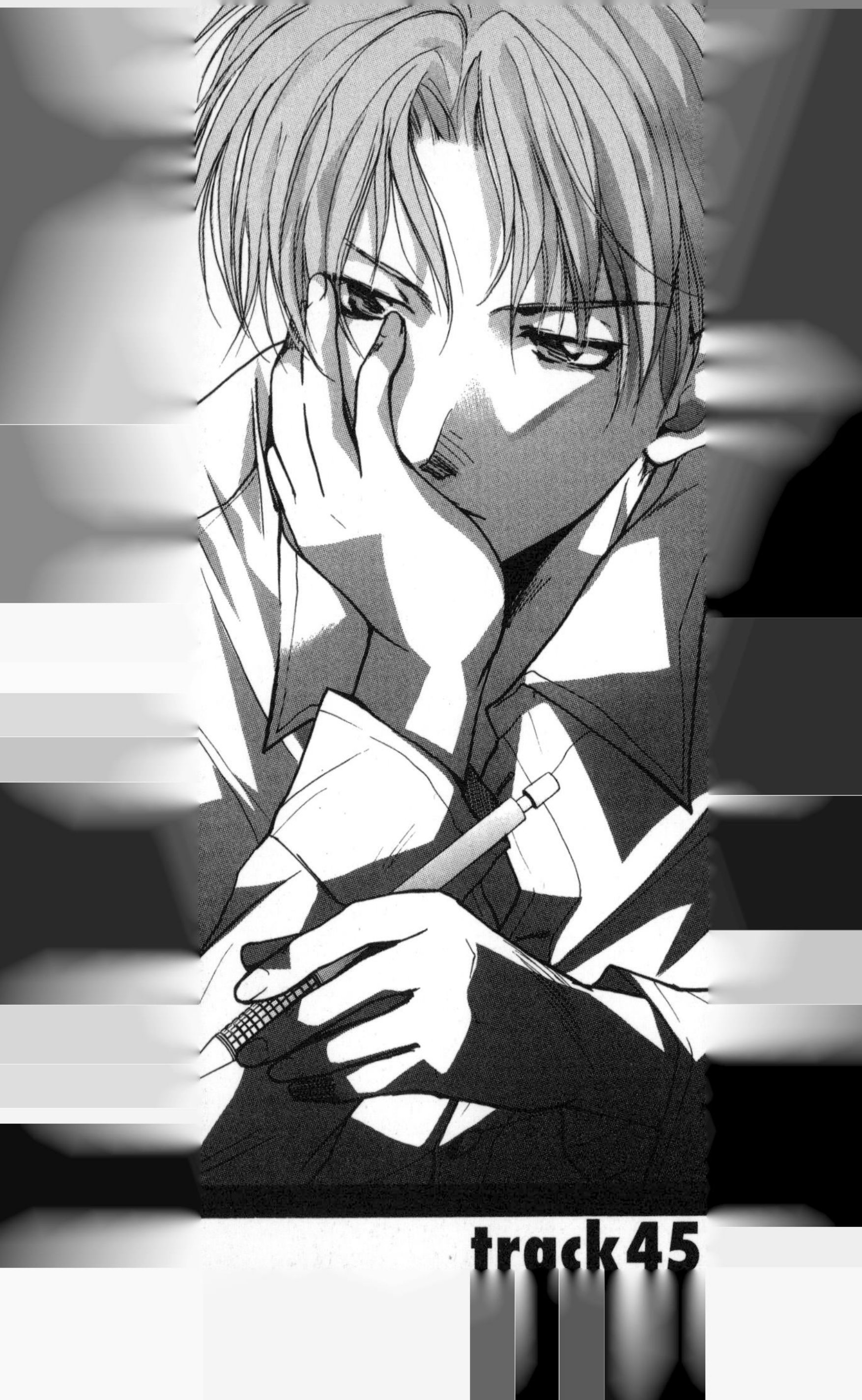

track45

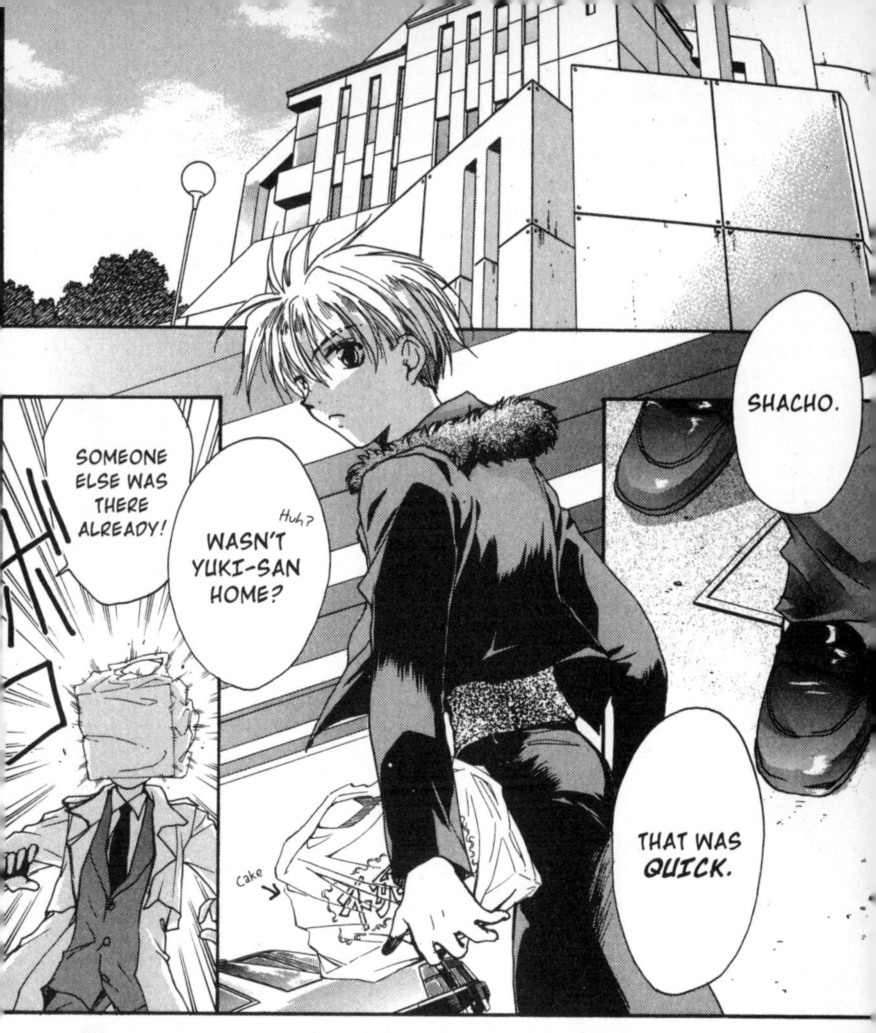
SHACHO.
THAT WAS **QUICK.**
Huh?
WASN'T YUKI-SAN HOME?
Cake
SOMEONE ELSE WAS THERE ALREADY!

ABOUT GRAVITATION TRACK 45

I've gotten used to using this autograph pen, and at first glance you might not even recognize my writing. What do you think? I also use a specialized G pen, but I have a hard time writing with that one, too. After all, they're autograph pens! But it's a pretty cheap way to go. Each pen costs about 100 yen, and it'll last about 100 pages. But it's not something to brag about. This is just a last resort, since I have nothing to write about in this space.

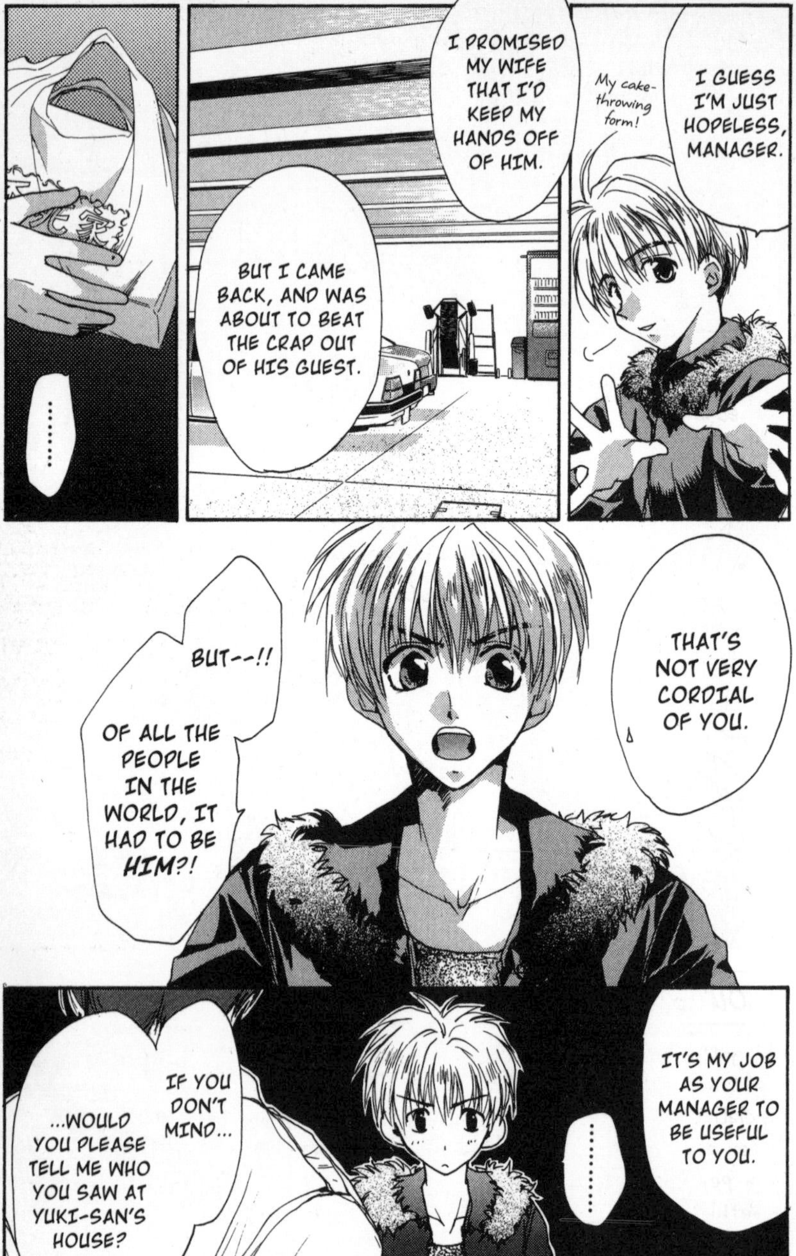
I GUESS I'M JUST HOPELESS, MANAGER.
My cake-throwing form!
I PROMISED MY WIFE THAT I'D KEEP MY HANDS OFF OF HIM.
BUT I CAME BACK, AND WAS ABOUT TO BEAT THE CRAP OUT OF HIS GUEST.
......
THAT'S NOT VERY CORDIAL OF YOU.
BUT--!!
OF ALL THE PEOPLE IN THE WORLD, IT HAD TO BE HIM?!
IT'S MY JOB AS YOUR MANAGER TO BE USEFUL TO YOU.
......
IF YOU DON'T MIND...
...WOULD YOU PLEASE TELL ME WHO YOU SAW AT YUKI-SAN'S HOUSE?

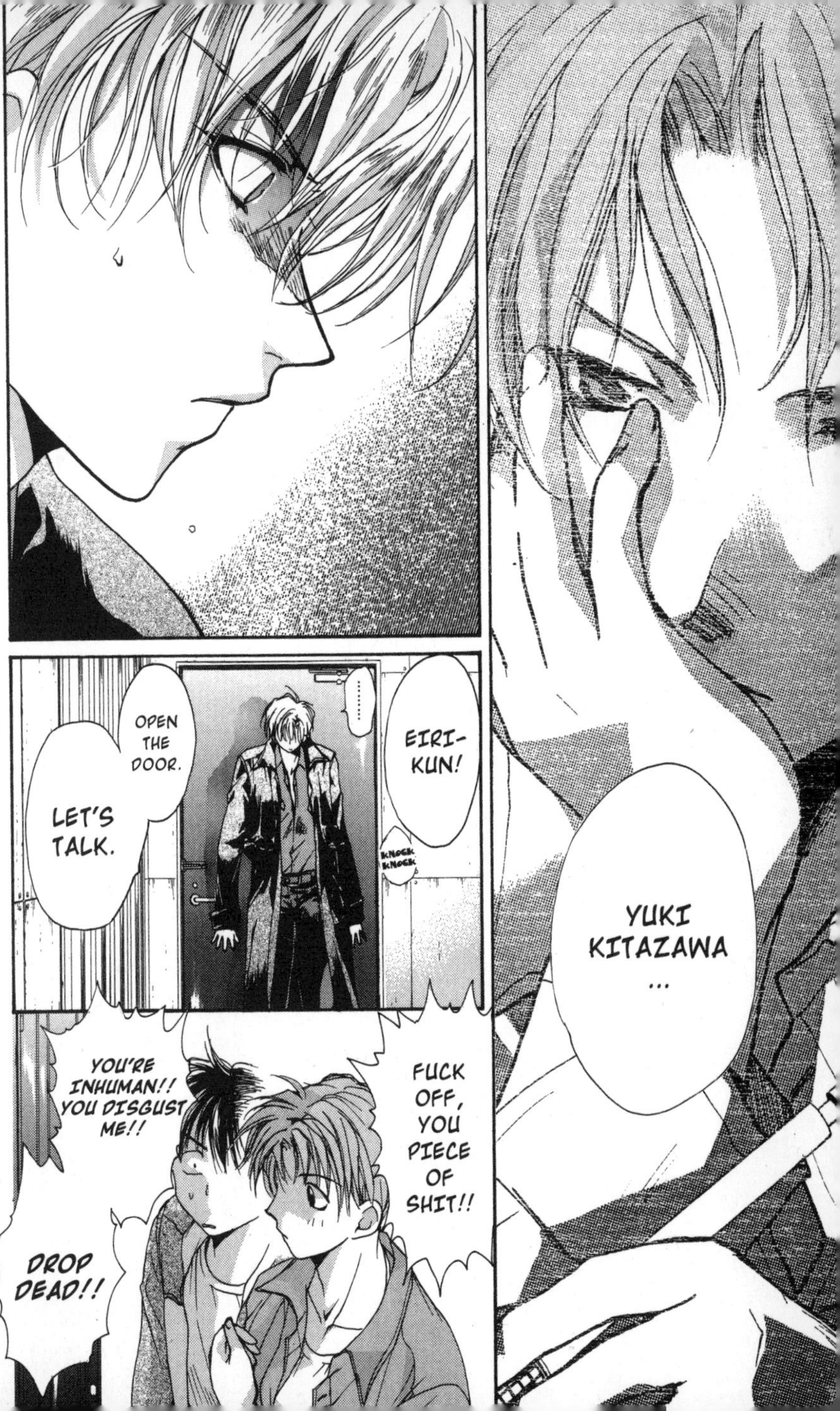
YUKI KITAZAWA ...
......
EIRI-KUN!
KNOCK KNOCK
OPEN THE DOOR.
LET'S TALK.
FUCK OFF, YOU PIECE OF SHIT!!
YOU'RE INHUMAN!! YOU DISGUST ME!!
DROP DEAD!!

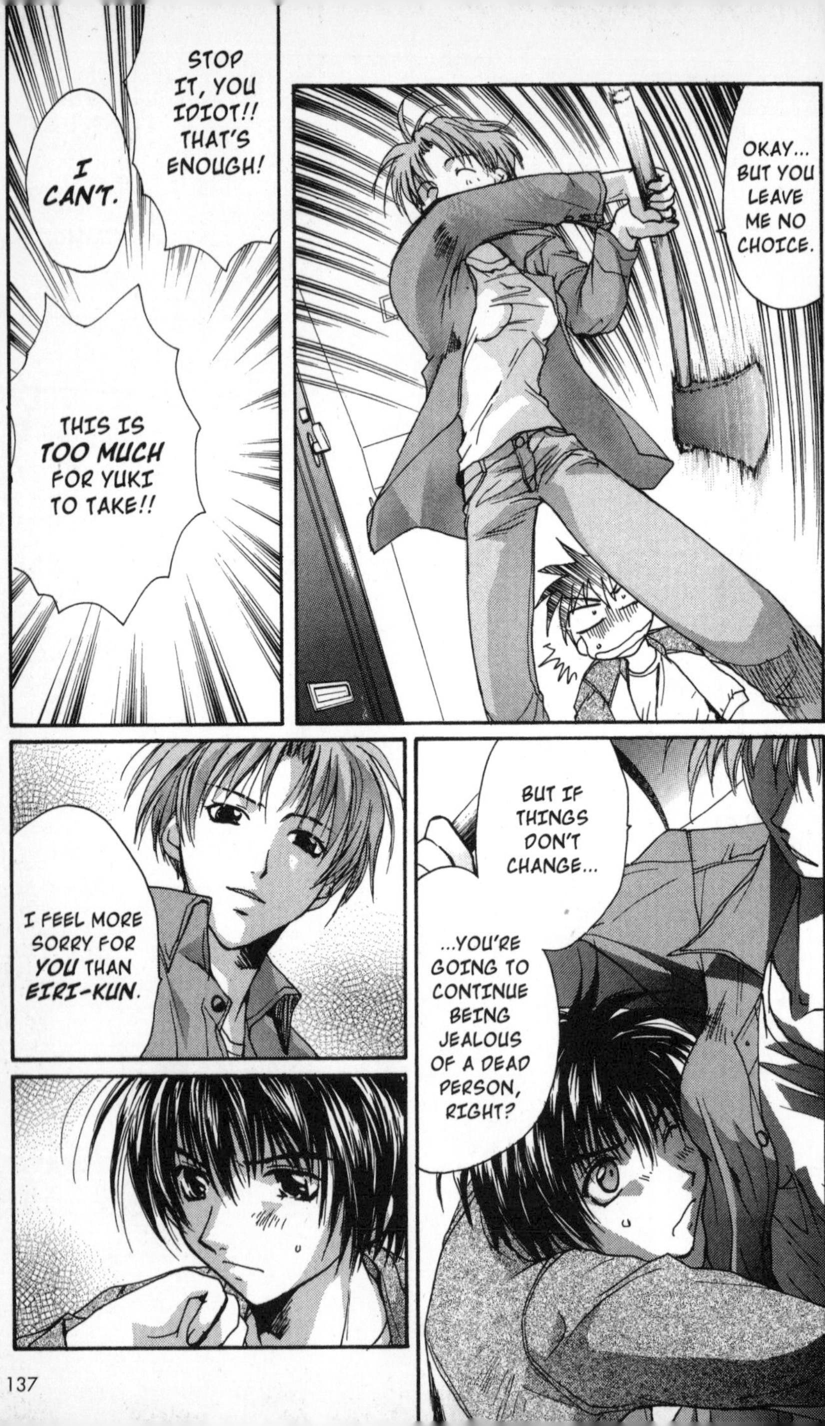
OKAY... BUT YOU LEAVE ME NO CHOICE.
STOP IT, YOU IDIOT!! THAT'S ENOUGH!
I CAN'T.
THIS IS TOO MUCH FOR YUKI TO TAKE!!
BUT IF THINGS DON'T CHANGE...
...YOU'RE GOING TO CONTINUE BEING JEALOUS OF A DEAD PERSON, RIGHT?
I FEEL MORE SORRY FOR YOU THAN EIRI-KUN.

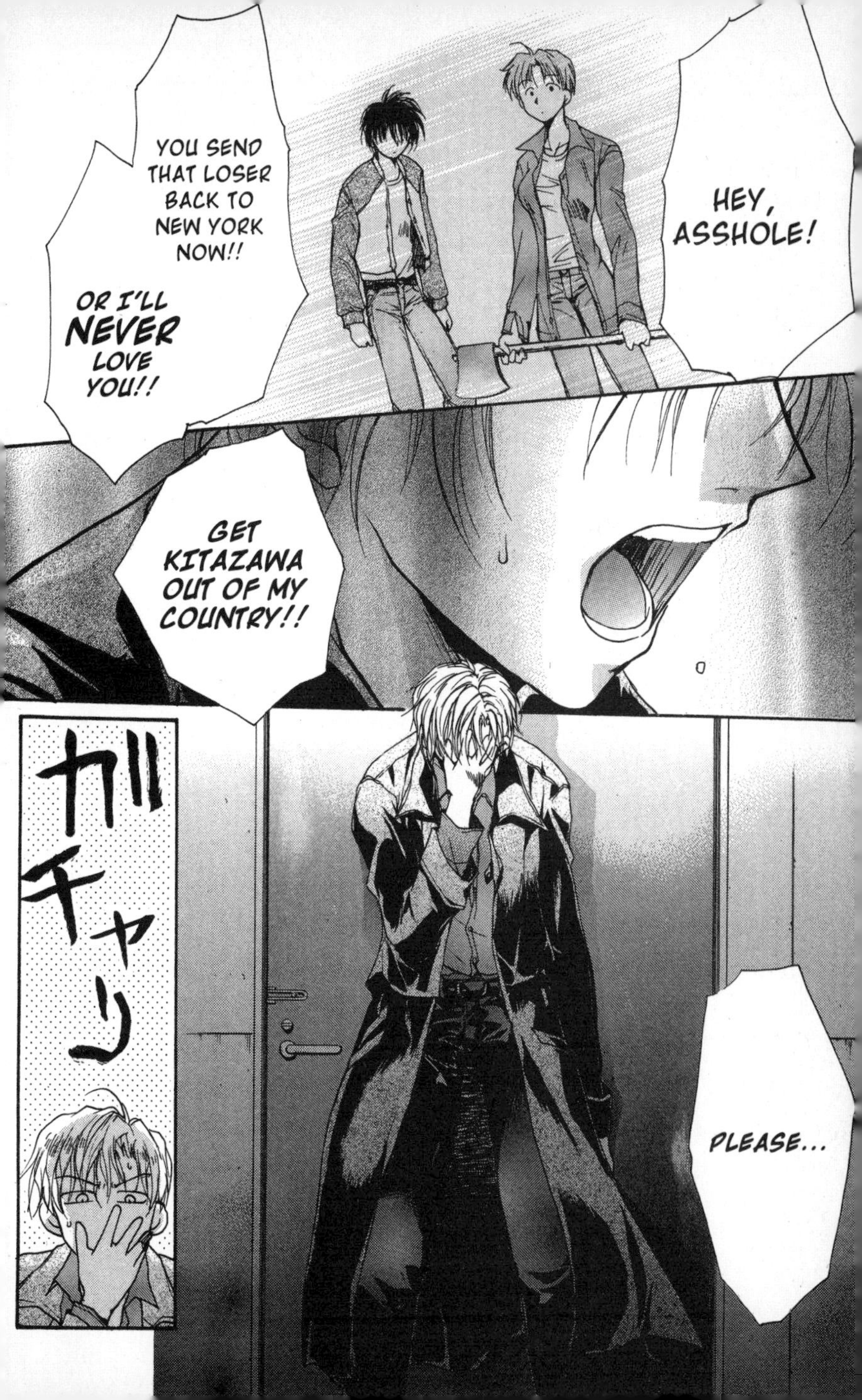
HEY, ASSHOLE!
YOU SEND THAT LOSER BACK TO NEW YORK NOW!!
OR I'LL **NEVER** LOVE YOU!!
GET KITAZAWA OUT OF MY COUNTRY!!
PLEASE...
ガチャリ

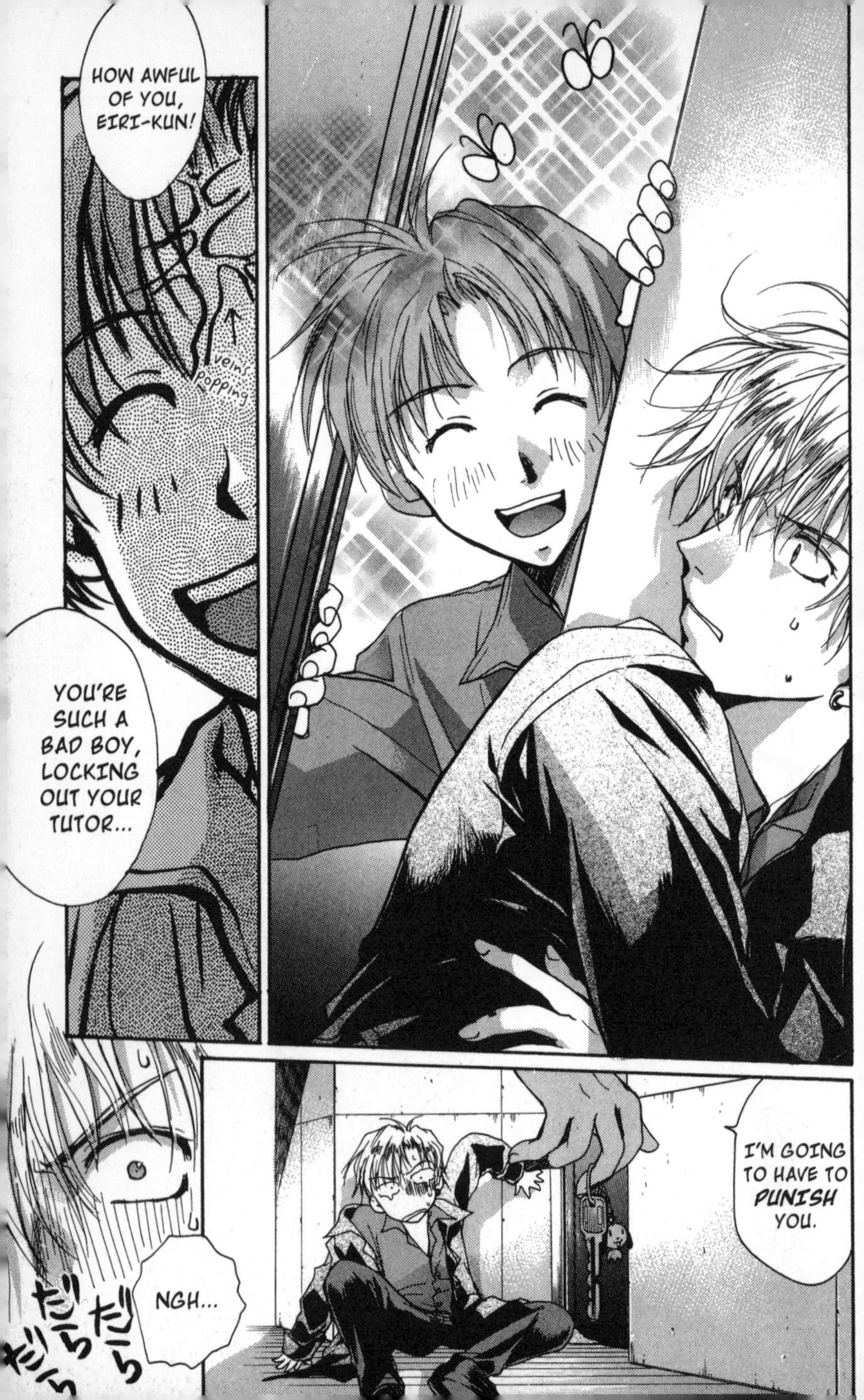
HOW AWFUL OF YOU, EIRI-KUN!
veins popping
YOU'RE SUCH A BAD BOY, LOCKING OUT YOUR TUTOR...
I'M GOING TO HAVE TO PUNISH YOU.
NGH...
だらだら
だらだら

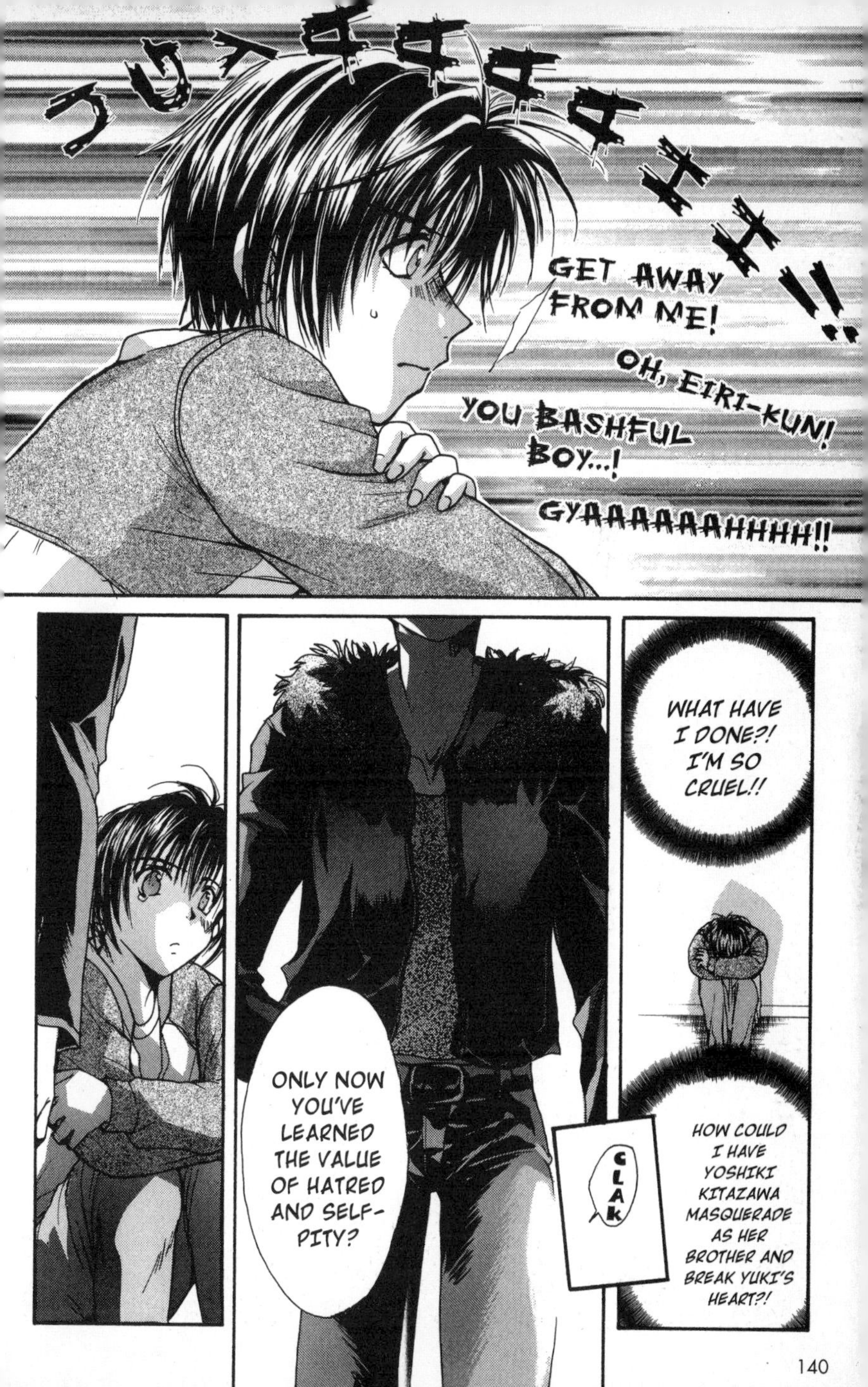
GET AWAY FROM ME!
OH, EIRI-KUN! YOU BASHFUL BOY...!
GYAAAAAAAAHHHHH!!
WHAT HAVE I DONE?! I'M SO CRUEL!!
HOW COULD I HAVE YOSHIKI KITAZAWA MASQUERADE AS HER BROTHER AND BREAK YUKI'S HEART?!
CLAK
ONLY NOW YOU'VE LEARNED THE VALUE OF HATRED AND SELF-PITY?

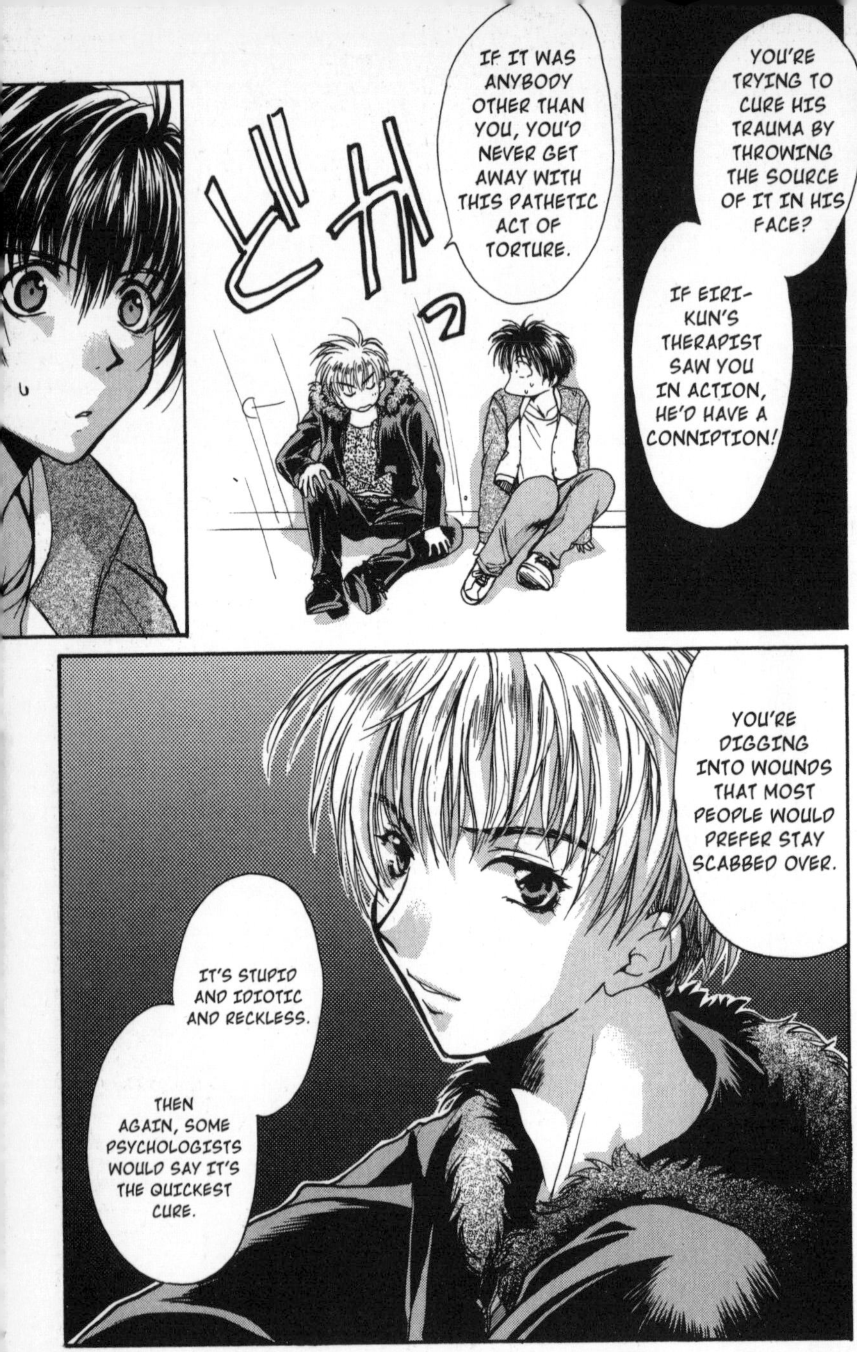
YOU'RE TRYING TO CURE HIS TRAUMA BY THROWING THE SOURCE OF IT IN HIS FACE?
IF EIRI-KUN'S THERAPIST SAW YOU IN ACTION, HE'D HAVE A CONNIPTION!
どかっ
IF IT WAS ANYBODY OTHER THAN YOU, YOU'D NEVER GET AWAY WITH THIS PATHETIC ACT OF TORTURE.
YOU'RE DIGGING INTO WOUNDS THAT MOST PEOPLE WOULD PREFER STAY SCABBED OVER.
IT'S STUPID AND IDIOTIC AND RECKLESS.
THEN AGAIN, SOME PSYCHOLOGISTS WOULD SAY IT'S THE QUICKEST CURE.

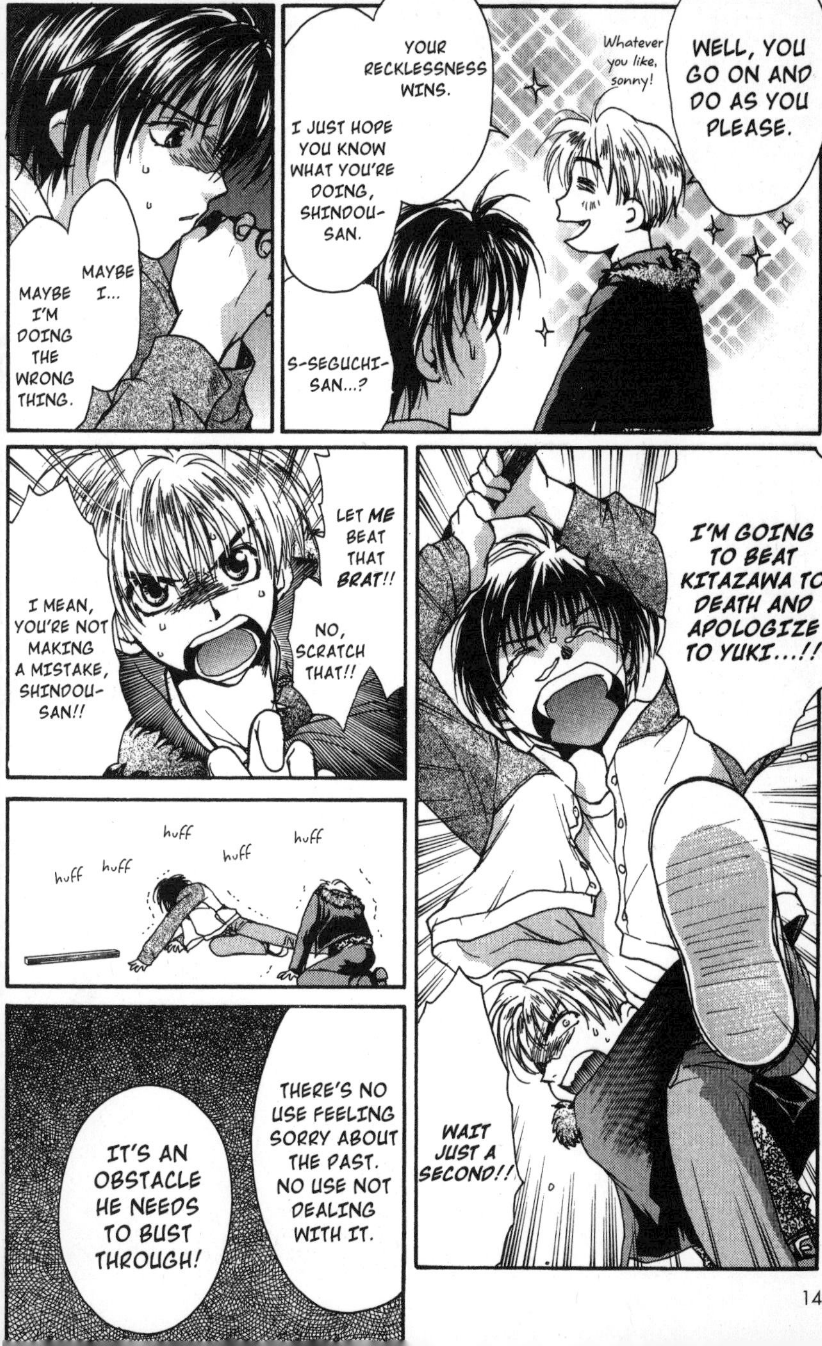
WELL, YOU GO ON AND DO AS YOU PLEASE.
Whatever you like, sonny!
YOUR RECKLESSNESS WINS.
I JUST HOPE YOU KNOW WHAT YOU'RE DOING, SHINDOU-SAN.
S-SEGUCHI-SAN...?
MAYBE I...
MAYBE I'M DOING THE WRONG THING.
I'M GOING TO BEAT KITAZAWA TO DEATH AND APOLOGIZE TO YUKI...!!
WAIT JUST A SECOND!!
LET ME BEAT THAT BRAT!!
NO, SCRATCH THAT!!
I MEAN, YOU'RE NOT MAKING A MISTAKE, SHINDOU-SAN!!
huff
huff
huff
huff
huff
THERE'S NO USE FEELING SORRY ABOUT THE PAST. NO USE NOT DEALING WITH IT.
IT'S AN OBSTACLE HE NEEDS TO BUST THROUGH!

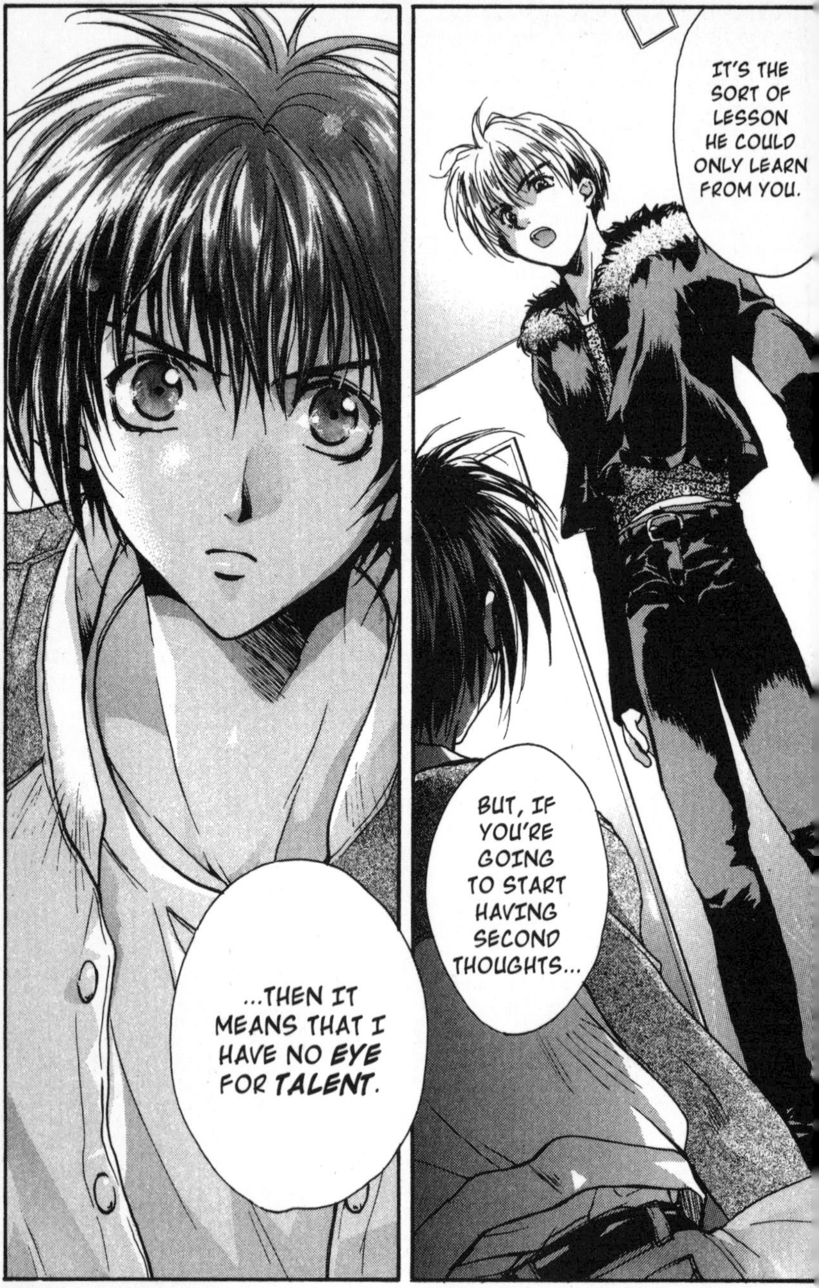
IT'S THE SORT OF LESSON HE COULD ONLY LEARN FROM YOU.
BUT, IF YOU'RE GOING TO START HAVING SECOND THOUGHTS...
...THEN IT MEANS THAT I HAVE NO EYE FOR TALENT.

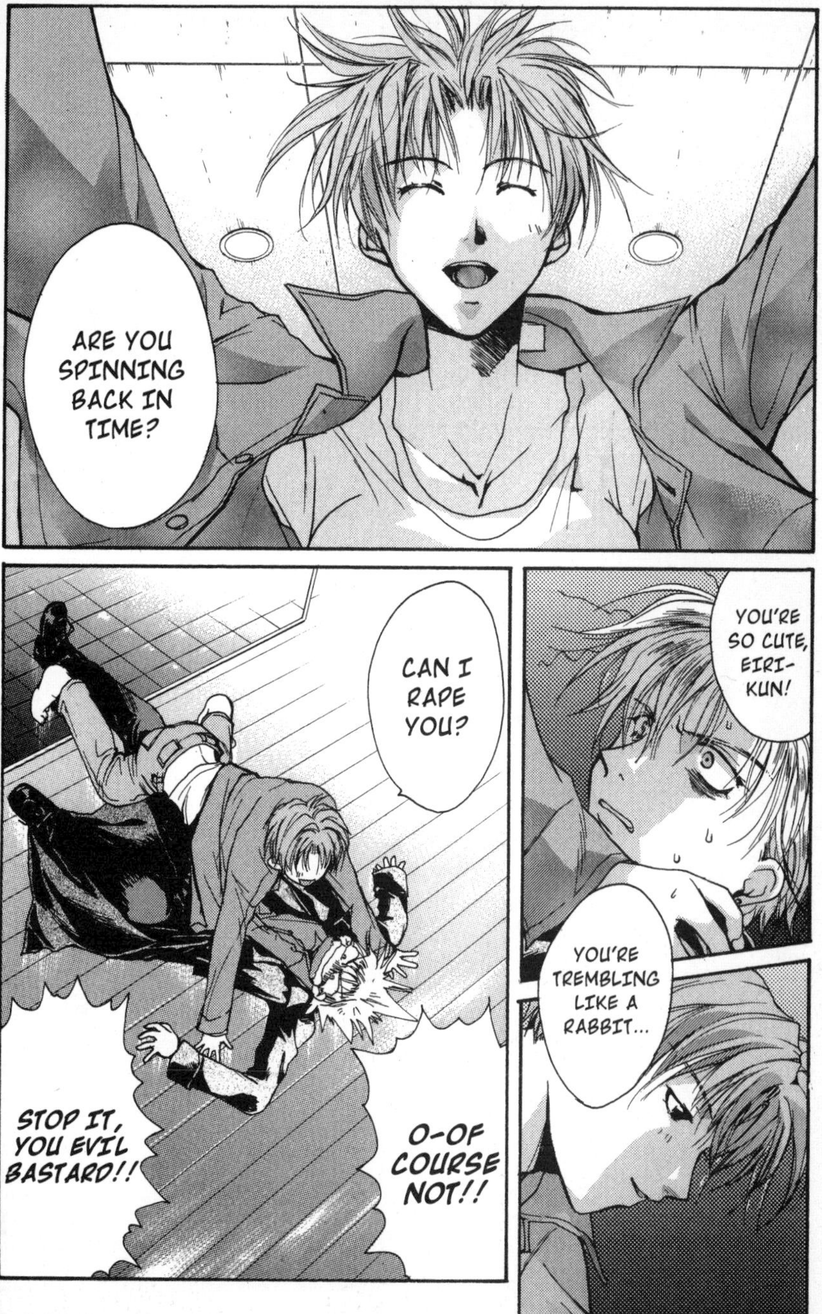
ARE YOU SPINNING BACK IN TIME?
YOU'RE SO CUTE, EIRI-KUN!
YOU'RE TREMBLING LIKE A RABBIT...
CAN I RAPE YOU?
O-OF COURSE NOT!!
STOP IT, YOU EVIL BASTARD!!

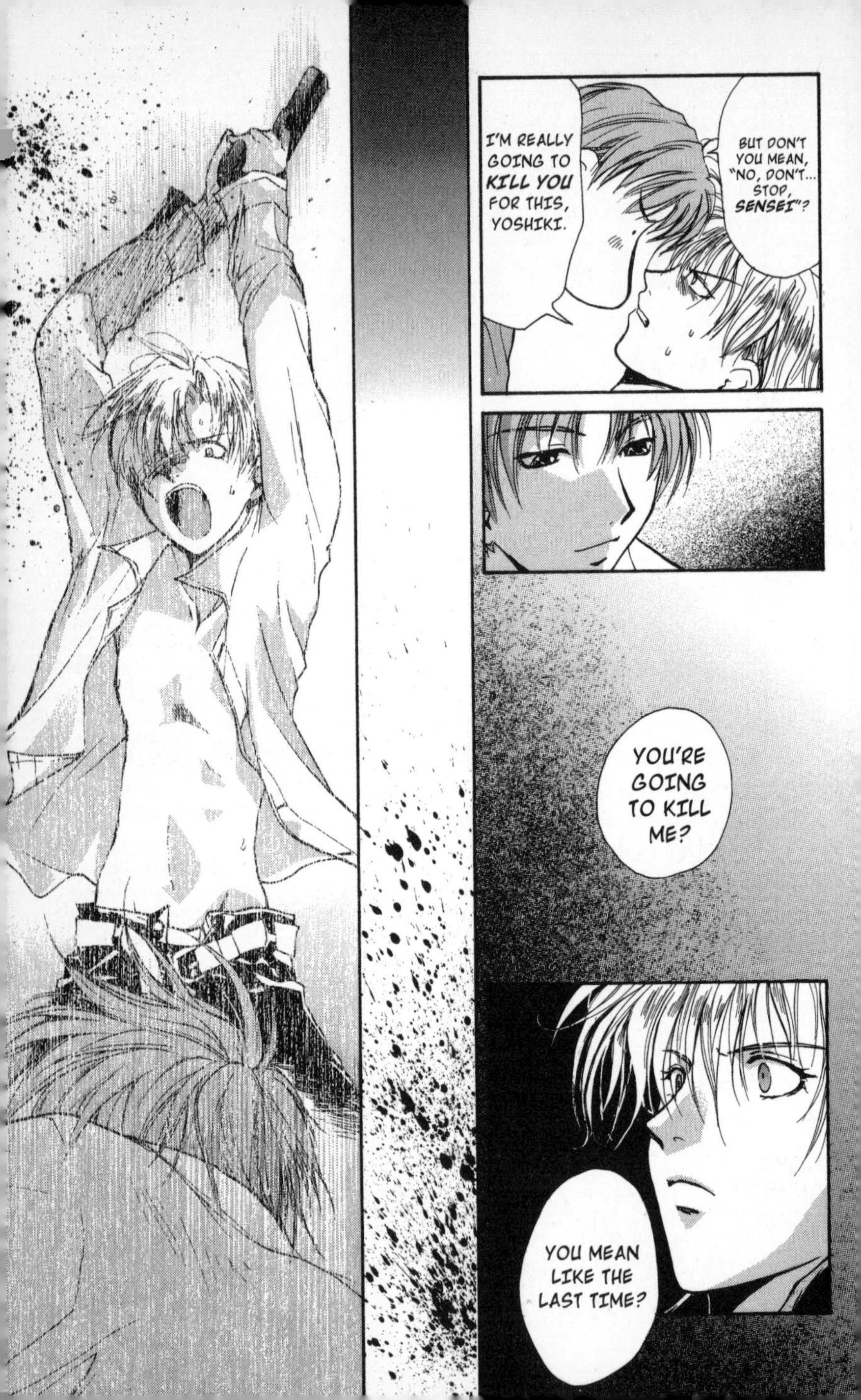
BUT DON'T YOU MEAN, "NO, DON'T... STOP, **SENSEI**"?
I'M REALLY GOING TO **KILL YOU** FOR THIS, YOSHIKI.
YOU'RE GOING TO KILL ME?
YOU MEAN LIKE THE LAST TIME?

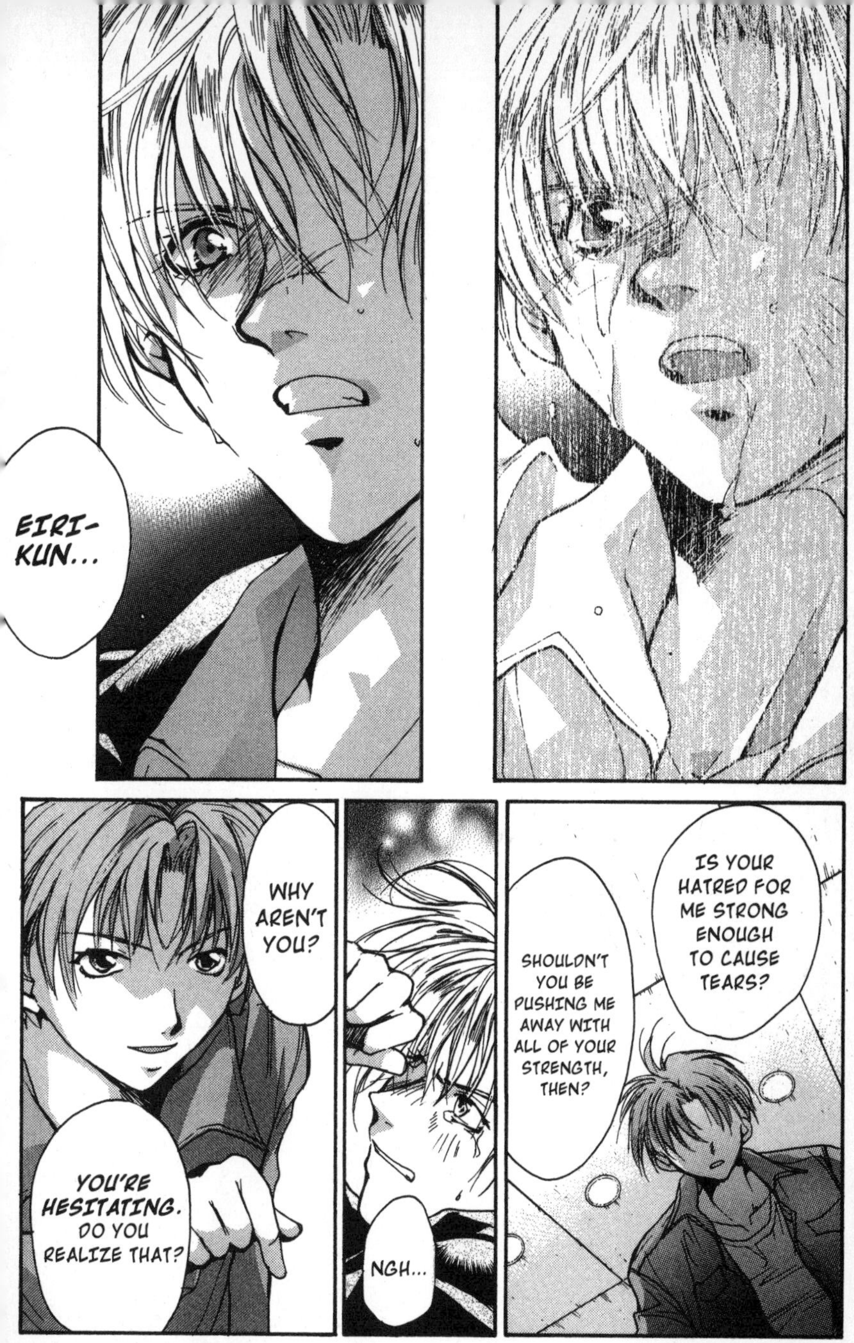
EIRI-KUN...
IS YOUR HATRED FOR ME STRONG ENOUGH TO CAUSE TEARS?
SHOULDN'T YOU BE PUSHING ME AWAY WITH ALL OF YOUR STRENGTH, THEN?
NGH...
WHY AREN'T YOU?
YOU'RE HESITATING. DO YOU REALIZE THAT?

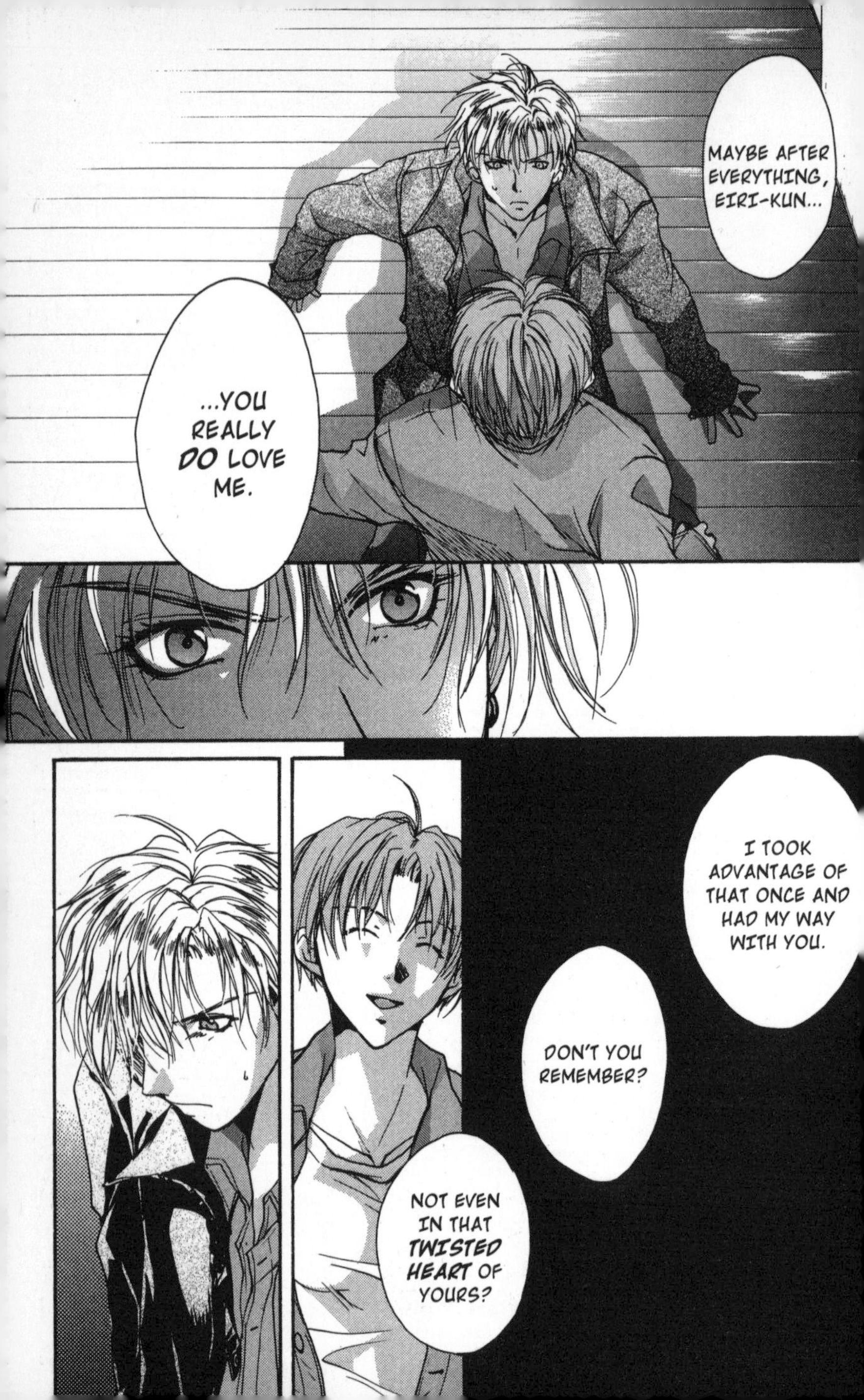
MAYBE AFTER EVERYTHING, EIRI-KUN...
...YOU REALLY DO LOVE ME.
I TOOK ADVANTAGE OF THAT ONCE AND HAD MY WAY WITH YOU.
DON'T YOU REMEMBER?
NOT EVEN IN THAT TWISTED HEART OF YOURS?

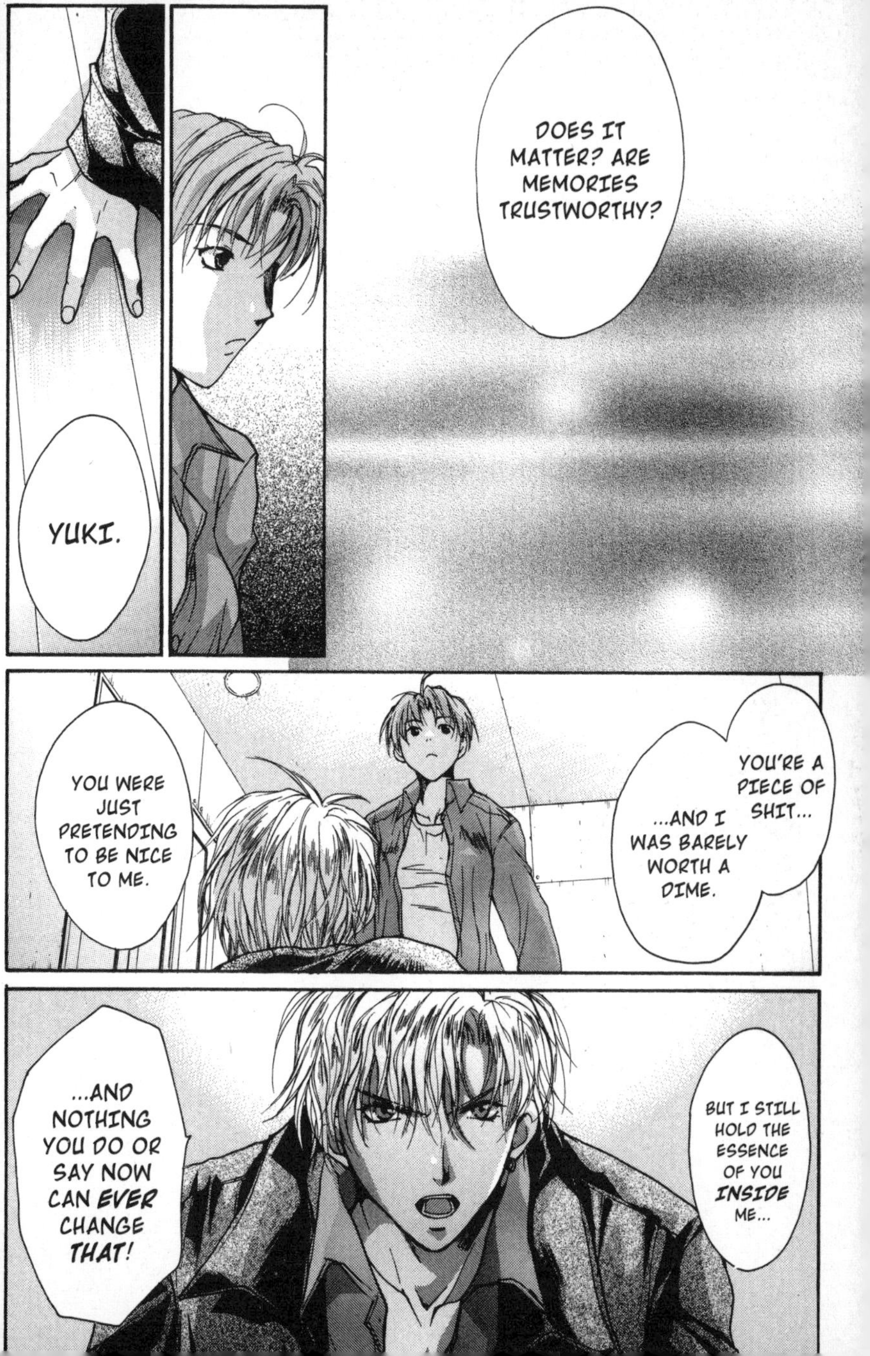
DOES IT MATTER? ARE MEMORIES TRUSTWORTHY?
YUKI.
YOU'RE A PIECE OF SHIT...
...AND I WAS BARELY WORTH A DIME.
YOU WERE JUST PRETENDING TO BE NICE TO ME.
BUT I STILL HOLD THE ESSENCE OF YOU *INSIDE* ME...
...AND NOTHING YOU DO OR SAY NOW CAN *EVER* CHANGE *THAT*!

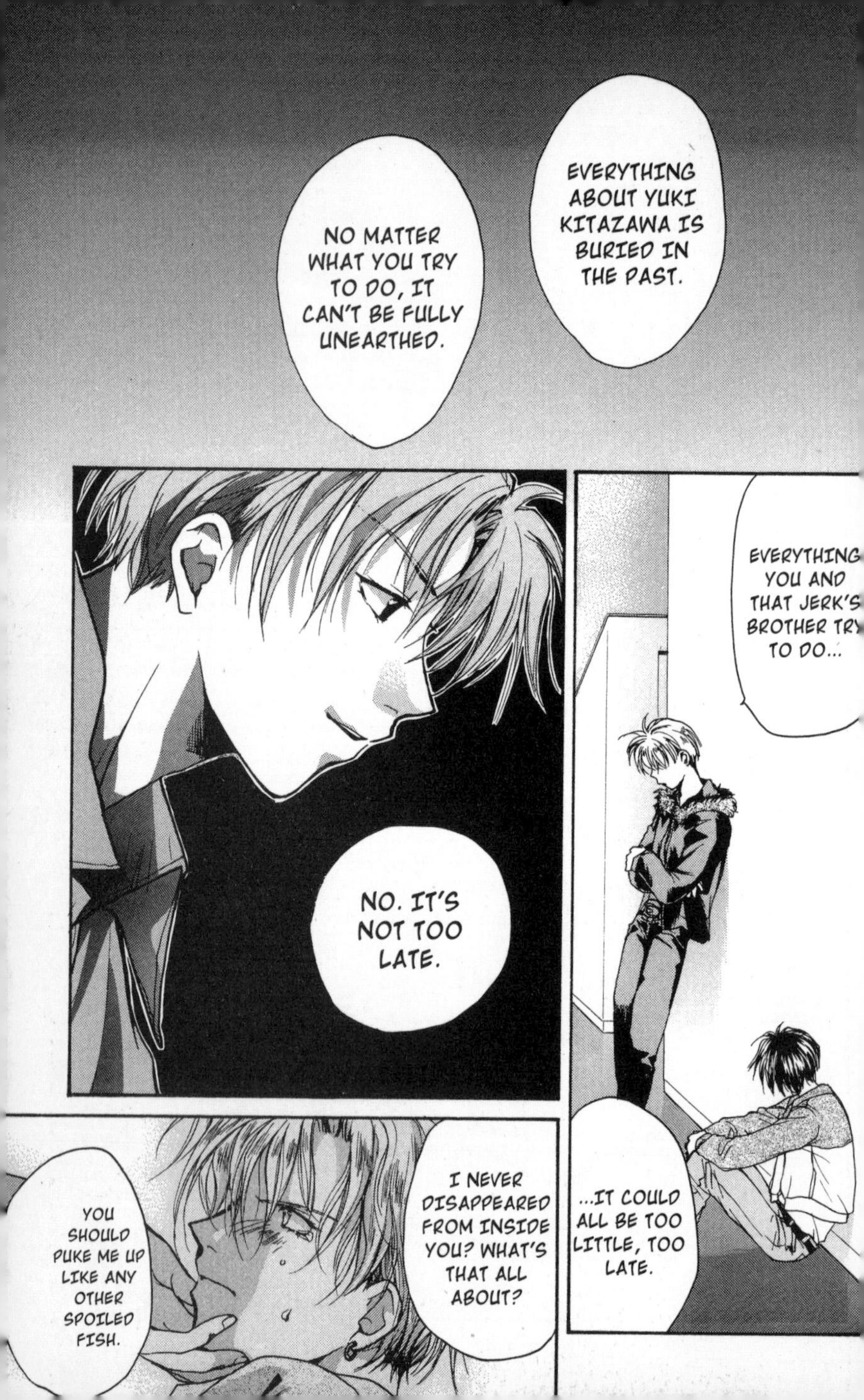
EVERYTHING ABOUT YUKI KITAZAWA IS BURIED IN THE PAST.
NO MATTER WHAT YOU TRY TO DO, IT CAN'T BE FULLY UNEARTHED.
EVERYTHING YOU AND THAT JERK'S BROTHER TRY TO DO...
...IT COULD ALL BE TOO LITTLE, TOO LATE.
NO. IT'S NOT TOO LATE.
I NEVER DISAPPEARED FROM INSIDE YOU? WHAT'S THAT ALL ABOUT?
YOU SHOULD PUKE ME UP LIKE ANY OTHER SPOILED FISH.

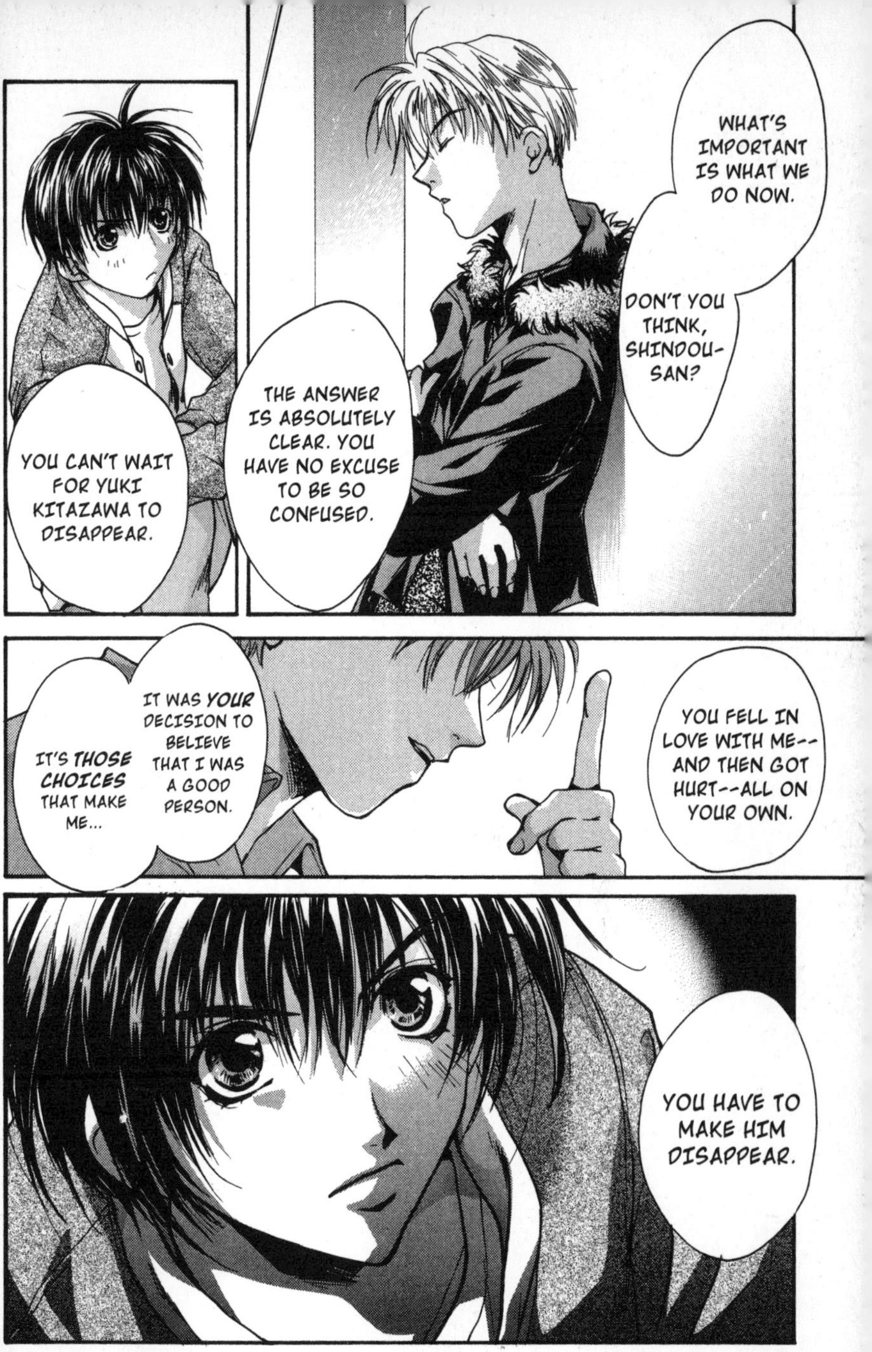
WHAT'S IMPORTANT IS WHAT WE DO NOW.
DON'T YOU THINK, SHINDOU-SAN?
THE ANSWER IS ABSOLUTELY CLEAR. YOU HAVE NO EXCUSE TO BE SO CONFUSED.
YOU CAN'T WAIT FOR YUKI KITAZAWA TO DISAPPEAR.
YOU FELL IN LOVE WITH ME--AND THEN GOT HURT--ALL ON YOUR OWN.
IT WAS *YOUR* DECISION TO BELIEVE THAT I WAS A GOOD PERSON.
IT'S *THOSE CHOICES* THAT MAKE ME...
YOU HAVE TO MAKE HIM DISAPPEAR.

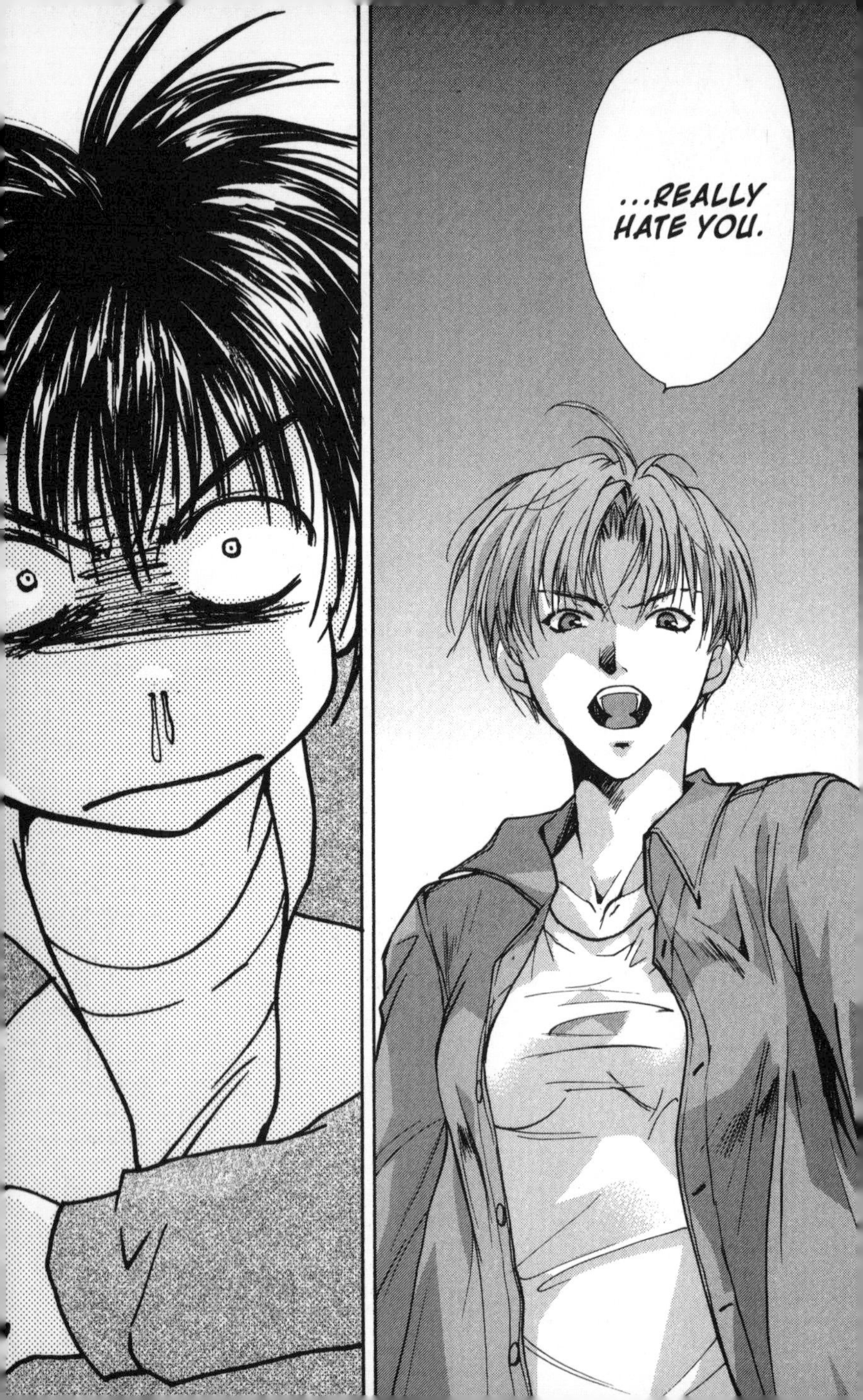
...REALLY HATE YOU.

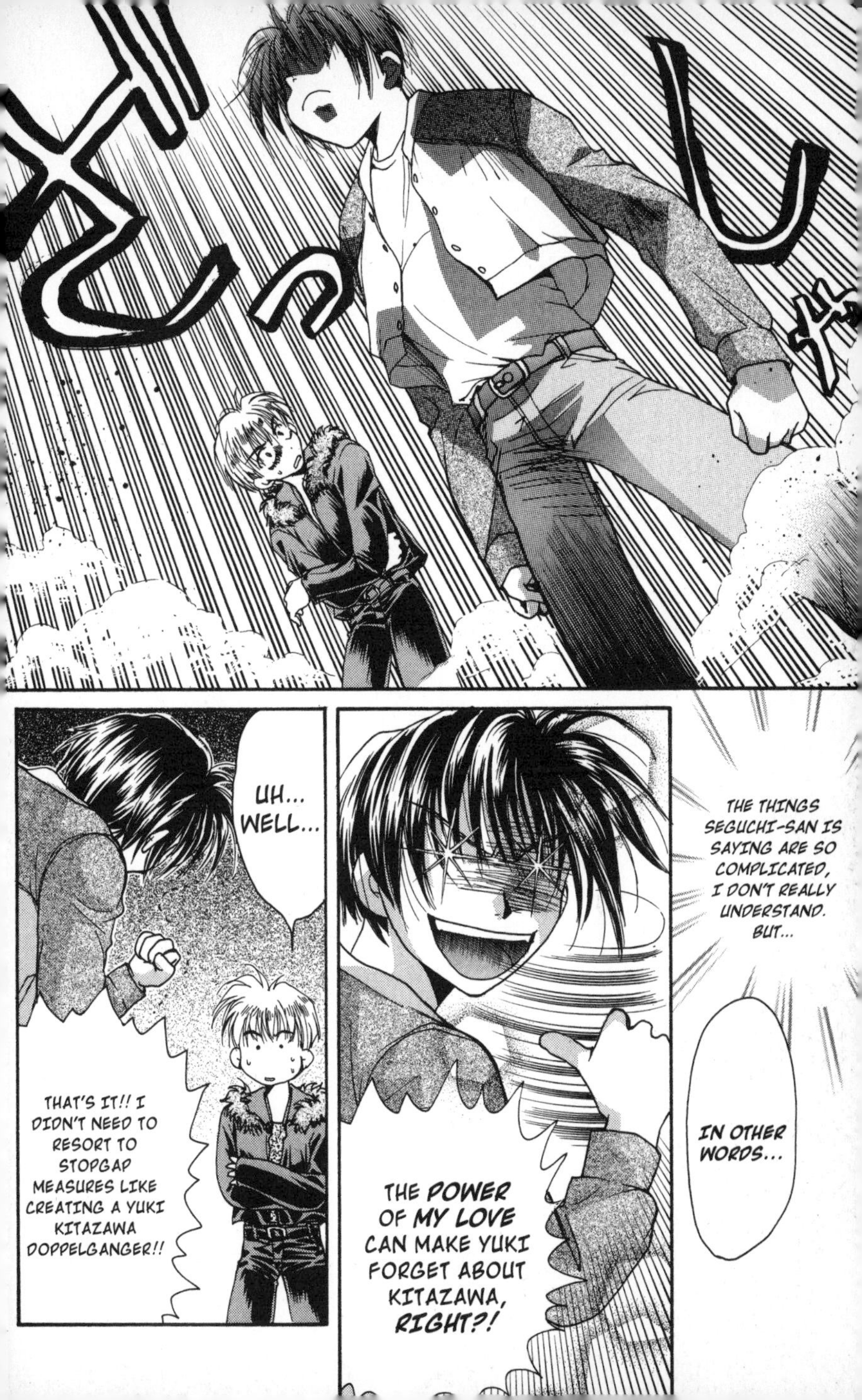
THE THINGS SEGUCHI-SAN IS SAYING ARE SO COMPLICATED, I DON'T REALLY UNDERSTAND. BUT...
IN OTHER WORDS...
THE *POWER* OF *MY LOVE* CAN MAKE YUKI FORGET ABOUT KITAZAWA, *RIGHT?!*
UH... WELL...
THAT'S IT!! I DIDN'T NEED TO RESORT TO STOPGAP MEASURES LIKE CREATING A YUKI KITAZAWA DOPPELGANGER!!

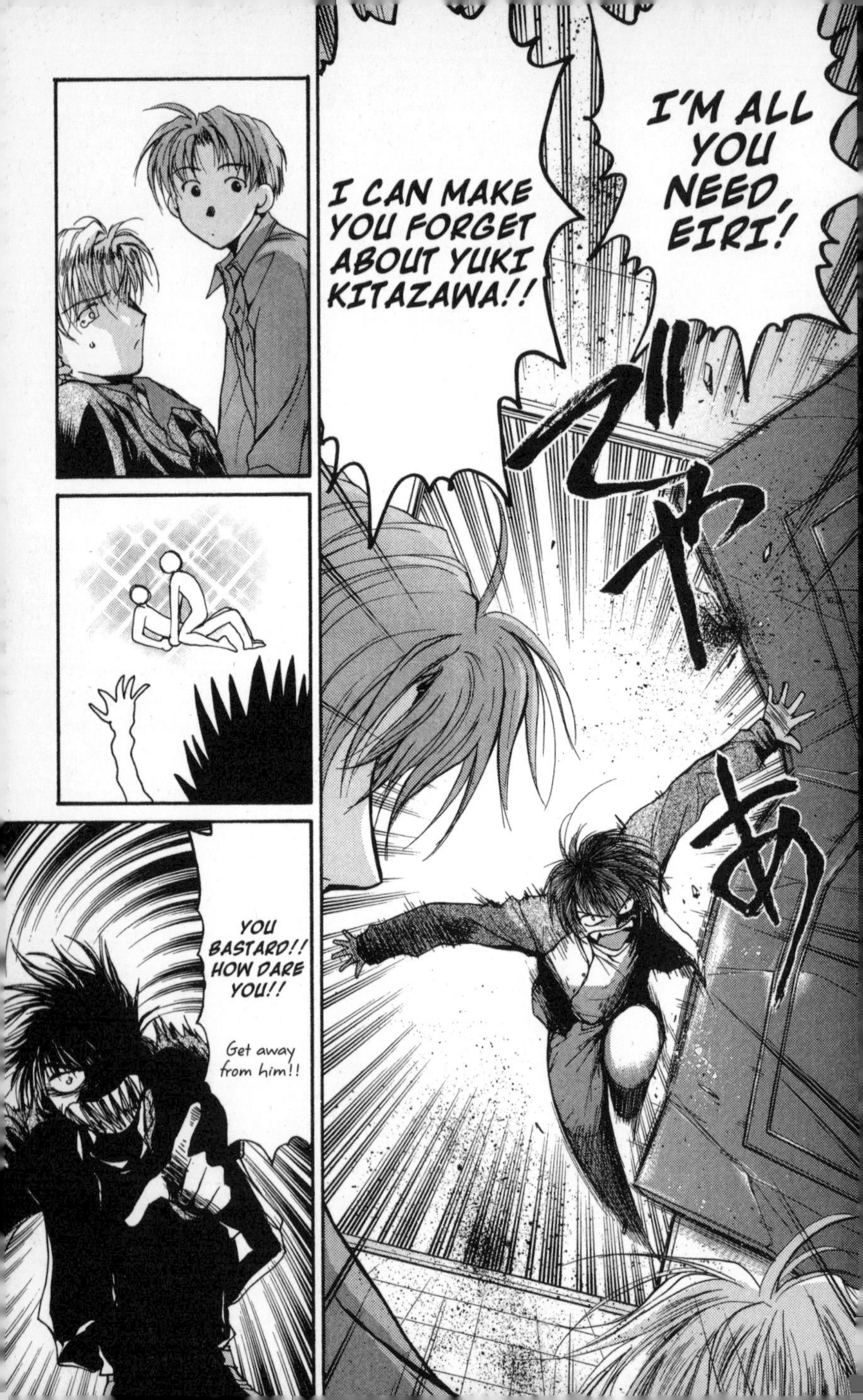
I'M ALL YOU NEED, EIRI!
I CAN MAKE YOU FORGET ABOUT YUKI KITAZAWA!!
YOU BASTARD!! HOW DARE YOU!!
Get away from him!!

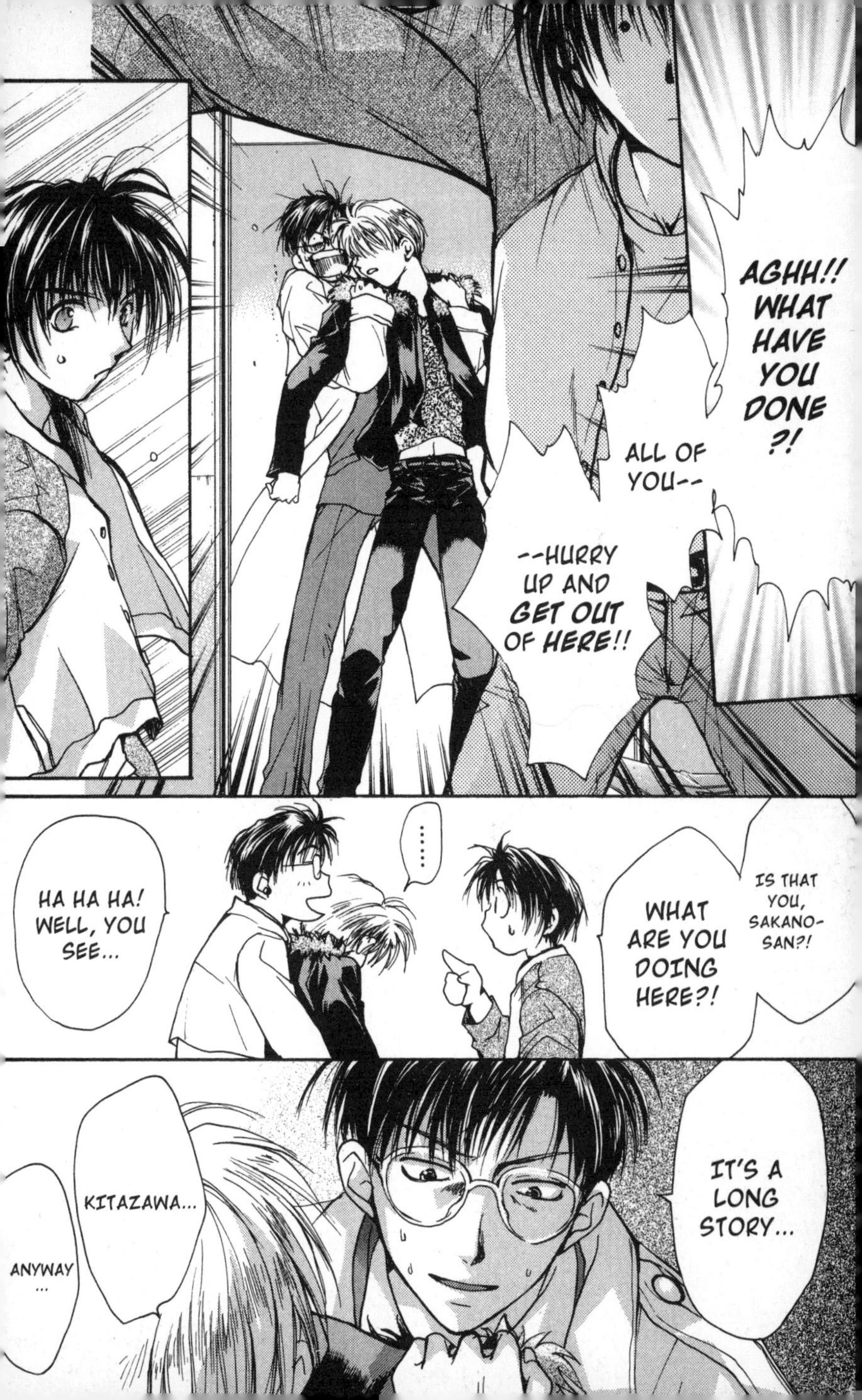
AGHH!! WHAT HAVE YOU DONE?!
ALL OF YOU--
--HURRY UP AND GET OUT OF HERE!!
IS THAT YOU, SAKANO-SAN?!
WHAT ARE YOU DOING HERE?!
......
HA HA HA! WELL, YOU SEE...
IT'S A LONG STORY...
KITAZAWA...
ANYWAY...

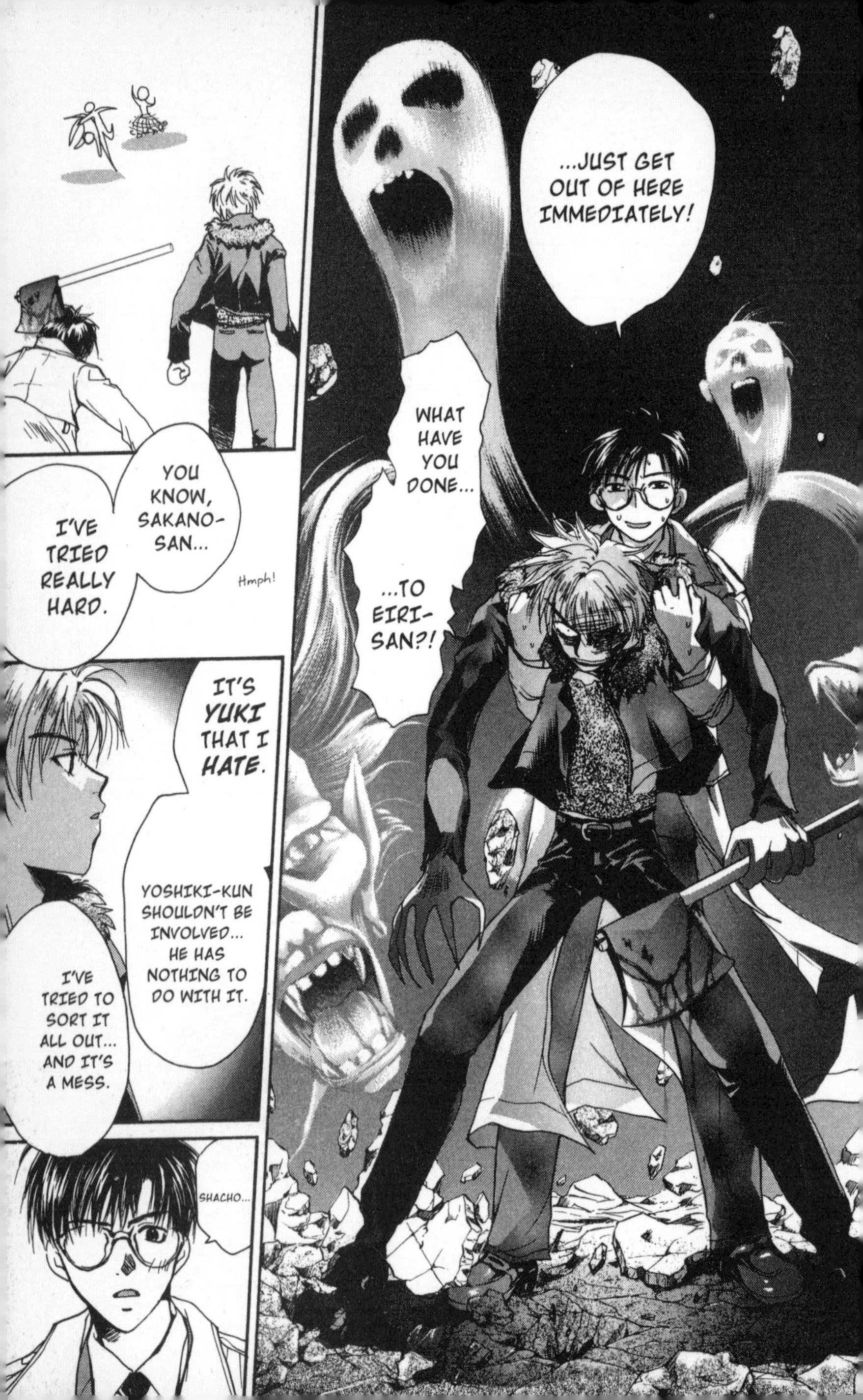
...JUST GET OUT OF HERE IMMEDIATELY!
WHAT HAVE YOU DONE...
...TO EIRI-SAN?!
YOU KNOW, SAKANO-SAN...
I'VE TRIED REALLY HARD.
Hmph!
IT'S *YUKI* THAT I *HATE*.
YOSHIKI-KUN SHOULDN'T BE INVOLVED... HE HAS NOTHING TO DO WITH IT.
I'VE TRIED TO SORT IT ALL OUT... AND IT'S A MESS.
SHACHO...

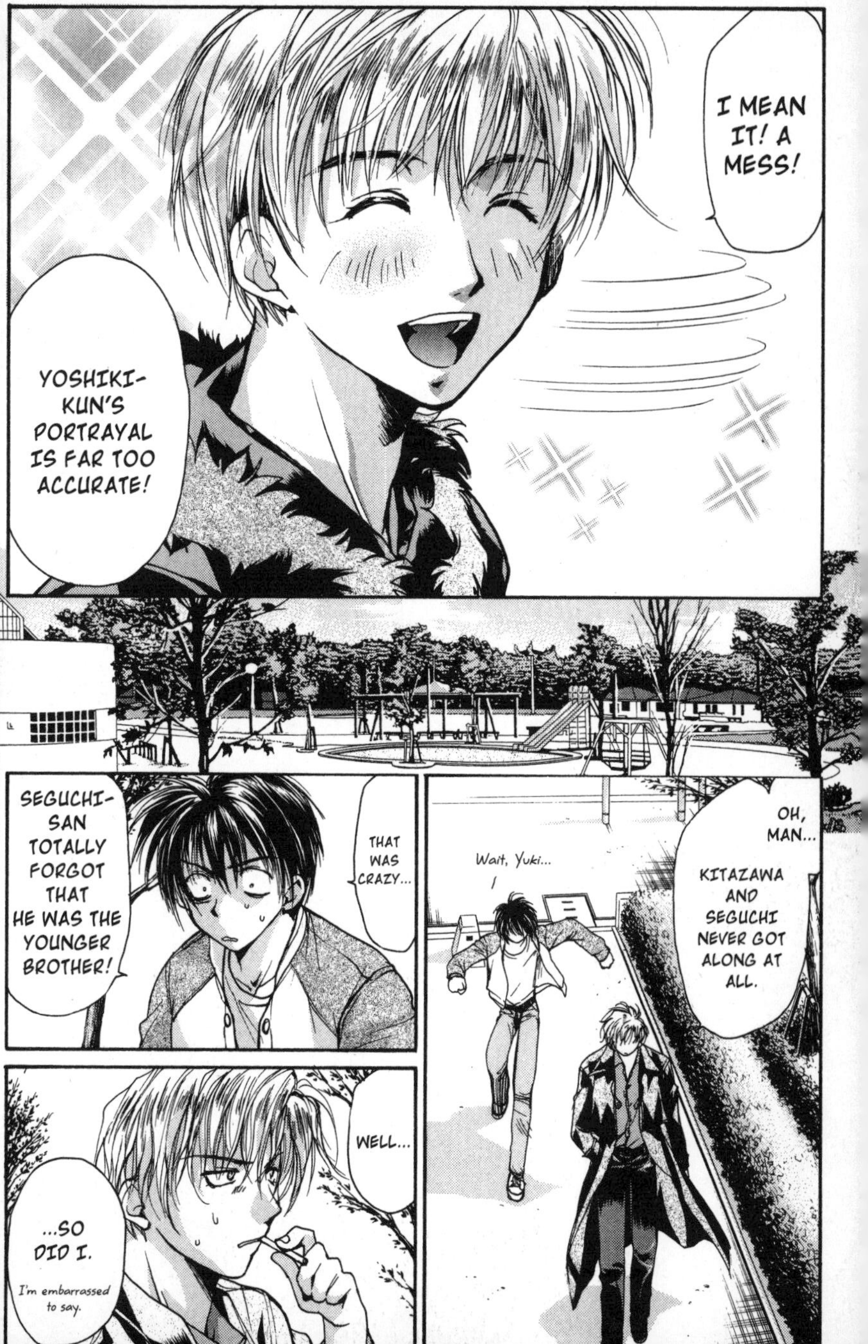
I MEAN IT! A MESS!
YOSHIKI-KUN'S PORTRAYAL IS FAR TOO ACCURATE!
OH, MAN...
KITAZAWA AND SEGUCHI NEVER GOT ALONG AT ALL.
Wait, Yuki...
THAT WAS CRAZY...
SEGUCHI-SAN TOTALLY FORGOT THAT HE WAS THE YOUNGER BROTHER!
WELL...
...SO DID I.
I'm embarrassed to say.

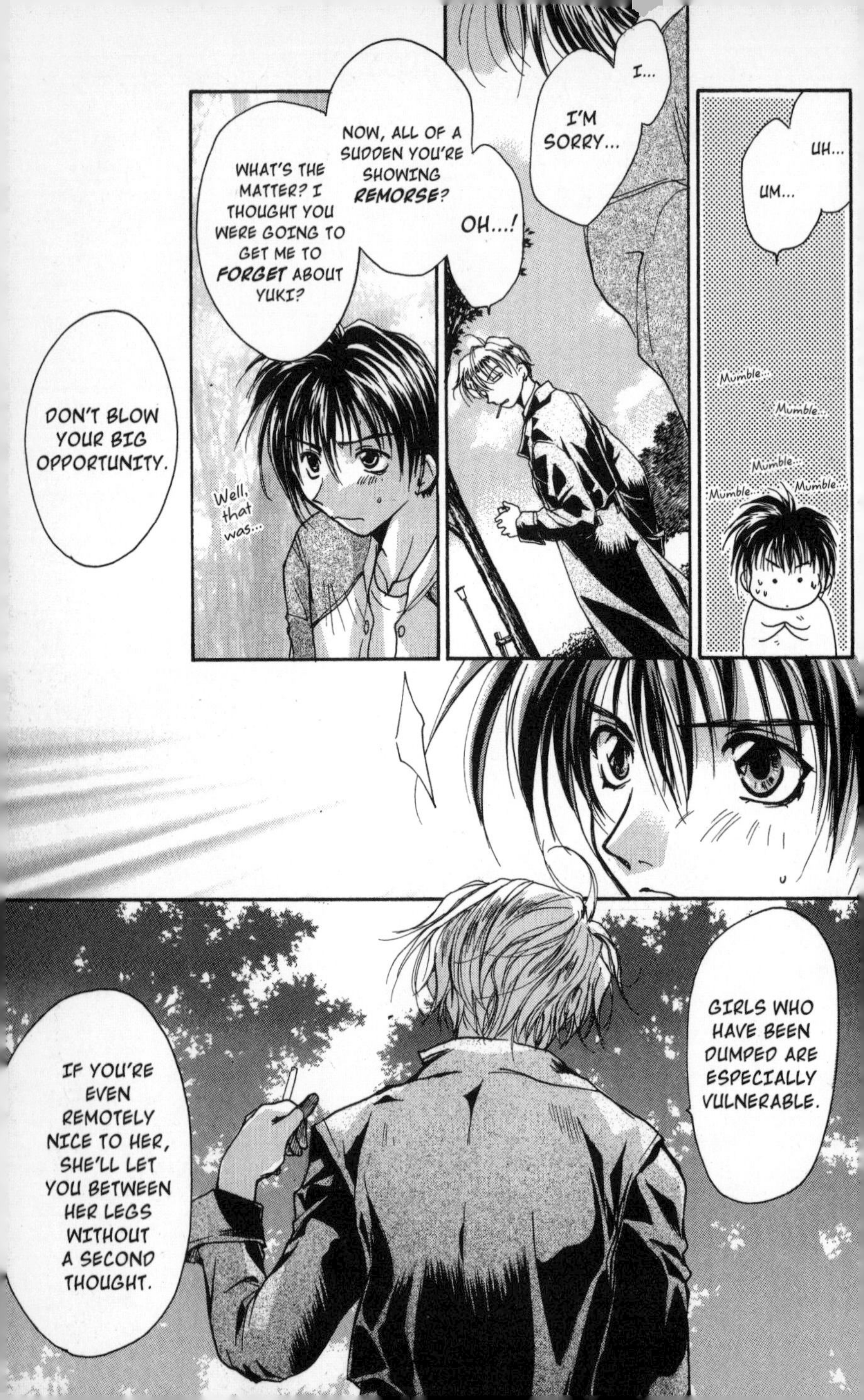
UH...
UM...
Mumble... Mumble... Mumble... Mumble... Mumble...
I...
I'M SORRY...
OH...!
NOW, ALL OF A SUDDEN YOU'RE SHOWING REMORSE?
WHAT'S THE MATTER? I THOUGHT YOU WERE GOING TO GET ME TO FORGET ABOUT YUKI?
Well, that was...
DON'T BLOW YOUR BIG OPPORTUNITY.
GIRLS WHO HAVE BEEN DUMPED ARE ESPECIALLY VULNERABLE.
IF YOU'RE EVEN REMOTELY NICE TO HER, SHE'LL LET YOU BETWEEN HER LEGS WITHOUT A SECOND THOUGHT.

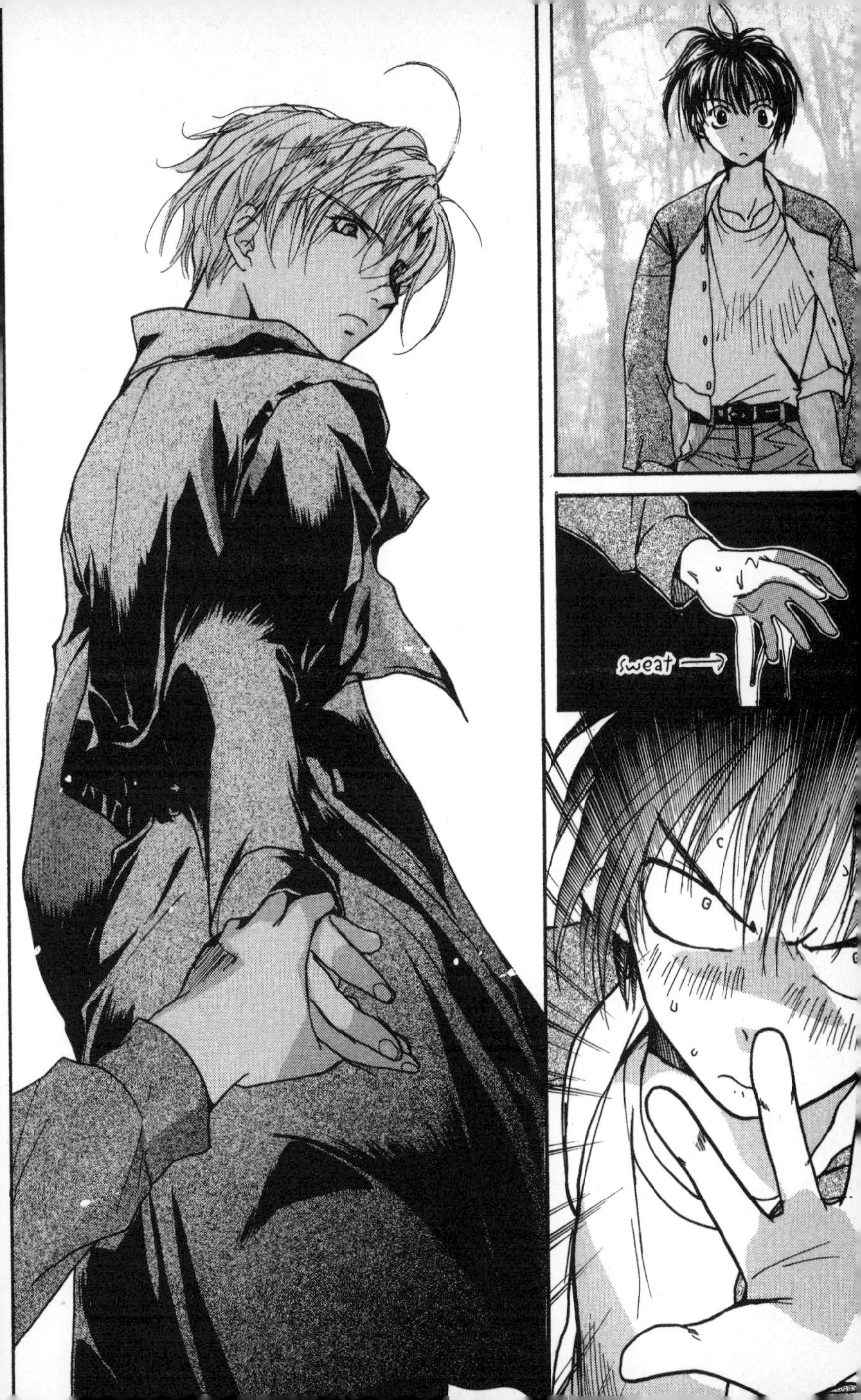
sweat

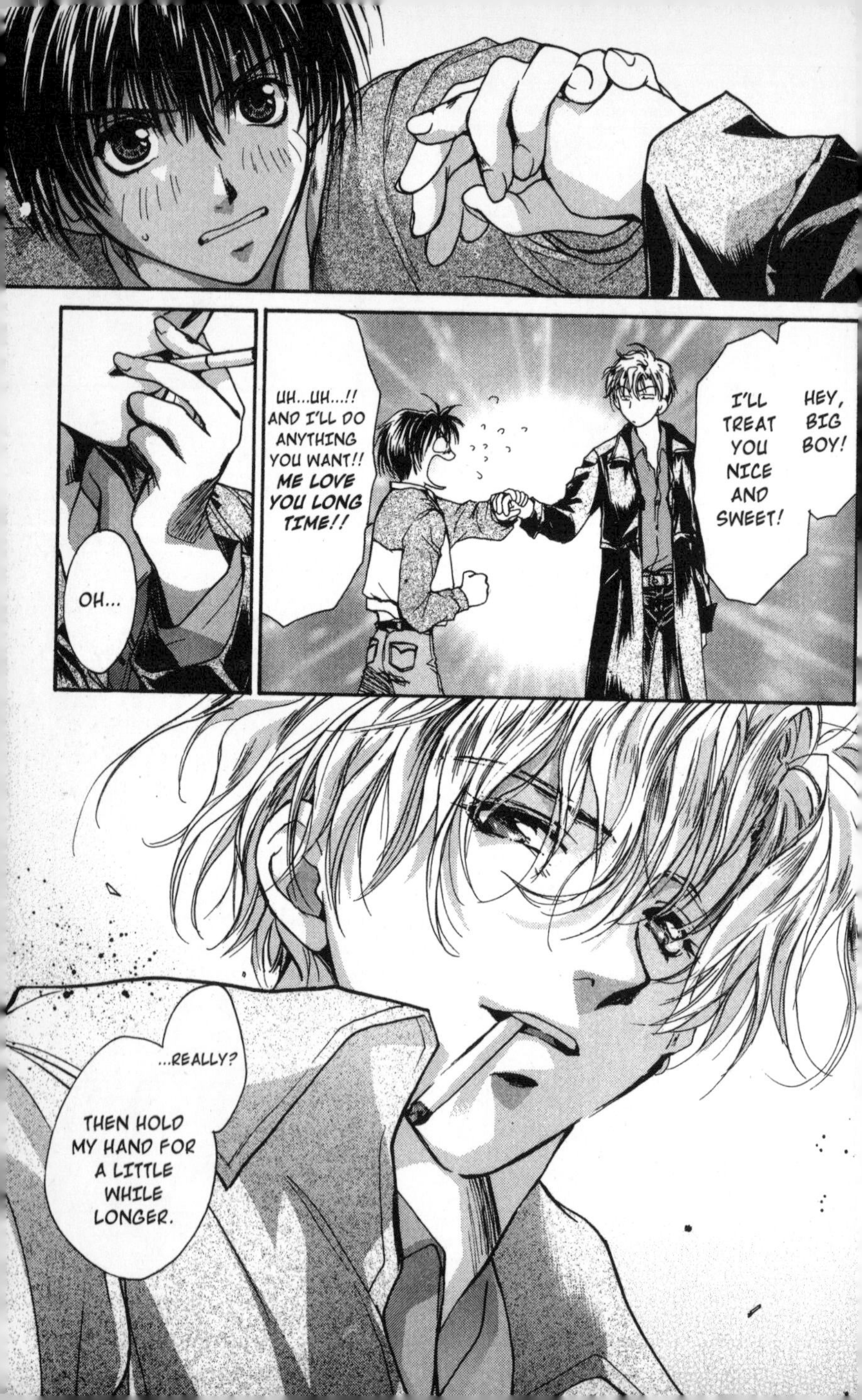
HEY, BIG BOY! I'LL TREAT YOU NICE AND SWEET!
UH...UH...!! AND I'LL DO ANYTHING YOU WANT!! ME LOVE YOU LONG TIME!!
OH...
...REALLY?
THEN HOLD MY HAND FOR A LITTLE WHILE LONGER.

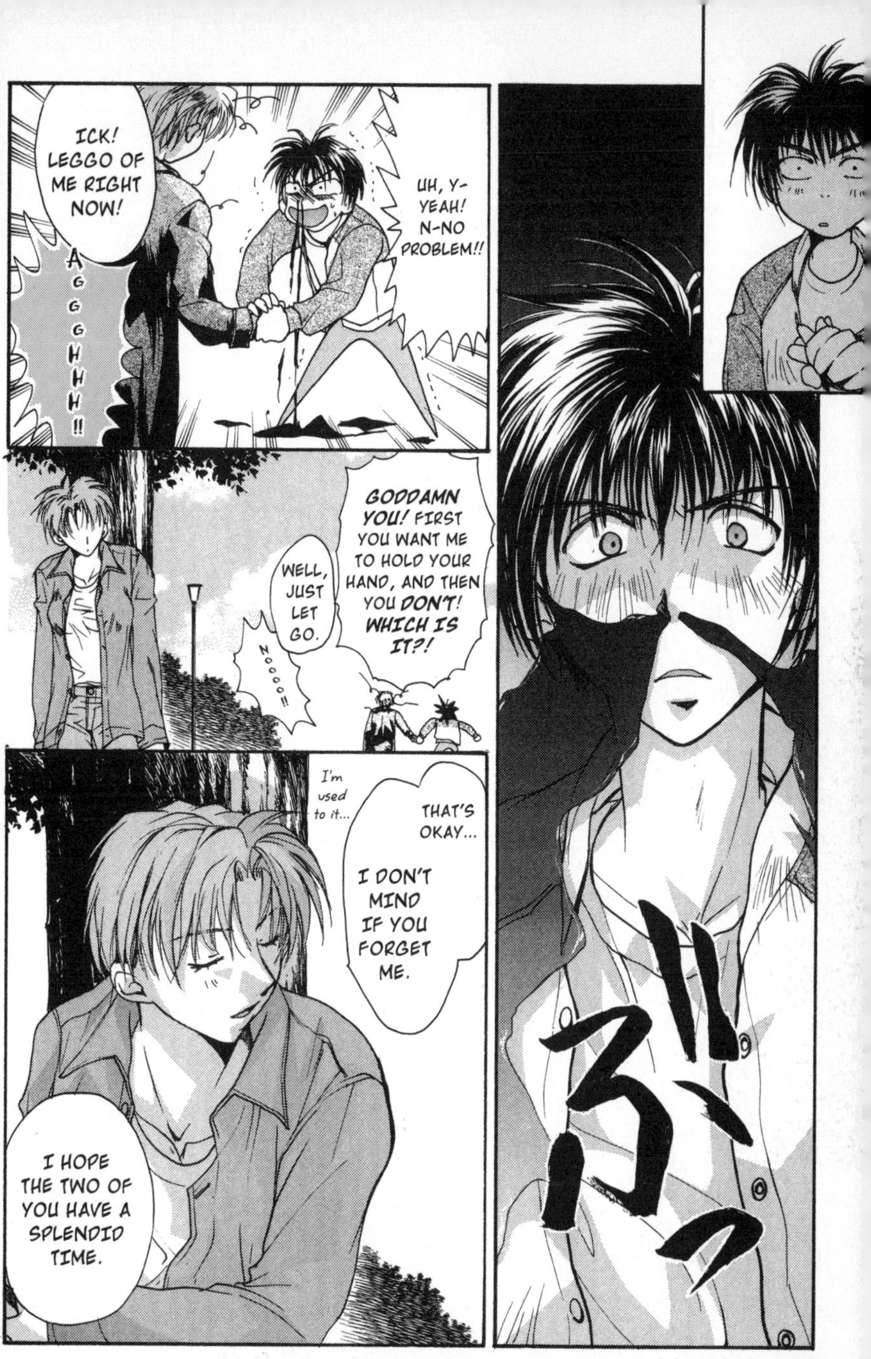
ぶっ
UH, Y-YEAH! N-NO PROBLEM!!
ICK! LEGGO OF ME RIGHT NOW!
AGGGHHHH!!
GODDAMN YOU! FIRST YOU WANT ME TO HOLD YOUR HAND, AND THEN YOU DON'T! WHICH IS IT?!
WELL, JUST LET GO.
NOOOOO!!
THAT'S OKAY... I DON'T MIND IF YOU FORGET ME.
I'm used to it...
I HOPE THE TWO OF YOU HAVE A SPLENDID TIME.

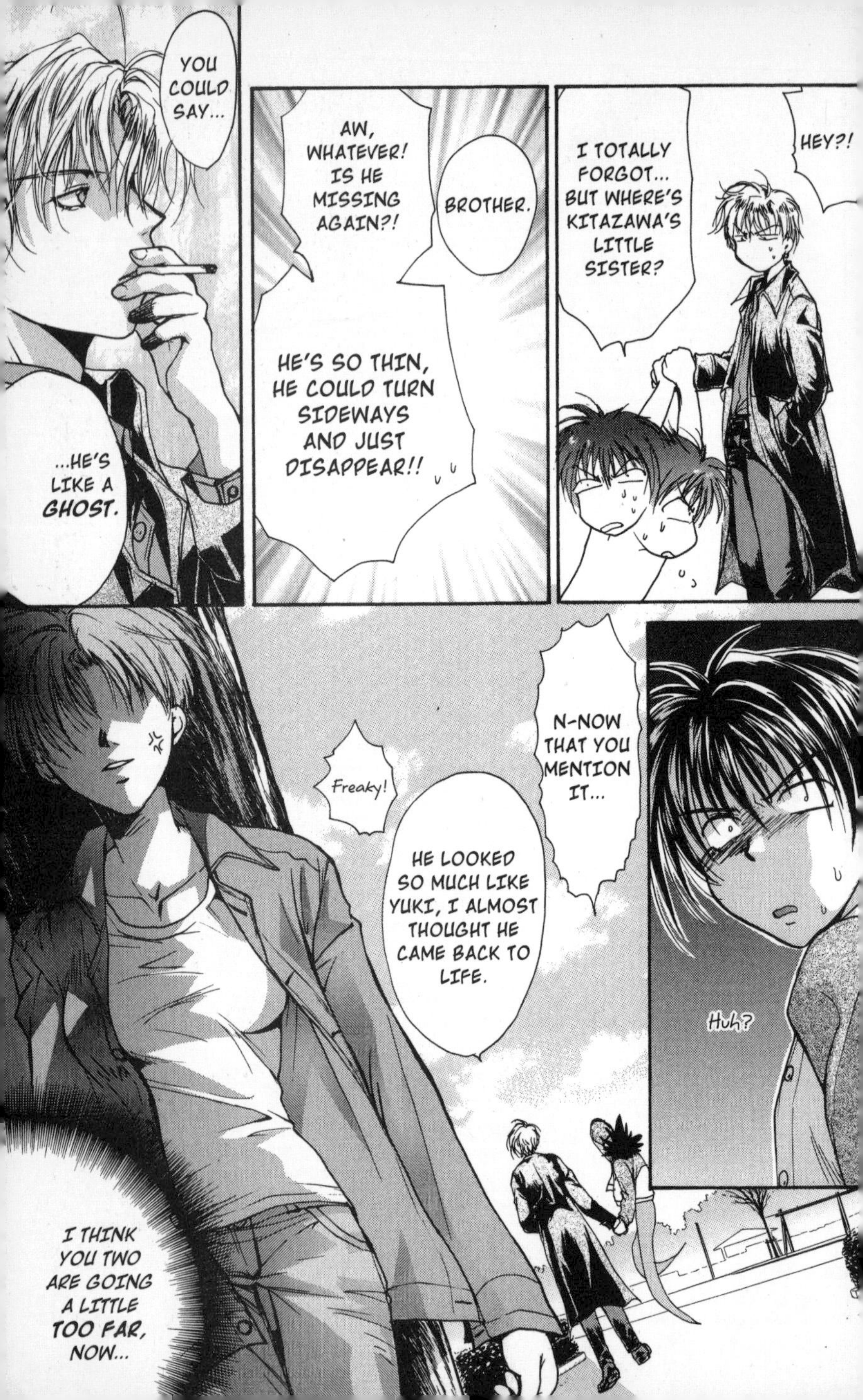
HEY?!
I TOTALLY FORGOT... BUT WHERE'S KITAZAWA'S LITTLE SISTER?
BROTHER.
AW, WHATEVER! IS HE MISSING AGAIN?!
HE'S SO THIN, HE COULD TURN SIDEWAYS AND JUST DISAPPEAR!!
YOU COULD SAY...
...HE'S LIKE A GHOST.
N-NOW THAT YOU MENTION IT...
Huh?
HE LOOKED SO MUCH LIKE YUKI, I ALMOST THOUGHT HE CAME BACK TO LIFE.
Freaky!
I THINK YOU TWO ARE GOING A LITTLE TOO FAR, NOW...

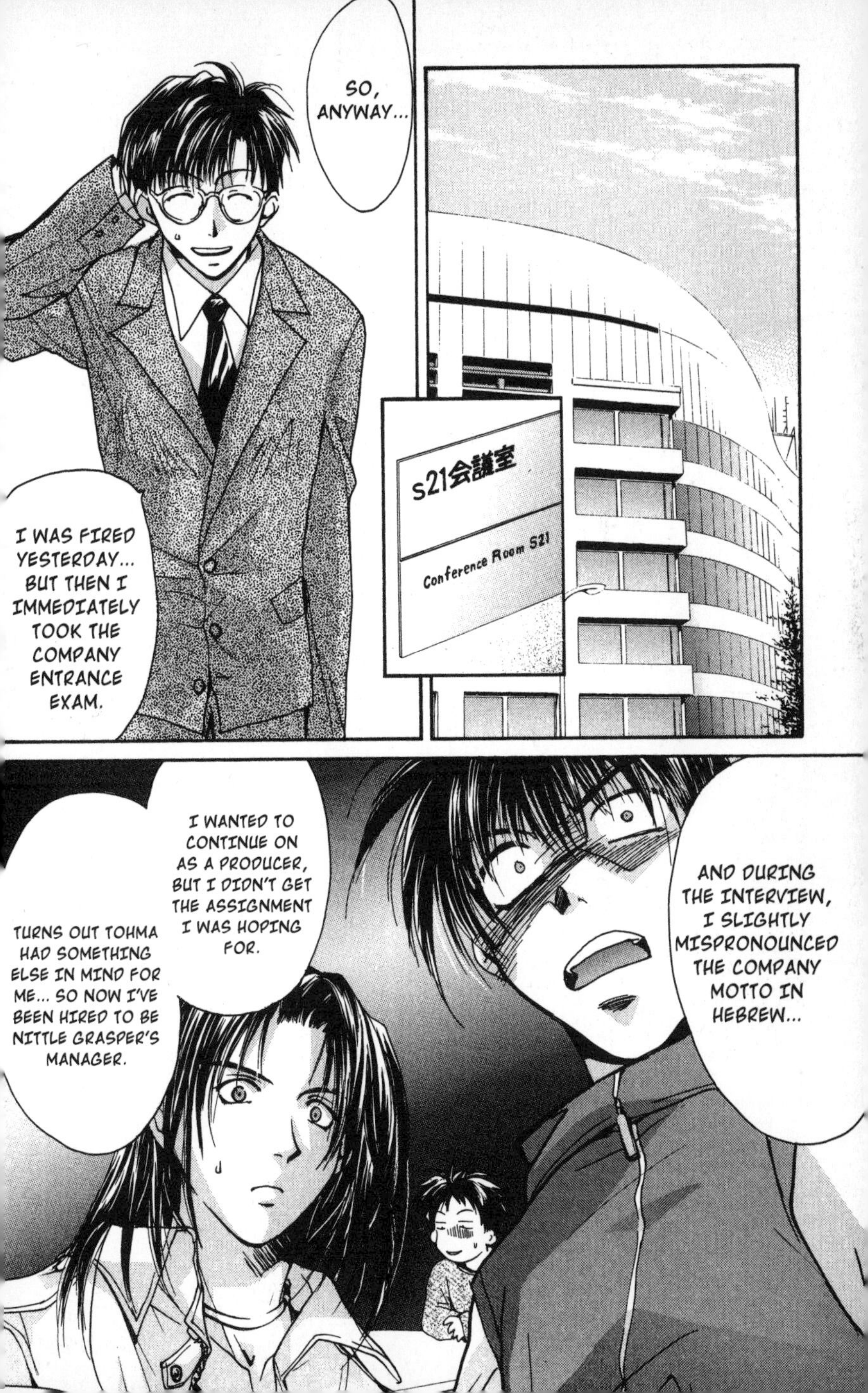
s21会議室
Conference Room S21
SO, ANYWAY...
I WAS FIRED YESTERDAY... BUT THEN I IMMEDIATELY TOOK THE COMPANY ENTRANCE EXAM.
AND DURING THE INTERVIEW, I SLIGHTLY MISPRONOUNCED THE COMPANY MOTTO IN HEBREW...
I WANTED TO CONTINUE ON AS A PRODUCER, BUT I DIDN'T GET THE ASSIGNMENT I WAS HOPING FOR.
TURNS OUT TOHMA HAD SOMETHING ELSE IN MIND FOR ME... SO NOW I'VE BEEN HIRED TO BE NITTLE GRASPER'S MANAGER.

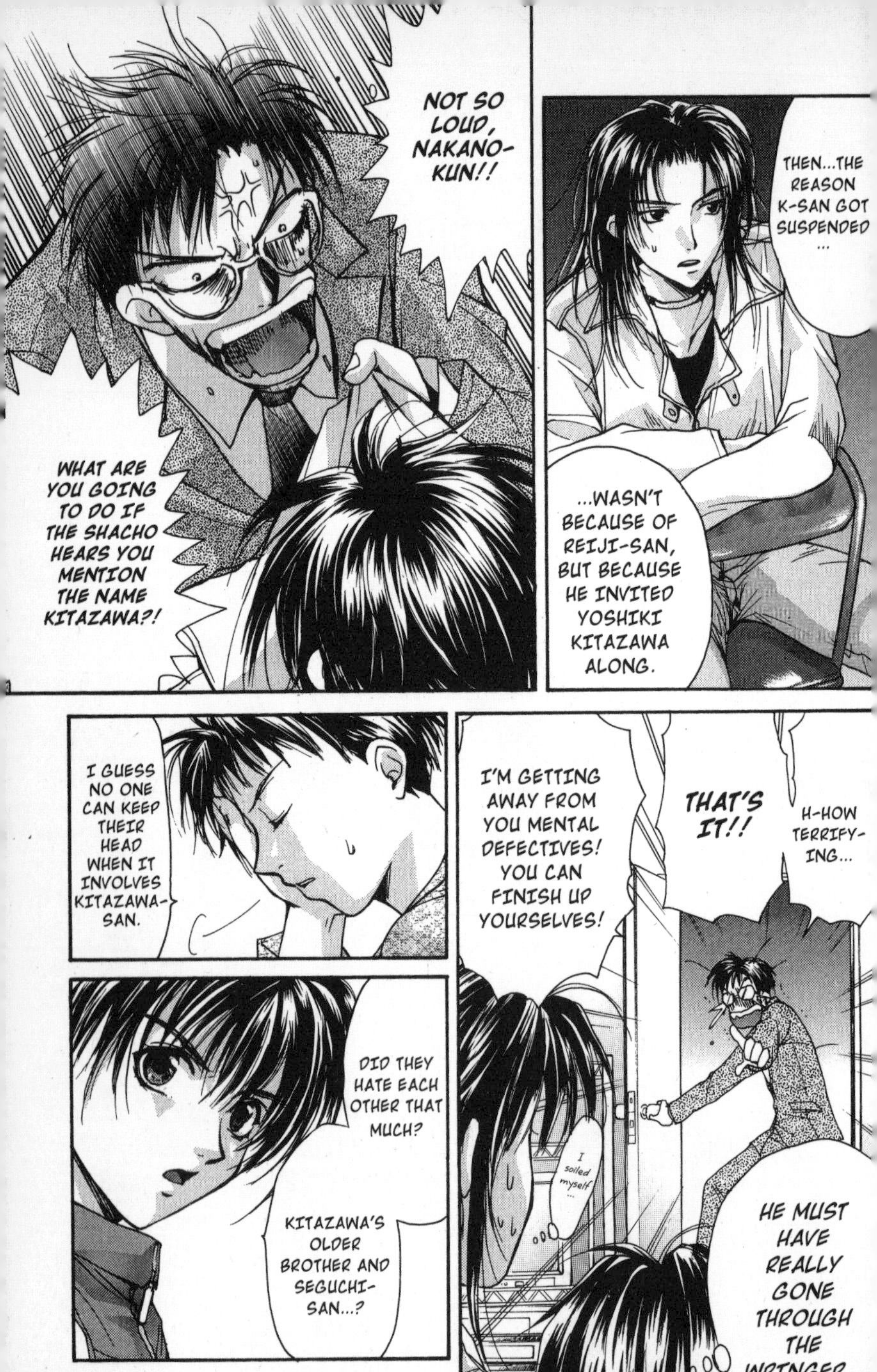
THEN...THE REASON K-SAN GOT SUSPENDED ...
...WASN'T BECAUSE OF REIJI-SAN, BUT BECAUSE HE INVITED YOSHIKI KITAZAWA ALONG.
NOT SO LOUD, NAKANO-KUN!!
WHAT ARE YOU GOING TO DO IF THE SHACHO HEARS YOU MENTION THE NAME KITAZAWA?!
H-HOW TERRIFYING...
THAT'S IT!!
I'M GETTING AWAY FROM YOU MENTAL DEFECTIVES! YOU CAN FINISH UP YOURSELVES!
I soiled myself ...
HE MUST HAVE REALLY GONE THROUGH THE WRINGER...
I GUESS NO ONE CAN KEEP THEIR HEAD WHEN IT INVOLVES KITAZAWA-SAN.
DID THEY HATE EACH OTHER THAT MUCH?
KITAZAWA'S OLDER BROTHER AND SEGUCHI-SAN...?

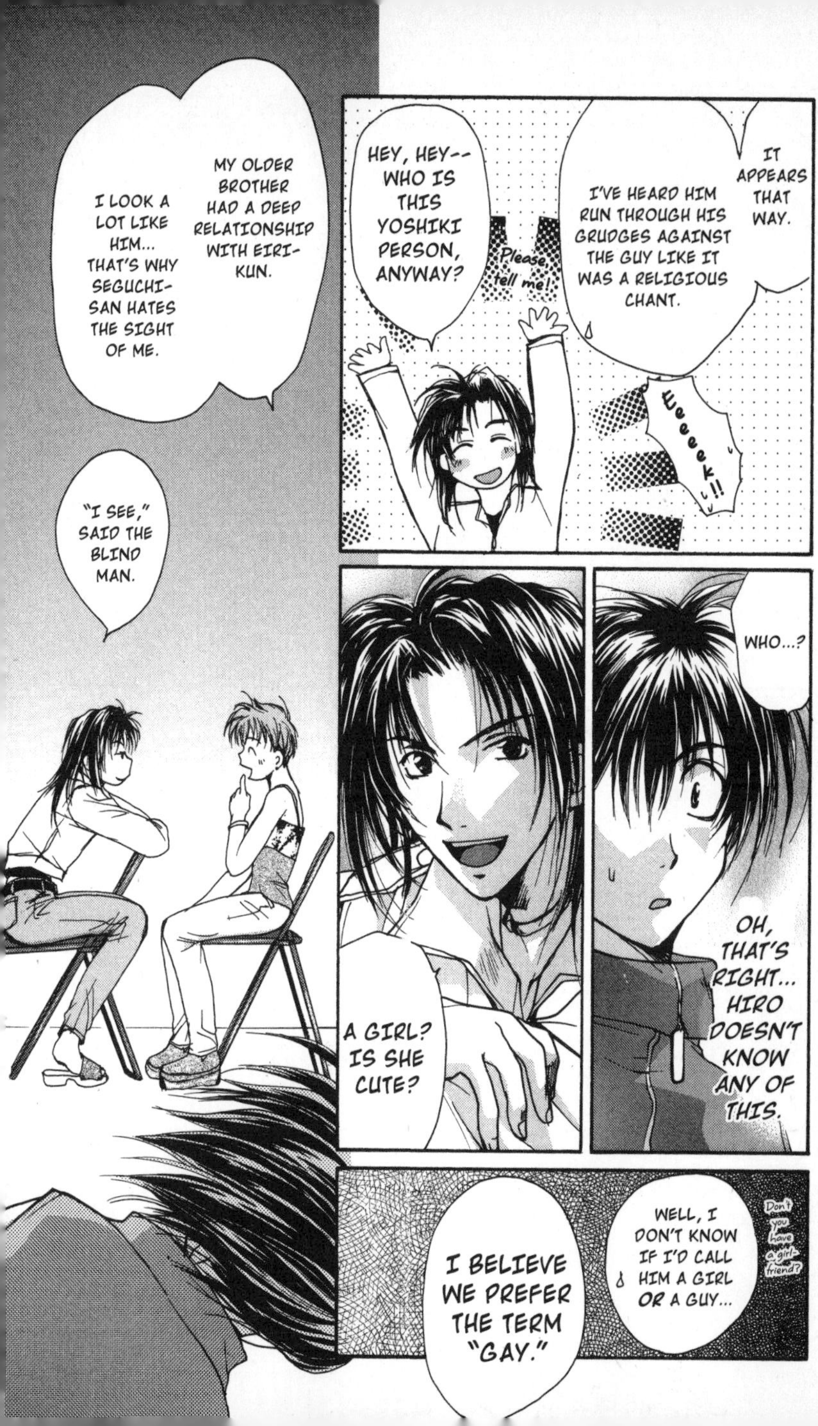
IT APPEARS THAT WAY.
I'VE HEARD HIM RUN THROUGH HIS GRUDGES AGAINST THE GUY LIKE IT WAS A RELIGIOUS CHANT.
HEY, HEY-- WHO IS THIS YOSHIKI PERSON, ANYWAY?
Please, tell me!
Weeeek!!
WHO...?
OH, THAT'S RIGHT... HIRO DOESN'T KNOW ANY OF THIS.
A GIRL? IS SHE CUTE?
Don't you have a girl-friend?
WELL, I DON'T KNOW IF I'D CALL HIM A GIRL OR A GUY...
I BELIEVE WE PREFER THE TERM "GAY."
MY OLDER BROTHER HAD A DEEP RELATIONSHIP WITH EIRI-KUN.
I LOOK A LOT LIKE HIM... THAT'S WHY SEGUCHI-SAN HATES THE SIGHT OF ME.
"I SEE," SAID THE BLIND MAN.

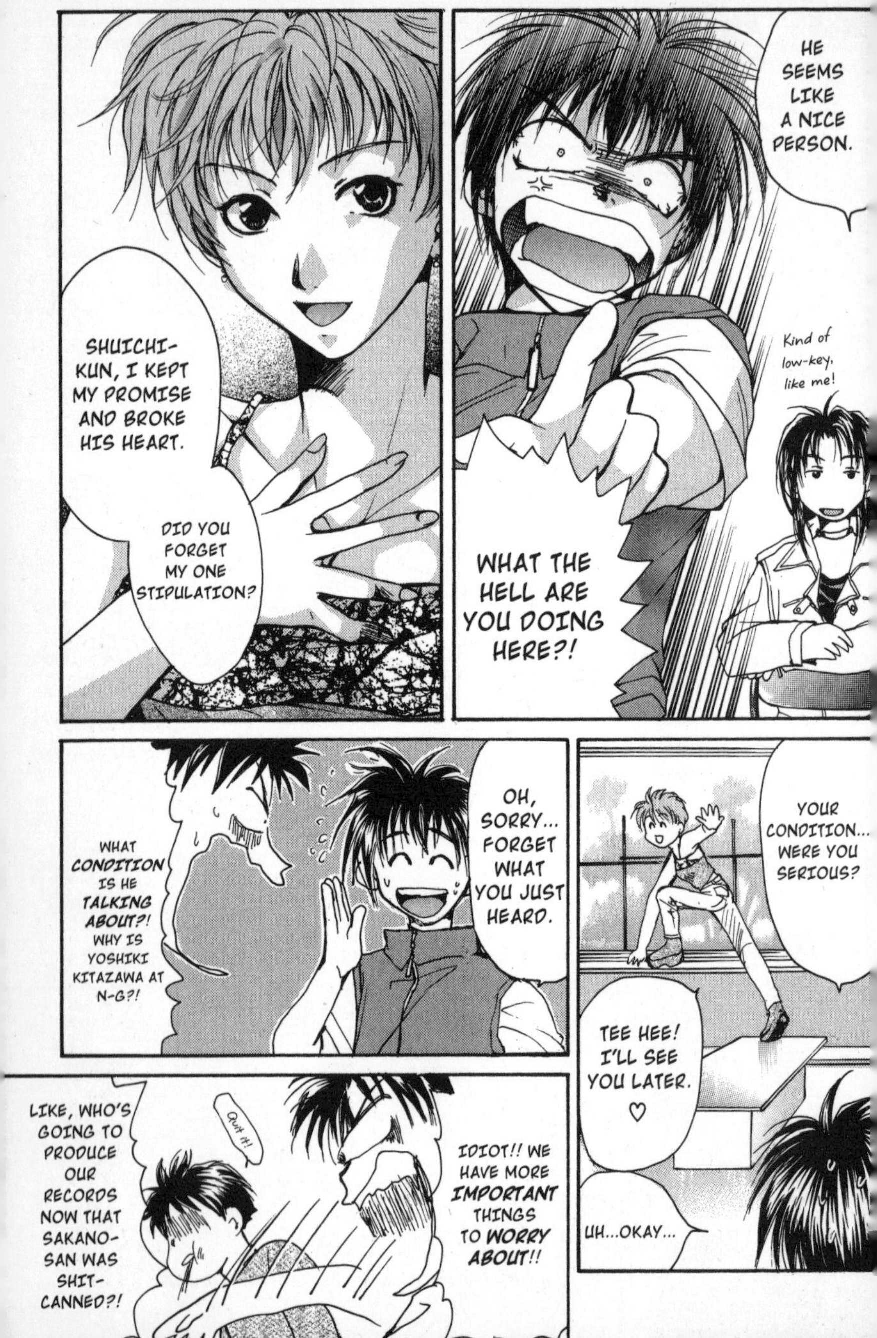
HE SEEMS LIKE A NICE PERSON.
Kind of low-key, like me!
WHAT THE HELL ARE YOU DOING HERE?!
SHUICHI-KUN, I KEPT MY PROMISE AND BROKE HIS HEART.
DID YOU FORGET MY ONE STIPULATION?
YOUR CONDITION... WERE YOU SERIOUS?
TEE HEE! I'LL SEE YOU LATER. ♡
UH...OKAY...
OH, SORRY... FORGET WHAT YOU JUST HEARD.
WHAT CONDITION IS HE TALKING ABOUT?! WHY IS YOSHIKI KITAZAWA AT N-G?!
IDIOT!! WE HAVE MORE IMPORTANT THINGS TO WORRY ABOUT!!
Quit it!
LIKE, WHO'S GOING TO PRODUCE OUR RECORDS NOW THAT SAKANO-SAN WAS SHIT-CANNED?!

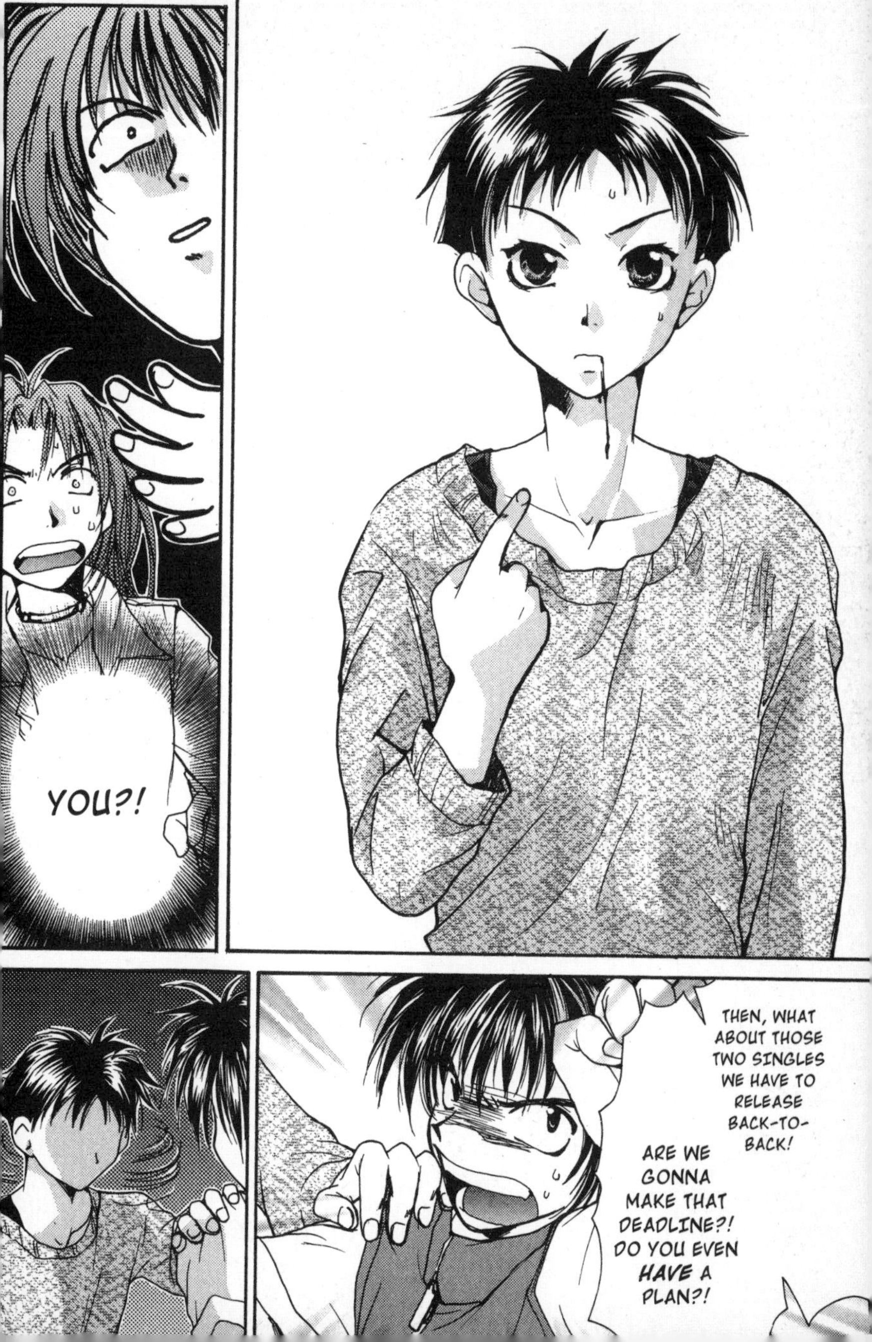
YOU?!
THEN, WHAT ABOUT THOSE TWO SINGLES WE HAVE TO RELEASE BACK-TO-BACK!
ARE WE GONNA MAKE THAT DEADLINE?! DO YOU EVEN **HAVE** A PLAN?!

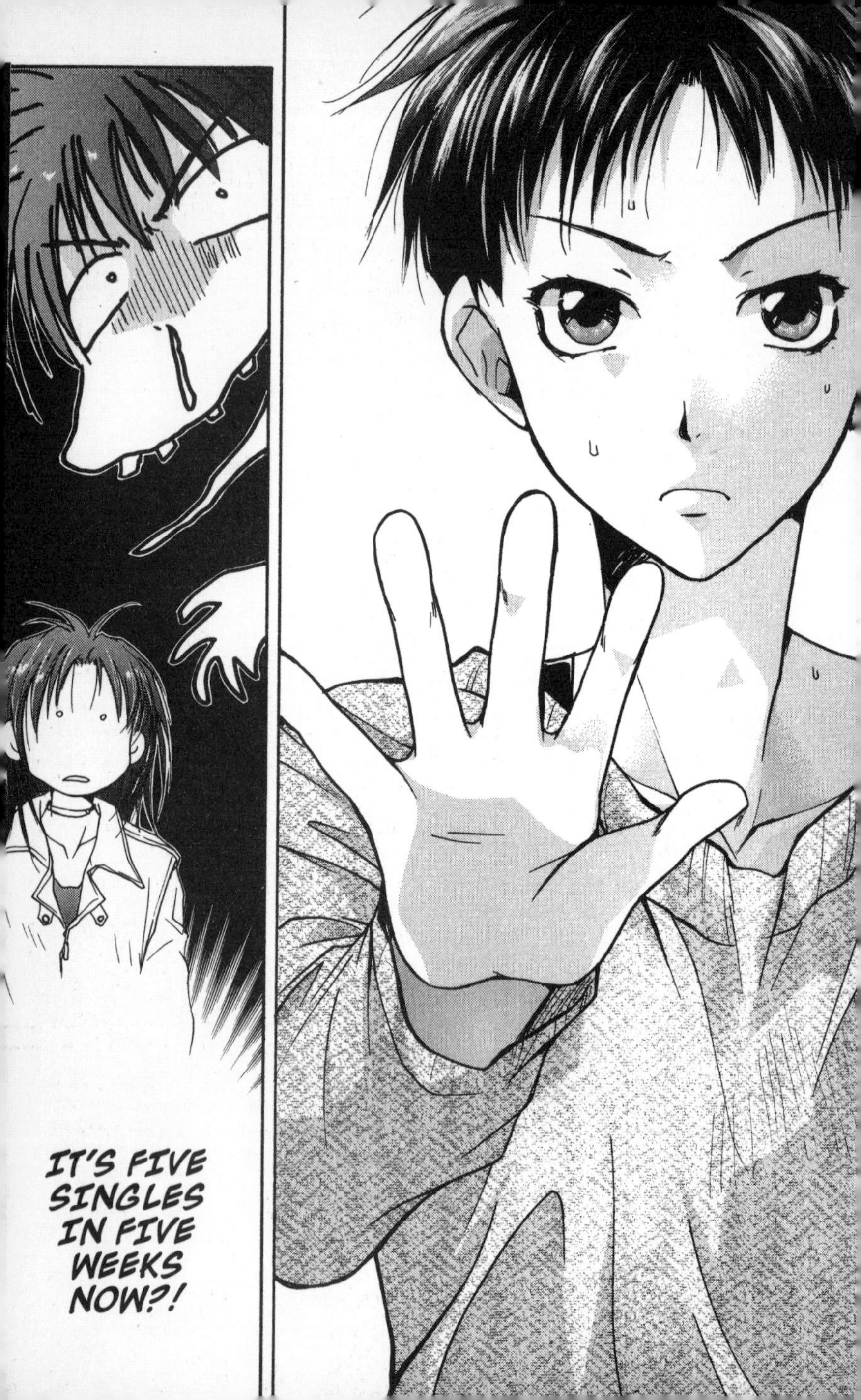
IT'S FIVE SINGLES IN FIVE WEEKS NOW?!

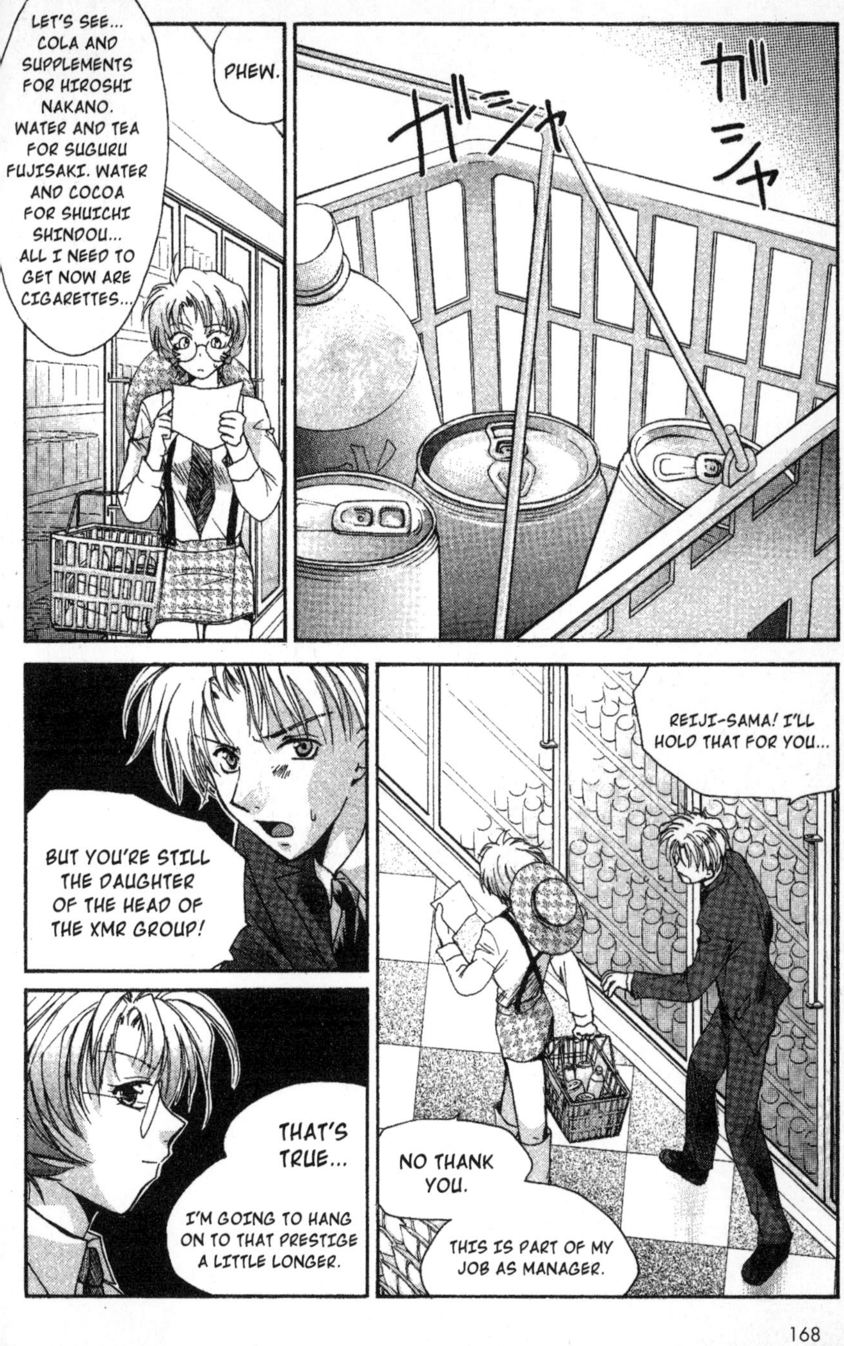
ガシャ
ガシャ
PHEW.
LET'S SEE... COLA AND SUPPLEMENTS FOR HIROSHI NAKANO. WATER AND TEA FOR SUGURU FUJISAKI. WATER AND COCOA FOR SHUICHI SHINDOU... ALL I NEED TO GET NOW ARE CIGARETTES...
REIJI-SAMA! I'LL HOLD THAT FOR YOU...
NO THANK YOU.
THIS IS PART OF MY JOB AS MANAGER.
BUT YOU'RE STILL THE DAUGHTER OF THE HEAD OF THE XMR GROUP!
THAT'S TRUE...
I'M GOING TO HANG ON TO THAT PRESTIGE A LITTLE LONGER.

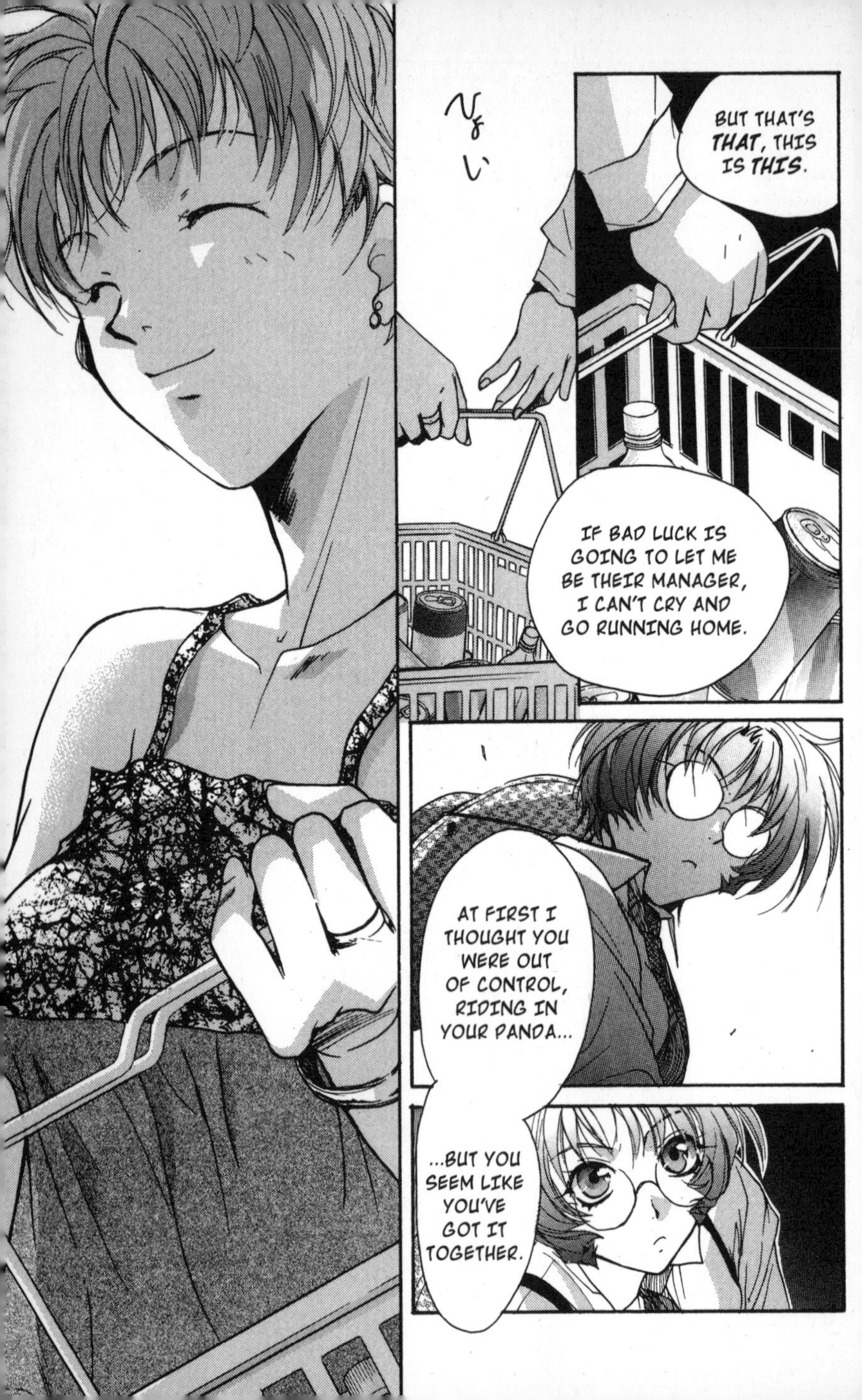
BUT THAT'S *THAT*, THIS IS *THIS*.
IF BAD LUCK IS GOING TO LET ME BE THEIR MANAGER, I CAN'T CRY AND GO RUNNING HOME.
AT FIRST I THOUGHT YOU WERE OUT OF CONTROL, RIDING IN YOUR PANDA...
...BUT YOU SEEM LIKE YOU'VE GOT IT TOGETHER.

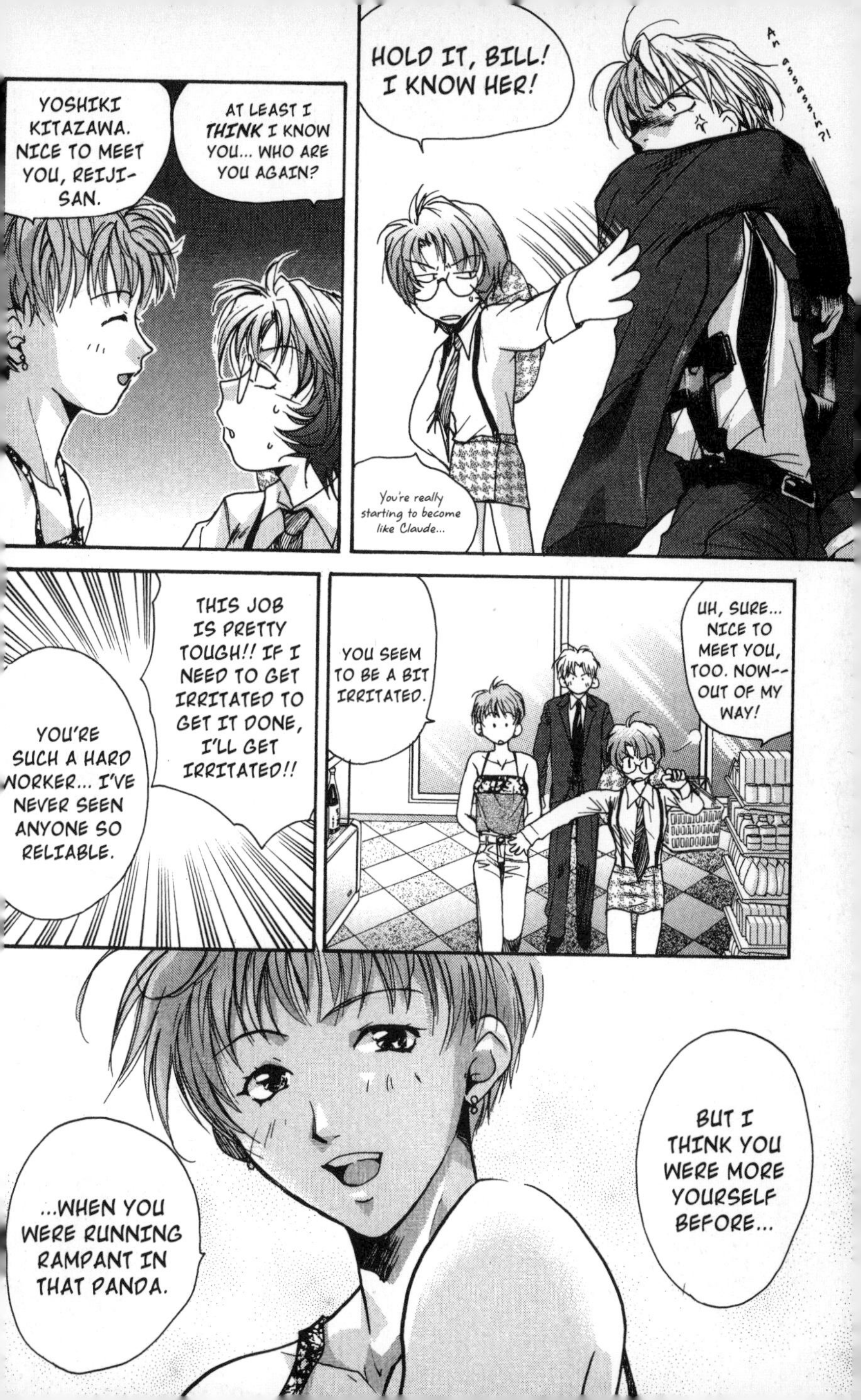
An assassin?!
HOLD IT, BILL! I KNOW HER!
You're really starting to become like Claude...
AT LEAST I *THINK* I KNOW YOU... WHO ARE YOU AGAIN?
YOSHIKI KITAZAWA. NICE TO MEET YOU, REIJI-SAN.
UH, SURE... NICE TO MEET YOU, TOO. NOW-- OUT OF MY WAY!
YOU SEEM TO BE A BIT IRRITATED.
THIS JOB IS PRETTY TOUGH!! IF I NEED TO GET IRRITATED TO GET IT DONE, I'LL GET IRRITATED!!
YOU'RE SUCH A HARD WORKER... I'VE NEVER SEEN ANYONE SO RELIABLE.
BUT I THINK YOU WERE MORE YOURSELF BEFORE...
...WHEN YOU WERE RUNNING RAMPANT IN THAT PANDA.

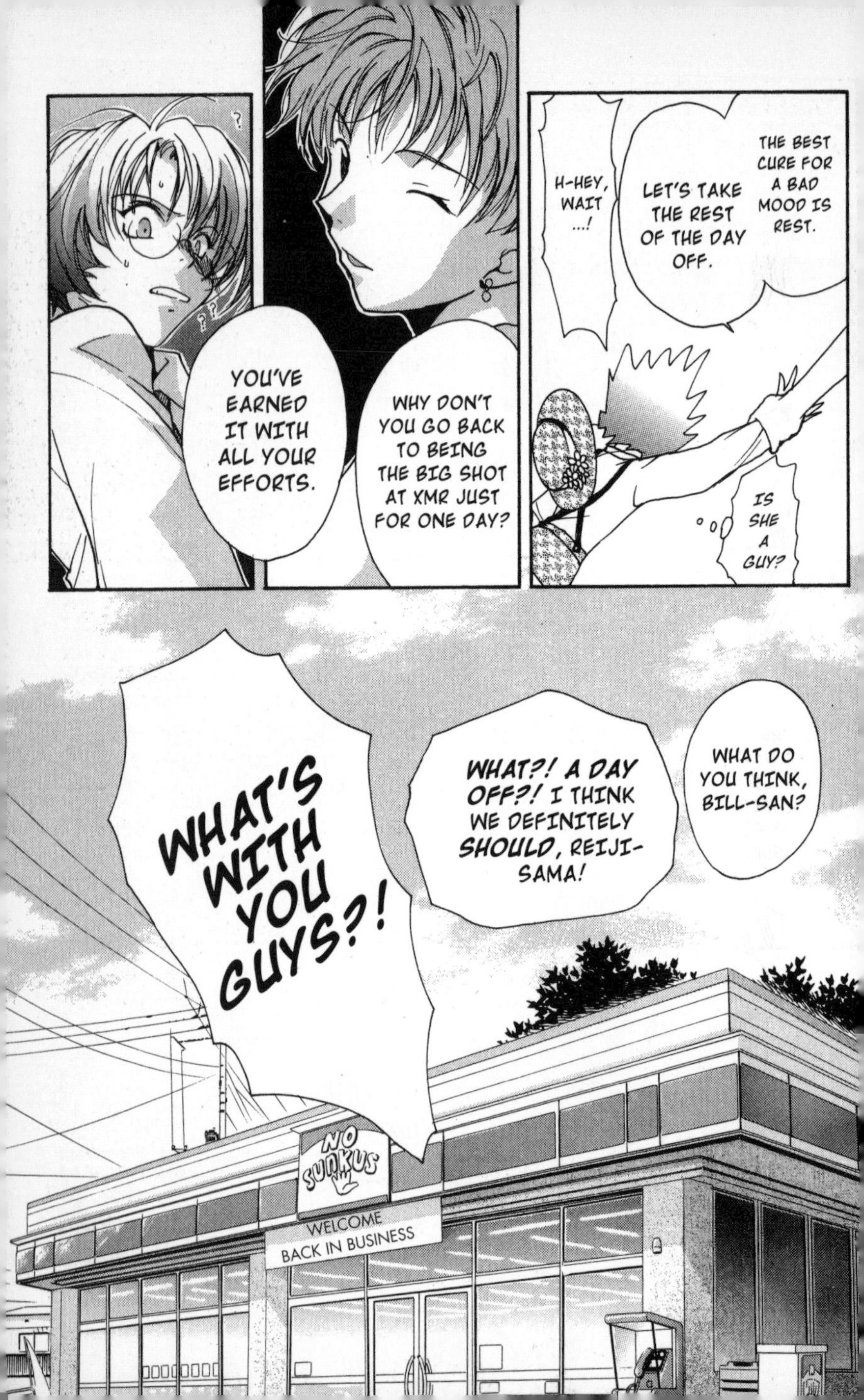
THE BEST CURE FOR A BAD MOOD IS REST.
LET'S TAKE THE REST OF THE DAY OFF.
H-HEY, WAIT ...!
IS SHE A GUY?
WHY DON'T YOU GO BACK TO BEING THE BIG SHOT AT XMR JUST FOR ONE DAY?
YOU'VE EARNED IT WITH ALL YOUR EFFORTS.
WHAT DO YOU THINK, BILL-SAN?
WHAT?! A DAY OFF?! I THINK WE DEFINITELY ***SHOULD***, REIJI-SAMA!
WHAT'S WITH YOU GUYS?!
NO SUNKUS
WELCOME
BACK IN BUSINESS

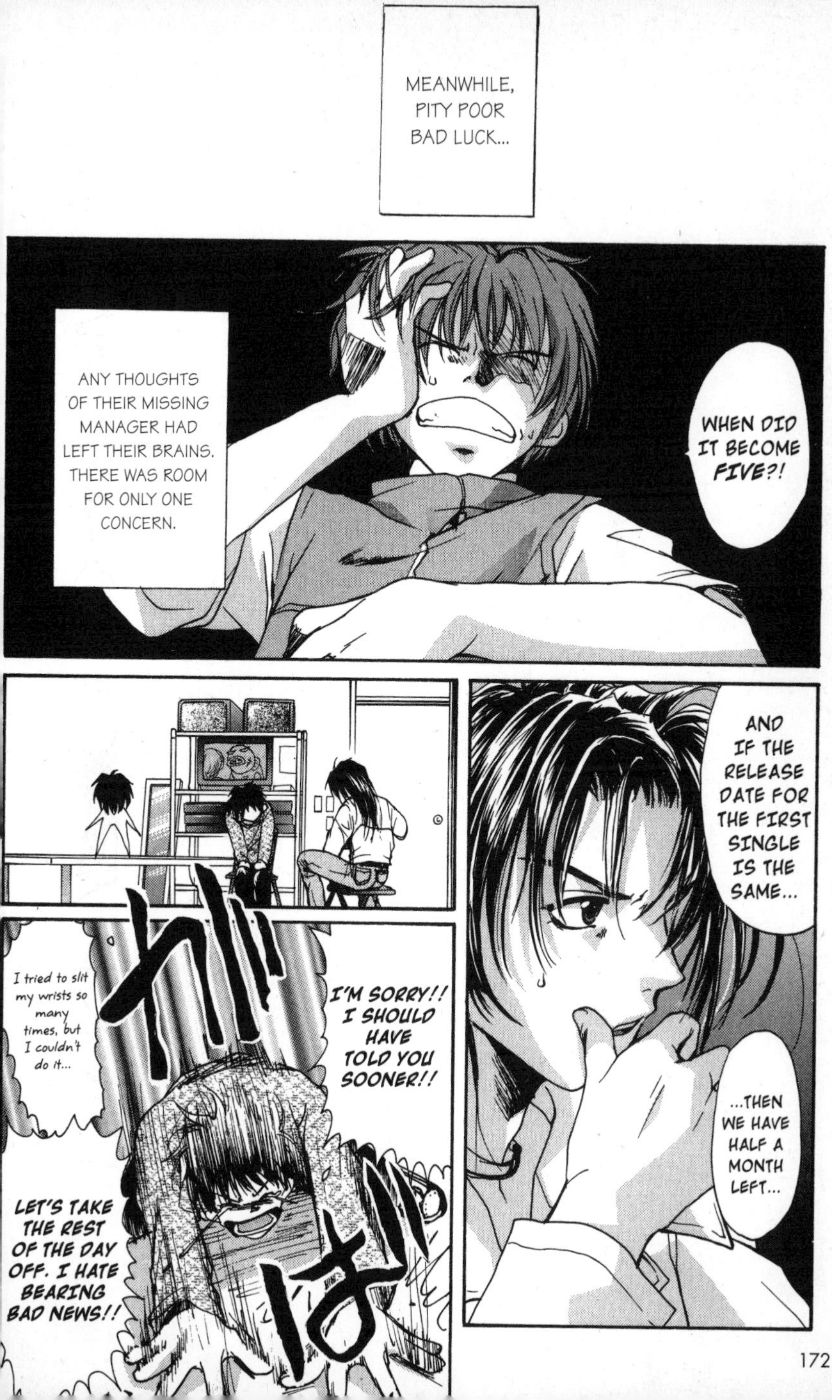
MEANWHILE, PITY POOR BAD LUCK...
WHEN DID IT BECOME FIVE?!
ANY THOUGHTS OF THEIR MISSING MANAGER HAD LEFT THEIR BRAINS. THERE WAS ROOM FOR ONLY ONE CONCERN.
AND IF THE RELEASE DATE FOR THE FIRST SINGLE IS THE SAME...
...THEN WE HAVE HALF A MONTH LEFT...
I'M SORRY!! I SHOULD HAVE TOLD YOU SOONER!!
I tried to slit my wrists so many times, but I couldn't do it...
LET'S TAKE THE REST OF THE DAY OFF. I HATE BEARING BAD NEWS!!

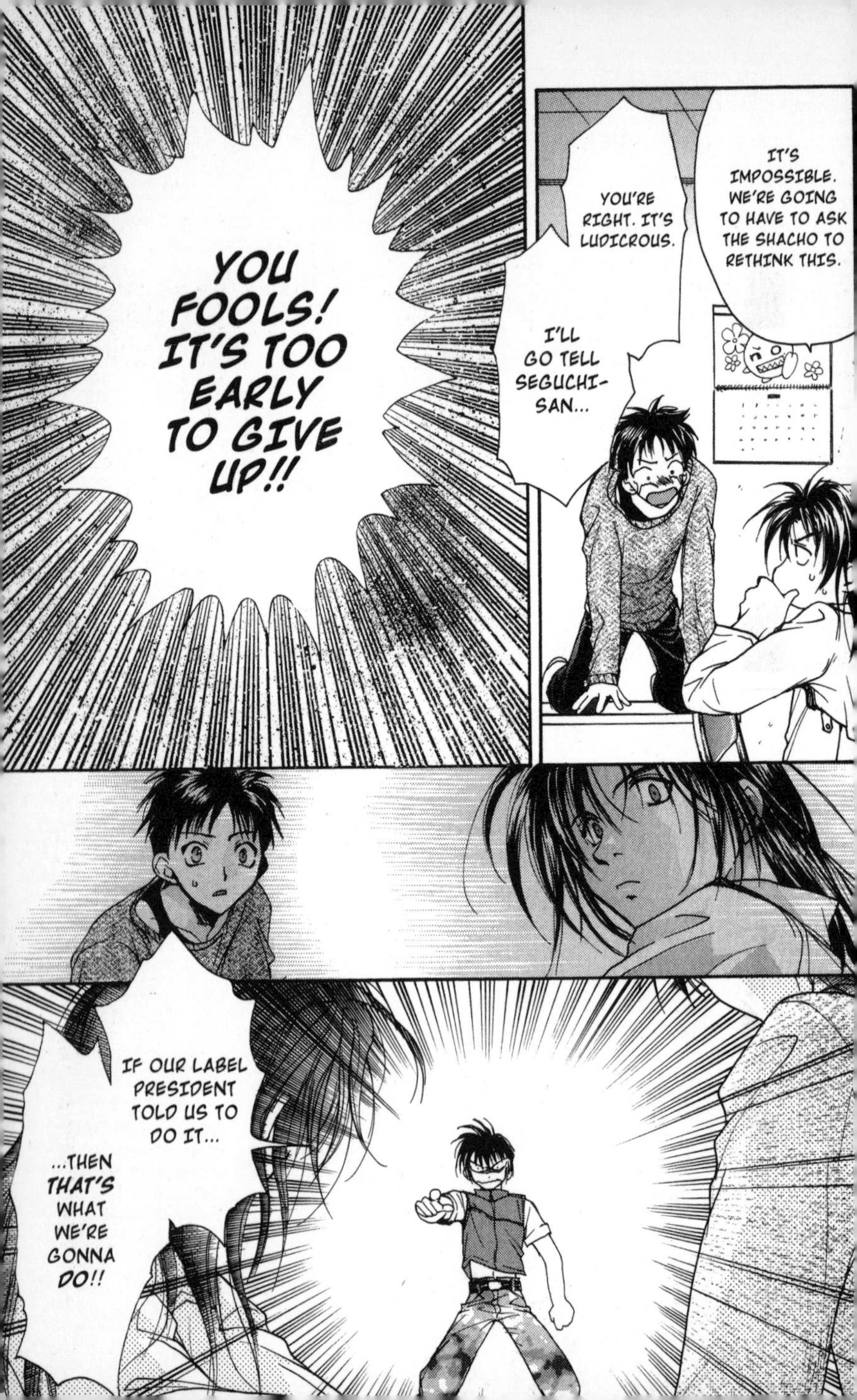
IT'S IMPOSSIBLE. WE'RE GOING TO HAVE TO ASK THE SHACHO TO RETHINK THIS.
YOU'RE RIGHT. IT'S LUDICROUS.
I'LL GO TELL SEGUCHI-SAN...
YOU FOOLS! IT'S TOO EARLY TO GIVE UP!!
IF OUR LABEL PRESIDENT TOLD US TO DO IT...
...THEN THAT'S WHAT WE'RE GONNA DO!!

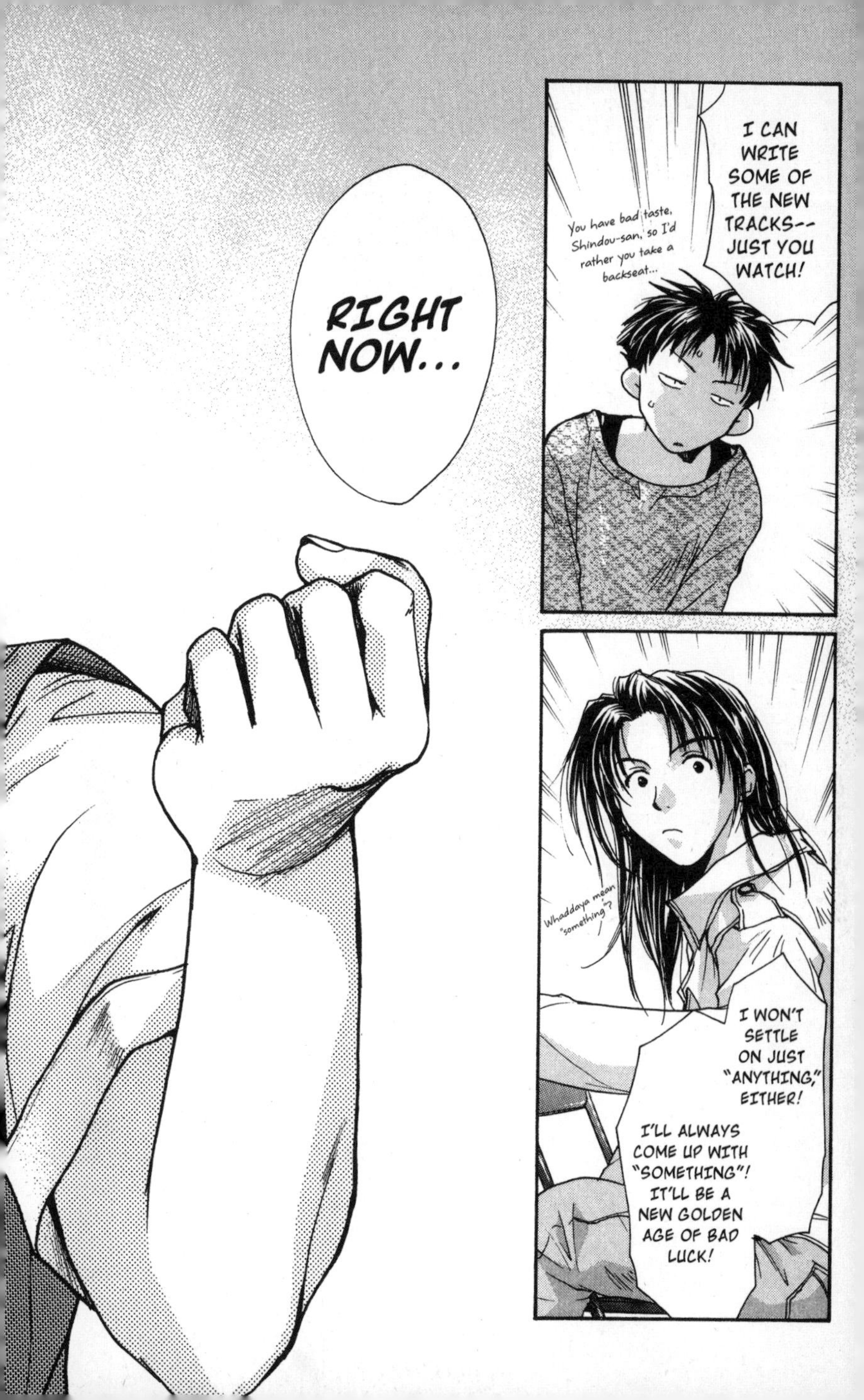
I CAN WRITE SOME OF THE NEW TRACKS--JUST YOU WATCH!
You have bad taste, Shindou-san, so I'd rather you take a backseat...
I WON'T SETTLE ON JUST "ANYTHING," EITHER!
I'LL ALWAYS COME UP WITH "SOMETHING"! IT'LL BE A NEW GOLDEN AGE OF BAD LUCK!
Whaddaya mean "something"?
RIGHT NOW...

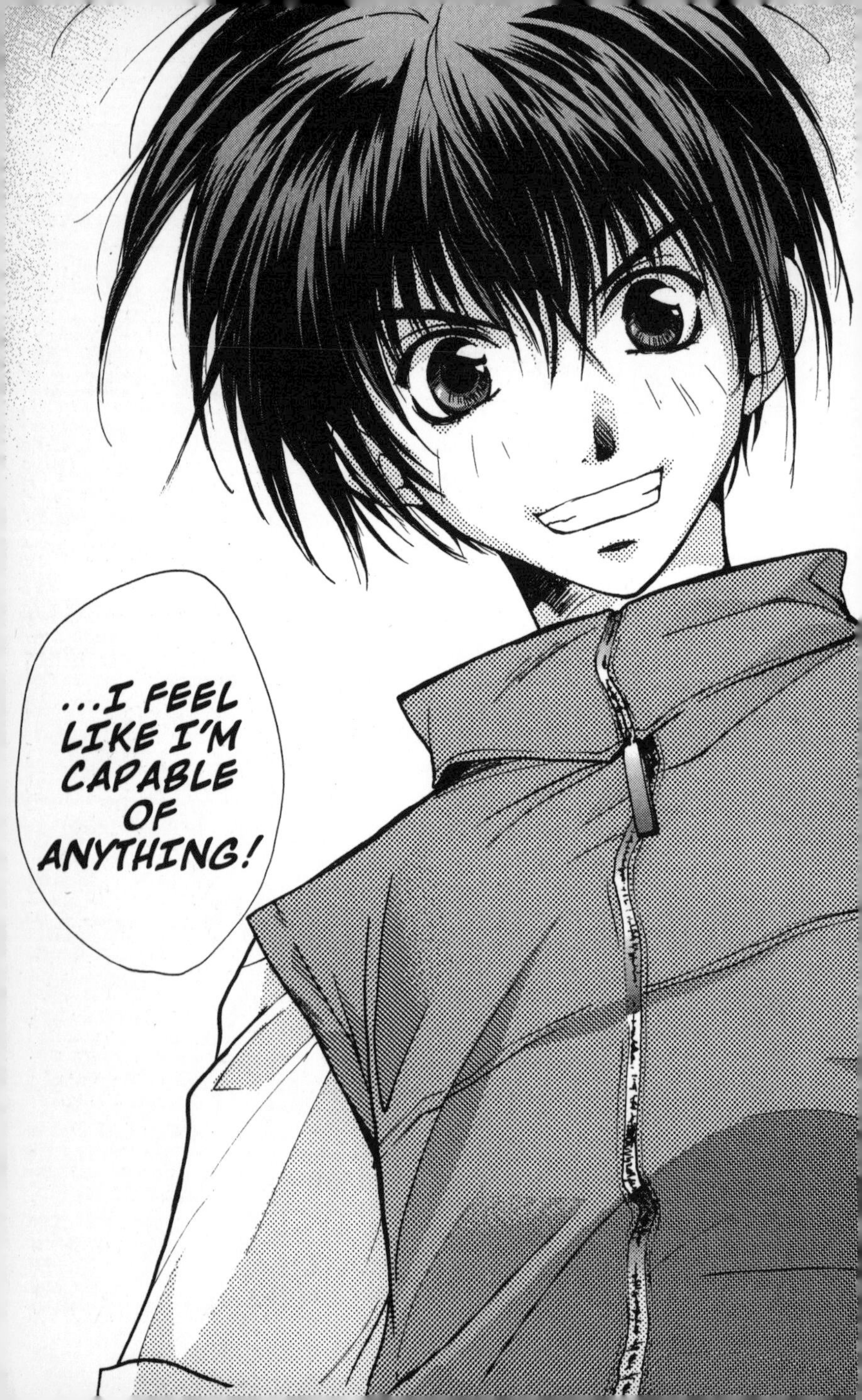
...I FEEL LIKE I'M CAPABLE OF ANYTHING!

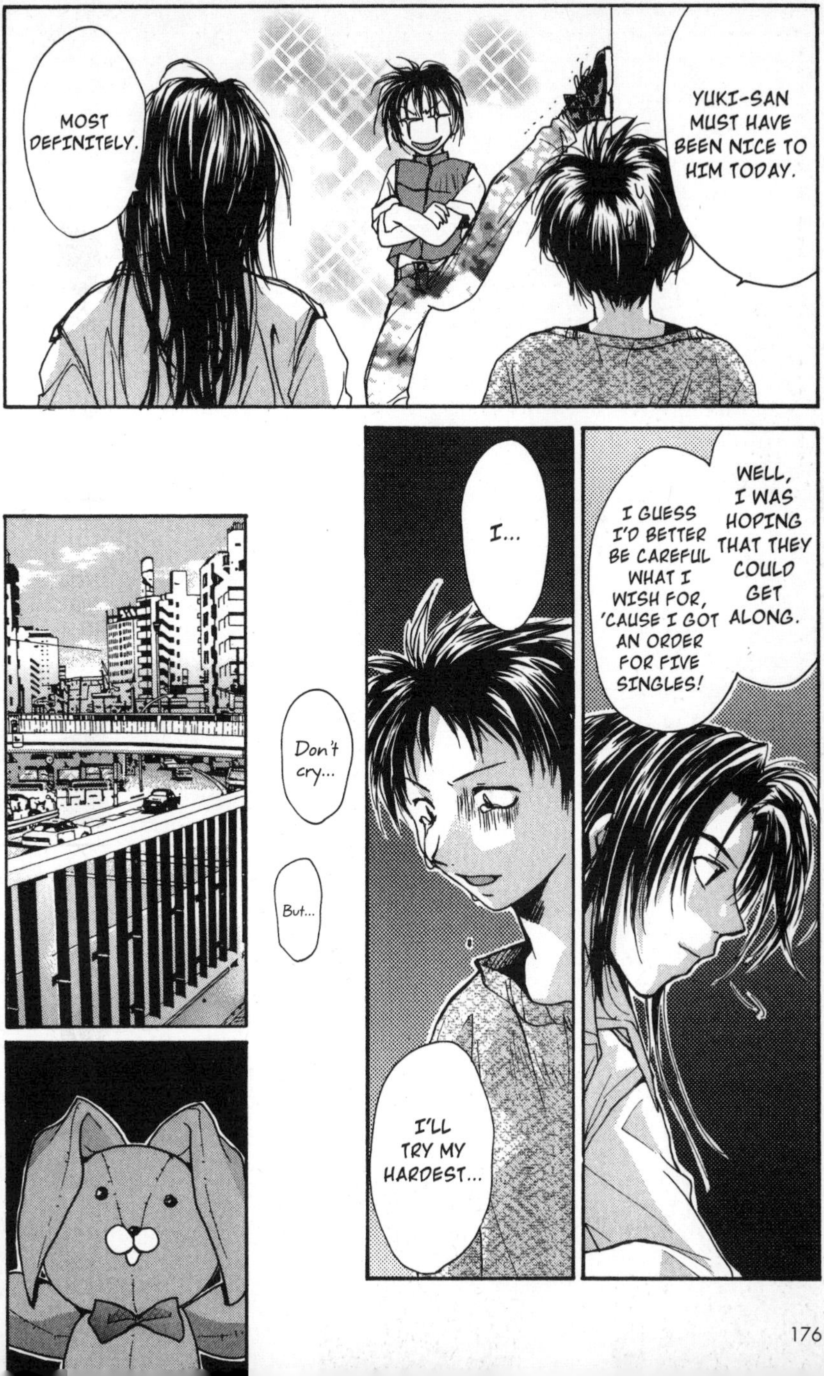
YUKI-SAN MUST HAVE BEEN NICE TO HIM TODAY.
MOST DEFINITELY.
WELL, I WAS HOPING THAT THEY COULD GET ALONG.
I GUESS I'D BETTER BE CAREFUL WHAT I WISH FOR, 'CAUSE I GOT AN ORDER FOR FIVE SINGLES!
I...
I'LL TRY MY HARDEST...
Don't cry...
But...

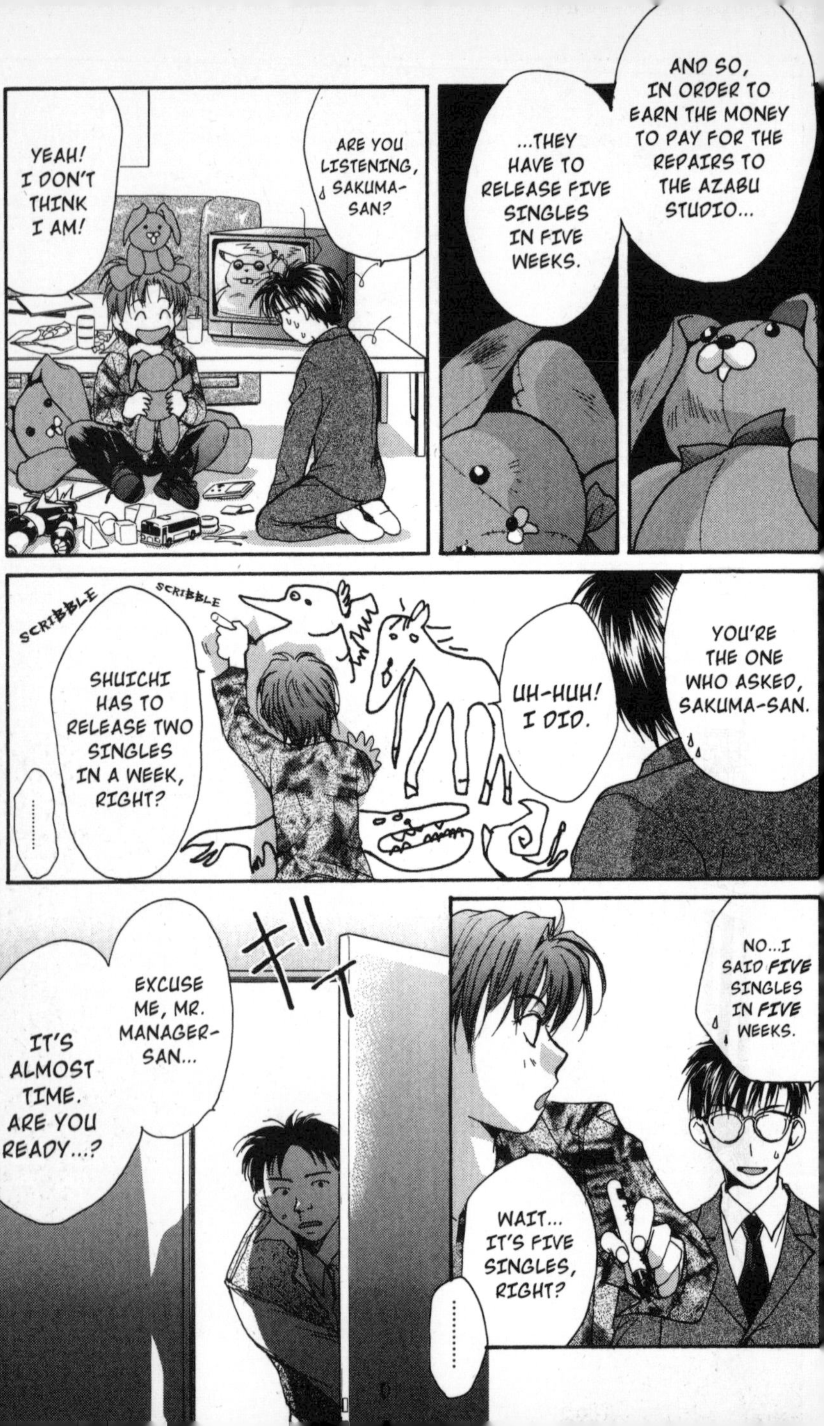
AND SO, IN ORDER TO EARN THE MONEY TO PAY FOR THE REPAIRS TO THE AZABU STUDIO...
...THEY HAVE TO RELEASE FIVE SINGLES IN FIVE WEEKS.
ARE YOU LISTENING, SAKUMA-SAN?
YEAH! I DON'T THINK I AM!
YOU'RE THE ONE WHO ASKED, SAKUMA-SAN.
UH-HUH! I DID.
SCRIBBLE
SCRIBBLE
SHUICHI HAS TO RELEASE TWO SINGLES IN A WEEK, RIGHT?
......
NO...I SAID *FIVE* SINGLES IN *FIVE* WEEKS.
WAIT... IT'S FIVE SINGLES, RIGHT?
......
ギイ
EXCUSE ME, MR. MANAGER-SAN...
IT'S ALMOST TIME. ARE YOU READY...?

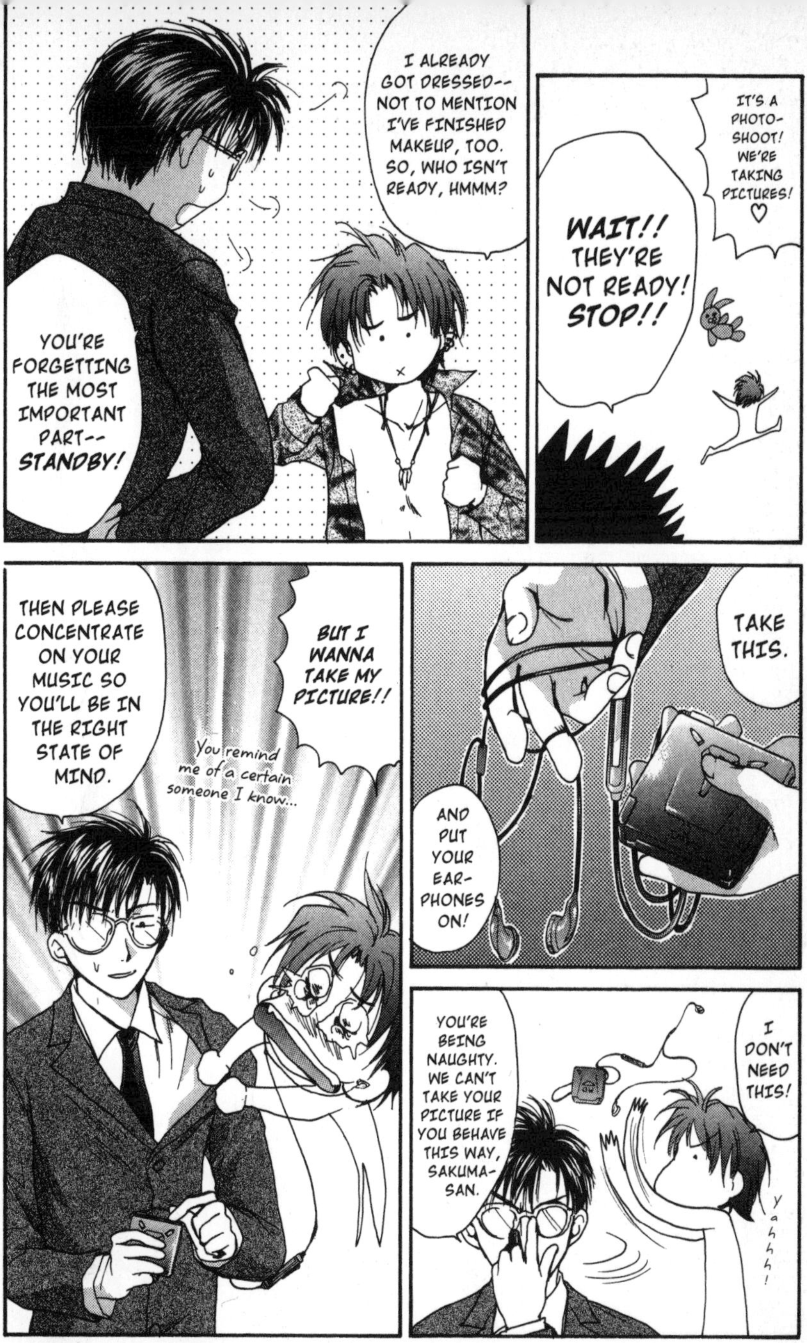
IT'S A PHOTO-SHOOT! WE'RE TAKING PICTURES! ♡
WAIT!! THEY'RE NOT READY! STOP!!
I ALREADY GOT DRESSED-- NOT TO MENTION I'VE FINISHED MAKEUP, TOO. SO, WHO ISN'T READY, HMMM?
YOU'RE FORGETTING THE MOST IMPORTANT PART-- STANDBY!
TAKE THIS.
AND PUT YOUR EAR-PHONES ON!
I DON'T NEED THIS!
YOU'RE BEING NAUGHTY. WE CAN'T TAKE YOUR PICTURE IF YOU BEHAVE THIS WAY, SAKUMA-SAN.
Yahhh!
BUT I WANNA TAKE MY PICTURE!!
THEN PLEASE CONCENTRATE ON YOUR MUSIC SO YOU'LL BE IN THE RIGHT STATE OF MIND.
You remind me of a certain someone I know...

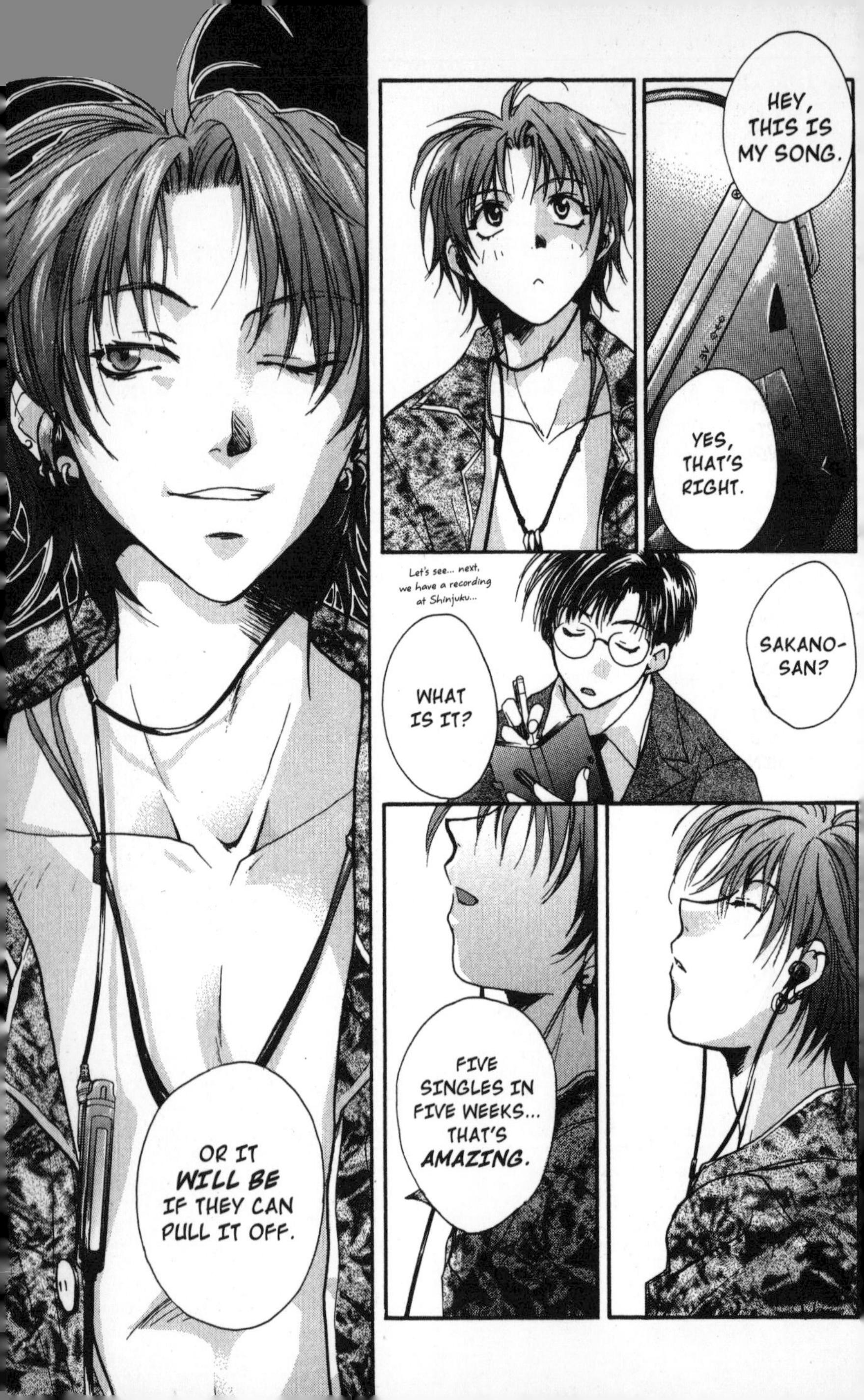
HEY, THIS IS MY SONG.
YES, THAT'S RIGHT.
SAKANO-SAN?
Let's see... next, we have a recording at Shinjuku...
WHAT IS IT?
FIVE SINGLES IN FIVE WEEKS... THAT'S AMAZING.
OR IT WILL BE IF THEY CAN PULL IT OFF.

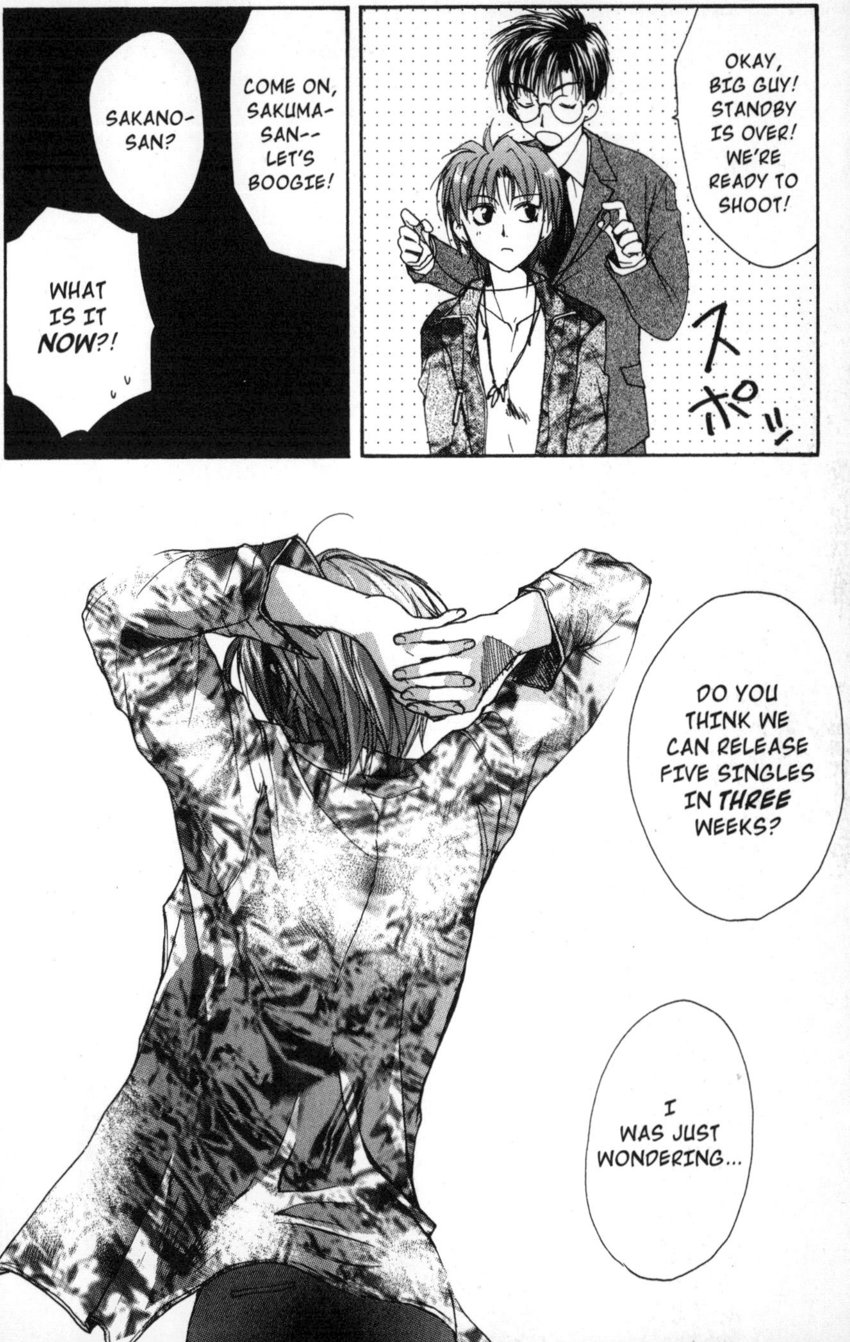
OKAY, BIG GUY! STANDBY IS OVER! WE'RE READY TO SHOOT!
スポッ
COME ON, SAKUMA-SAN-- LET'S BOOGIE!
SAKANO-SAN?
WHAT IS IT NOW?!
DO YOU THINK WE CAN RELEASE FIVE SINGLES IN THREE WEEKS?
I WAS JUST WONDERING...

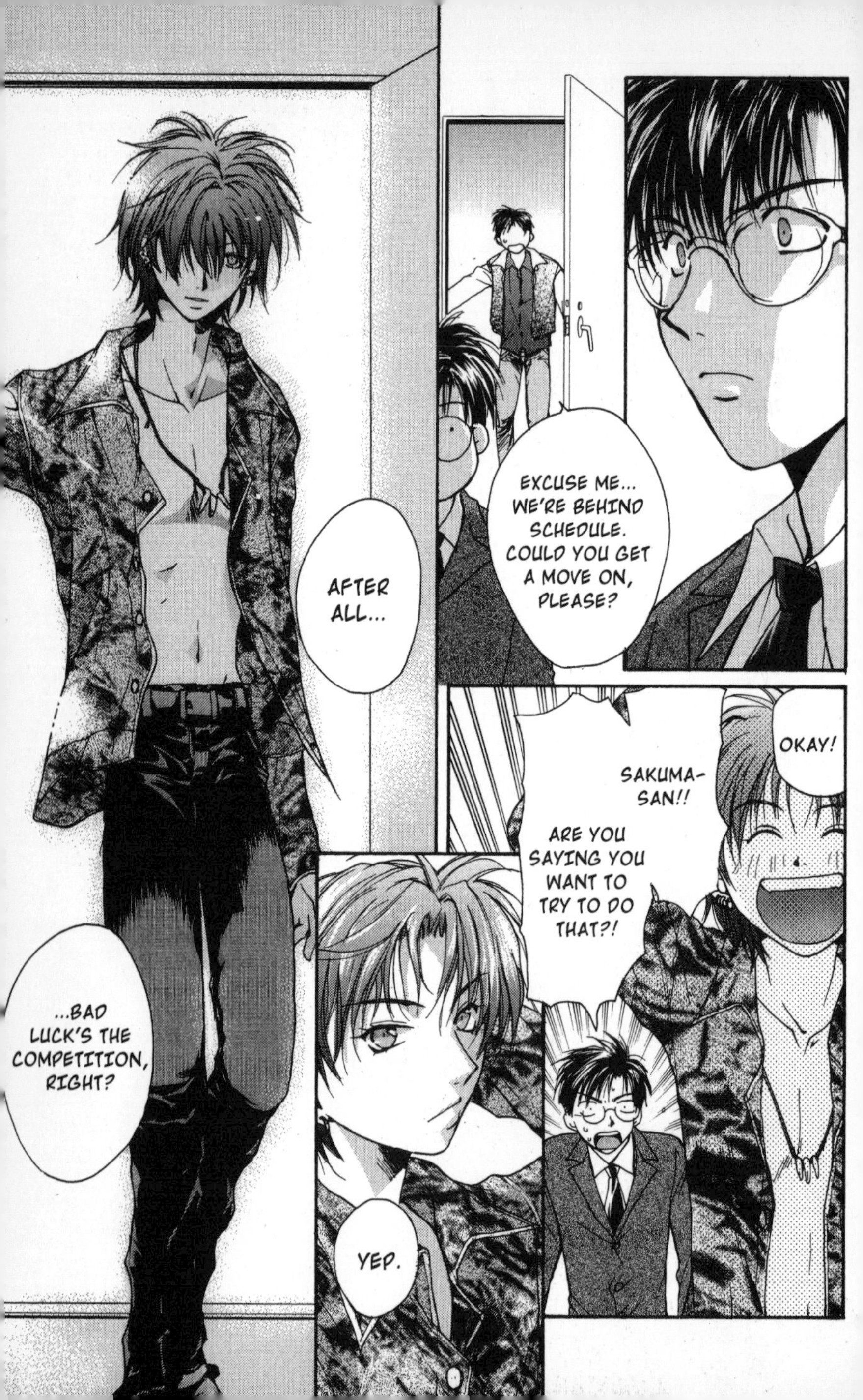
EXCUSE ME... WE'RE BEHIND SCHEDULE. COULD YOU GET A MOVE ON, PLEASE?
OKAY!
SAKUMA-SAN!!
ARE YOU SAYING YOU WANT TO TRY TO DO THAT?!
YEP.
AFTER ALL...
...BAD LUCK'S THE COMPETITION, RIGHT?

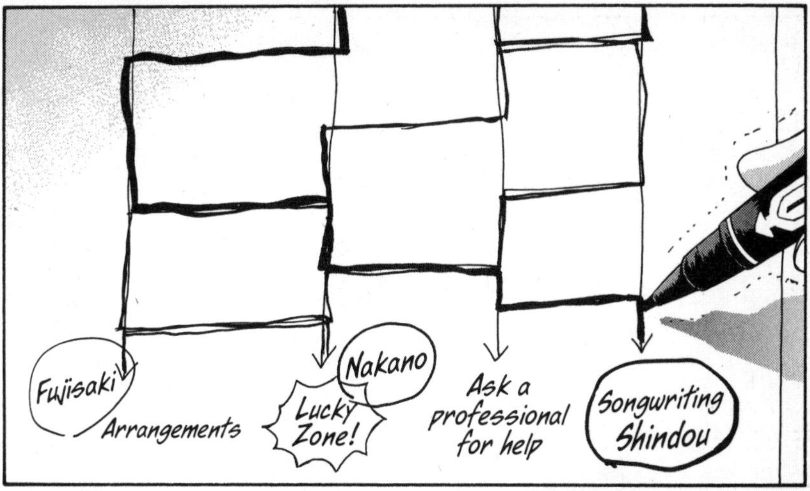
Songwriting Shindou
Ask a professional for help
Nakano
Lucky Zone!
Fujisaki
Arrangements

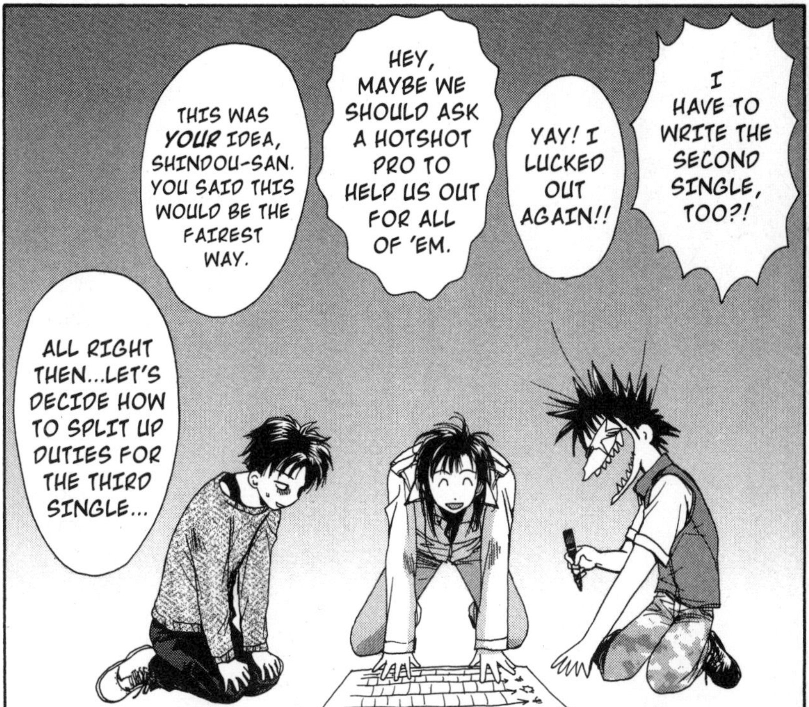
I HAVE TO WRITE THE SECOND SINGLE, TOO?!
YAY! I LUCKED OUT AGAIN!!
HEY, MAYBE WE SHOULD ASK A HOTSHOT PRO TO HELP US OUT FOR ALL OF 'EM.
THIS WAS *YOUR* IDEA, SHINDOU-SAN. YOU SAID THIS WOULD BE THE FAIREST WAY.
ALL RIGHT THEN...LET'S DECIDE HOW TO SPLIT UP DUTIES FOR THE THIRD SINGLE...

track45 ▶ END

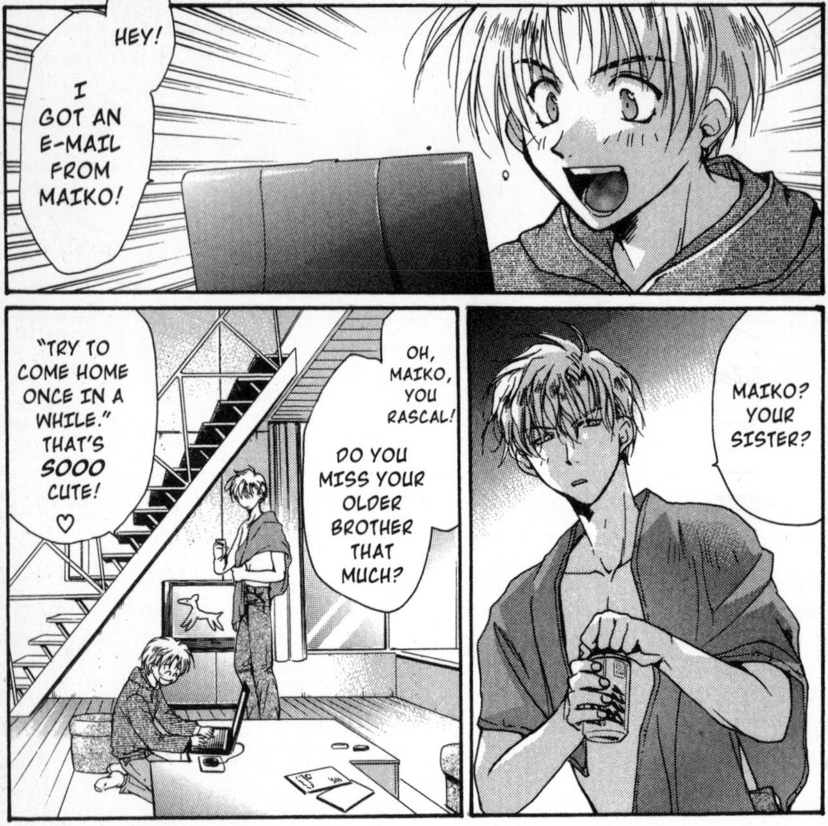
HEY!
I GOT AN E-MAIL FROM MAIKO!
MAIKO? YOUR SISTER?
"TRY TO COME HOME ONCE IN A WHILE." THAT'S SOOO CUTE! ♡
OH, MAIKO, YOU RASCAL!
DO YOU MISS YOUR OLDER BROTHER THAT MUCH?

Gravitation

BONUS TRACK!

To Oni-chan!

My first e-mail!
Are you getting along with Yuki-san?
I'm studying for entrance exams,
but I decided to start some
extracurricular activities!
I joined the softball team.
It's a lot of work, but it's fun.
I got home late after
practice yesterday.
On the way home...

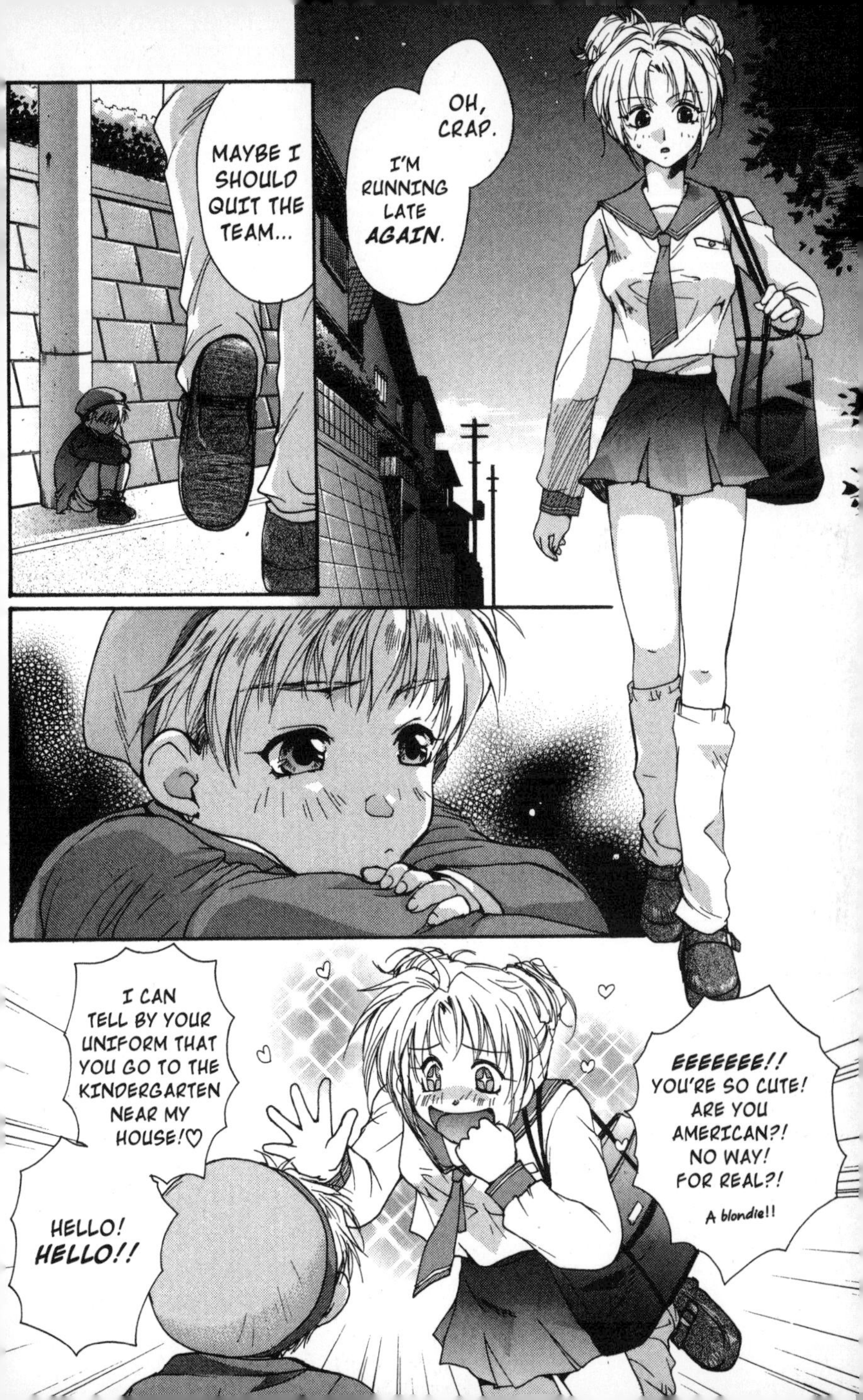
OH, CRAP.
I'M RUNNING LATE AGAIN.
MAYBE I SHOULD QUIT THE TEAM...
EEEEEEE!! YOU'RE SO CUTE! ARE YOU AMERICAN?! NO WAY! FOR REAL?!
A blondie!!
I CAN TELL BY YOUR UNIFORM THAT YOU GO TO THE KINDERGARTEN NEAR MY HOUSE!♡
HELLO! HELLO!!

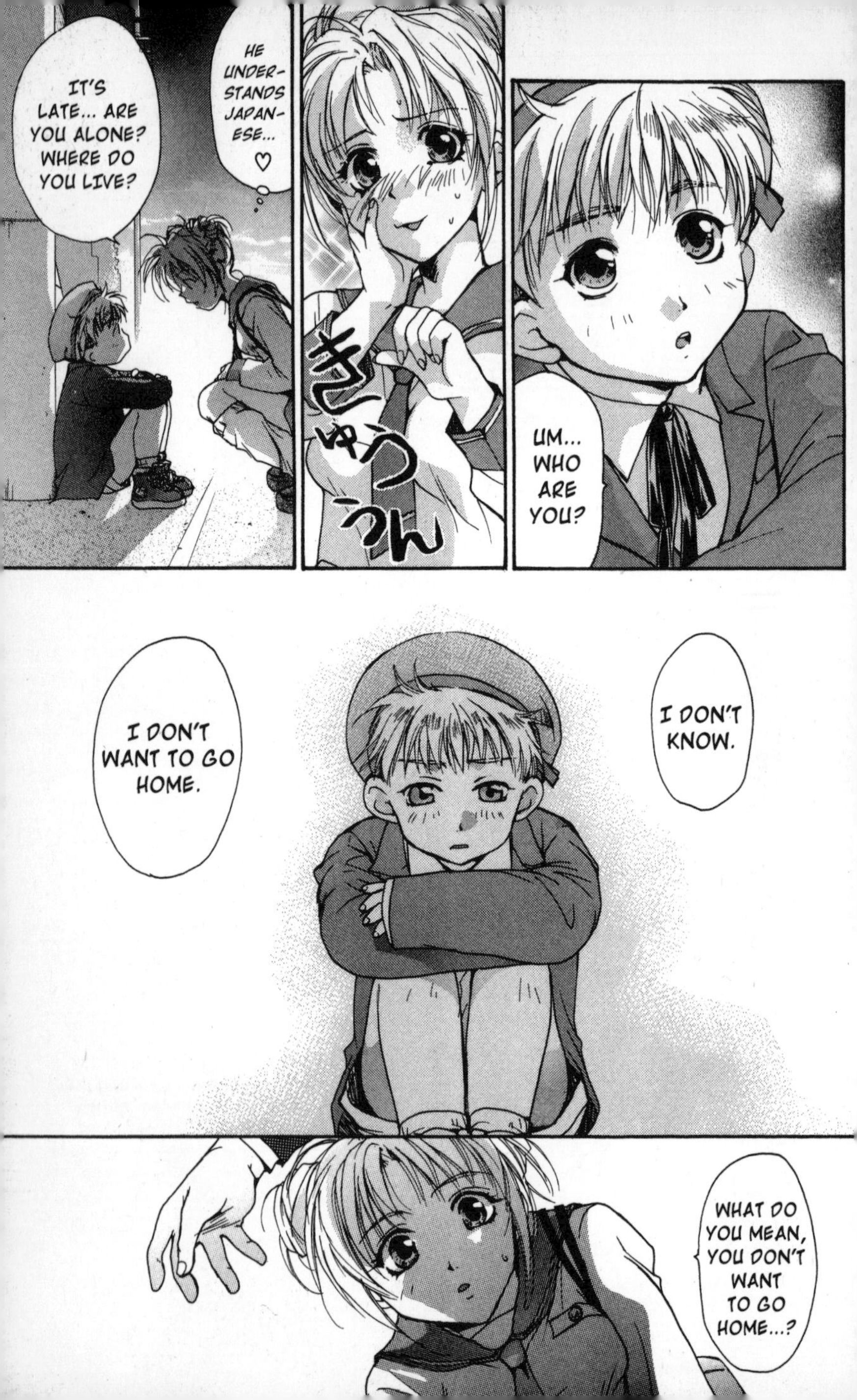
UM... WHO ARE YOU?
きゅうつん
HE UNDER-STANDS JAPAN-ESE... ♡
IT'S LATE... ARE YOU ALONE? WHERE DO YOU LIVE?
I DON'T KNOW.
I DON'T WANT TO GO HOME.
WHAT DO YOU MEAN, YOU DON'T WANT TO GO HOME...?

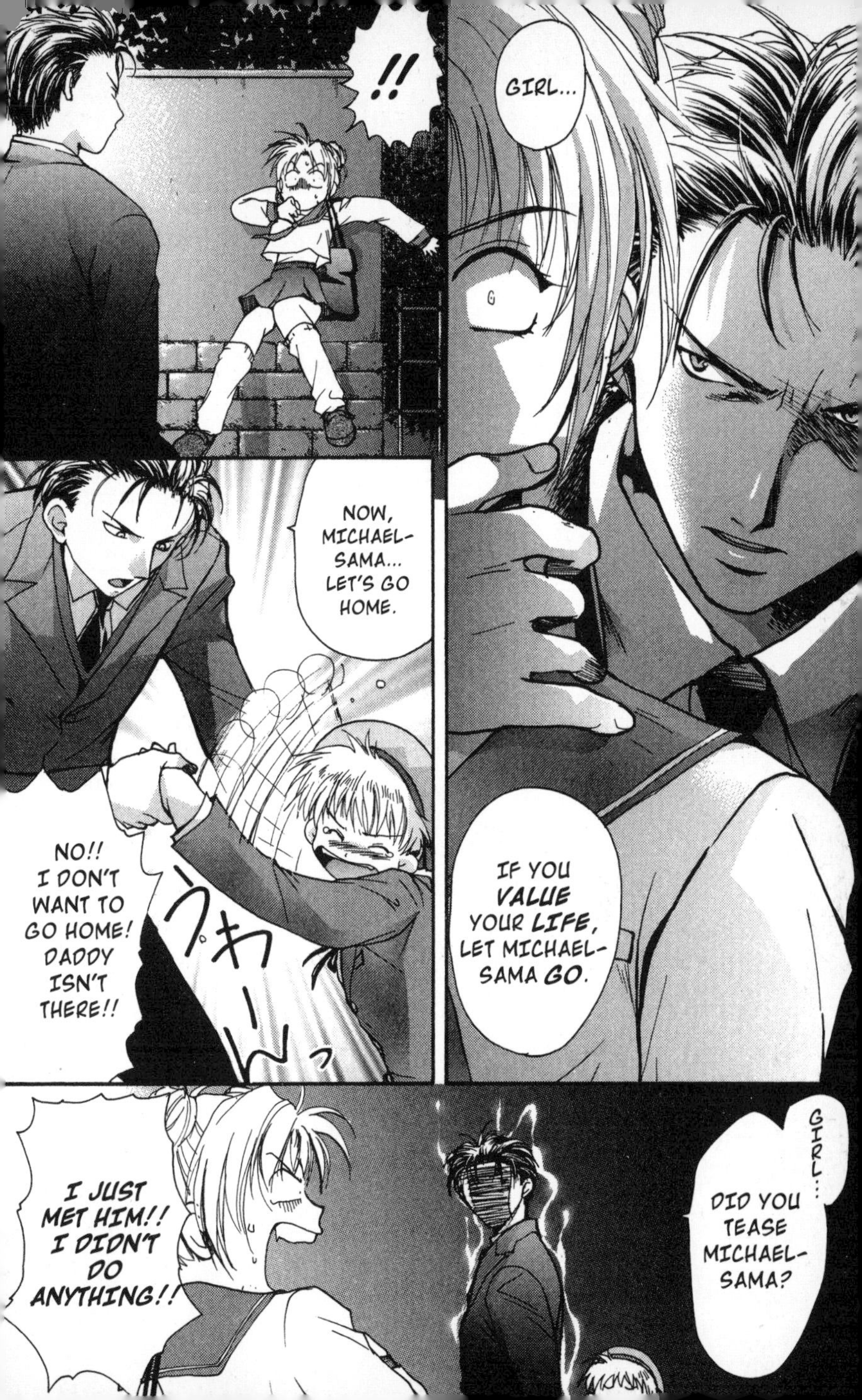
GIRL...
IF YOU VALUE YOUR LIFE, LET MICHAEL-SAMA GO.
!!
NOW, MICHAEL-SAMA... LET'S GO HOME.
NO!! I DON'T WANT TO GO HOME! DADDY ISN'T THERE!!
うわーん
GIRL...
DID YOU TEASE MICHAEL-SAMA?
I JUST MET HIM!! I DIDN'T DO ANYTHING!!

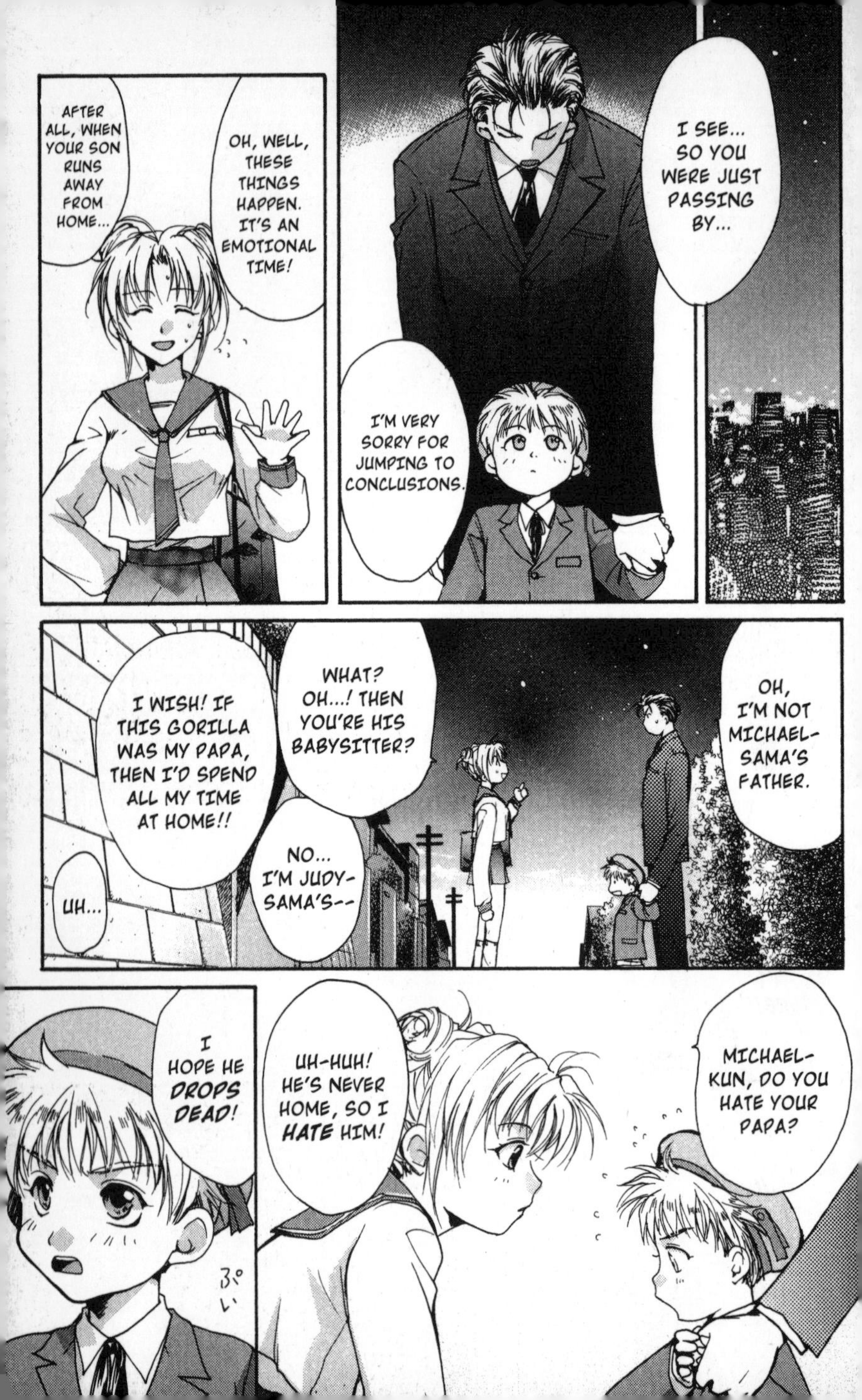
I SEE... SO YOU WERE JUST PASSING BY...
I'M VERY SORRY FOR JUMPING TO CONCLUSIONS.
OH, WELL, THESE THINGS HAPPEN. IT'S AN EMOTIONAL TIME!
AFTER ALL, WHEN YOUR SON RUNS AWAY FROM HOME...
OH, I'M NOT MICHAEL-SAMA'S FATHER.
WHAT? OH...! THEN YOU'RE HIS BABYSITTER?
NO... I'M JUDY-SAMA'S--
I WISH! IF THIS GORILLA WAS MY PAPA, THEN I'D SPEND ALL MY TIME AT HOME!!
UH...
MICHAEL-KUN, DO YOU HATE YOUR PAPA?
UH-HUH! HE'S NEVER HOME, SO I HATE HIM!
I HOPE HE DROPS DEAD!
ぷい

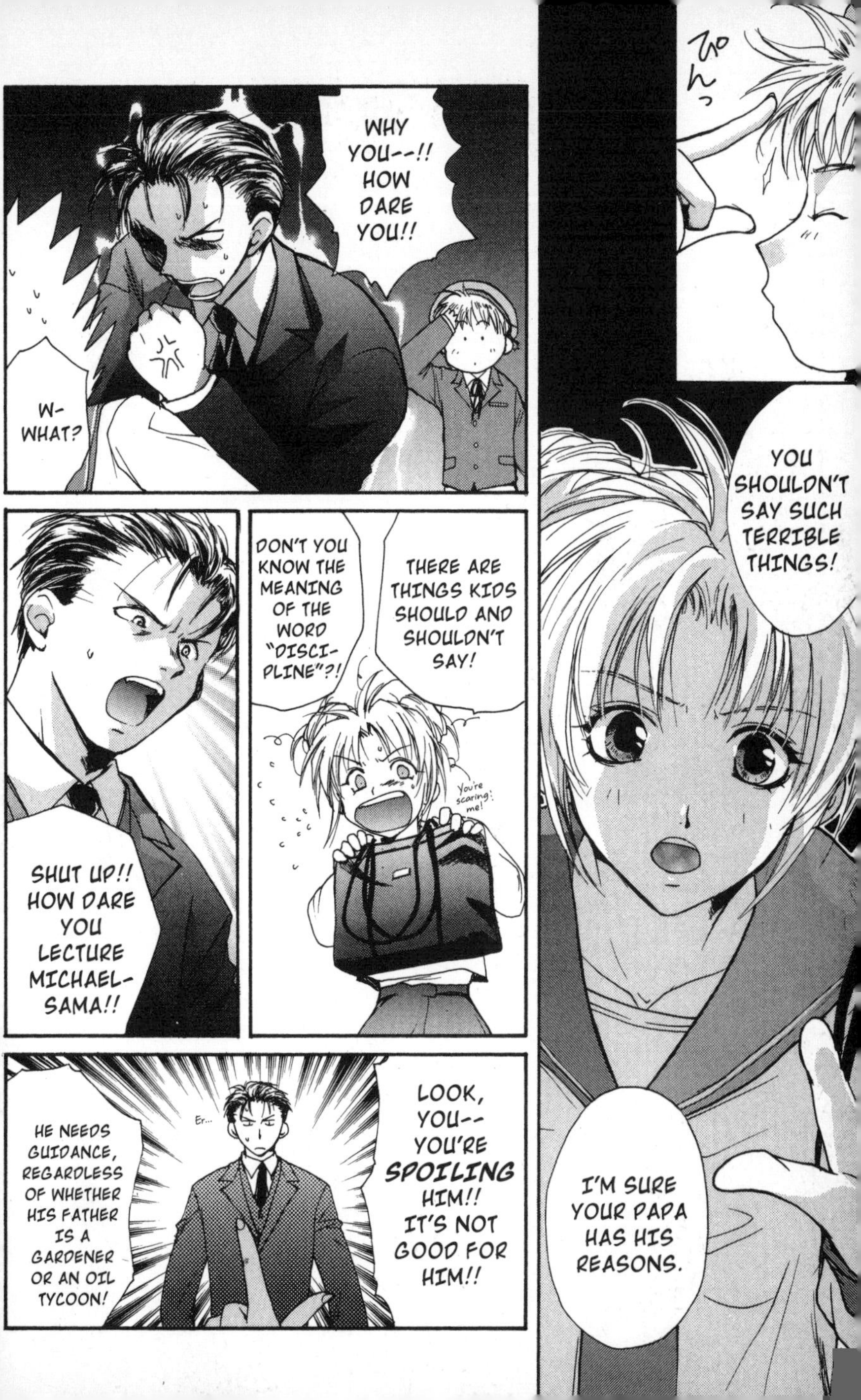
ぴんっ
YOU SHOULDN'T SAY SUCH TERRIBLE THINGS!
I'M SURE YOUR PAPA HAS HIS REASONS.
WHY YOU--!! HOW DARE YOU!!
W-WHAT?
THERE ARE THINGS KIDS SHOULD AND SHOULDN'T SAY!
DON'T YOU KNOW THE MEANING OF THE WORD "DISCI-PLINE"?!
You're scaring me!
SHUT UP!! HOW DARE YOU LECTURE MICHAEL-SAMA!!
LOOK, YOU-- YOU'RE SPOILING HIM!! IT'S NOT GOOD FOR HIM!!
Er...
HE NEEDS GUIDANCE, REGARDLESS OF WHETHER HIS FATHER IS A GARDENER OR AN OIL TYCOON!

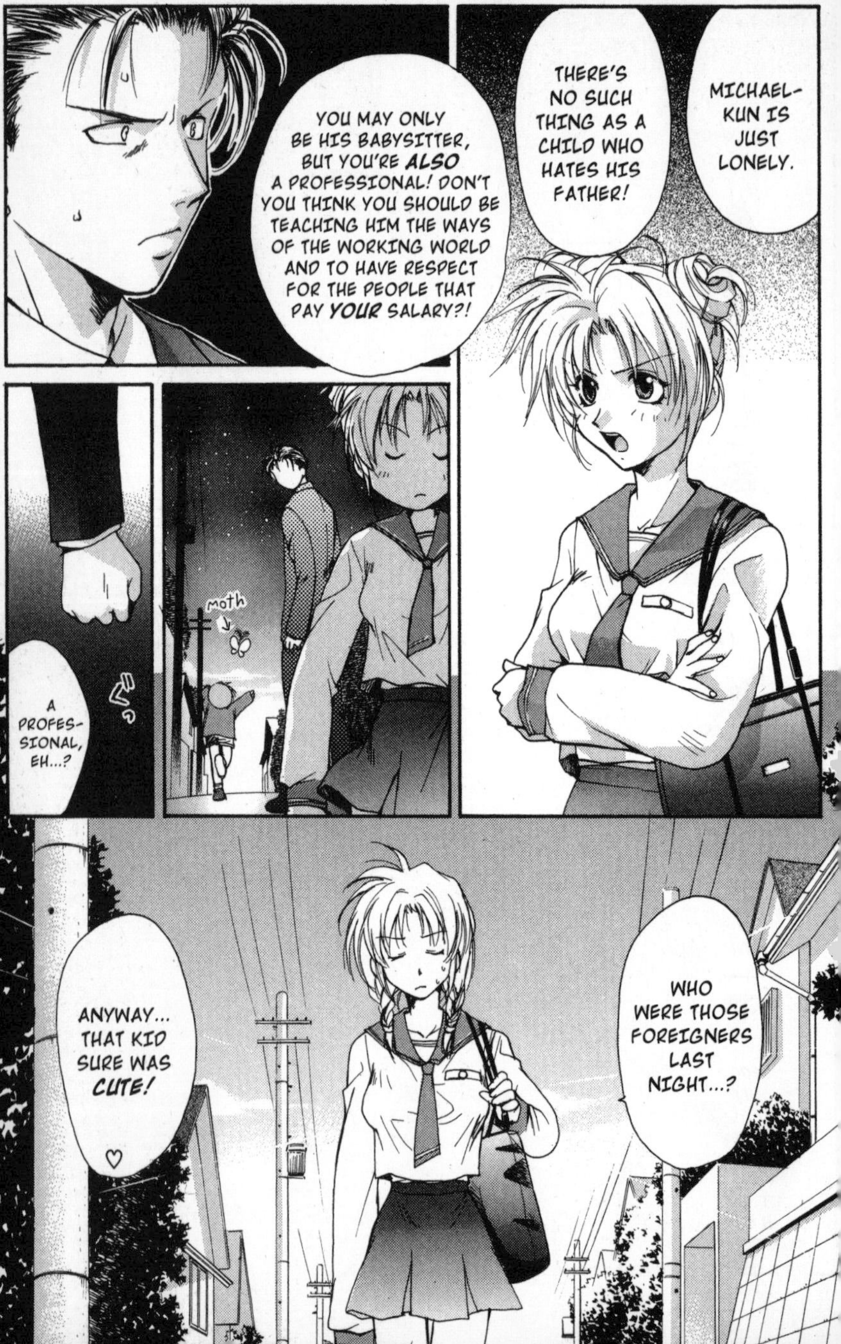
MICHAEL-KUN IS JUST LONELY.
THERE'S NO SUCH THING AS A CHILD WHO HATES HIS FATHER!
YOU MAY ONLY BE HIS BABYSITTER, BUT YOU'RE ALSO A PROFESSIONAL! DON'T YOU THINK YOU SHOULD BE TEACHING HIM THE WAYS OF THE WORKING WORLD AND TO HAVE RESPECT FOR THE PEOPLE THAT PAY YOUR SALARY?!
moth
A PROFES-SIONAL, EH...?
WHO WERE THOSE FOREIGNERS LAST NIGHT...?
ANYWAY... THAT KID SURE WAS CUTE! ♡

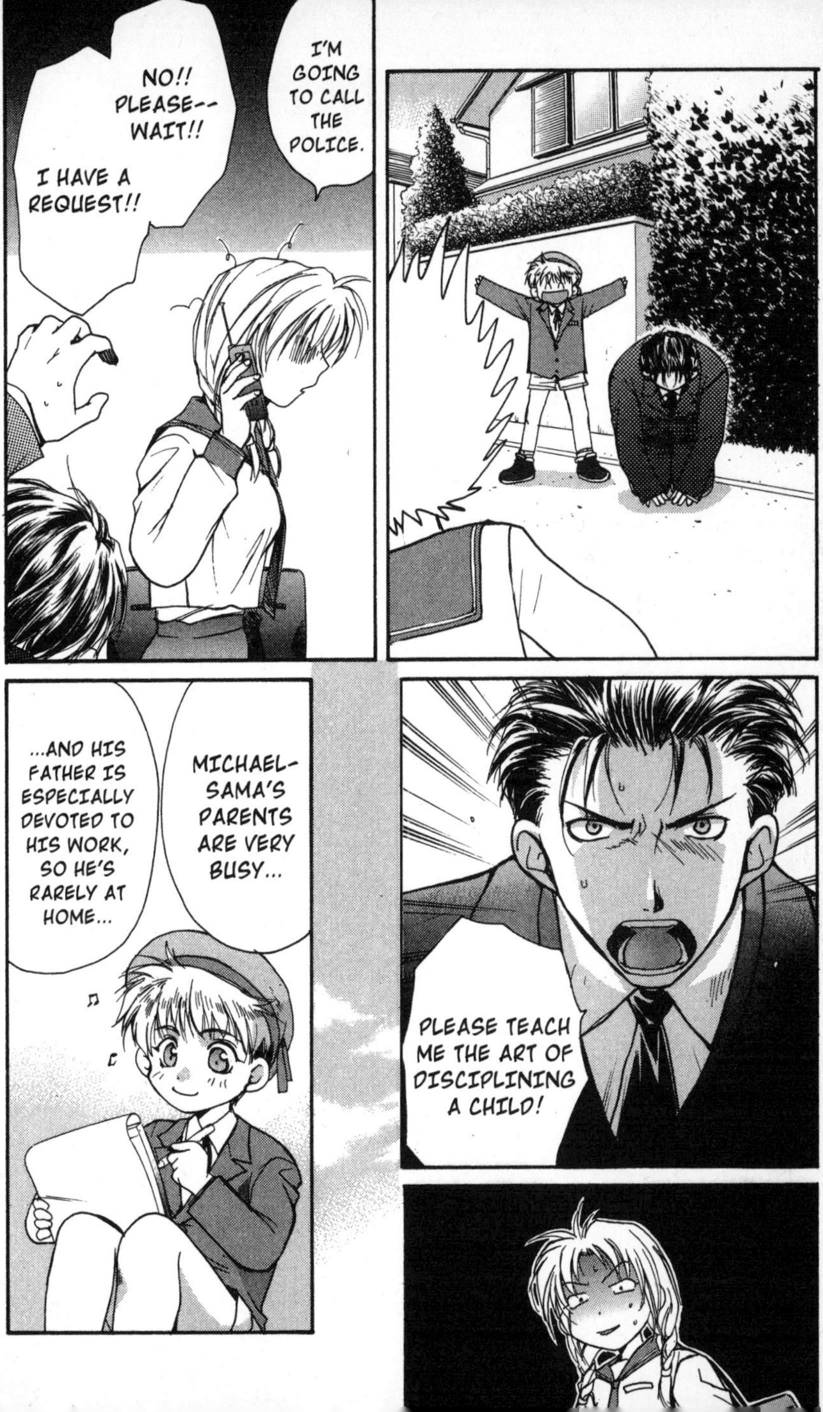
I'M GOING TO CALL THE POLICE.
NO!! PLEASE--WAIT!!
I HAVE A REQUEST!!
PLEASE TEACH ME THE ART OF DISCIPLINING A CHILD!
MICHAEL-SAMA'S PARENTS ARE VERY BUSY...
...AND HIS FATHER IS ESPECIALLY DEVOTED TO HIS WORK, SO HE'S RARELY AT HOME...

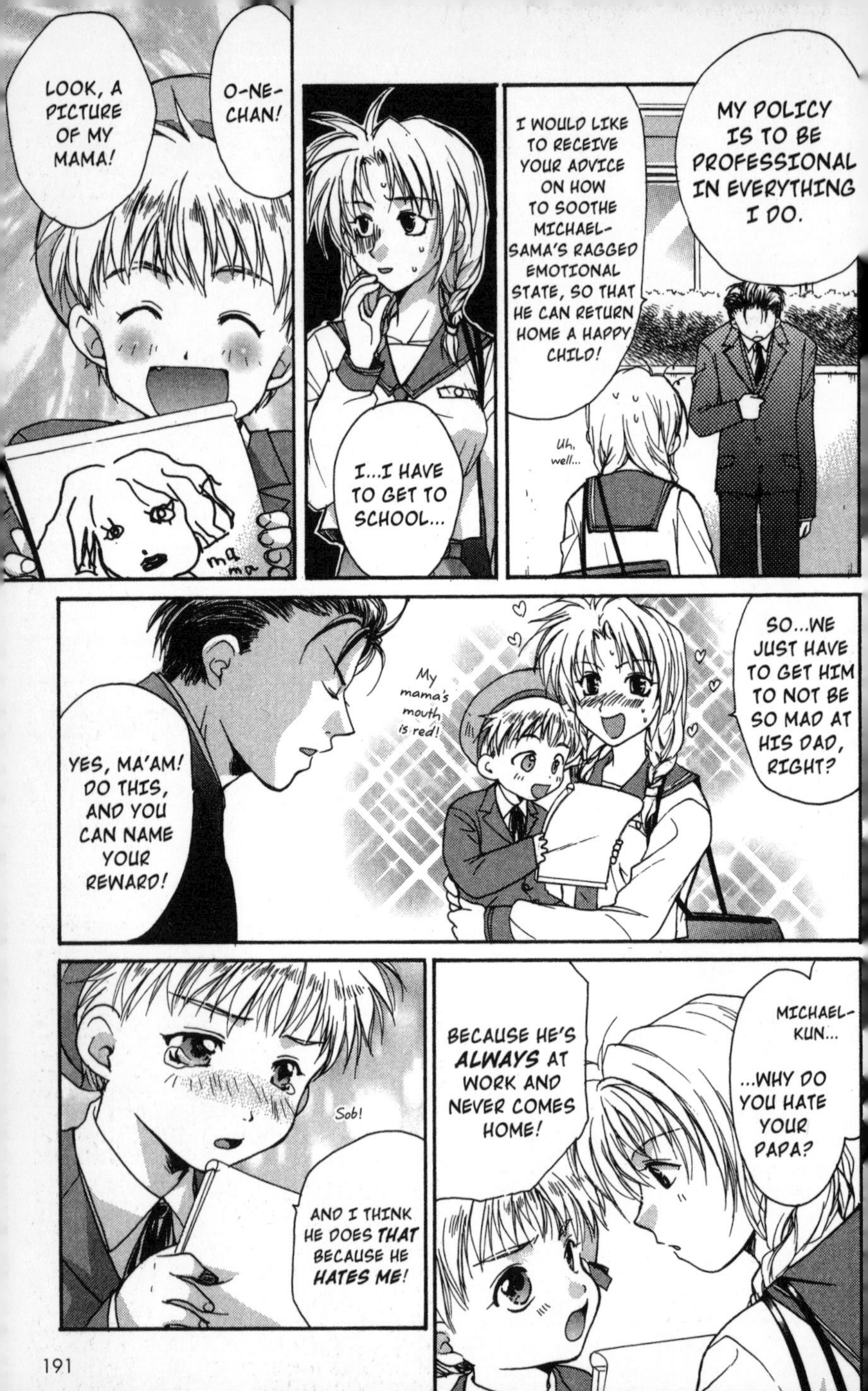
MY POLICY IS TO BE PROFESSIONAL IN EVERYTHING I DO.
I WOULD LIKE TO RECEIVE YOUR ADVICE ON HOW TO SOOTHE MICHAEL-SAMA'S RAGGED EMOTIONAL STATE, SO THAT HE CAN RETURN HOME A HAPPY CHILD!
Uh, well...
I...I HAVE TO GET TO SCHOOL...
O-NE-CHAN!
LOOK, A PICTURE OF MY MAMA!
ma ma
SO...WE JUST HAVE TO GET HIM TO NOT BE SO MAD AT HIS DAD, RIGHT?
My mama's mouth is red!
YES, MA'AM! DO THIS, AND YOU CAN NAME YOUR REWARD!
MICHAEL-KUN...
...WHY DO YOU HATE YOUR PAPA?
BECAUSE HE'S ALWAYS AT WORK AND NEVER COMES HOME!
Sob!
AND I THINK HE DOES THAT BECAUSE HE HATES ME!

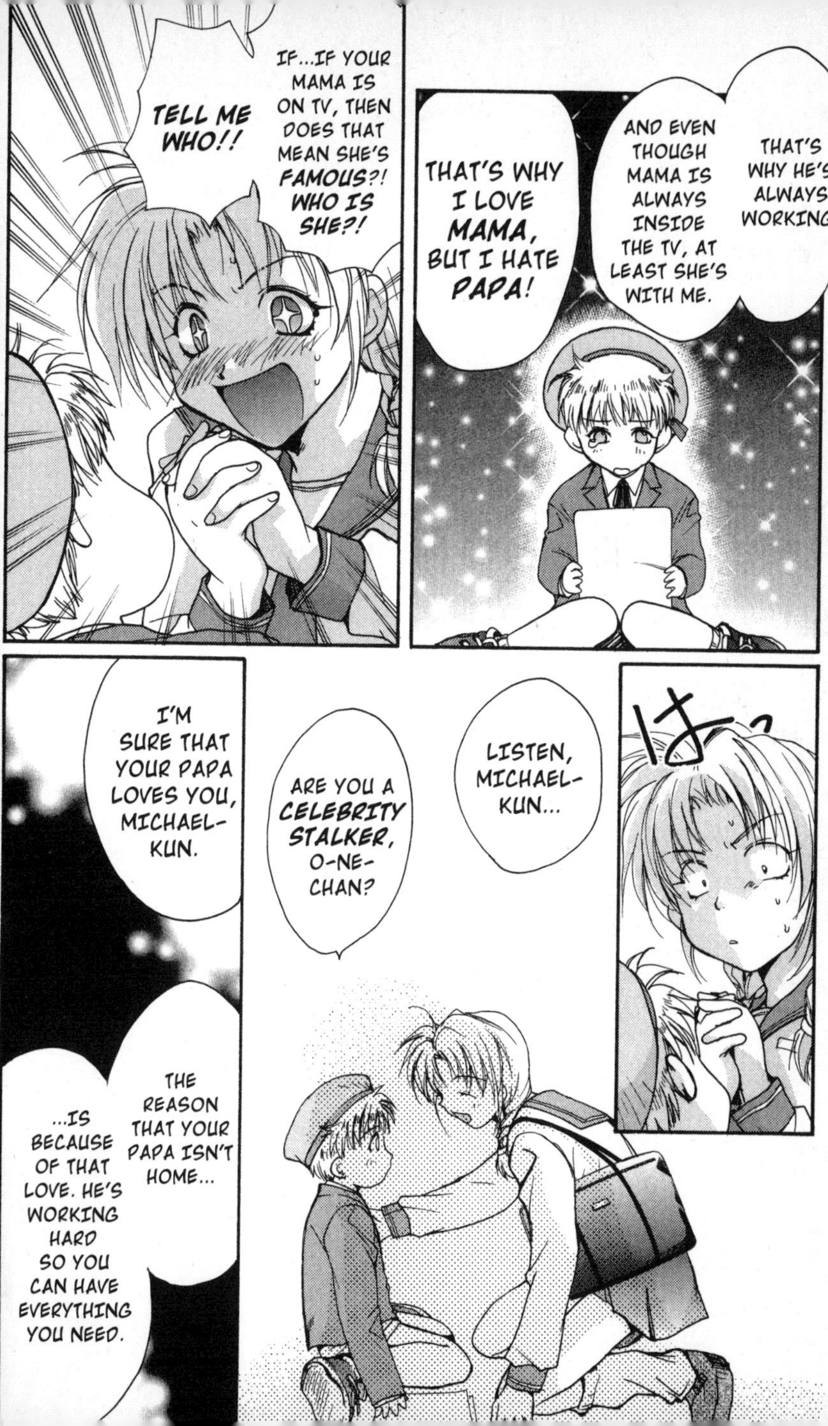
THAT'S WHY HE'S ALWAYS WORKING.
AND EVEN THOUGH MAMA IS ALWAYS INSIDE THE TV, AT LEAST SHE'S WITH ME.
THAT'S WHY I LOVE MAMA, BUT I HATE PAPA!
IF...IF YOUR MAMA IS ON TV, THEN DOES THAT MEAN SHE'S FAMOUS?! WHO IS SHE?!
TELL ME WHO!!
はっ
LISTEN, MICHAEL-KUN...
ARE YOU A CELEBRITY STALKER, O-NE-CHAN?
I'M SURE THAT YOUR PAPA LOVES YOU, MICHAEL-KUN.
THE REASON THAT YOUR PAPA ISN'T HOME...
...IS BECAUSE OF THAT LOVE. HE'S WORKING HARD SO YOU CAN HAVE EVERYTHING YOU NEED.

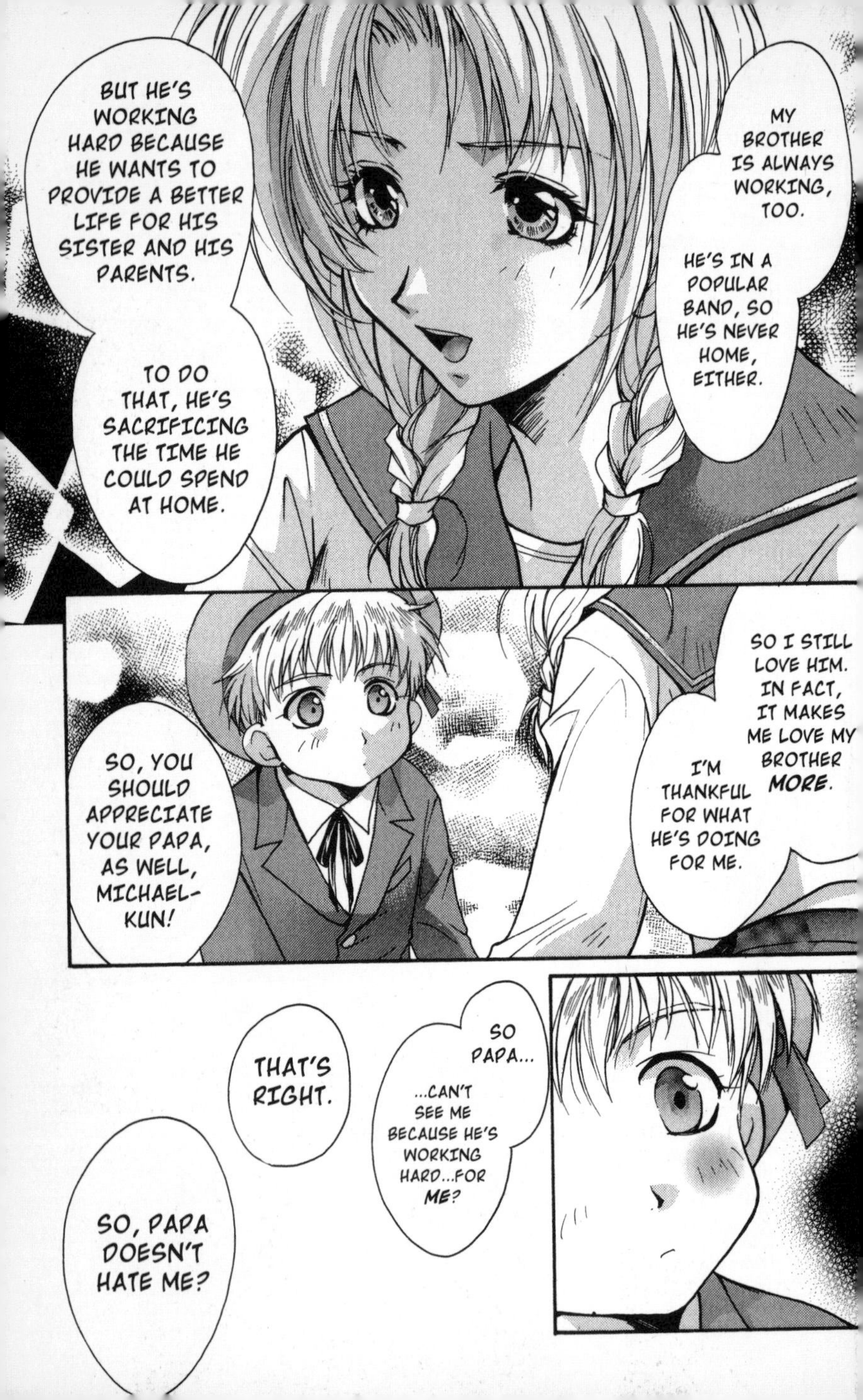
MY BROTHER IS ALWAYS WORKING, TOO.
HE'S IN A POPULAR BAND, SO HE'S NEVER HOME, EITHER.
BUT HE'S WORKING HARD BECAUSE HE WANTS TO PROVIDE A BETTER LIFE FOR HIS SISTER AND HIS PARENTS.
TO DO THAT, HE'S SACRIFICING THE TIME HE COULD SPEND AT HOME.
SO I STILL LOVE HIM. IN FACT, IT MAKES ME LOVE MY BROTHER *MORE*.
I'M THANKFUL FOR WHAT HE'S DOING FOR ME.
SO, YOU SHOULD APPRECIATE YOUR PAPA, AS WELL, MICHAEL-KUN!
SO PAPA...
...CAN'T SEE ME BECAUSE HE'S WORKING HARD...FOR *ME*?
THAT'S RIGHT.
SO, PAPA DOESN'T HATE ME?

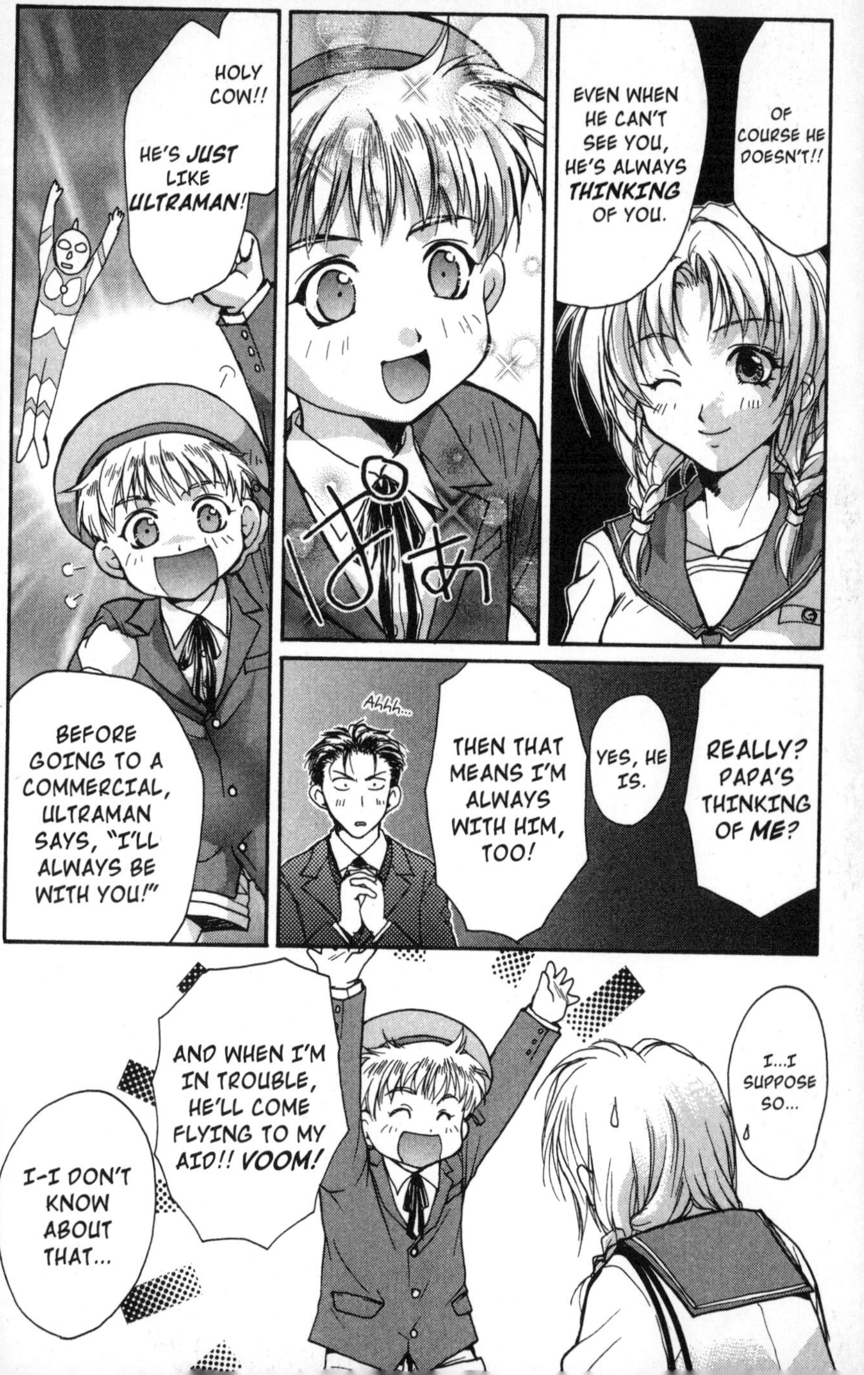
OF COURSE HE DOESN'T!!
EVEN WHEN HE CAN'T SEE YOU, HE'S ALWAYS THINKING OF YOU.
ぱあ
REALLY? PAPA'S THINKING OF ME?
YES, HE IS.
THEN THAT MEANS I'M ALWAYS WITH HIM, TOO!
Ahhh...
HOLY COW!!
HE'S JUST LIKE ULTRAMAN!
BEFORE GOING TO A COMMERCIAL, ULTRAMAN SAYS, "I'LL ALWAYS BE WITH YOU!"
AND WHEN I'M IN TROUBLE, HE'LL COME FLYING TO MY AID!! VOOM!
I...I SUPPOSE SO...
I-I DON'T KNOW ABOUT THAT...

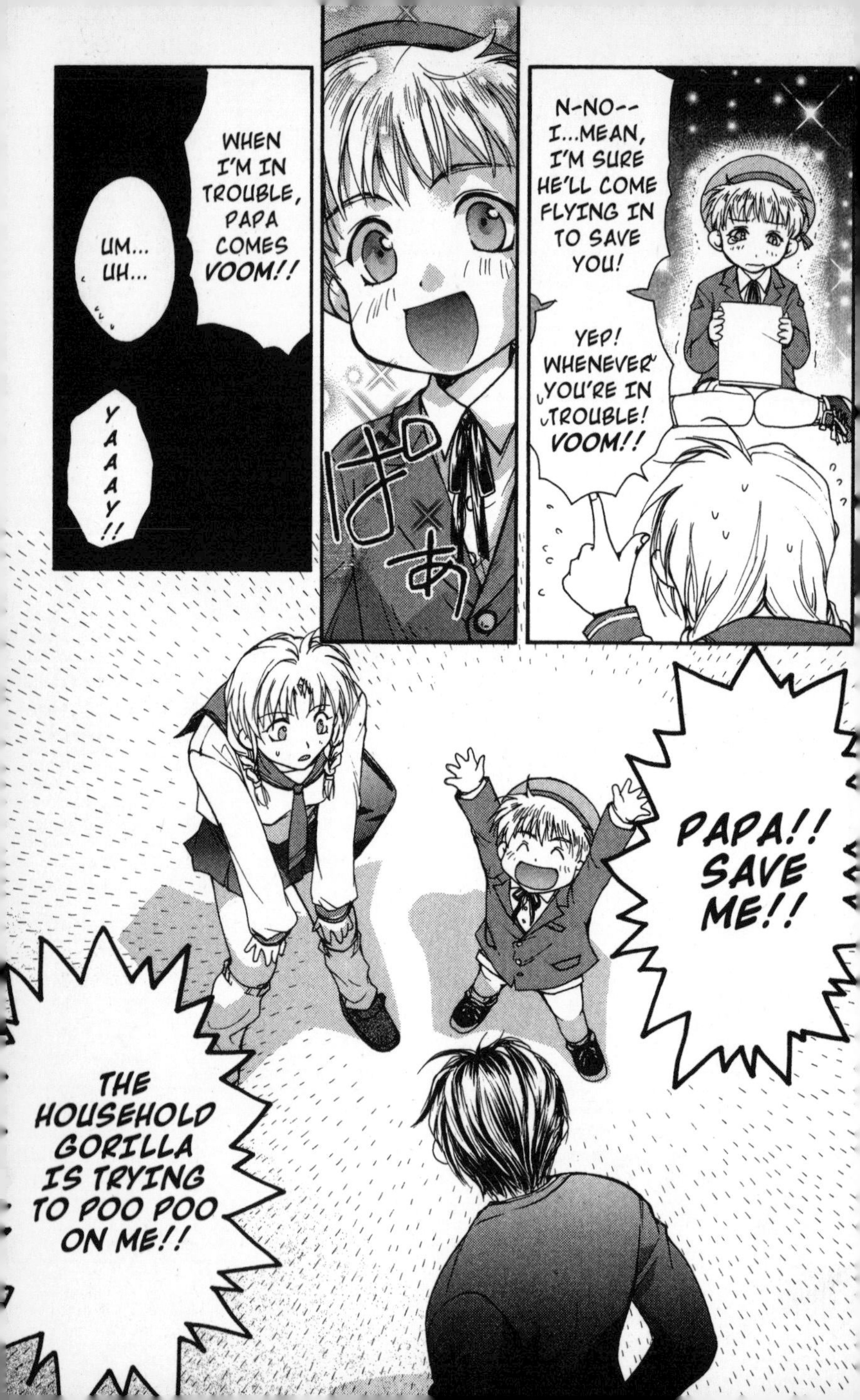
N-NO-- I...MEAN, I'M SURE HE'LL COME FLYING IN TO SAVE YOU!
YEP! WHENEVER YOU'RE IN TROUBLE! VOOM!!
ぱあ
WHEN I'M IN TROUBLE, PAPA COMES VOOM!!
UM... UH...
YAAAAY!!
PAPA!! SAVE ME!!
THE HOUSEHOLD GORILLA IS TRYING TO POO POO ON ME!!

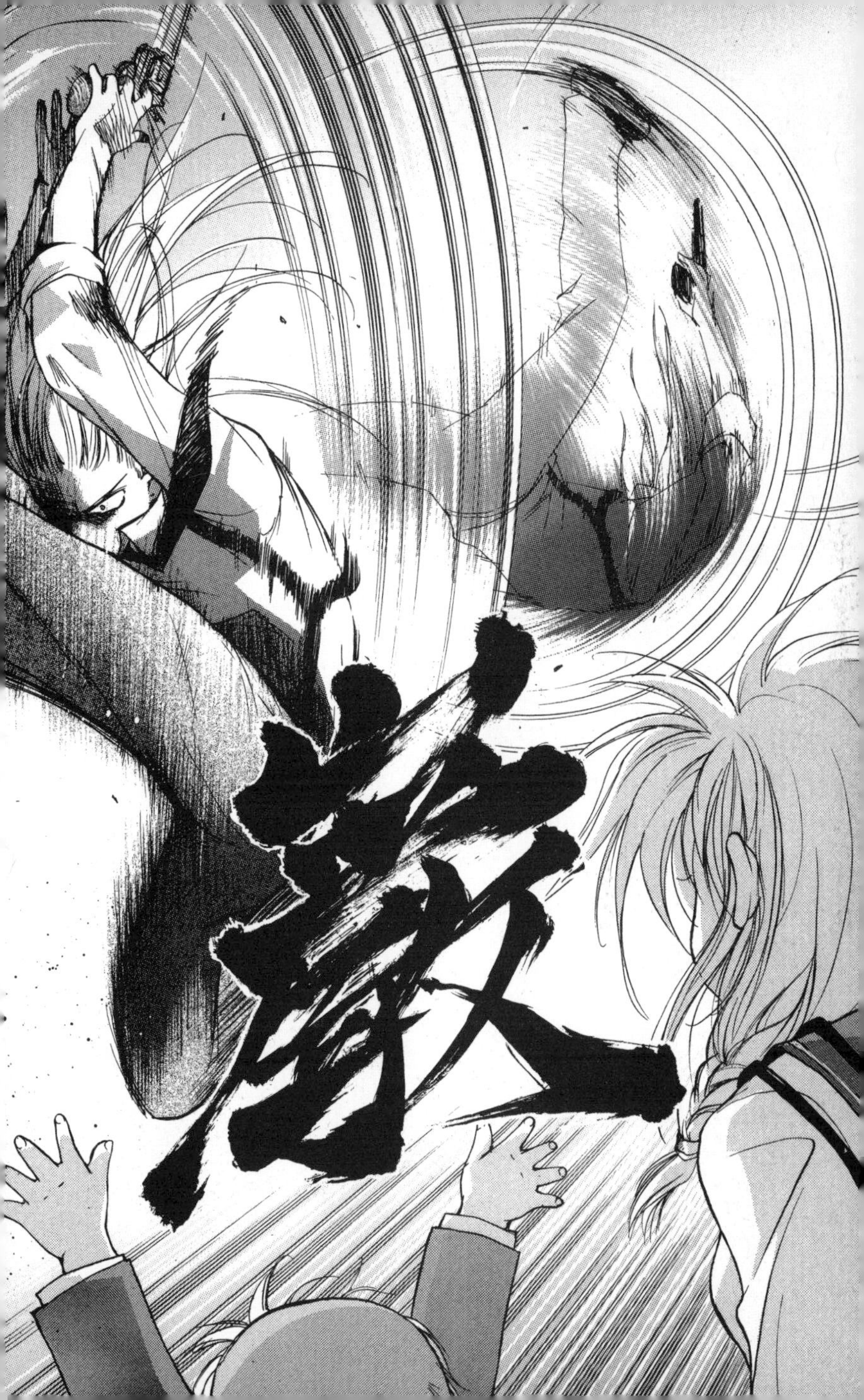
激

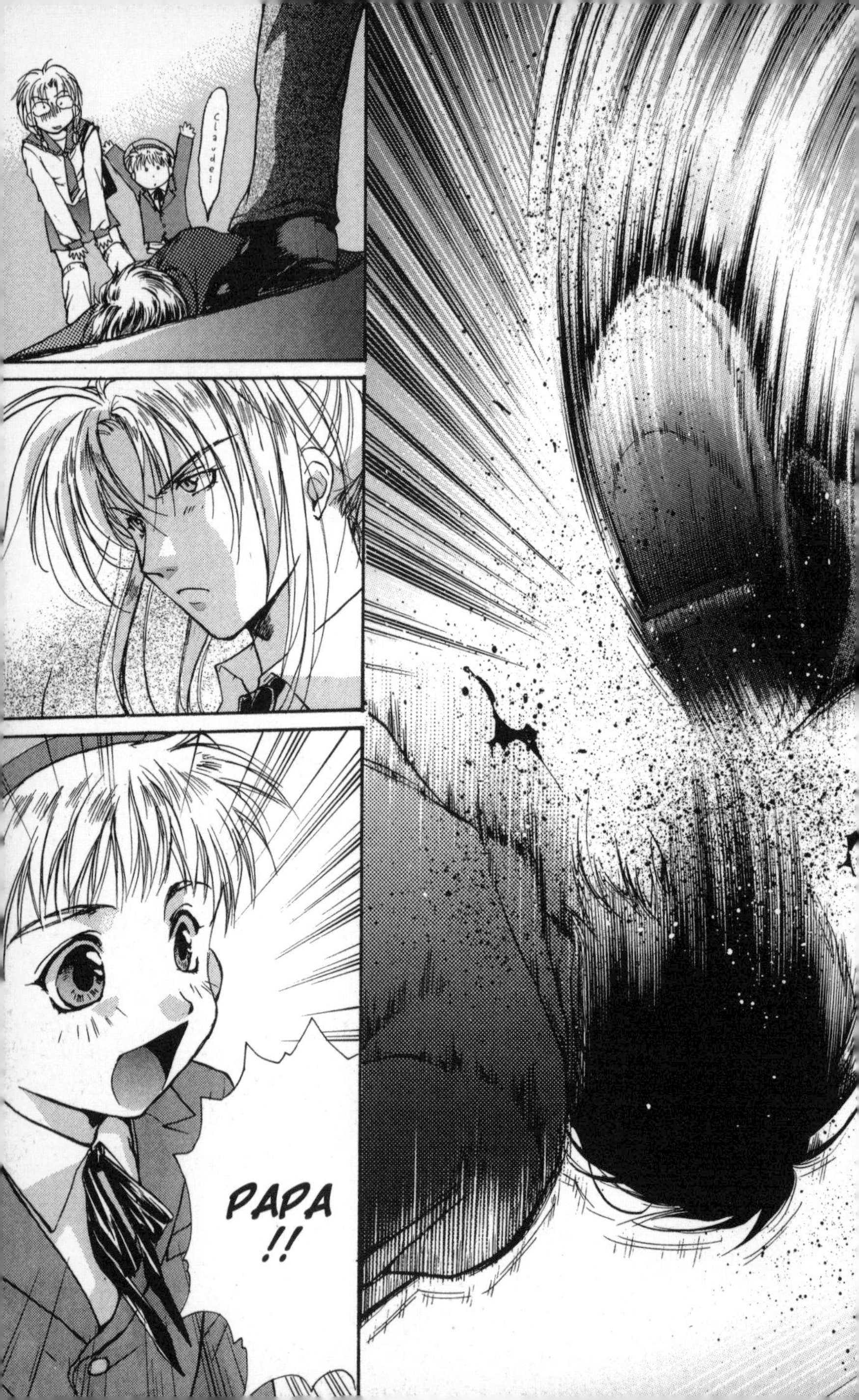
Claude!!
PAPA !!

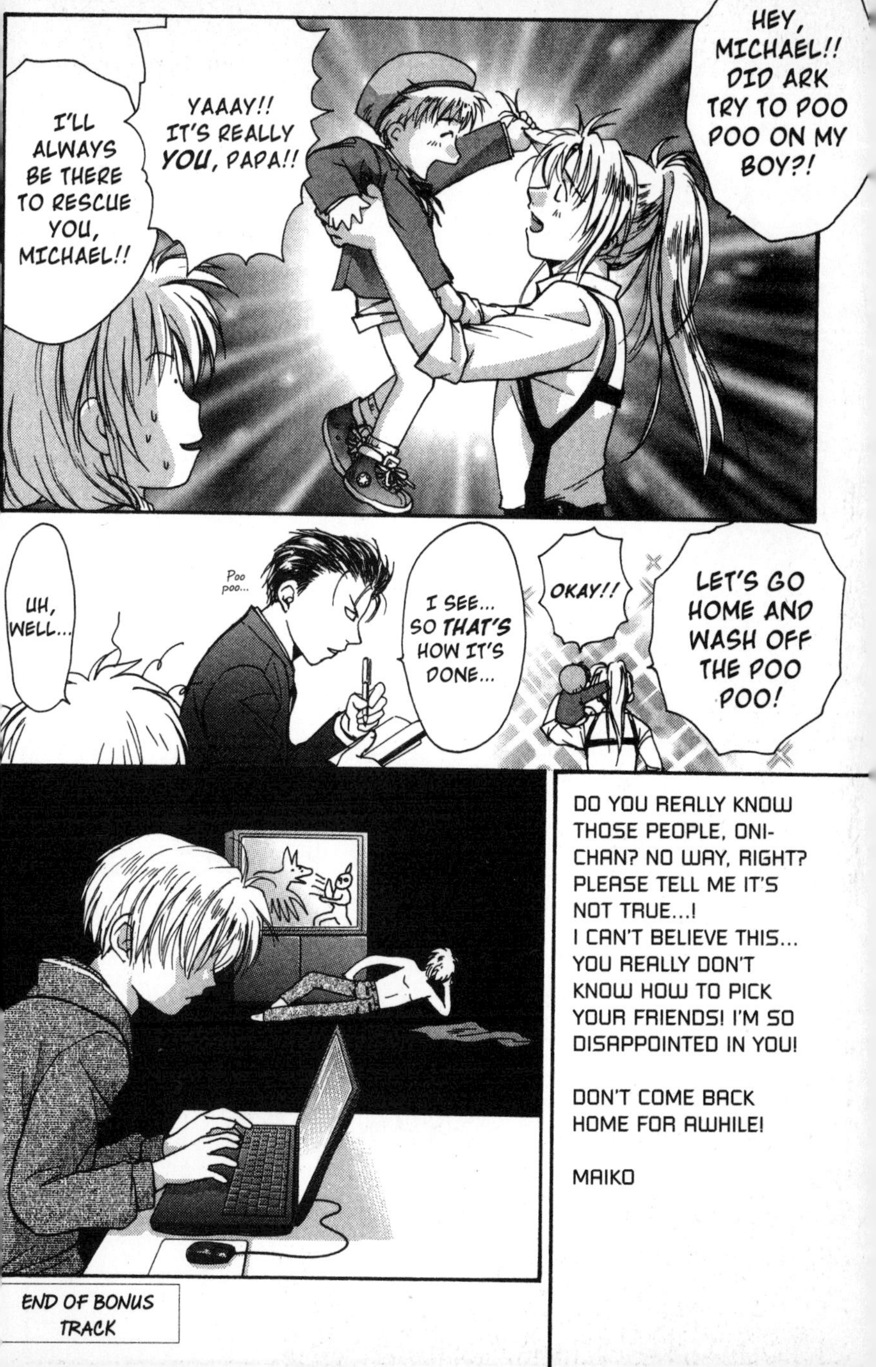
HEY, MICHAEL!! DID ARK TRY TO POO POO ON MY BOY?!
YAAAY!! IT'S REALLY YOU, PAPA!!
I'LL ALWAYS BE THERE TO RESCUE YOU, MICHAEL!!
LET'S GO HOME AND WASH OFF THE POO POO!
OKAY!!
I SEE... SO THAT'S HOW IT'S DONE...
Poo poo...
UH, WELL...
DO YOU REALLY KNOW THOSE PEOPLE, ONI-CHAN? NO WAY, RIGHT? PLEASE TELL ME IT'S NOT TRUE...! I CAN'T BELIEVE THIS... YOU REALLY DON'T KNOW HOW TO PICK YOUR FRIENDS! I'M SO DISAPPOINTED IN YOU!
DON'T COME BACK HOME FOR AWHILE!
MAIKO
END OF BONUS TRACK

COMMENT CORNER
(WHERE WE SPEAK WITH PEOPLE WHO JUST HAPPENED TO BE IN THE AREA)
TODAY'S SUBJECT: "PRAISE ME"

RESPECTIVE SELF-PORTRAITS

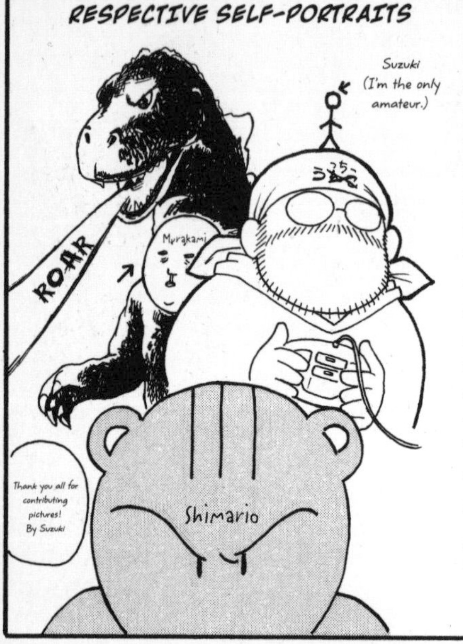

Suzuki
(I'm the only amateur.)
ROAR
Murakami
Shimario
Thank you all for contributing pictures! By Suzuki

Murakami-san has cable at her mansion (condo). She can even listen to satellite radio in her bathtub. Shimario-san was all excited when the man came to turn the cable on. But, when someone is taking a bath, the rule is never to play audio books, shows that give love advice, or bad news about the business world.The mini-discs are all organized into titles and categories like, "various", "trendy" (From when?), "for Murakami" (in red and blue)... but there aren't too many labeled "sucks". Out of those, you definitely won't find too many like, "You choose, Suzuki-san," or "Next time, choose wisely, okay?" (But they're all Murakami-san's MDs...)I'm so happy to be working at Murakami-san's place. I've become an even greater fan (really, truly).Assistant (for food), Suzuki.

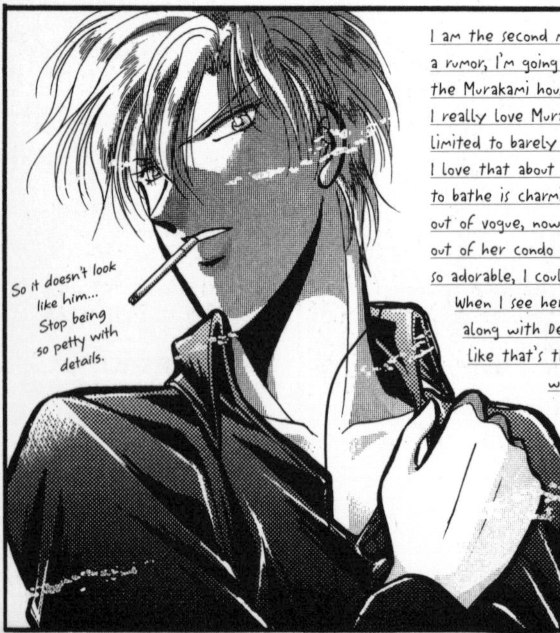

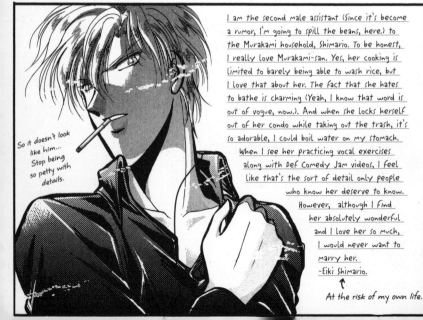

So it doesn't look like him... Stop being so petty with details.

I am the second male assistant (Since it's become a rumor, I'm going to spill the beans, here.) to the Murakami household, Shimario. To be honest, I really love Murakami-san. Yes, her cooking is limited to barely being able to wash rice, but I love that about her. The fact that she hates to bathe is charming (Yeah, I know that word is out of vogue, now.). And when she locks herself out of her condo while taking out the trash, it's so adorable, I could boil water on my stomach. When I see her practicing vocal exercises along with Def Comedy Jam videos, I feel like that's the sort of detail only people who know her deserve to know. However, although I find her absolutely wonderful and I love her so much, I would never want to marry her.

-Eiki Shimario.

At the risk of my own life...

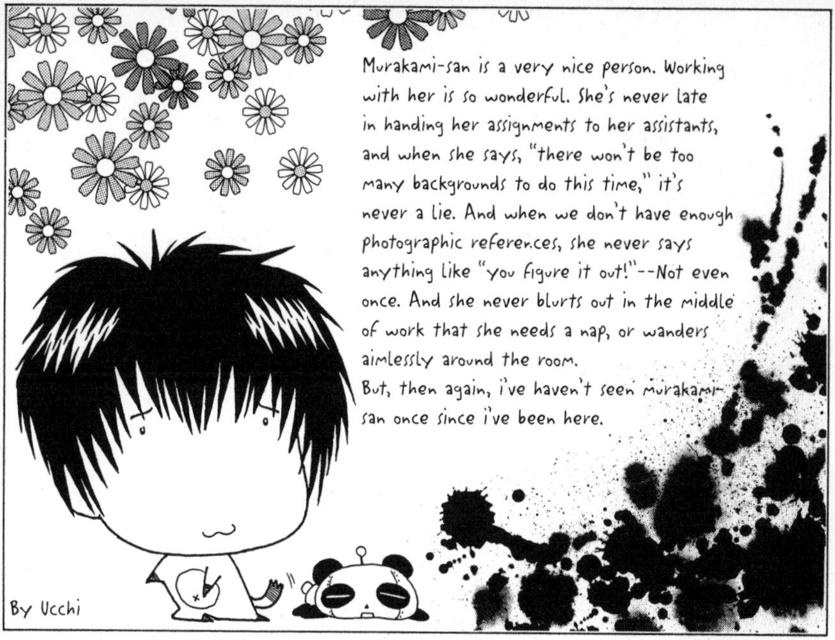
Murakami-san is a very nice person. Working with her is so wonderful. She's never late in handing her assignments to her assistants, and when she says, "there won't be too many backgrounds to do this time," it's never a lie. And when we don't have enough photographic references, she never says anything like "you figure it out!"--Not even once. And she never blurts out in the middle of work that she needs a nap, or wanders aimlessly around the room.
But, then again, i've haven't seen Murakami-san once since i've been here.
By Ucchi

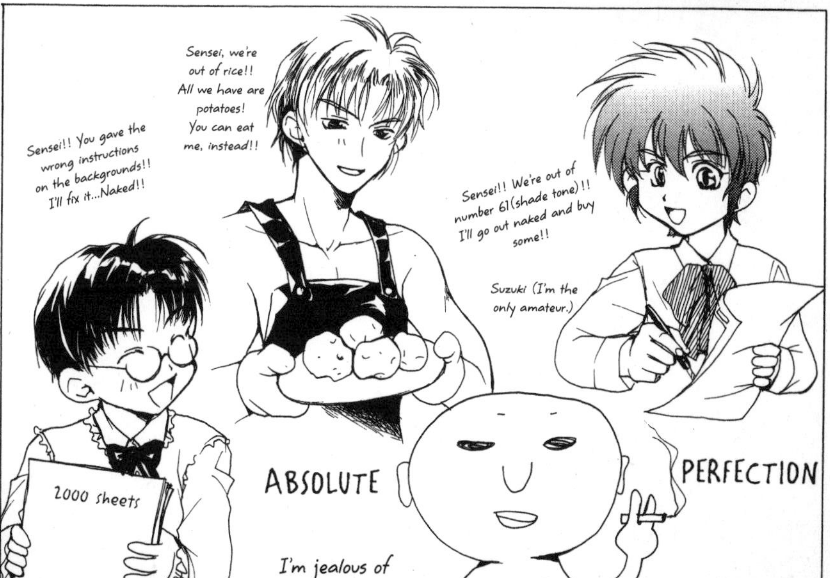
Sensei!! We're out of number 61(shade tone)!! I'll go out naked and buy some!!
Suzuki (I'm the only amateur.)
Sensei, we're out of rice!! All we have are potatoes! You can eat me, instead!!
Sensei!! You gave the wrong instructions on the backgrounds!! I'll fix it...Naked!!
2000 sheets
PERFECTION
ABSOLUTE
I'm jealous of Murakami-san!
By Run-chan

Thank you very much for reading! I hope to see you again in Book 11!

Of course, I'm praying that Book 11 will make it on the stands without any hassle...

Maki Murakami

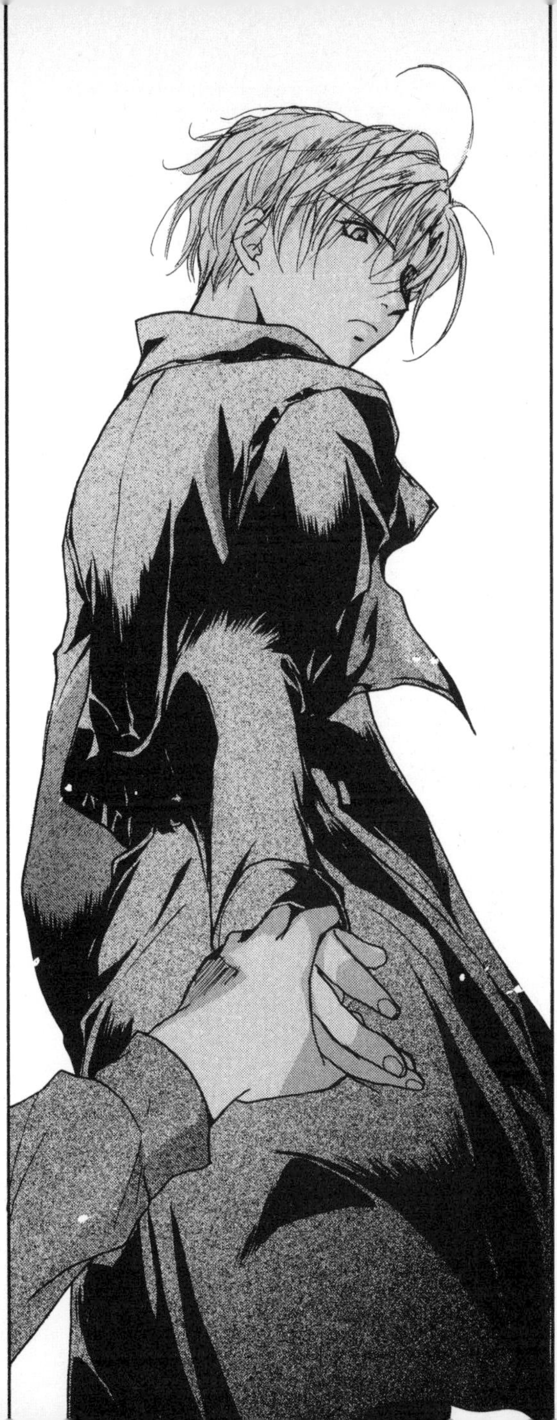

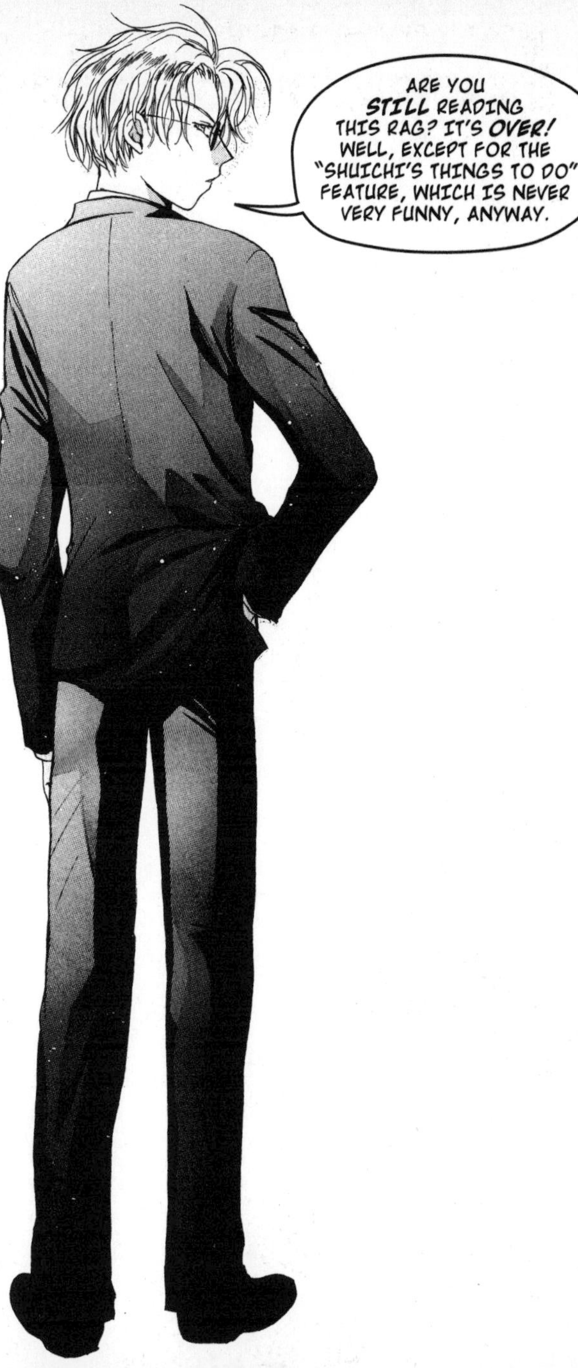
ARE YOU STILL READING THIS RAG? IT'S OVER! WELL, EXCEPT FOR THE "SHUICHI'S THINGS TO DO" FEATURE, WHICH IS NEVER VERY FUNNY, ANYWAY.

Gravitation

SAVE THAT ENERGY FOR YOUR PERFORMANCE, CUPCAKE!
DAMMIT!! IF SOCIETY IS TO SURVIVE, YOU NEED TO BE ELIMINATED!

Graduate from "Rock, Paper, Scissors" to "Bazooka, Tear Gas, Butcher Knife...

Tell K that his wake-up calls are getting out of hand...

TRAGEDY! HE MIGHT HAVE BEEN KIDNAP-PED!!
MY HEART IS BEATING A DISTRESS SIGNAL! YUKI'S IN DANGER!!

Rescue the abducted Yuki from his mysterious captor...

HOW DOES TYING ME UP HELP YOUR MOOD?
IT DOESN'T. I JUST LIKE IT.

Combine love of driving with love of bondage...

YOU HAVE ZERO TALENT.
CALL IT QUITS...
...WHILE YOU STILL HAVE SOME DIGNITY.

Suffer writer's block...but get an encouraging pep talk from Yuki!

Available April 2005!

Shuichi's things to do in Volume 11...

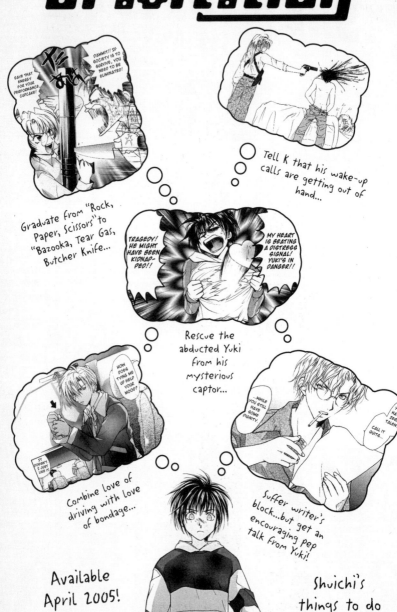

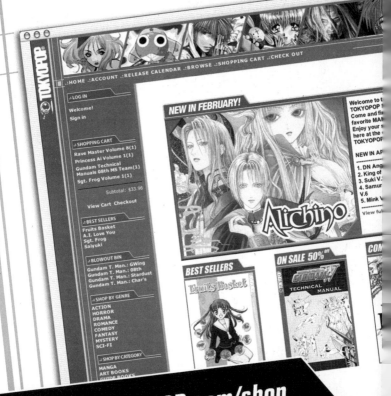